The Psychology of
TEACHING
PHYSICAL EDUCATION

FROM THEORY TO PRACTICE

Bonnie Tjeerdsma Blankenship

PURDUE UNIVERSITY

Holcomb Hathaway, Publishers
Scottsdale, Arizona

Library of Congress Cataloging-in-Publication Data

Blankenship, Bonnie Tjeerdsma.
    The psychology of teaching physical education : from theory to practice /
Bonnie Tjeerdsma Blankenship.—1st ed.
       p. cm.
   ISBN 978-1-890871-86-4
  1. Physical education teachers—Psychology.   2. Physical education and
training—Study and teaching.   I. Title.
   GV361.B55 2008
   613.701'9—dc22

                                        2008004442

DEDICATION

To the honor and glory of my Lord and Saviour, Jesus Christ

Holcomb Hathaway, Publishers, Inc.
6207 North Cattletrack Rd.
Scottsdale, Arizona 85250
480-991-7881
www.hh-pub.com

10 9 8 7 6 5 4 3 2 1

ISBN 978-1-890871-86-4

Printed in the United States of America

CONTENTS

Modeling   53

Moral Development   83

Achievement Goals   117

Self-Perceptions   149

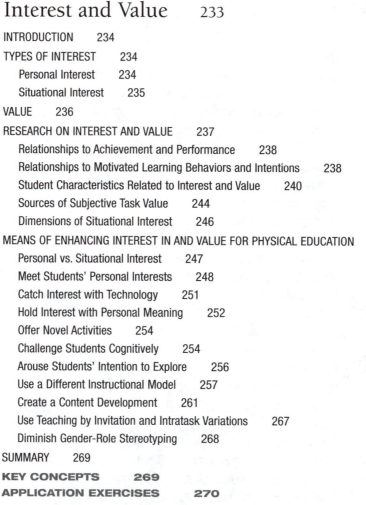

Physical Activity and Lifestyle Enhancement   299

Appendix A

Appendix B

Physical educators usually have multiple goals for their students: motor skill learning, fitness, knowledge of movement and fitness concepts, sportspersonship, personal and social responsibility, enhanced self-esteem, and lifelong participation in physical activity. Teachers must try to accomplish these goals in classrooms of moving and quite diverse students—often in higher numbers than a regular classroom and sometimes when meeting only once or twice a week. In fact, elementary physical education teachers usually teach all of the students in the school, not just students from one grade level. Is it any wonder that beginning and even experienced physical educators often feel overwhelmed with all they must understand and do? One area that can help teachers be more effective is the discipline of psychology.

Many topics within sport and exercise psychology have the potential to provide great assistance to physical educators in achieving their goals and dealing with individual students. Thus, this book focuses on the psychology of teaching physical education. It presents the study of human behavior in physical education, and the practical application of that knowledge in physical education settings. This book includes only that information studied in psychology and sport and exercise psychology that can help physical educators specifically enhance student learning and enjoyment in physical education classes. It is not meant to directly parallel current sport and exercise psychology textbooks.

For both preservice and practicing teachers, studying the psychology of teaching physical education offers several benefits:

- Helping address teacher concerns, such as classroom management, disciplining students, and increasing motivation toward and enjoyment of physical activity;
- Achieving program goals, such as meeting the NASPE national content standards, enhancing student fitness levels, helping students acquire responsible social behaviors, and enabling them to learn skills and movement concepts more effectively; and
- Establishing a positive learning environment that is focused on student learning, making the experience more enjoyable for both students and the teacher.

Text Progression

Chapter 1 provides an introduction to the psychology of teaching physical education and a rationale for the book's chapters. Subsequent chapters are organized around three major areas: social factors in teaching physical education, student factors that may affect physical education teaching, and factors related to the enhancement of students' physical activity participation and lifestyles.

Chapters 2 through 4 focus on three social factors that are important to teaching in physical education: reinforcement, modeling, and moral development. The first two factors—reinforcement and modeling—are important social processes physical educators use to promote learning. I describe theories and research examining the most effective ways of providing reinforcement and modeling. Moral development, or the learning of prosocial behaviors such as cooperation and responsibility, is an important social outcome of quality physical education programs (NASPE, 2004b). This outcome is greatly affected by reinforcement and modeling; thus, the inclusion of the chapter on moral development.

Chapters 5 through 9 examine student factors that may affect their participation and learning in physical education, including achievement goals, self-perceptions, attributions, interests/value, and motivation. These personal characteristics are intrinsic to and may be very different for each student. These chapters examine both the processes by which these personal characteristics affect student participation and learning as well as how physical educators can positively impact these student factors.

The final chapter, Chapter 10, is dedicated to the enhancement of physical activity and a physically active lifestyle. Regular participation in physical activity and the development of a physically active lifestyle are two very important outcomes of quality physical education programs (NASPE, 2004b). Due to the extreme importance of these outcomes and the current low physical activity levels of school-age children and adults in the United States, a separate chapter on physical activity seemed imperative. Because the enhancement of students' physical activity participation and lifestyles can be greatly affected by the aforementioned social processes as well as all of the student factors, this topic is covered in the culminating chapter.

Chapter Organization

Chapters 2 through 10 are divided into three primary sections: explanation of theories, description of related research, and practical applications.

After an opening scenario illustrating a common situation in physical education, I present an explanation of the theory or theories that are related to the situation. The theories chosen for inclusion are those believed to be most helpful in teaching physical education. As readers progress through the theory section, they should relate the concepts and theories described to students or situations they have encountered or heard about; this will help them understand, remember, and apply the information more effectively.

Following the explanations of theories, I describe research that has been conducted related to the topic and theories. As with the previous section, readers will benefit most from this section if they attempt to relate the research results to their own particular experiences. Although the research review is extensive, it is not meant to be exhaustive. Every attempt was made to include the most relevant and important research on the topic or theories. Whenever possible, research performed in physical education settings with school-age children (i.e., pre-kindergarten through high school) is included. Research conducted in youth sport, general education, and other settings and with older individuals has been included when research in physical education settings with school-age children is lacking, or when it helps further understanding of a topic or theory.

The final section of Chapters 2 through 10 is a description of ways to apply the information learned in the theory and research sections to teaching in physical education. Many of these practical applications have already been implemented by physical educators across the United States. So, whenever possible, I have included descriptions of how these teachers applied these strategies. This will help readers see that these are indeed methods they can implement. Real-world physical educators who have actually used these practical applications (described in the recurring "Real World" feature) are referred to using their first name and last initial to distinguish them from the fictitious teachers described in the chapter-opening scenario (who are identified as Mr. or Ms. Last Name). As they read the practical strategies described in this section, readers should consider which strategies will work best in their situation and how best to implement these techniques.

Special Features

Chapter-Opening Scenarios

C hapters 2 through 10 begin with a scenario that illustrates a common situation in physical education with physical education teachers and/or students as the focus. These scenarios represent situations often encountered by preservice teachers and experienced physical educators. The scenario is revisited periodically throughout the theoretical and practical application sections as the information being presented is applied to the scenario. Readers should keep this scenario in mind as they go through the chapter so they can see how the chapter's content can assist with frequently experienced situations in physical education.

Focus Points

Embedded within each chapter are **Focus Points** describing important principles or applications of the chapter's concepts, theories, and research. The Focus Points are especially helpful in the research sections because they provide concise summaries of the studies described. These key points will help readers focus on and keep track of the most important conclusions and principles presented among the chapter's detailed information.

Connected Concepts

Also interspersed throughout each chapter is a feature I've called **Connected Concepts.** Many of the theories, research, and instructional strategies within the text relate to more than one topic and can help physical education teachers in several ways. For example, self-efficacy theory is explained in detail in Chapter 6 to help readers understand the development of students' self-perceptions, but it also has relevance to reinforcement (Chapter 2) and modeling (Chapter 3). The Connected Concepts within the chapters will help readers recognize these important connections among topics and identify goals that can be accomplished using various methods.

Key Concepts and Glossary

Key concepts are boldfaced within the chapter text, and each of these terms is defined in the glossary in the back of the book. To help students review and identify these important key concepts, at the end of each chapter I include a list of those discussed in that chapter, in the order in which they appear. This list of key concepts provides readers with a concise visual summary of the most important concepts described in that chapter. The glossary can then be used as a quick way to recall the basic premise of a concept; the glossary will also be helpful to readers when they come across a concept in one chapter that was described in detail in a previous chapter.

Application Exercises

Each chapter concludes with several application exercises. These exercises are meant to challenge the reader to go beyond simply understanding the concepts and theories to trying to apply the information to their own situation. Completing these exercises after reading the chapter will help the readers develop a more in-depth, practical, and perhaps personal understanding of the information presented.

Studying the psychology of teaching physical education specifically can be quite valuable to future and practicing physical educators—they obtain practical means of helping them address their concerns, achieve their goals, and create a positive learning environment, while also acquiring an understanding of why such strategies can be successful in physical education.

ACKNOWLEDGMENTS

A project like this could not be produced without the assistance of many people. Sincere thanks and gratitude are extended to:

- My editor, Colette Kelly; thank you for your patience and advice along the way. You really are the best!

- All of the teachers and preservice teachers named in the book; thanks for putting many of these ideas into action.

- All of the scholars, researchers, and authors of the referenced studies and papers; collectively, your creative ideas and hard work have created a powerful body of knowledge that really can help teachers help students in physical education learn motor skills and enjoy physical activity.

- All of the reviewers of this book, both in its early and later stages; they include: Debra A. Ballinger, Towson University; Melissa A. Chase, Miami University; Matthew Cummiskey, Central Connecticut State University; Jessica L. Daw, Northern State University; Karen Fredenburg, Baylor University; Mary Fry, University of Memphis; Jeffrey Martin, Wayne State University; Tom Martinek, University of North Carolina-Greensboro; Kirk E. Mathias, Central Washington University; Moira E. Stuart, Northern Illinois University; Lavon Williams, Guilford College; and Ping Xiang, Texas A&M University. Your valuable suggestions significantly enhanced the quality of this book.

- My friends and former colleagues, Mike and Terry Metzler and Deborah Shapiro; you were there when this book was just an idea, and you encouraged me to make it a reality. Deborah, thanks for all your support and advice on students with disabilities or other challenges.

- My friends and colleagues at Purdue University: Carole DeHaven, Susan Flynn, Kristi Serra, and Tom Templin; thanks for being such wonderful colleagues, letting me bounce ideas off of you, providing teacher names, and being willing to work together to produce the best physical education teachers possible. Al Smith, thanks for being a sounding board and providing many valuable ideas and suggestions.

- My NYSP buddies, Kim Lehnen, Jon Laswell, and Bill Harper; you have taught me what it means to be truly dedicated to a cause, and I only hope I can live up to your superb examples. Bill, thank you especially for being so supportive of my talents and for your willingness to utilize my skills in the best ways possible.

- My parents, Don and Marj Tjeerdsma; you always believe in me, even though you don't always understand what it is I do.

- My husband, Chris; thanks for loving me, keeping me grounded, and making me laugh!

The Importance of Psychology
to the Physical Educator

introduction ▶

Teaching physical education is a complex endeavor. Physical education teachers must have an in-depth understanding of many activities and movements, as well as organization and management skills. Various instructional techniques and methods must be mastered. Physical education teachers usually have multiple goals for their students: motor skill learning, fitness, knowledge of movement and fitness concepts, sportspersonship, personal and social responsibility, enhanced self-esteem, and desire for and motivation to participate in lifelong physical activity. The teacher must try to accomplish these goals in a classroom of moving and quite diverse students—often in greater numbers than a regular classroom and when only meeting once or twice a week. In fact, physical education teachers often teach all of the students in the school, not just one classroom of students. Is it any wonder that beginning and even experienced physical education teachers often feel overwhelmed with all they must understand and do? One area that can help physical educators be more effective is the discipline of psychology.

What Is the Psychology of Teaching Physical Education?

Psychology is the study of the mind and behavior (American Psychological Association, n.d.). A subdiscipline within the field of kinesiology that has its roots in psychology and that contributes to the psychology of teaching physical education is sport and exercise psychology. **Sport and exercise psychology** is "the scientific study of human behavior in sport and exercise, and the practical application of that knowledge in sport and exercise settings" (Gill, 2000, p. 7). Research in and practical applications of topics in sport and exercise psychology address the impact of psychological factors on sport and exercise performance (e.g., how does confidence affect one's exercise participation) as well as how sport and exercise participation affects psychological factors (e.g., can participation in youth sport enhance a child's confidence; Weinberg & Gould, 2003). A wide variety of topics comprises the field of sport and exercise psychology, such as personality, confidence, exercise adherence, reinforcement, modeling, team cohesion, burnout, psychological skills training, motivation, and goal setting.

Many topics within sport and exercise psychology have the potential to provide great assistance to physical educators in achieving their goals and dealing with individual students. Thus, the **psychology of teaching physical education** is the study of human behavior in physical education, and the practical application of that knowledge in physical education settings. It includes only that information studied in psychology and sport and exercise psychology that can help physical education teachers specifically enhance student learning and enjoyment in physical education classes.

Why Study the Psychology of Teaching Physical Education?

To Help Teachers Address Their Concerns

As teachers develop throughout their careers, their needs and abilities change. One way the development of teachers has been conceptualized is by changes in their concerns, which are proposed to occur in three stages:

1. concerns about self,
2. concerns about the task, and
3. concerns about impact on students (Fuller, 1969).

Early in their careers, teachers are believed to focus on their own adequacy and survival as teachers and how others perceive them: How do I get control of my class? Do the students like me? Do other teachers respect me? Does my supervisor think I'm doing a good job? With experience, those concerns are believed to shift from oneself to concerns about the routines and daily tasks of teaching: How do I deal with so many students at once? How do I teach this unit with only half a gym and little equipment? How can I get everything done? Eventually teachers' concerns are believed to shift to concerns about having an impact on students: How can I motivate students? How do I meet the needs of the high-skilled and low-skilled students in the same unit, as well as students with disabilities? How do I make sure students are learning what I want them to learn? Although researchers have not yet confirmed this developmental shift in physical education teachers' concerns (Behets, 1990; Boggess, McBride, & Griffey, 1985; Fung, 1993; Meek, 1996; Rikard & Knight, 1997; Wendt & Bain, 1989), it seems a safe conclusion that beginning and experienced physical education teachers could share many of same concerns.

In fact, similar to other teachers, physical educators cite class control and management as some common concerns (Behets, 1990; Boggess et al., 1985; McBride, 1984; McBride, Boggess, & Griffey, 1986; Rikard & Knight, 1997). Physical education teachers, even experienced ones, worry about their ability to maintain order in the classroom and to discipline students. Another frequently named concern that is related to class control is being able to motivate students (Behets, 1990; McBride, 1984; Rikard & Knight, 1997); when students are motivated to participate and learn, class control is usually less of a problem. Other concerns include being valued as a teacher, working with large numbers of students, inadequate time and equipment, and student learning and enjoyment (Behets, 1990; Boggess et al., 1985; Fung, 1993; McBride, 1993; McBride et al., 1986; Rikard & Knight, 1997).

Understanding the psychology of teaching physical education can help teachers address many of these concerns, sometimes directly but often in a preventive fashion. For instance, teachers can address concerns about motivating students by implementing numerous strategies such as enhancing students' self-perceptions, establishing a task-involving climate, helping students make adaptive attributions. Classroom control, appropriate student behavior, and student enjoyment are often less of a worry when students are motivated, so utilizing strategies specific to the psychology of teaching physical education to increase motivation will help prevent some of these problems. Other school staff and administrators will often have greater respect and appreciation for physical educators when those physical educators are using the principles and applications of the psychology of physical education to enhance student learning of motor skills and physical activity participation.

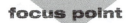

focus point

Many commonly cited concerns of physical education teachers can be addressed by studying the psychology of teaching physical education.

To Achieve Program Goals

Quality physical education programs strive to develop physically educated individuals, and these individuals have the following characteristics (National Association for Sport and Physical Education [NASPE], 2004b, p. 11):

- Demonstrate competency in the motor skills and movement patterns needed to perform a variety of physical activities;
- Demonstrate understanding of movement concepts, principles, strategies, and tactics as they apply to the learning and performance of physical activities;
- Participate regularly in physical activity;
- Achieve and maintain a health-enhancing level of physical fitness;
- Exhibit responsible personal and social behavior that respects self and others in physical activity settings; and
- Value physical activity for health, enjoyment, challenge, self-expression, and/or social interaction.

These characteristics are, in fact, the national standards of achievement for quality physical education programs (NASPE, 2004b). Studying the psychology of teaching physical education can help teachers achieve these national content standards, which will also address their concerns for student learning. For instance, knowing the most effective ways to give reinforcement and feedback to students in physical education can directly influence students' learning of motor skills and movement concepts and their enjoyment of physical activity. In turn, achievement of those standards could lead students to participate regularly in physical activity, which can enhance their fitness levels. Appropriately applying reinforcement principles can also help students acquire responsible social behaviors. Similarly, learning about theories and means of enhancing student motivation and interest in physical education may help students participate more regularly in class, enjoy and value physical activity more, and thus learn skills and movement concepts more effectively.

To Establish a Positive Learning Environment

Most people, including teachers, prefer to work in a positive environment rather than a negative environment. Students prefer to attend classes they find enjoyable rather than ones that are not; in fact, students probably learn better in positive environments than negative ones. For many students (especially some middle school and high school students), physical education can be a negative experience; they may dislike sports, competition, dressing out, and some wouldn't be there if they didn't have to be. Many topics that are part of the psychology of teaching physical education can help physical educators create a positive environment that is focused on student learning, making the experience more enjoyable both for students and the teacher. For instance, creating a task-involving climate (see Chapter 5) can focus students on improving their own performance rather than doing better than others. Most students can improve performance and find a task-involving climate more enjoyable than just competing against others (which will still happen in physical education even in this task-involving climate). When students are enjoying class, it is more enjoyable and pleasant for the teacher as well.

To Acquire Information and Applications Specific to Physical Education

Another motive for studying the psychology of teaching physical education is related to the information presented in sport and exercise psychology textbooks, which often do not provide specific guidance for physical education teachers. The reasons for this lack of guidance are twofold. First, the focus often tends to be on sport and, to a somewhat lesser degree, exercise. These settings are usually quite different than physical education settings. Even though sport and exercise are both content areas within physical education, participation in the two areas tends to be voluntary (e.g., involvement in a professional/amateur sport or working out in a health club), while physical education participation is usually required. Also, the focus of sport and exercise psychology is often on elite

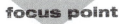

focus point

Studying the psychology of teaching physical education can help teachers achieve the NASPE national content standards for quality physical education programs.

focus point

The creation of a positive learning environment can result from studying the psychology of teaching physical education.

athletes or adults. Both are major factors that could impact the effectiveness of various psychological principles in physical education. Moreover, sport and exercise are not the only content areas included in physical education; dance, adventure education, outdoor education, leisure activities, fundamental motor skills, and movement concepts are also part of physical education.

Second, most of the theory and research discussed in sport and exercise psychology textbooks usually include only a few examples of how to apply the psychological concepts and theories to teaching physical education, unless the research was specifically conducted in physical education settings. Most applications described are quite general; instructional methods that are specific to physical education settings are not provided. For example, an instructional model called peer teaching is an excellent means of giving students in physical education some leadership and responsibility opportunities, which can help develop prosocial behaviors. And doing a set induction at the beginning of a lesson is a good way to increase student interest in and value for a lesson. But such instructional methods are seldom mentioned in sport and exercise psychology textbooks as strategies for enhancing student responsibility and interest in physical activity.

To provide physical educators with the information they need, this book focuses on the psychology of teaching physical education. It is not meant to directly parallel current sport and exercise psychology textbooks. Several topics included in such texts are either not relevant to the physical education setting or have not been examined sufficiently in research in physical education settings (e.g., athlete burnout, attentional styles, psychological skills training). In addition, physical education-specific topics and instructional methods, not focused on in current sport and exercise psychology textbooks, are included in this text.

Chapter Organization

The remaining chapters in the book are divided into three sections: an explanation of theories, description of related research, and practical applications.

Theory Explanation

After an opening scenario that illustrates a common situation in physical education, an explanation follows of the theory or theories that are related to the problem presented in the scenario. A **theory** is simply "a system of ideas explaining something" (Urdang, 1995, p. 597). Thus, theories can be very helpful in physical education as they can help explain a problem we might encounter—lack of motivation—or help us best understand how

focus point

Sport and exercise psychology theoretical explanations and applications often fail to provide information specific to the physical education setting and most helpful to physical education teachers.

to use a teaching skill—feedback or demonstrations. Theories help us organize our thoughts and research related to a problem—a student's low self-esteem—and even help us develop means of addressing a problem. Although you can teach physical education without knowledge of psychological theories, such knowledge enables you to go beyond random strategies for dealing with situations to organized, thoughtful methods and increases your chance of success. The theories chosen for inclusion in the chapters are those believed to be most helpful in teaching physical education. As you progress through this section, try to relate the described concepts and theories to students or situations you have encountered or heard about; this will help you understand, remember, and apply the information more effectively.

Research Description

Following the theory explanation is a description of the research related to the topic and theories. It is important to review relevant research as it helps us discover which aspects of theories are most likely true, as well as provides insights into how best to apply the theoretical constructs to teaching physical education. As with the theory section, you will benefit most from this section if you attempt to relate the research results to your own experiences. For instance, some research shows that children with motor coordination difficulties or with obesity tend to have lower perceptions of physical competence in physical education than children without these characteristics; knowing about this research finding might help a preservice or practicing teacher better understand why these students are reluctant to participate in class.

In presenting the research, every attempt was made to include the most relevant and important research on the topic or theories. It makes sense that the most relevant and useful research is that which has been conducted in situations most similar to the target situation (Silverman & Ennis, 2003). Therefore, research performed in physical education settings with school-aged children and adolescents (i.e., pre-kindergarten through high school) is included whenever possible. Research conducted in youth sport, general education, and other settings and with older individuals was included when research in physical education settings with school-aged children is lacking, or when it helps further our understanding of a topic or theory. So, the type of research included in each chapter varies somewhat. For example, the vast majority of research included in Chapter 5, Achievement Goals, was performed in physical education settings, because many studies on students' achievement goals in physical education have been conducted. Conversely, the research reviewed in Chapter 2, Reinforcement, is from the fields of physical education, youth sport, and motor learning.

Practical Applications

The final section of each chapter describes ways to apply the information learned in the theory and research sections to teaching in physical education. Many of these practical applications have already been implemented by physical education teachers across the United States. So, whenever possible, descriptions of how these teachers applied these strategies are included to help you see that these are methods that you can implement. In addition, the scenario from the beginning of the chapter is referenced, suggesting ways those fictitious teachers can address the problem in that situation. Real-world physical education teachers who have actually used these practical applications are referred to using their first name and last initial to distinguish them from the fictitious teachers described in the chapter-opening scenario (who are identified as Mr. or Ms. Last Name). As strategies are described in this section, readers should consider which of these strategies will work best in their situation and how best to implement these techniques.

Study Tools

To help you understand the theories and research related to the psychology of physical education and help you apply them in your teaching, the book includes several study tools.

Scenario

Each chapter that follows begins with a teaching scenario that illustrates a common situation in physical education, with physical education teachers and/or students as the focus of these scenarios. These scenarios represent situations often encountered by preservice teachers and experienced physical educators. The scenario is revisited periodically throughout the theoretical and practical application sections, as the information being presented is applied to the scenario. Keep this scenario in mind as you read the chapter so you can see how the chapter's content can assist with a frequently experienced situation in physical education.

Focus Points

Embedded within the chapters are Focus Points that describe important principles or applications of the concepts, theories, and research presented. These Focus Points are especially helpful when reading the research sections because they provide concise summaries of the studies described. These key points will help you keep track of the most important conclusions reached and principles presented in the studies.

Connected Concepts

Also interspersed throughout the chapters are Connected Concepts boxes. Many of the theories, research, and instructional strategies within the text relate to more than one topic and can help physical education teachers in several ways. For instance, the self-efficacy theory explained in detail in Chapter 6 to help readers understand the development of students' self-perceptions also has relevance to reinforcement (Chapter 2) and modeling (Chapter 3). The Connected Concepts will help you see all of the connections among topics and identify all of the goals that can be accomplished using various methods.

Key Concepts and Glossary

Key concepts are set in boldfaced type within the chapters. At the end of each chapter is a list of these terms in the order they were presented in that chapter. Each of these terms is then defined in the glossary in the back of the book. The list of terms provides you with a concise visual means of reviewing the most important concepts discussed. The glossary can be used as a quick way to recall the basic premise of a concept; this might be especially helpful when you come across a concept in one chapter that was described in detail in a previous chapter.

Application Exercises

Each chapter concludes with several application exercises. These exercises are meant to challenge you to go beyond simply understanding the concepts and theories to trying to apply the information to your own situation or a hypothetical teaching situation. Completing these exercises will help you develop a more in-depth, practical, and perhaps more personal understanding of the information presented.

Summary

Studying the psychology of teaching physical education specifically can be quite valuable to you as a physical educator. My goal is to help you obtain the practical means to address your concerns, achieve your goals, and create a positive learning environment, while also acquiring an understanding of why such strategies can be successful in physical education.

To emphasize the relevance of this material to you as a physical educator, whenever possible I will address you directly. Thus, instead of saying, for example, "Teachers should reinforce . . .," I will say "Reinforce . . .," and instead of saying "teacher," I say "you." At times a more general discussion may refer to "teachers" instead of "you," but my goal is to address you directly when feasible.

Enough talk! Let's get started on the journey of learning about the psychology of teaching physical education!

KEY concepts

Key concepts are presented in the order they appear in the chapter, rather than in alphabetical order.

Psychology

Sport and exercise psychology

Psychology of teaching physical education

Theory

Reinforcement

Last year Ms. Brown, frustrated with the lack of effort put forth by many of the 9th graders in her basic required fitness class, developed a reward system for their cardio-vascular workouts. During the 20 minutes allotted in class for walking and running, students could earn an Eagle Point for each quarter mile completed (the school mascot is the eagle). Eagle Points could be accumulated to purchase school merchandise, such as Eagle T-shirts, caps, and so forth. Most students were quite excited about the reward program, and the program really enhanced their effort. But for other students like Sarah and Al, who were working hard without the reward system, the program seemed to decrease their effort. This year Ms. Brown has many of the same students in a sport-specific conditioning class, and their effort is low again. They keep asking Ms. Brown for prizes like they had the previous year, but the Eagle Points reward system was quite expensive for Ms. Brown and she can't afford to do that again. Are such reward systems worth the time and effort? What might make a reward system like that more effective in the long run?

introduction

External rewards like the one described above are one type of reinforcement frequently used in physical education to help motivate students and enhance their performance and learning. Other reinforcements include praise and corrective information from the teacher, recognition for accomplishments, and partic-ipation in special activities. Besides influencing student motivation and performance, reinforcements can also influence student self-perceptions and even socially desirable behaviors like punctuality, sportspersonship, and on-task behaviors. But what kind of reinforcements work best to positively impact students? And can punishments be as effective as rein-forcements in achieving these goals? In this chapter, the principles of behavioral theory and behavior modification, for which reinforcement is an important element, will be examined. Cognitive evaluation theory, which addresses the impact of external rewards on intrinsic motivation, will also be explored. Research that examines the impact of teacher feedback and external rewards on children's motor skill performance, self-perceptions, and prosocial behaviors in physical activity settings will be described. Finally, ways to effectively use reinforcements and punishments in physical education, based on the theories and research, will be presented.

Reinforcement Theories

Reinforcement is central to behavioral theory (Skinner, 1953, 1974) and behavior modification. Another theory, cognitive evaluation theory (Deci & Ryan, 1985; Ryan & Deci, 2000), attempts to explain how extrinsic rewards can influence intrinsic motivation.

Behavioral Theory

According to **behavioral theory,** behaviors and skills are learned via interactions between individuals and the environment (Skinner, 1953, 1974); essentially, the consequences that follow a behavior will determine whether that behavior is repeated and learned or not. Behavioral theory generated **behavior modification,** which is the deliberate and systematic use of reinforcement to develop desirable behaviors and eliminate undesirable behaviors. Other terms used in the literature to describe this process include behavior management and contingency management; in youth sport literature, it is called behavioral coaching.

Reinforcement vs. punishment

Behavior modification is built on the element of **reinforcement**—any stimulus that *increases* the occurrence of a behavior it closely follows. Reinforcers can be positive or negative.

In **positive reinforcement,** a behavior increases because the person received something perceived as positive (e.g., candy, a certificate, a gold star, or a T-shirt) after performing the behavior. Ms. Brown was using positive reinforcement in the Eagle Points reward system to increase her students' effort. In addition to such tangible rewards, positive reinforcers can also be intangible, such as watching the golf ball go in the hole, being praised by the teacher, being able to lift more weight than before, or the enjoyment of being outdoors.

When a behavior increases or is strengthened because something negative or aversive to the individual is removed, that is **negative reinforcement.** The physical education teacher who lets his students skip the push-ups in their warm-up one day if they run their warm-up laps without any walking is using negative reinforcement, as his students do not like to do push-ups. A student who performs a jump rope skill so the rope no longer slaps and hurts him is also experiencing negative reinforcement;

connected **CONCEPTS**

Reinforcement is also an important part of social learning theory, competence motivation theory, and self-efficacy theory. In social learning theory, reinforcement, along with observational learning and social comparison, influences the learning of behaviors (see Chapters 3 and 4). According to competence motivation theory, reinforcement and feedback from significant others can influence a person's perceptions of competence and control, as well as their motivational and goal orientations (see Chapter 6). In self-efficacy theory, verbal persuasion from significant others (reinforcement) is one of six sources an individual uses to judge their competence level (see Chapter 6).

focus point

Reinforcements, either positive or negative, are designed to increase a behavior, while punishment is meant to decrease a behavior.

the pain he experienced when performing the skill incorrectly is removed when he performs the skill correctly.

Whereas reinforcements are designed to increase the occurrence of a behavior, **punishments** are meant to *decrease* the occurrence of a behavior. This can happen either by presenting something to an individual that the person finds aversive or negative or by taking away something the person perceives as positive. A teacher who scolds a student for forgetting her "gym" shoes is attempting to use punishment, as is a teacher who does not give the 5th graders their normal Friday "free day" because they were disrespectful to each other earlier in the week. Although many people equate negative reinforcement with punishment, the two elements have different purposes; negative reinforcement is designed to increase a behavior, while punishment is given to decrease a behavior.

Exhibit 2.1 summarizes these behavior modification terms.

Categories of reinforcers

The number of elements or events that can be used as reinforcers is practically limitless. Yet, reinforcers basically fall into one of four categories (Weinberg & Gould, 2003), as described in the list on the following page.

EXHIBIT 2.1	Behavior modification terms—purposes and means of accomplishing.

TERM	PURPOSE	MEANS OF ACCOMPLISHING	EXAMPLE
Positive Reinforcement	Increase a behavior	Present something positive	Student hears "good job" or receives a certificate after improving her PACER test score.
Negative Reinforcement	Increase a behavior	Take away something negative	Students don't have to do push-ups, which they don't like, because they ran their laps without stopping.
Punishment	Decrease a behavior	(1) Present something negative	(1) Student has to write a report about flexibility because she forgot her physical education clothes.
		(2) Take away something positive	(2) Students don't get to participate in "free day" because they showed poor sportspersonship.

1. *Material reinforcers* are tangible items that a student might find desirable, such as a T-shirt, certificate, trophy, CDs, money, or Ms. Brown's Eagle Points system.

2. *Social reinforcers* are less tangible events or behaviors that indicate approval from others. Examples include verbal praise, a high-five, a smile, or a thumbs-up from someone important to the individual. Being recognized for accomplishments is also a social reinforcer; for example, having your name called during morning announcements or seeing your name in the newspaper or on a poster for achievements are social reinforcers.

Verbal feedback from the teacher is an important social reinforcer and can take many forms. For instance, the teacher may generally praise a student by saying "good job" or may specifically praise the student by saying "I like the way you had your racket back that time."

3. *Activity reinforcers* are activities or events in which a student enjoys participating. For example, younger children might enjoy helping the teacher put away equipment. Other activity reinforcers physical education teachers might use include allowing students to choose activities, playing a game students enjoy, or allowing students to lead an activity like stretching. If activity reinforcers are used, ensure that the activity is still educational and safe and uses skills the students have practiced. For example, dodgeball should not be used as an activity reinforcer, even though students enjoy it, because dodgeball is dangerous and is not considered acceptable by the National Association for Sport and Physical Education (NASPE, 2004c).

4. *Special outings* can also serve as reinforcers. For example, a teacher might reward her students for their accomplishments by going to a park, spending time on a hiking trail, or golfing on an actual golf course. However, these may be difficult to arrange for physical education classes and, thus, are probably used sparingly.

Shaping

Shaping is the "development of a new behavior by the successive reinforcement of closer approximations . . . of the behavior" (Martin & Pear, 2003, p. 123). With shaping, a teacher first reinforces a behavior that vaguely resembles the one desired. Once that behavior is established, the teacher then reinforces behaviors closer to the one desired, until the target behavior develops. Shaping is especially useful when students learn complex or difficult skills or behaviors. For instance, when teaching the basketball layup, the teacher first rewards students for standing on both feet beside the basket and aiming at the correct spot on the backboard, then for standing on the inside foot and correctly laying the ball off the backboard, next for walking up and correctly shooting the ball off the correct foot, and finally for running and doing a layup correctly. In another exam-

focus point

There are four categories of reinforcers: material, social, activity, and special outings.

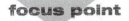

focus point

Shaping can be helpful when students are learning complex or difficult skills or behaviors.

ple, Madeline, a 9th grade student in Ms. Brown's class, is often tardy for class. Ms. Brown can shape Madeline's behavior by initially rewarding Madeline for showing up no later than 5 minutes after class starts, and gradually require her to be in class 4 minutes, 3 minutes, 2 minutes, and 1 minute after class starts, and then on time in order to get the reward.

Fading

Fading is the process of gradually changing the reinforcer that controls a behavior so the behavior eventually occurs in response to a new reinforcer (Martin & Pear, 2003). Often, this means removing tangible rewards and replacing them with intangible or internal reinforcers, with the hope of yielding more internal motivation for the behavior. One possible reason why Ms. Brown's students lacked motivation and effort for running when the reward system was not in place was because Ms. Brown did not fade the use of the external rewards. She could have gradually changed the reinforcer by requiring students to complete more laps to earn Eagle Points. Or the prizes that the students bought with their Eagle Points could have cost more points. In either case, Ms. Brown should concurrently praise students for their accomplishments and remind them of the intangible benefits they are gaining from completing laps (e.g., losing weight, looking fit) so that those elements might become new reinforcers for the students.

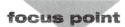

focus point

Fading is a good technique to use when trying to prevent students from becoming dependent on tangible rewards and to move them toward internal sources of motivation.

Schedules of reinforcement

Important to behavior modification are the various **schedules of reinforcement,** or the timing and frequency with which a person is reinforced, and how these affect the learning and maintenance of behaviors (Martin & Pear, 2003; Skinner, 1953, 1974). With **continuous reinforcement,** a person is reinforced every time the desired behavior is produced. If, for example, Ms. Brown was trying to change Madeline's tardiness with a continuous reinforcement schedule, Madeline would receive a reward every day she showed up to class on time. When some instances of a behavior are reinforced but others are not, reinforcement is **intermittent.** In a **fixed ratio schedule,** the behavior must be exhibited a set number of times before being reinforced. With this reinforcement schedule, Madeline only receives a reward if she shows up on time for class at least 3 days per week. With a **variable ratio schedule,** the number of times a person must produce the desired behavior in order to earn a reward is unpredictable, so the person doesn't know when the reward will be received. With this kind of schedule, Madeline doesn't know how many days she has to be on time in order to get the reward; sometimes it is 3 days, sometimes 5 days, sometimes 1 day. This is the principle that drives gambling—you don't win very often, but you keep playing because the next bet might be the one that wins big!

focus point

Although using a continuous reinforcement schedule is best in the early stages of learning a skill or behavior, an intermittent schedule of reinforcement, particularly a variable schedule, is most effective in maintaining that behavior after it has been learned.

According to behavioral theory, a continuous reinforcement schedule is helpful in the early stages of learning a skill or behavior. But once the learner has the basic idea of the movement, an intermittent schedule of reinforcement, particularly a variable schedule, is most effective in maintaining that behavior (Martin & Pear, 2003).

The complexity of behavior modification

It sounds so simple—if a physical education teacher wants students to learn certain skills or display particular behaviors, those skills and behaviors should be positively or negatively reinforced. If the students are exhibiting skills or behaviors the teacher doesn't want, those actions should be punished. Yet, the principles of behavior modification are quite complex, for several reasons (Martens, Christina, Harvey, & Sharkey, 1981):

- *Not all students react the same way to reinforcers and punishments.* A punishment for one child may be a reinforcer for another. For instance, one 6th grader might view being put in time-out as a punishment because he enjoys the soccer activity being practiced that day, while time-out is a reinforcer for another student because he doesn't like soccer.

- *Some skills or behaviors that are reinforced may not be repeatable by the student.* A student who is rewarded when she gets a strike while bowling may try very hard to get another strike, but may not have the ability to repeat the behavior.

- *It is very difficult to know all of the reinforcers in an environment and how much a student values them.* While the physical education teacher is reinforcing one behavior, the student may be receiving other reinforcements from friends or family for other behaviors; if the student values the other reinforcers more than those from the teacher, the teacher's reinforcers will be ineffective. For example, the rewards that are part of the contingency system Ms. Brown set up to help Madeline be on time to class may not be as valuable to Madeline as the reward of spending that time with her boyfriend, and so Ms. Brown's reward system to improve her punctuality will likely not be effective.

Intrinsic Motivation and Extrinsic Rewards

In the chapter's opening scenario, Sarah and Al were two students who participated in running before the Eagle Points reward system was implemented because they enjoyed running and liked improving themselves, demonstrating that they had high intrinsic motivation for running. **Intrinsic motivation** is an internal desire to show competence and be self-determining; individuals with high intrinsic motivation will perform an

focus point

The principles of behavior modification are difficult to apply because children react differently to the same reinforcers, a child may not be able to repeat a behavior that was reinforced, and there may be unknown reinforcers in the environment more valuable to the child than those from the teacher.

activity for its own sake, for the pleasure and excitement derived from participation, and for the desire to master a task (Ryan & Deci, 2000). In contrast, **extrinsic motivation** is when someone performs a task or behavior in order to receive some outcome separate from the activity (Ryan & Deci, 2000). Intrinsic motivation is more desirable than extrinsic motivation because intrinsic motivation is more long-lasting and doesn't require the use of external rewards. The increased effort displayed by many students in Ms. Brown's fitness class seemed to be from extrinsic motivation, because their effort disappeared when the reward was removed. You might think that the addition of an external motivator for performing an already intrinsically motivating activity would further enhance motivation. Unfortunately, as evidenced by their behavior, once Sarah and Al received Eagle Points for running, intrinsic motivation and effort actually decreased.

Several classic studies demonstrate the negative impact that external rewards can have on intrinsic motivation. In one study (Lepper & Greene, 1975), nursery school children performed an intrinsically motivating activity, drawing with felt pens, under one of three conditions. In the "expected reward" condition, the children were told they would receive a Good Player certificate for drawing with the pens. Children in the "unexpected reward" condition were not told about the certificate, but received a certificate after the session. The children in the "no reward" condition were not promised a reward, neither did they receive one when they finished. One week after these sessions, the children were observed during a free-choice situation to see whether the rewards affected their intrinsic motivation for felt pen drawing. The children who received the expected reward for drawing showed a decline in intrinsic motivation for drawing, while the children in the other two groups spent as much time drawing with the pens as before.

Cognitive Evaluation Theory

Why do external rewards decrease intrinsic motivation? Will this decline happen every time extrinsic rewards are given? **Cognitive evaluation theory** (Deci & Ryan, 1985; Ryan & Deci, 2000) describes the complex relationship between extrinsic rewards and intrinsic motivation.

According to this theory, the effects of external rewards on intrinsic motivation depend on how the reward influences someone's perceptions of competence and self-determination. Every external reward—including Eagle Points, free day, being recognized on a poster, and even verbal praise and corrective feedback—has two aspects that can affect intrinsic motivation:

1. Every reward has a *controlling* aspect, and this aspect conflicts with an individual's desire to be self-determining. If a person perceives that a reward is given in order to control her behavior, it leads to a more external perception of control, which decreases her sense of self-determination and thereby decreases intrinsic motivation.

2. Every reward has an *informational* aspect that can affect a person's perceptions of competence. If the reward is believed to provide positive information about one's ability, then intrinsic motivation will be enhanced—as long as the controlling aspect is low. Conversely, failure to receive a reward, or receiving some rewards very easily, can convey negative information about one's competence, and decrease intrinsic motivation.

The key to whether an external reward enhances or harms intrinsic motivation depends on which aspect of the reward is more salient or important to the receiver. If a student believes the controlling aspect of a reward is high, intrinsic motivation will decrease. If the informational aspect is high, the controlling aspect is low, and the information about one's competence is positive, intrinsic motivation will increase. In the felt pen study described earlier, intrinsic motivation was not harmed with the unexpected reward because it was not perceived as controlling. But intrinsic motivation will be harmed if the informational aspect is high and the information obtained about one's competence is negative. This theory indicates that reward systems set up by physical education teachers will enhance student motivation if teachers decrease the controlling aspect of the reward and increase the positive informational aspect.

Let's use these principles to understand how Ms. Brown's Eagle Points reward system affected Sarah and Al's intrinsic motivation. These two students, already intrinsically motivated to run, may have thought the reward system was meant to control their behavior. Although the amount of points they earned could give them positive information about their ability, they didn't need this information because they already thought they were competent. For Sarah and Al, the reward's controlling aspect was higher than the informational aspect, so their intrinsic motivation decreased. Perhaps if Ms. Brown emphasized the positive information the points gave students about their fitness, pointing out to students like Sarah and Al how their fitness levels improved over the semester, the negative impact on intrinsic motivation might not have materialized.

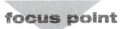

focus point

According to cognitive evaluation theory, external rewards will decrease intrinsic motivation if the controlling aspect of a reward is high and the informational aspect is low, or the informational aspect is high and the information obtained about one's competence is negative.

Reinforcement Research

Reinforcement may take on many different forms: verbal feedback from the teacher, tangible rewards for accomplishments, or even seeing written records of task attempts. Sometimes reinforcement is very systematic, as in behavioral coaching programs based on the principles of behavior modification that are often seen in youth sport (e.g., Smith & Smoll, 1996). Reinforcement in forms like these has long been the subject of research in physical education and youth sport, as well as related fields like motor learning. In this section, some of that research will be reviewed, focusing on studies in which children were the participants.

Student Characteristics Related to the Use of Teacher Feedback

One factor that has been examined in research on reinforcement is which kinds of students are more likely to use feedback from significant adults like the physical education teacher to decide on their competence level.

■ *Age.* Some studies show that feedback from significant adults is more important to elementary children than older children. In a summer physical activity camp (Horn & Hasbrook, 1986; Horn & Weiss, 1991) as well as in physical education (McKiddie & Maynard, 1997), children 11 and 12 years old and younger used feedback from significant adults like the teacher to decide on their ability level more so than older children. Another researcher found that while 13 and 14 year olds in physical education did use some verbal feedback to judge their competence, they also used information gleaned from their coach's behaviors, like where players are positioned (e.g., poorer players are put in right field, bat near the end of the order), when deciding their competence level (Chase, 1998).

■ *Experience with an activity.* Amorose and Smith (2003) found that female youth sport participants between 7 and 14 years old with no previous softball playing experience were more likely than girls with at least one year of playing experience to use feedback from a coach to judge the ability level of girls they watched on video batting a ball.

These studies indicate that elementary students place more importance on teacher feedback than older students, but that adolescents will still use teacher verbal feedback, as well as their teachers' behaviors, to determine their competence. Physical educators' actions must imply a belief that all students can improve. For instance, all students, not just the highly skilled, should be used to demonstrate tasks. Teachers should be especially mindful of giving feedback to children with less experience with skills, because those students rely on that feedback.

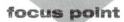

focus point

Students who are more likely to use teacher feedback to determine their competence level are elementary students and those with little experience with a skill.

Reinforcement and Students' Motor Skill Performance

Two aspects of reinforcement and motor skill performance have been investigated in research: (1) verbal feedback and (2) reinforcement as part of behavioral coaching programs based on behavior modification principles. Research conducted in physical education pedagogy and motor learning reveals important information about the impact of verbal feedback on children's motor skill performance (see Exhibit 2.2 for a list of terms used in these two areas for the types of verbal feedback). Most studies on behavioral coaching programs were conducted in youth sport and physical activity settings.

	Terms used in pedagogy and motor learning to describe various types of feedback.	**EXHIBIT**	**2.2**

TERM	DEFINITION	EXAMPLES
General	Conveys that something was done correctly or incorrectly; doesn't specify what or how to improve	"Good job." "That's right." "That's wrong." "Don't hit it that way."
Specific	Describes precisely what was done correctly or incorrectly, or how to improve	"Nice job of stepping on the opposite foot." "You didn't step forward on the opposite foot that time." "Next time make sure you step on the opposite foot."
Positive	Communicates pleasure or satisfaction	"Good job." "Thank you for sharing the ball." "Good job of following through that time."
Negative	Communicates displeasure or dissatisfaction	"I told you a thousand times to step on the other foot!" "I've seen 1st graders who can kick better than that."
Neutral	Conveys neither satisfaction or dissatisfaction (tone of voice can influence whether a feedback statement is positive, negative, or neutral)	"That's right/wrong." "You missed/hit it."
Evaluative	Conveys a judgment regarding the correctness of a skill	"Good job." "I like how you really extend your arms when you're finished." "That's not right." "You didn't extend that time."
Corrective	Provides the learner information on how to perform the movement correctly in the future	"Make sure you throw the ball to the shortstop first." "It helps you get under the ball if you drag your toe a bit."
Congruent	Matches the focus of the task	*"Good screen." "Make sure you set your feet firmly when you make your screen."
Incongruent	Doesn't match the current focus of the task	*"Good shot." "Get your hands up, defense!"
Contingent	Matches the performance level of the student	"You're doing great" (when a student is being successful). "Try keeping the racket level as you swing— you're angling it too much" (when a student is having trouble).
Noncontingent	Doesn't match the performance level of the student	"You're doing great." "Keep up the good work" (when a student is not being successful).
Motivational	Statements meant to encourage/ motivate students	"Keep trying, you'll get it." "You're working so hard— I really appreciate it." "That's allright— this skill is hard—it takes awhile to master it."

(continued)

EXHIBIT   2.2   Terms used in pedagogy and motor learning to describe various types of feedback, *continued.*

TERM	DEFINITION	EXAMPLES
Descriptive	Describes specifically what a student did correctly or incorrectly on a skill just performed	"Great job of knowing where your teammates are." "You didn't pay attention to where your teammates were."
Prescriptive	Describes specifically what a student needs to do in the future to correctly perform a skill	"Next time look around so you can see where your teammates are."
Augmented	Any information that a performer receives about a movement from an outside source	Time it takes to swim 50 meters; any verbal feedback from the teacher about a movement; watching a video of performance.
Intrinsic	Information that a performer receives about a movement through the senses, just by making the movement	Seeing the bowling ball go into the gutter; feeling the sting in the hands after hitting a ball with a bat incorrectly; hearing the bat hit only air after swinging and missing a ball.
Continuous	Learner receives information about the skill on every task attempt	Teacher watches every task attempt by a student and gives her feedback after each attempt.
Intermittent	Learner receives information about the skill periodically throughout practice	Teacher watches a student make several attempts, gives her feedback, watches a few more, gives feedback again.
Concurrent (guidance)	Information given to a learner about a skill during a task attempt	"Make sure you shoot with your outside hand" (spoken as the student attempts a layup).
Immediate	Information given to a learner about a skill immediately after making a task attempt	"You stepped on the correct foot that time." "Make sure you step on the opposite foot next time." (Each spoken immediately after a student finishes an overhand throw.)
Delayed	Teacher allows some time** to lapse before giving the learner feedback about a task attempt (or several)	Teacher watches a student roll 2 or 3 frames in bowling, then may ask the student to describe to her what to do to make the ball roll straight, ask if she is doing that, and then say, "When you release the ball, your hand is pointed straight for the gutter. Make sure you follow through with your hand pointed toward the head pin."

*The task in the basketball lesson is to set a screen on the defender guarding the person with the ball so that person can get free and shoot.
**The amount of time is relative; it may be a few seconds, a minute, several minutes, etc. It just doesn't happen immediately.

Pedagogy research on teacher verbal feedback

One reason physical educators give students praise and corrective information is because they believe it will enhance students' motor skill learning. But in a review of the research on the effects of teacher feedback, Lee, Keh, and Magill (1993) concluded that teacher feedback is not always related to long-term student motor skill achievement. These reviewers found that feedback had small, zero, or even detrimental effects on student achievement.

Other researchers shed further light on the usefulness of teacher feedback. Some studies demonstrate that feedback has a more immediate impact on student practice success that, in turn, could help them learn the skills (e.g., Pellet & Harrison, 1995; Rikard, 1991; Silverman, Woods, & Subramaniam, 1999; Stroot & Oslin, 1993). For example, the practice success of low-ability elementary students improved immediately after receiving feedback from the teacher (Rikard, 1991). It may be that certain kinds of feedback must be given to have a positive impact. Feedback about the outcome of task attempts (Silverman, Tyson, & Krampitz, 1992), specific feedback about errors (Stroot & Oslin, 1993), a critical cue repeated in task instructions and feedback (Masser, 1993), and specific, corrective, congruent feedback (Pellet & Harrison, 1995) have all been shown to positively affect students' immediate practice success.

Although it is unclear if teacher feedback positively impacts long-term student learning, the feedback probably positively affects students' short-term practice and performance. Specific and corrective feedback (e.g., "Make sure you step with your opposite foot next time") may be most helpful. **Congruent feedback,** that which matches the task's focus, seems important to practice success. So if a teacher asks students to work on stepping with the opposite foot as they throw, the teacher's feedback to students should be about stepping on the opposite foot, not about other behaviors or skills.

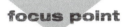

focus point

While pedagogy research indicates that teacher feedback may not affect student learning, it may affect students' short-term practice, especially if it is specific, corrective, and congruent.

Motor learning research and augmented feedback

The pedagogy studies just described examined the teacher's verbal feedback given to children learning motor skills in instructional settings. In the field of motor learning, researchers have conducted laboratory studies of **augmented feedback,** which is any information a person receives about a movement from an outside source. Measuring the time it takes to swim 50 meters is one kind of augmented feedback, as is a teacher's verbal feedback to a student. Augmented feedback is different than **intrinsic feedback,** which is information a performer receives about a movement through the various senses just by making the movement. For instance, a student knows she did something wrong when she sees the bowling ball go into the gutter; a student knows an error was made in batting when he feels the sting in his hands. Augmented feedback can be redundant with intrinsic feedback, as when a teacher tells a student, "You made a basket," something the student can see for herself. But it can also provide unrecognized information to the student, as when a teacher tells a student where the golf ball landed when the student cannot see the ball after a tee shot, or tells a student how fast she swam 50 meters.

Most motor learning research on augmented feedback uses laboratory tasks unlike any motor skill tasks that would actually be practiced in physical education in order to control the many variables that can influence performance and learning. In addition, most of that research has been done with adults and not children. Because of these restrictions, specific motor learning studies will not be reviewed; rather, conclusions based on this research will be presented. Keep in mind that these principles are tentative, pending the satisfactory testing of these principles in actual teaching situations. Motor learning research has addressed three important questions: Is augmented feedback (e.g., teacher verbal feedback) necessary for motor skill learning to occur? How often should augmented feedback be given? When should augmented feedback be given?

Augmented feedback and motor skill learning. Some motor learning researchers have examined whether augmented feedback is necessary for motor skill learning to occur. After all, students receive intrinsic feedback when they see that they made a basket or feel if the ball rolled off their fingertips correctly; is the teacher's feedback redundant? According to Richard Magill (2004), renowned motor learning researcher, the relationship between augmented feedback and motor skill learning can be described four ways:

1. *Augmented feedback is essential for learning motor skills in some situations.* This is true in three situations: (a) if intrinsic feedback is not available to the student from the task (e.g., hitting a golf ball off of a tee and not seeing where it lands, or determining the time in a 50-meter swim); (b) if the student cannot detect sensory feedback due to physical disability (e.g., sight or hearing loss); and (c) if the person is unable to use intrinsic feedback due to lack of experience with the skill (e.g., even though a student can feel how a basketball rolls off her fingers, she doesn't know enough about shooting to notice and use her tactile sense to help correct her shot).

2. *Some motor skills can be learned without augmented feedback.* Very simple skills, like kicking a stationary playground ball from a stationary position for distance, sometimes can provide enough intrinsic feedback so learners can detect their own errors and make adjustments. According to Magill, these skills must have an external referent in the environment that the student can use to assess his initial actions, make changes, and judge new actions. For instance, for the kicking task, the teacher can set up markers at various distances so the students can accurately detect how far they kicked.

3. *Augmented feedback can enhance the learning of some motor skills.* Even though some skills can be learned without augmented feedback, often skills can be learned faster or to a higher level if augmented feedback is received. This principle applies to skills in which a person is learning to move quickly, like using starting blocks in track. Other skills for which augmented feedback can enhance learning include complex skills that require the coordination of several limbs, like the tennis serve or basketball layup.

4. *Augmented feedback can hinder learning of some motor skills.* One way this happens is if the teacher gives a student incorrect or incomplete information about a movement. For example, a teacher tells a student to make sure to follow through to the target when he kicks the ball, but the student has no idea what that means (i.e., incomplete information). Augmented feedback can also hinder learning if students become dependent on the teacher's feedback. They may perform well when the teacher provides feedback, but when the teacher is not available, performance declines. In such cases, the learner is not learning to detect and use intrinsic feedback from her senses about the movement. This happens when the teacher gives the student verbal feedback too often and doesn't give the learner a chance to use her own senses to detect errors. It can also happen when the teacher consistently gives **concurrent feedback,** feedback given to a student while a movement is made, which also prevents the learner from detecting his own sensory information.

Frequency of augmented feedback about errors. Some beginning physical educators believe they must see and give students feedback about every task attempt in order for students to learn best (a continuous reinforcement schedule). To accomplish this, a teacher may arrange students in a single line and have them perform a skill one by one, allowing the teacher to observe and give feedback on each attempt. However, such an arrangement results in many students standing around and prevents them from actually practicing skills. Furthermore, motor learning research strongly indicates that feedback about errors does not need to be given on every task attempt (Magill, 2004; Salmoni, Schmidt, & Walter, 1984; Schmidt & Lee, 2005). In most studies, participants who received information about errors on every attempt performed the skill better while receiving that feedback than those who received feedback less frequently. But when asked to reproduce the movement later without any feedback (a better measure of learning), the participants who received feedback on every trial did worse.

When learners receive feedback about errors on every task attempt (continuous feedback), they can become dependent on that feedback for information about how to improve (Magill, 2004; Schmidt & Lee, 2005). They may not engage in the type of learning strategies they do when they do not receive feedback on every attempt. As mentioned previously, only when learners are first attempting a skill should they receive continuous

focus point

The type of skill (quick, simple, complex), whether or not the student is capable of detecting and using intrinsic feedback (due to either experience level or physical disabilities), and whether or not external referents are available to help determine an action's appropriateness all influence whether or not augmented feedback is important to student learning.

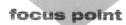

feedback. Once students have acquired the basic idea of a movement, it is actually beneficial for students to make some task attempts without information from the teacher about their errors. What we do not know yet is specifically how often feedback should be given; we only know that it shouldn't be given on every trial. Magill (2004) cautions that this principle relates to feedback about errors; learners may still need periodic feedback to motivate them, especially early in learning.

Timing of augmented feedback about errors. Another question related to augmented feedback is when to give it; is it ok to give feedback while a student is attempting a skill, or should a teacher wait until the student is finished? And should a teacher give the feedback right away or wait a bit? Concurrent feedback is similar to **verbal guidance** from the teacher, which studies reveal can hinder learning because it takes the learner's attention away from intrinsic feedback that is detectable while performing the task. This in turn hurts performance when the teacher's feedback is not available (Schmidt & Lee, 2005). Thus, verbal guidance, given while a student performs a skill, should be given sparingly and only in the very early stage of learning.

Motor learning research indicates that **immediate feedback** (given immediately after a task attempt) usually hinders learning, while **delayed** augmented feedback (delayed for a period of time after a task attempt) does not (Magill, 2004; Salmoni et al., 1984; Schmidt & Lee, 2005). The question remains about the optimum length of this delay. Delays of a few seconds, minutes, and even one week have been examined in studies, with no or small negative effects on learning. A small delay gives learners the opportunity to process intrinsic feedback about the movement before receiving external information, which then prevents dependency. Magill (2004) even suggests that, while waiting to receive feedback about their errors, students should try to verbally describe their own errors to ensure they are processing error information on their own.

Teaching implications. The results of motor learning research have several implications for physical educators and the process of giving students verbal feedback about performance errors.

1. Discern situations and skills in which learning will occur faster and better with feedback and those where it will not. When students learn simple motor skills that may be learned without feedback, ensure that an external referent is available and set up the situation to maximize practice. Then, let students practice without much verbal feedback. This can be a very difficult for teachers!

2. Avoid task structures in which only one student at a time attempts a task. It appears that after students have the basic idea of a move-

ment, they do not have to receive feedback on every task attempt for optimal learning.

3. Use verbal guidance, verbally cueing the student during performance of a skill, only when the student is first learning a skill.

4. Avoid informing students about their errors immediately following task attempts. Rather, as Magill (2004) suggests, question students regarding their perception of their task attempts and possible errors.

5. Remember that all of these principles relate to feedback about motor skill errors. Other types of feedback are still necessary, such as specific praise for successful task attempts or high effort, and encouraging comments to motivate students.

Research on behavioral coaching programs

Several researchers have examined the effectiveness of behavioral coaching programs based on behavior modification principles on children's motor skill performance in youth sport and physical activity settings. The main difference between these programs and traditional instruction of motor skills is that the use of reinforcement, verbal instructions, demonstrations, and practice is deliberate and systematic (as done in behavior modification programs); a specific procedure to follow for correct and incorrect performances is created before practice begins.

One of the first investigations of behavioral coaching was the classic study Komaki and Barnett (1977) conducted with 9- and 10-year-old boys on a Pop Warner football team. The program was designed to improve the boys' accuracy in completing three football plays. Each play was broken down into five stages, which were explained to the boys, modeled by the coach, and put on a checklist. After attempting the targeted play during scrimmages, successful stages in the play were marked on the checklist. The checklist was shown to the boys, and they received feedback and recognition immediately for correct and incorrect stages. Performance during games was reinforced in the same manner, but not until the first practice after the game. Each play was progressively targeted over the season. The researchers found the behavioral coaching program improved the boys' accuracy in completing the plays, with each play improving after the program was introduced for that play but not before.

Other studies also indicate that behavioral coaching programs can enhance the motor skill performance of children of various ages (preschool children to high school students) in a wide range of activities: swimming, soccer, dance, ballet, football, gymnastics, tennis, track, and recreational games (Allison & Ayllon, 1980; Arntzen, Halstadtro, & Halstadtro, 2003; Brobst & Ward, 2002; Buzas & Ayllon, 1981; Fitterling & Ayllon, 1983; Koop & Martin, 1983; Rush & Ayllon, 1984; Shapiro & Shapiro, 1985; Vintere, Hemmes, Brown, & Poulson, 2004). In many studies, positive reinforcements were simple social reinforcers like praise, public postings, smiles, or a thumbs-up. Most of these programs also used instructional cues, corrective feedback, and modeling of correct form. Two programs were even administered by peers instead of the coach (Arntzen et al., 2003; Rush & Ayllon, 1984). For instance, a 5-year-old boy with developmental disabilities learned to play organized games with his peers after participating in a behavioral program in which his 4- and 5-year-old peers were trained to give him social reinforcers (e.g., smiles, nods, thumbs-up) each time he displayed correct behaviors (Arntzen et al., 2003).

The main limitation of this research is that these programs were conducted with only a few children at a time; we still need to determine how well such programs work with large groups of children, as in physical education.

Teacher Feedback and Student Self-Perceptions

The results of various studies provide specific ideas about the types of feedback most likely to enhance self-perceptions. Positive comments, information about one's performance, and motivational statements are related to higher self-perceptions, especially after good performances (e.g., Allen & Howe, 1998; Amorose & Smith, 2003; Amorose & Weiss, 1998; Black & Weiss, 1992; Fredenburg, Lee, & Solmon, 2001; Koka & Hein, 2003; Vallerand, 1983). But following unsuccessful performances, encouragement and specific information about how to improve is needed (e.g., Amorose & Smith, 2003; Amorose & Weiss, 1998; Black & Weiss, 1992).

Low self-perceptions are associated with criticism ("Come on! That was awful!") that lacks specific corrective information following failure (Amorose & Smith, 2003; Amorose & Weiss, 1998). One study indicated **contingent feedback** (that which matches the student's performance level) enhances self-perceptions; in that study, 12- to 15-year-old female softball players with low ability got more praise from their coaches, but had lower self-perceptions than did high-ability players who received more criticism and technical information (Horn, 1985). The researcher believed these results were because the criticism/information was contingent to the girls' performance, while the praise was not. Perhaps the coaches set lower performance standards for the lower-skilled girls, since they were praised a lot but received less helpful information.

Teaching implications

Physical educators can help children perceive higher levels of ability by praising them when successful (e.g., "Way to go, Sarah!"), while giving them technical, corrective information and encouraging them when they are not successful (e.g., "Your arm wasn't straight, Sarah. Next time extend your arm to get a full swing. You can do it."). Conversely, criticizing students when they fail (e.g., "That was a poor shot. What a bad decision!") or only giving technical information with success (e.g., "You extended your arm correctly that time") contributes to lower perceptions of ability. It is important that the feedback you give to students matches their performance level, because excessive praise for very low performance levels suggests that you lack faith in a student's ability, and contributes to low perceptions of competence. But giving technical, corrective information conveys confidence in the child's ability to improve.

focus point

Children's perceptions of competence can be enhanced with contingent feedback such as praise for success and technical, corrective information for unsuccessful attempts.

Reinforcement, Behavior Management, and Prosocial Behaviors

Prosocial behaviors are those that society generally deems desirable and that help one function in and contribute to society, such as being attentive, punctual, helpful, and cooperative.

Punctuality, task persistence, and effort

Researchers, mostly in youth sport, have examined the impact of behavioral coaching programs based on behavior modification principles on behaviors like punctuality, task persistence, and effort. In an early classic study, McKenzie and Rushall (1974) used shaping to improve the punctuality, attendance, and effort of youth sport swimmers at practices. In the first phase, the swimmers were reinforced by receiving a check by their name on a publicly displayed attendance board, along with praise from the coach, if they simply came to practice. In the next phase, they got the check and praise only if they were on time to practice, and in the third phase, swimmers had to be on time and swim the entire session to get the check and praise. Attendance improved at each phase. A public workout board was also used in the program; the swimmers checked off each lap they completed of their programmed workout. This public recognition, a form of reinforcement, increased the number of laps completed, and thus effort, by 27 percent.

Other studies show that behavioral coaching can increase the number of task attempts and the effort children make (DeLuca & Holborn, 1992; Wolko, Hrycaiko, & Martin, 1993) and can decrease their off-task behaviors (Hume, Martin, Gonzalez, Cracklen, & Genthon, 1985). Techniques used in those studies included goal setting by the coach, public display and private self-recording of goals and task attempts, graphing of task attempts, and activity and material rewards.

Attentiveness and disruptive behaviors

A behavior management program conducted with three 6- and 7-year-old children with attention deficit hyperactivity disorder (ADHD) in a summer program enhanced attentiveness while decreasing disruptive behaviors

(Reitman, Hupp, O'Callaghan, Gulley, & Northup, 2001). During kickball games, the children earned poker chips for attentive behavior (i.e., being in ready position before each pitch; answering a question about the current game situation after each pitch). The chips were exchanged for prizes, like stickers and stuffed toys. This token economy was slightly more effective than medication in increasing attentive behavior in these children, while the biggest improvement in attentive behavior came with a combination of the token economy and medication.

Off-task behaviors

Researchers have found that students' off-task behaviors decrease when teachers give verbal praise for appropriate behavior and motor skill performance (van der Mars, 1989), when feedback of any kind is given to students on the opposite side of the gym (Ryan & Yerg, 2001), or when such feedback is amplified using a public address system (Ryan, Ormond, Inwold, & Rotunda, 2002). Similarly, giving students at least one specific skill-related feedback statement each minute, regardless of how close the teacher was to the students, increased students' on-task behaviors (Sariscsany, Darst, & van der Mars, 1995).

Teaching implications

focus point

Reinforcement in various forms, including shaping, can decrease children's off-task, disruptive behaviors, and increase prosocial behaviors.

These studies indicate that physical educators can use reinforcements to positively affect students' prosocial behaviors. Reinforcement may take various forms: points or tokens exchanged for tangible rewards or fun activities, teacher praise, systematic recordkeeping and visual representation of target behaviors by the teacher or student (public or private), or verbal feedback given to other students. Shaping, as done by McKenzie and Rushall (1974), can also help students acquire new prosocial behaviors. A variety of behaviors may be affected using these systematic reinforcement techniques; off-task, inappropriate, disruptive behaviors may be decreased, while attention, effort, punctuality, and attendance may be increased.

Reinforcement, Behavior Management, and Physical Activity

A major goal of most physical education programs is to get children physically active, both inside and outside of physical education. Some research shows that systematic behavior management programs that include a reinforcement element can enhance children's physical activity levels outside of physical education. For example, in one study parents were trained by the researcher to establish a contract with their child, monitor the child's activity level and points earned for activity, and gradually extinguish material rewards the child earned for reaching a weekly activity point criterion (Taggart, Taggart, & Siedentop, 1986). In another study with 6- to 17-year-old children with intellectual disabilities (Katz & Singh, 1986), visual signs of the school mascot (a frog) participating in ball and jungle gym play were placed around the playground; the supervisors used these to remind the children to play. Play was reinforced with praise and by taking pictures of the children at play and placing the pictures on a display board. Fading occurred by gradually decreasing the number of pictures taken per day and reminders to look at the sign; eventually the signs were removed. The treatment significantly increased the number of children participating in these activities and nearly tripled the amount of time the children played. Most important, these gains were maintained over 12 weeks of gradually fading the prompts and pictures.

It is encouraging that behavior management programs using reinforcement can be developed to enhance the physical activity levels of children outside of physical education. These studies show that

- such programs don't need to be expensive (i.e., taking pictures and putting up signs);
- the programs can be successful with children with intellectual disabilities; and
- parents and physical educators can work together to enhance children's activity levels.

Cognitive Evaluation Theory Research

Several studies have been conducted in physical activity settings with children to test the principles of cognitive evaluation theory.

External rewards

In one study, the impact of two elementary schools' running programs on running performance and motivational variables was investigated (Xiang, Chen, & Bruene, 2005). At one school, 4th grade children earned external rewards (stickers, certificates, trophies, etc.) for running laps, and the number of laps completed were publicly displayed. In the other school, running was integrated into the regular motor skill development process; children received no external rewards for running but were encouraged to practice running to improve their skills. The results showed that the children who did not receive external rewards focused more on running to improve their own performance, and less on comparing their performance to their peers,

connected   CONCEPTS

Task involvement, in which the focus is on improving one's own performance, tends to produce greater effort and persistence than ego involvement, in which one's performance is compared to others (see Chapter 5).

than the children who received external rewards. Such a focus can result in greater task persistence.

Information about competency levels

Another principle of cognitive evaluation theory is that external events providing positive information about one's competence will increase motivation, while events providing negative information about competence will decrease motivation. This was confirmed by Whitehead and Corbin (1991), who found that students who were told that their time on an agility run was in the top 20 percent of children their age (i.e., received positive information) had higher levels of intrinsic interest in the task than students who were told they were in the bottom 20 percent (i.e., received negative information).

Contingent rewards

Because contingent rewards are those that are received only if a specified level of performance is reached, and noncontingent rewards are received regardless of performance level, contingent rewards should provide more information about one's competence than noncontingent rewards, thereby increasing intrinsic motivation more. Indeed, competitive teenaged swimmers who earned a contingent reward (i.e., listening to music) showed greater improvements in productive behaviors and more dramatic decreases in nonproductive behaviors during practice than swimmers who received the reward noncontingently (Hume & Crossman, 1992). Other researchers found that noncontingent rewards motivated 5-year-old boys to work on a task, but 9-year-old boys were most motivated by a contingent reward (Thomas & Tennant, 1978).

Teaching implications

focus point

Cognitive evaluation research indicates that external rewards can decrease children's intrinsic motivation, but giving rewards contingently can help minimize this negative effect.

These studies on cognitive evaluation have several implications for physical educators. First, you should be aware that external rewards can decrease intrinsic motivation. Second, if you want to use external rewards, the rewards should be given contingently; students should only receive rewards if they earn them. Contingent rewards provide more positive information about students' ability levels, so are more likely to enhance their intrinsic motivation. Although noncontingent rewards may enhance the motivation of young children (i.e., preschool to 2nd grade), you will be more consistent if rewards given to students of all ages are contingently earned. Third, based on Whitehead and Corbin (1991), you as a physical educator might be better off using fitness tests that do not use percentile-based interpretations of the students' results, because negative information can harm the children's interest in the tasks. Many fitness tests use self-improvement or health-based criteria for receiving awards;

these types of tests have the potential to provide positive information to all children, unlike the percentile-based tests.

Practical Guidelines for Reinforcement in Physical Education

Theories and research related to reinforcement provide teachers with valuable guidelines for using punishment, giving verbal feedback and extrinsic rewards, and creating a behavior management system. In the following section, those guidelines will be described, along with an instructional model that can enhance the provision of feedback during physical education.

Guidelines for Using Punishment

You may have noticed that punishments are rarely mentioned in reinforcement research. That is because reinforcement should be used much more than punishment in physical education; in fact, Kauss (1980) proposed that punishment should be used only 5 percent of the time and only for intolerable behaviors. Punishment can arouse a fear of failure in students; this fear causes them to focus more on the unpleasant consequences of mistakes when learning skills than on how to perform the skill correctly, which can lead to more mistakes. Moreover, excessive use of punishment produces an unpleasant, aversive learning environment (Smith & Smoll, 1996). As a physical educator, strive to "catch students being good" and reinforce such skills and behaviors, rather than catching students doing wrong and punishing that behavior.

However, for those times when punishment is used, here are some guidelines to help increase its effectiveness (Martens et al., 1981):

- Make it clear that it is the student's behavior that is unacceptable ("Madeline, this is the third day this week that you've been late; that needs to change"), and not the student who is unacceptable ("Madeline, you are just no good! You can't even get to class on time!").
- Administer punishments without anger and in an impersonal way; do not punish students to retaliate and make you feel better.
- Punishment should be corrective; make sure students understand appropriate behavior.
- Unless the student's behavior is putting other students or staff in danger, give the student one warning before punishing.
- Administer punishments consistently—if one student is punished for a behavior, other students should also be punished for that behavior.

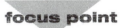

focus point

Punishment should be used sparingly in physical education class, as it creates an unpleasant learning environment and can develop a fear of failure in students, which can actually lead to more mistakes.

And if a behavior is punished one day, it should also be punished on other days.

■ Make sure the punishment is viewed negatively by the student, and not as a positive reinforcement. For instance, a time-out for a 6th grader who is off-task may be viewed positively by that student if he really doesn't want to participate in the activity.

■ Once a punishment has been completed, do not continue to punish the student by having a negative attitude toward the student; resume normal, positive interactions immediately.

■ Do not punish a student for making errors while learning a skill. This likely occurs most often when students are learning to control a skill. For example, when students first learn the tennis backhand, it is difficult to control the ball. Do not punish students who cannot control the backhand, as when the ball is hit over a fence.

■ Physical activity/exercise should not be used as punishment! You are in the business of helping students enjoy physical activity; using it as a punishment will lead students to view it negatively and decrease their desire to be physically active in the future. The Centers for Disease Control (CDC, 1997) cites the importance of avoiding the use of physical activity as punishment. The National Association for Sport and Physical Education (NASPE) has published position statements explaining why physical activity should not be used as punishment in physical education (NASPE, 2000, 2001, 2004a; visit www.aahperd.org/naspe/template.cfm?template=peappropriatepractic e/index.html and go to the elementary, middle, and high school appropriate practices documents).

real world

A teacher who effectively uses punishment in physical education is Carolyn J., who teaches at an elementary school in the southern United States. She rarely punishes, focusing instead on students' positive behaviors. When a student is punished, the student goes to the time-out area, where she completes a worksheet describing the inappropriate behavior for which she is being punished, as well as the appropriate behavior she should exhibit. Carolyn administers punishments in an impersonal way, and makes sure to praise the student for something positive shortly after returning to practice. She doesn't punish students for skill errors, and never uses physical activity as a punishment. Carolyn admits, however, that some of her older 5th grade students probably view the time-out positively (as it gets them out of practice); but Carolyn works very hard to make the tasks enjoyable enough so all students want to participate.

Like Carolyn, Ms. Brown rarely uses punishment in class. When she was a beginning teacher, she used to punish students (e.g., for being late, swearing, incorrect dress) by having them run extra laps or do push-ups because that's what her former coaches did. But she quickly learned that students in physical education are more motivated by positive reinforcement, and she strives to use it whenever possible.

Guidelines for Giving Teacher Verbal Feedback

Physical educators give students verbal feedback to help them learn motor skills, to enhance their self-perceptions, and to help them learn prosocial behaviors. Theories and research give us ideas about the type of feedback that best accomplishes each goal.

Verbal feedback to enhance motor skill learning and performance

Factors that influence the impact of teacher feedback on student performance and learning of motor skills include the timing and situations in which feedback is given, the task structure, if feedback is withheld at appropriate times, and types of feedback given (see Exhibit 2.3).

Guidelines for giving teacher verbal feedback to improve students' motor skill performance.	**EXHIBIT 2.3**

- Recognize skills and situations in which learning is enhanced with feedback about errors and give it
  - Intrinsic feedback isn't available to students due to the task itself, a disability, or lack of experience with the skill
  - Learning to move quickly
  - Complex skills coordinating several limbs
- Concurrent and continuous feedback should only be given early in learning; both should be removed quickly and replaced with intermittent feedback
- Wait a few seconds before giving students feedback about errors, or ask them what they did right or wrong before giving feedback
- Set up tasks to maximize student practice, not to watch and give feedback on every attempt
- Avoid giving feedback when students practice very simple motor skills that have an external referent they can use to assess and adjust their performance
- Give specific, corrective, congruent feedback
- Reinforce the process of motor performance rather than the outcome

When to provide feedback. Even though pedagogical research indicates that the total amount of feedback given to students does not appear to affect motor skill learning, it likely enhances students' short-term performance and practice success. Motor learning research further suggests there are situations in which information from you about errors can help your students learn motor skills. As a physical educator, recognize and give students corrective feedback

1. when intrinsic feedback about a motor task isn't available to students (e.g., not being able to see where a tee shot in golf landed; not being able to tell how fast a mile was run);

2. when intrinsic feedback isn't available to students due to a physical disability (e.g., a student with cerebral palsy cannot sense how far her arm reaches back on a tennis forehand);

3. when students lack sufficient experience with a skill to use intrinsic information (e.g., a student can see that an overhand volleyball serve went into the net and that she hit it too low, but she doesn't know enough about serving to know that she needs to contact the ball higher); and

4. when students are learning to move quickly or learning complex skills in which several limbs are coordinated (e.g., cross-country skiing or punting).

Make it your goal to decrease student dependency on teacher verbal feedback about errors; you want students to eventually perform well without your input. With this in mind, concurrent feedback or verbal guidance (given during performance of a skill) and continuous feedback (feedback after every attempt) should be given only when students are first learning a motor skill, if it is even possible to do so. But very quickly, remove concurrent and continuous feedback about errors and adopt a more intermittent and variable schedule for feedback. You can also decrease student dependency on teacher feedback if you avoid giving feedback immediately after a task attempt. Instead, wait a few seconds before giving students feedback. Or, better yet, ask students to tell you what they think they did right or wrong on an attempt before you tell them. Delaying feedback in these ways allows students to use their own intrinsic feedback to process their own errors. Be sure to teach the students clear cues related to the motor skill they are practicing, as this will guide them in detecting any errors.

Effective task structures for providing feedback. One important finding from motor learning research is that once students have a basic idea of a movement, they learn better when they do not get information from you about errors on every try (continuous feedback). This relieves you from needing to see and give feedback to students on every attempt, and frees you to set up tasks to maximize students' practice time. So, the task structure where one student performs at a time, under your watchful eye, isn't the best for student learning. Organize tasks to give students as many attempts as possible. To do that, set up tasks so only the minimum number of students necessary is used. For instance, if students are working on dribbling a ball, every student should have a ball and dribble simultaneously; avoid having students wait in lines for a turn. If the task is to dribble against a defender and then pass to a teammate, then three students is the minimum needed. If you don't have enough "official" equipment (e.g., basketballs for dribbling), use other types of equipment (e.g., volleyballs or playground balls). Allow enough space for maximum participation to occur safely.

When not to provide feedback. As a physical educator, learn to recognize situations and skills in which learning occurs best without your feedback. This includes very simple motor skills, as long as you set up the task so students have an external environmental referent to use to make adjustments to their actions. For instance, if students are learning to underhand toss a beanbag various distances, cones may be set up at different distances from a target, and the children practice tossing at each distance. Students can readily use their own sensory feedback to adjust the force with which they toss the bag. With these types of tasks, you can minimize teacher feedback and let students detect and correct their own errors.

Types of feedback to provide. Feedback that is specific and corrective seems to help students perform better, so tell students specifically what they need to do to improve ("Trisha, contact the ball further out in front of your body"). Moreover, the feedback should be congruent to the focus of the task; if you are focusing on correct overhand throw form, for example, don't give feedback about the throw's distance or accuracy. Or if you are focusing on stepping on the opposite foot in a throwing task, give feedback about stepping on the opposite foot, not about the follow-through or getting the arm back.

When verbally reinforcing students about their motor skills, reinforce the process of motor skill performance more than the outcome (Weinberg & Gould, 2003). That means praising students more often for exhibiting correct form when performing a skill ("Good job of stepping on the opposite foot"), rather than the result of the skill ("What a long throw!"). It also means praising students for their performance during games ("You got 80 percent of your first serves in that game—good job, Trisha!"), rather than whether or not they won the game ("You beat Angela, Trisha—good job!"). Students have greater control over their own performance than the outcome, so reinforcing specific parts of their performance is more motivating and more likely to enhance performance than praising the outcome.

real world

Giving effective feedback about motor skill errors is difficult. A teacher must know when to give information and when to stay quiet, and what type of information to give. A physical education teacher who seems to have mastered this skill is Jeremy S., who teaches elementary students in a Midwestern U.S. town. When skills are simple, Jeremy stands back and lets students try the skill on their own, without interruption from him. But in situations that require feedback, Jeremy makes sure it is congruent with the current focus of the task, giving students specific information about their errors. For instance, when he asked students practicing cartwheels to make sure they alternated "hand–hand–foot–foot," he gave feedback only on that, not on keeping their legs straight or landing softly. Even during game play, Jeremy's feedback is about the process of student performances (e.g., "Good quick changes of direction in that tagging game, Scott!"), not about whether they got tagged or won the game. Jeremy structures tasks to maximize practice time, meaning he cannot give feedback on every task attempt. Jeremy also uses questions when he gives feedback; he asks students what they think they did right or wrong on task attempts before he gives them feedback. These strategies decrease the chances his students will become dependent on his feedback. As with many physical education teachers, Jeremy has trouble giving students continuous feedback when they are first learning a skill.

Verbal feedback to enhance students' self-perceptions

Research shows that reinforcement and feedback from significant others can influence student self-perceptions. Although researchers found that feedback from teachers is more important to elementary students than older students (who prefer information from their peers), adolescents still use teacher feedback as well as teacher actions when deciding their self-perceptions. Theories and research on feedback suggest some guidelines for giving feedback to students in physical education that can positively affect their self-perceptions (see Exhibit 2.4).

Give contingent feedback. One basic principle is to give contingent feedback; that is, make sure the feedback given to students matches their performance levels. Quite simply, that means if students are successful, you should praise them specifically (e.g., "Good job, Tom! Your fake was much quicker that time!"), and when students are not successful, you should give them technical, corrective information to help them improve (e.g., "That's ok, Tom. Your fake was kind of weak. Next time really make it look like you're going the other way and you'll get by that defender"). Giving contingent feedback also means avoiding excessive praise when students are successful at easy tasks, because that implies you do not believe the student can improve. Furthermore, strive to praise students when they are success-

Guidelines for giving teacher verbal feedback to enhance students' self-perceptions.	**EXHIBIT**	**2.4**

- Give contingent feedback

- Praise students for success

- Avoid excessive praise for success on easy tasks

- Avoid only giving technical, corrective information for success

- Use the "sandwich" approach after unsuccessful task attempts
    - Give a positive statement
    - Give future-oriented technical instruction
    - Give a compliment

- Avoid criticizing students for unsuccessful attempts

- Avoid behaviors that imply a belief that students have low ability

ful; it can be discouraging for students to continually receive technical, corrective information without ever being praised when they do well.

Avoid criticism of unsuccessful attempts. Avoid criticizing students for unsuccessful attempts (e.g., "Tom, I can't believe you didn't get by the defender. I've shown you how to do a good fake—why can't you do it?!"). In fact, it's probably a good idea to use the **sandwich approach** (Smith & Smoll, 1996) to give students feedback after unsuccessful attempts. This approach comprises three sequential elements:

1. *A positive statement.* The sandwich starts with a positive statement, which makes the listener more receptive to the next part of the sandwich, the technical instruction: "Good try, Tom."; "Tom, you almost got by him that time."

2. *Future-oriented technical instructions.* Now give the student corrective, technical information about the skill for the student to try on his next attempt: "Next time make your fake realistic—really look like you're going the opposite way"; "Angela, be sure to keep your back elbow up when you swing at the ball."

3. *A compliment.* The sandwich ends with a compliment, a statement about something the student did well so the student feels good. This compliment can be an encouraging statement about effort or improvement: "Keep trying, Tom. You'll get it"; "That's ok, Angela, you're getting better." Or it can specifically describe something technical the

student performed correctly: "You did a good job of keeping the dribble on the outside. Way to go!"; "You're stepping into the pitch correctly now, Angela. Keep that up!"

Avoid behaviors and actions that suggest negative judgments of student ability. As a physical education teacher, strive to avoid behaviors and actions that suggest you believe some students have lower ability than others, especially when working with adolescents. Avoid actions such as always putting low-skilled students in right field during softball games, or only using high-skilled students to demonstrate or be coaches in sport education units.

real world

One teacher who does a great job of giving feedback to enhance students' self-perceptions is Jean R., who teaches at an urban elementary school in the southern United States. She often uses the sandwich approach and is keenly aware of students who lack confidence. For instance, during a 3rd grade rope jumping lesson, she told a boy who was frustrated with his low success: "Damond, you almost got it! Try moving only your wrists as you turn the rope and that will control it. You are working so hard—I know you're going to get this trick!" Jean gives contingent feedback and will not praise students unless they earn it; she also carefully watches students before giving feedback so she makes truthful positive statements in the sandwich. Jean is well-known in her school as a teacher who positively impacts her students' self-perceptions and is respected by her students.

Verbal feedback to enhance prosocial behaviors

Teacher verbal feedback can enhance a variety of prosocial behaviors, including student effort, punctuality, attendance, on-task behaviors, and attentiveness (see Exhibit 2.5 for guidelines). Teachers often assume stu-

EXHIBIT 2.5	Guidelines for giving teacher verbal feedback to enhance students' prosocial behaviors.

- Clearly define in observable terms and demonstrate prosocial behaviors

- Verbally praise students for exhibiting appropriate behaviors

- Verbal praise for successful motor skill performances and information about motor skill errors can decrease off-task behaviors

- When appropriate, make sure other students can hear any feedback you give to a student, because simply hearing feedback given to other students can keep students on-task

dents know what appropriate behavior is, when many times they do not. Clearly define in observable terms the specific prosocial behaviors you want students to show.

One important principle to remember when trying to enhance students' prosocial behaviors is to catch them being good. Verbally praise students when they show the appropriate behaviors that have been clearly defined for them ("Thank you for congratulating the other team, Shelly"; "Good job keeping your hands to yourself, Jerry"). Too often the only time teachers comment about prosocial behaviors is when reprimanding a student who exhibits inappropriate behaviors.

Feedback of any kind, including skill-related feedback, can decrease off-task behaviors. Moreover, a student can be positively affected (i.e., decrease her off-task behaviors) even if she doesn't directly receive the feedback, but can hear the feedback given to other students. Consider using an amplification system if you teach in large spaces with large groups of students, or in noisy environments. This system could be used to do task presentations, but also to provide feedback as students practice, because simply hearing feedback of any kind can keep students on-task.

real world

Elizabeth B. is a physical educator in an urban middle school in the southern United States that has many at-risk students. Yet, Elizabeth has a real knack for "catching students when they're good." The rules for class are posted on the gym wall, but appropriate behaviors are still somewhat vague. So Elizabeth, who wants her students to demonstrate sportspersonship in her classes, actually does skits with her students that demonstrate the specific behaviors she desires. For instance, in one two-part skit Elizabeth played the part of a high-skilled student playing volleyball with teammates. In Part A of the skit, she ran all over the court, stepped in front of classmates to hit the ball, and yelled at them when they made mistakes (illustrating inappropriate behavior); in Part B, she played her position only, encouraged her teammates when they made mistakes, and even showed them how to do skills (appropriate behavior). Such skits are done at the start of the year and periodically throughout the year. Although it decreases time for motor skill practice, prosocial goals are important to Elizabeth, so she thinks it is worth it. Elizabeth also makes a conscious, consistent effort all year to praise students when they exhibit appropriate behavior. For example, when a student who is often late for class is on time, Elizabeth thanks the student.

Now let's apply the principles for giving effective feedback to Ms. Brown and her students. The main type of feedback Ms. Brown gives is general praise. "Good job" and "good try" are common phrases she uses, whether in reaction to students' motor skill attempts or prosocial behaviors. Hence, students do not receive the specific, corrective information about the process of performance needed to improve, they do not know why they are praised, and they are praised even when they don't do well. Ms. Brown should give more contingent, specific feedback; she should tell students specifically what they do well when they are successful or show appropriate prosocial behaviors, and she needs to give students specific, corrective feedback for unsuccessful motor skill attempts and inappropriate behaviors. Her feedback must match their performance levels (i.e., be contingent). "Good job" can become "Nice steady pace, Chris," "Thank you for getting to class on time, Madeline." The sandwich approach should be used to give corrective feedback, so "good try" becomes "Good try, Jeanie, your golf swing is looking much smoother. Keep watching the ball and that will help you get solid contact. But you brought your club back this time!" Ms. Brown should also ask students to explain what they think they did wrong on incorrect attempts before she explains what she saw. Any of these feedback techniques will help her give feedback that more positively affects her students' motor skill performances, self-perceptions, and prosocial behaviors than the general, noncontingent praise she currently gives.

Guidelines for Giving Extrinsic Rewards

Like Ms. Brown, many physical educators use extrinsic rewards in their programs. Following are guidelines, gleaned from the cognitive evaluation theory and related research, to enhance the effectiveness of such rewards. See Exhibit 2.6.

EXHIBIT 2.6   Guidelines for giving extrinsic rewards.

- Choose effective reinforcers (ones that are desired by the students)
- Clearly define the target behavior in observable, measurable terms
- Establish clear criteria for earning the reward
- Criteria for earning rewards should be individually based or based on self-improvement, when possible
- Minimize giving rewards based on the performance of others
- Make sure rewards are contingently earned
- Let the reward system be optional for students, or obtain input from students
- Verbal praise for student accomplishments should accompany extrinsic rewards
- Use fading

Choose effective reinforcers

Even if a teacher thinks a reward is great, it won't be effective if students do not perceive the reward positively. Try to determine the types of rewards students desire. You may give students a survey at the start of the school year on which they check the types of rewards they value (see Appendix A.1). This type of survey is better than just asking students the open-ended question, "What type of rewards for good performance in physical education would you like to earn?" because you may include on the checklist only the types of rewards you are willing to give. Once you know the rewards students like, rewards can even be individualized for students, because not all students react similarly to the same reward.

Clearly define the target behavior in observable, measurable terms

The behavior to be developed in students needs to be clearly explained and demonstrated for them so that they know unmistakenly when they exhibit the behavior. If, for instance, you want your upper elementary students to develop correct disk throwing skills, the target behavior can be defined by these critical elements: (1) thumb on top, fingers underneath the disk; (2) reach across the body; (3) step toward target; (4) snap wrist on release; and (5) point to target on follow-through. You may decide students need to exhibit all five critical elements in order to correctly display the target behavior, or maybe only four out of the five need to be seen. The target behavior might be a critical element of a skill with which students are having trouble, like "hit the ball out of the hand, do not toss it up" in the underhand volleyball serve. Or, if you want your high school students to be out of the locker room more quickly at the start of each class, the target behavior might be defined as sitting in their assigned position within 6 minutes after the bell rings, by the gym clock. In all of these examples, the target behavior is very clear. Unclear target behaviors might be to "show correct form in throwing the disk" or "get out of the locker room more quickly."

Establish clear criteria for earning the reward

How many times, and within what time period, must the target behavior be displayed in order to earn the reward? For the above target behavior, showing four of the five critical elements when throwing a disk, students might perform ten throws for a classmate in a class period. The classmate has a checklist with the critical elements and a place to mark for each throw if the classmate showed each critical element. The reward is earned if a student shows four of the five critical elements on eight of ten throws that day. Or you might decide that eight out of ten need to be reached in three class periods in a week. Whatever is decided, the criteria should be clearly explained to students before the task begins.

Criteria for earning rewards should be individually based or based on self-improvement, when possible

In the above example, some elementary students might already demonstrate all five critical elements on most of their throws before any instruction is even given, so the eight out of ten criteria may be too easy for them and not motivating. Other students may not even be able to hold a disk correctly, and for them, the eight out of ten criteria is too hard. Although it is harder to organize than having the same criteria for everyone, it may be best to either create different criteria for different students to earn rewards, or base rewards on improvement rather than a set standard. For disk throwing, for example, at the start of a unit, the students could make 10 throws and get evaluated on his or her form. Then you can set standards for students individually and specifically (e.g., "Lance, your goal the next time we do the test is to try to use 3 of the 5 critical cues in 5 out of 10 throws. Laurie, your goal is to show all 5 cues in 8 out of 10 throws"), or more generally by self-improvement (e.g., "Class, to earn the reward today you need to increase from your first attempt the number of throws out of 10 in which you show all 5 critical cues"). Individualizing criteria for students will increase the positive informational aspect of rewards, which according to cognitive evaluation theory enhances the effectiveness of rewards.

Minimize giving rewards based on the performance of others

An integral part of sports is the outcome of contests (i.e., winning a game; where one places in a race or tournament). Such outcomes, however, are partially based on the performance of others, which is less controllable by a student than his own performance or that of his team. So although you might reward the team that places first in the culminating tournament during a sport education volleyball unit, for example, you should also reward teams for improving the percentage of accurate serves or getting a certain number of three-hit sequences in game play. Similarly, rewards given for performance on fitness tests are more motivational and give more positive information about students' performance if the rewards are based on health-related criteria or

connected CONCEPTS

Rewards based on the performance of others invokes ego involvement, which tends to be less motivating than rewards based on one's own improvement (task involvement; see Chapter 5).

individual improvement, rather than percentile-based criteria. The latter are based on how others performed and limit the number of students who can achieve at a certain percentile, unlike trying to reach a certain health standard or improve one's fitness level.

Make sure rewards are contingently earned

Rewards should not be given to students unless they have met the criteria and earned them. Resist the temptation to give students a reward because they "got close" or they "tried hard" or because some students earned the reward but others did not. Giving students rewards contingently increases your credibility. Students learn that you really mean what you say. When students receive rewards they haven't earned, they learn they cannot trust what you say. Giving rewards contingently also increases the informational aspect of a reward, which is important to effective rewards. Receiving the reward means that the student did something well; it provides the student with positive information about her competence, which noncontingent rewards fail to do.

Let the reward system be optional for students, or obtain input from students

Increasing the informational aspect of rewards in the ways just described decreases the controlling aspect. Another way to decrease the controlling aspect is to make the reward system optional for students. Present the idea to students and let them choose to participate or not. You may also ask students for input on the reward system. These strategies help students perceive more control and decrease the perception that you are trying to control them.

Provide praise for student accomplishments to accompany extrinsic rewards

This enhances the possibility that students will exhibit the target behavior after the extrinsic rewards are removed. This is part of the fading process, in which the reinforcer that controls a behavior (e.g., an extrinsic reward) is gradually changed to a new reinforcer (e.g., teacher praise, pride in accomplishments, enjoyment of activity). Besides praising students for accomplishments, also point out the benefits of the target behavior. For instance, verbally praise students who reach the criteria for hitting the ball out of the hand in the volleyball underhand serve for their achievements, but also remind them how they are now better volleyball players and can enjoy the game more because their serve is more accurate.

Use fading

In addition to praising students while giving the extrinsic reward, fading also involves gradually making it harder to receive a reward. The idea is to move the students' focus from the extrinsic reward to less tangible reinforcers of teacher praise and internal reinforcers like enjoyment and satisfaction. If, for example, students first received a reward if they exhibited four of the five critical elements for disk throwing in eight out of ten throws in a single class period, require them to perform those critical elements on nine of ten throws in the next class period, or to display four critical elements in eight of ten throws for two class periods in a row.

Example of the Effective Use of Extrinsic Rewards

real world

Kristi S., physical education instructor at a university in the Midwestern United States, worked with a local elementary principal to establish a walking program that included a rewards system to encourage student physical activity during recess. Kristi painted a walking trail around the perimeter of the school's playground area (approximately one-quarter mile). During noon recess, students who choose to participate in the program that day get their walking card stamped for every lap completed. Once a student has 20 stamps on the first card (meaning he has completed 20 laps), he trades his card in for a chain and a token (a plastic running foot to place on the chain). For each card completed after that, the student receives another token for his chain, with the tenth token being glow-in-the-dark. When a student turns in his eleventh card, he starts over with a new chain. Kristi's university students administer the program; they stamp the walking cards, organize the cards by grade level and teacher, and award students with tokens. However, a physical education teacher might recruit assistance from classroom teachers who are supervising the playground. Kristi believes 90 percent of the school's students participated in the program at some point. The principal claims that, besides increasing student activity, less bullying and fewer injuries occur during recess, because students are spread over a greater area on the playground instead of just all around the basketball courts or jungle gyms. Kristi admits, however, that she doesn't have a plan for fading these rewards and wonders what will happen to the students' activity levels when the tokens disappear.

Ms. Brown follows many of these guidelines for her reward system. The target behavior is defined in measurable, observable terms (1 Eagle point per one-quarter mile); there are clear criteria for obtaining rewards (she has a list of prizes along with the number of points needed to earn each prize); other students' performances don't affect whether a student earns a reward; and points and rewards are given to students only if they meet the criteria. Even though Ms. Brown doesn't survey students to discover the types of rewards they like, she uses a variety of prizes, so students can choose something they actually want. She could have an extra incentive in the system for individual improvement; for example, students who complete 5 percent more laps this week than last week get 5 extra points. She could decrease the controlling aspect of the rewards by making it optional, or getting students' ideas about the system. As stated earlier in the chapter, Ms. Brown could use fading by requiring students to complete more laps in order to earn Eagle points or requiring them to pay more points for prizes. She needs to praise them more often for their accomplishments and remind them of the intangible benefits gained from completing laps (e.g., losing weight, looking fit) so those elements become new reinforcers for students.

Create a Behavior Management Program

Once a teacher knows the principles for effective verbal feedback and extrinsic rewards, he or she can use those principles to set up a behavior management program. Such a program can help develop those motor skills that children may have difficulty learning, or help them learn specific prosocial behaviors like punctuality, dressing out, praising peers instead of demeaning them, staying on-task, or using appropriate language. Such a program can be created for individual students, small groups, or an entire class. Remember that many reinforcements in programs used in research projects are not material reinforcers; rather, they are simple checklists, specific teacher praise, or charts showing progress on a target behavior. The key to a behavior management program is the deliberate and systematic use of reinforcement, verbal instructions, demonstrations, and practice; the program is decided upon before instruction begins and closely followed.

Behavior management programs are often developed when a student or group of students is having a difficult time learning a particular motor skill or prosocial behavior. Shaping is a good strategy in such instances, because the students don't have to exhibit the target behavior right away. At first, only a vague resemblance of the target behavior is reinforced; the students are required to exhibit closer and closer approximations of the target behavior in order to be reinforced, until eventually the target behavior is necessary for reinforcement.

The research reviewed earlier shows that student peers, even as young as kindergarten, and parents can be enlisted to administer a behavior management program. For example, 9th graders skilled at the tennis serve could help their classmates who are having trouble with the serve; 2nd graders whose classmate with autism refuses to play with others can be

focus point

An effective behavior management program can use shaping, should clearly outline all the specific details of the program, and can use peers and parents to administer the program, as long as they as sufficiently trained.

taught to praise him when he interacts with them. In such instances, it is very important that all details of the program be specifically outlined and made clear to the peer or parent administrators; they must understand the importance of sticking to the established program (e.g., not giving reinforcements when they weren't earned). It will also be helpful, especially when using peers as administrators, to train the students how to conduct the program by role-playing the steps with them.

Earlier we met Madeline, a 9th grader who was often tardy to Ms. Brown's class. Ms. Brown could set up a behavior management program to help Madeline improve her punctuality. For example, Ms. Brown asked Madeline about rewards she might like and found out that she enjoys listening to her iPod but her parents won't let her use it in the evenings because of her low grades (including her low grade in physical education). Ms. Brown created a program with Madeline's parents whereby they would reward Madeline with 15 minutes of iPod listening time in the evenings if she met the criteria Ms. Brown set each week for punctuality to class. Ms. Brown used shaping to establish the criteria to receive the reward. The first week, Madeline could be no more than 5 minutes tardy to class each day. Each subsequent week, the number of minutes Madeline could be tardy to class each day and still receive the reward decreased by 1 minute, until she had to be in class on time 5 days a week to earn iPod time.

Use the Personalized System of Instruction Model

Although studies show students seem to learn better when they don't receive feedback from the teacher on every task attempt, it is important students receive continuous feedback when first learning a new skill. Students also need to receive regular feedback because feedback enhances student motivation and self-perceptions. But when physical educators follow effective teaching skills like maximizing student practice time by having all students practice at once, they find it hard to adequately reinforce their students. In fact, giving students too much feedback is rarely a problem in physical education. An instructional model that may help students receive sufficient reinforcement is the **personalized system of instruction** (PSI).

The PSI model, based on the principles of behavioral theory, was developed by Fred Keller (1968; Keller & Sherman, 1982) as a way to individualize instruction and consistently reinforce students. In this

connected CONCEPTS

Peer teaching is another instructional model that can increase the amount of feedback students receive (see Chapter 3).

model, first determine the skills and knowledge needed to participate in an activity, and then design a sequence of learning tasks for learning those elements. Task presentations, task structures, common performance errors, and performance criteria are all determined by you. What distinguishes this instructional model from others is that you don't present the tasks to the students in person, but via a written workbook, videos, or other instructional media. This frees you to give individualized instruction and feedback to students. When students reach a certain performance level (via the criteria you determine) on a task, they are reinforced by being allowed to move onto the next task. Students must have a sufficient level of reading ability to comprehend the task presentations and structures described in their PSI workbook, as well as have sufficient personal responsibility to work independently; thus, the PSI model is probably best used with middle school students and older (Metzler, 2005).

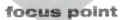

Among the teachers who have successfully used the PSI model in physical education is Tamara A. While a student teacher at a suburban high school in the southern United States, she designed a PSI badminton unit. Tamara designed a workbook with learning task modules on the short and deep serve, three types of clears, forehand and backhand drive shots, overhead smash, and forehand and backhand drop shots. On the first day of the unit, she explained to the students the premise of the PSI unit and important procedures. Students then began working at their own pace on the tasks. In the following class periods, students entered the gym at the start of class, picked up their workbook, and proceeded to work on the task they were working on at the end of the previous class period. Tamara spent the class period clarifying skills and task structures for students, observing students for attaining the criteria, and giving feedback to students about the skills.

The use of the PSI model allows students to work at their own pace, sometimes without any teacher assistance, and to receive regular reinforcement (either verbally from you or by moving on to the next module) through the completion of the modules. The creation of a PSI unit requires much preparation before the unit, but once the unit begins, lesson plans aren't necessary because instruction is individualized. Additional information on the PSI model can be found in Metzler (2005), while complete PSI units on several sports are available in the *Personalized Sport Instruction Series* by Metzler and Sebolt (1998).

Using the PSI model might help Ms. Brown give more effective feedback. The required basic fitness class for 9th graders is an excellent course in which to use the PSI model. Modules could be developed for individual practice and knowledge related to each fitness area: cardiovascular

focus point

The personalized system of instruction (PSI) is an instructional model that can help teachers individualize instruction and consistently reinforce students.

fitness, flexibility, muscular strength, muscular endurance, and body composition. For example, in the muscular strength module, tasks could be developed to help students learn cognitive information about developing muscular strength, as well as proper form on specific weight training equipment exercises. Completing that module might require students to pass a written quiz about how to develop muscular strength and another one about displaying proper form (quizzes would be obtained from Ms. Brown). Students should have to demonstrate for Ms. Brown the proper form on each muscular strength exercise in order to pass this module. The last module could be on how to develop a complete exercise program, using all components of fitness from the previous modules. Once all modules are successfully completed by a student, the student then proceeds to work on the program developed in the last module. Using the PSI model in this way allows Ms. Brown to give lots of feedback to students first learning this information, while giving less feedback to students who might already know this information.

Summary

Reinforcement of various kinds is frequently used in physical education. In behavior modification, a product of behavior theory, desirable behaviors can be enhanced and undesirable behaviors eliminated through the deliberate and systematic use of reinforcement. Applying the principles of behavioral theory in behavior management programs is difficult, however, because students react differently to the same reinforcers, they cannot always duplicate the behavior for which they were reinforced, and reinforcers outside of the program may be acting on the students. According to cognitive evaluation theory, extrinsic rewards negatively impact intrinsic motivation if the controlling aspect of the reward is perceived to be greater than the positive information about one's competence received by earning the reward. Conversely, extrinsic rewards are proposed to positively impact intrinsic motivation if the controlling aspect of the reward is low and the reward provides positive information about one's competence.

Research indicates that teacher verbal feedback can positively influence students' motor skill learning, self-perceptions, and prosocial behaviors, as long as that feedback is of a certain type and given with a specific timing and frequency. Other research shows that other types of reinforcers (e.g., material rewards, praise from peers, graphs of target behaviors) can also have a positive effect in those three areas, as long as some basic principles are followed. Remember that reinforcement is preferred over punishment as a means of yielding positive changes in students' motor skill performance, self-perceptions, or prosocial behaviors, and that punishment should rarely be used. The PSI instructional model could enhance the frequency and quality of reinforcement students receive for their skill attempts.

KEY concepts

Behavioral theory	Extrinsic motivation
Behavior modification	Cognitive evaluation theory
Reinforcement	Congruent feedback
Positive reinforcement	Augmented feedback
Negative reinforcement	Intrinsic feedback
Punishment	Concurrent feedback
Shaping	Verbal guidance
Fading	Immediate feedback
Schedules of reinforcement	Delayed feedback
Continuous reinforcement	Contingent feedback
Intermittent reinforcement	Prosocial behaviors
Fixed ratio schedule	Sandwich approach
Variable ratio schedule	Personalized system of
Intrinsic motivation	instruction (PSI)

application exercises

1. Four high school physical education teachers have the same problem: their students are not wearing appropriate clothing (e.g., shorts, T-shirts, sneakers) for class. Each teacher creates a different plan to increase the number of students dressing out, or decrease the number of students not dressing out: Teacher A's plan uses positive reinforcement; Teacher B's uses negative reinforcement; Teacher C punishes students by presenting them with something aversive; and Teacher D's plan is to punish by taking away something positive. Discuss each program: will it be successful or unsuccessful in regard to getting the students to dress out? Why?

2. In Mr. Finn's reward system for his 7th graders, each class earns points for displaying sportsperson-like behaviors during lessons; points are taken away for unsportsperson-like behaviors. When a certain number of points are earned, the class earns a "You choose" day, where students can individually choose an activity in which to participate for the day. Use cognitive evaluation theory to explain why this specific program enhances Joe's sportsperson-like behaviors, but isn't affecting Brannon's level of sportsperson-like behaviors.

3. In a 4th grade lesson on the cartwheel, describe and give specific examples of the verbal feedback you would give students if you are trying to: (a) enhance performance; (b) enhance self-perceptions; and (c) enhance prosocial behaviors during the lesson.

4. Describe in detail a behavior management program with shaping or fading you could use to help students learn a folk or line dance. Be sure to use the principles for giving effective verbal feedback and/or rewards, or for establishing behavior management programs.

Modeling

Mr. Todd is a beginning physical educator at an urban middle school who is very frustrated. While in the teachers' lounge, he says, "My students aren't learning skills the way I know they can. They just don't pay attention. I show them at the beginning of class how to do a skill, but then they can't do it. I try yelling at them to work harder, but they just don't get any better. Playing games with them is no fun because they can't control their tempers. Every day their games get interrupted with students arguing with each other about some rule violation—and they scream at the top of their lungs! I yell at them to get them to stop, but they just do it again the next day. These kids are just impossible!"

introduction

Modeling, or demonstrating, is an important part of physical education instruction; it is very common for a teacher, like Mr. Todd, to visually show students how to do a skill or what to do in a task. Besides demonstrating to improve motor skill learning and performance, teachers often model prosocial behaviors like sharing and sportspersonship, as well as psychological skills such as controlling anxiety or anger or developing self-confidence. **Modeling** is communicating a visual or auditory representation of a motor skill, prosocial behavior, or psychological skill to someone in order to convey information about performing that skill or behavior. **Demonstration,** another term for modeling, is frequently used in physical education to describe the visual presentation of how to perform a motor skill or task. A related term often used is **observational learning,** which is the process of learning to perform a motor skill, prosocial behavior, or psychological skill by watching someone perform the skill or behavior. Modeling can take many forms, including a live demonstration by a teacher, student, or other respected person; a videotape; pictures; or even written diagrams or figures representing the movement. In this chapter, theories that involve modeling will be described, along with research related to modeling's impact and factors surrounding modeling. Finally, the most effective ways of using modeling in physical education will be presented.

Modeling Theories

One theory in which modeling plays an important part is social learning theory. Cognitive mediation theory, which explains how modeling influences learning, is derived from social learning theory. Each theory is described, and what is learned by observing a model is discussed.

Social Learning Theory

According to **social learning theory,** we learn skills and behaviors through our social interactions. This learning occurs via three processes: observational learning or modeling, reinforcement, and social comparison (Bandura, 1977, 1986). Thus, a physical education student might learn to jump rope by watching another student (modeling), particularly if the model is similar to the student (e.g., same gender, race, skill level, etc.) and the student likes and respects the model (social comparison). Learning will also be enhanced if the student is reinforced for her skill attempts. The same process could occur for learning psychological skills like self-confidence or prosocial behaviors like sportspersonship; a student sees a friend who is similar praise an opponent for a good move, and then hears the behavior reinforced when the teacher praises his friend for being a good sport.

connected CONCEPTS

Another theory in which modeling plays a vital role is self-efficacy (see Chapter 6). According to self-efficacy theory, one of the six factors that influence a person's self-efficacy is vicarious experiences, or seeing other individuals perform a skill or behavior (i.e., modeling). When a student sees someone who is similar to him successfully perform a skill, the student starts to believe that he can perform the skill, too.

Social learning theory might explain why Mr. Todd's students aren't learning skills like he wants. Because Mr. Todd always demonstrates the skills and tasks at the start of each class, perhaps his students cannot relate to him as well as if a classmate modeled the skills. It might also explain why Mr. Todd's students display poor sportspersonship; Mr. Todd himself is modeling lack of control when he yells at them for their poor displays of sportspersonship and skill, and they are learning to yell at each other from observing his behavior.

focus point

According to social learning theory, skills and behaviors can be learned when an observer sees a model who is similar to and/or respected by the observer perform the behavior, and then is either reinforced for performing the behavior or sees the model be reinforced for it.

Cognitive Mediation Theory

Although social learning theory emphasizes the importance of modeling to learning motor skills, prosocial behaviors, and psychological skills, it does not explain *how* modeling influences the learning of such skills and behaviors. **Cognitive mediation theory** (Bandura, 1986), which is derived from social learning theory, proposes four processes by which modeling affects learning: (1) attention, (2) retention, (3) behavior reproduction, and (4) motivation (see Exhibit 3.1).

Attention process

In the first process of modeling, the learner must pay attention to the model in order for the demonstration to be effective. Physical educators must ensure students are watching and directing their full attention to the demonstration. This process is affected by characteristics of the skill or behavior, the model, and the observer. The more complex the skill or behavior being modeled, the more important it is for the teacher to direct

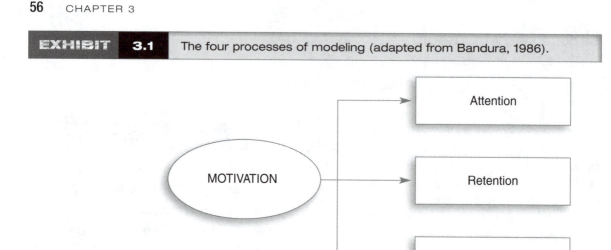

EXHIBIT 3.1 The four processes of modeling (adapted from Bandura, 1986).

the students' attention to the most critical parts of the skill being demonstrated. This helps the learners extract the most vital information. For example, if a teacher has a student demonstrate the handstand for the class, the teacher should ask students before the demonstration begins to watch for the cue "shoulders over knuckles." Then during the demonstration, the teacher should point out how the shoulders are over the knuckles. Without these specific prompts, the students may attend to other elements of the demonstration that are irrelevant to performing the skill.

In addition to the complexity of the skill or behavior, characteristics of the observer and model can influence the attentional process. For instance, children's attentional, visual, and auditory skills are not fully mature until about 12 years of age (Gallagher, French, Thomas, & Thomas, 2002). In fact, children between 6 and 12 years of age are generally in the overinclusive phase of attention development, meaning they attend to many environmental cues and are easily distracted by environmental factors (Gallagher et al., 2002). Such characteristics make it more important for teachers to point out critical elements of a skill in demonstrations so children will focus on the correct ones. Concerning model characteristics, observers will attend to a model they respect and admire, such as a well-known athlete, a well-liked classmate, and the teacher.

focus point

Although it is important in the attention process of modeling to point out the critical aspects of a demonstration to all observers, it is especially important when the task is complex and the observers are below 12 years of age.

Retention process

But simply attending to the critical elements of a skill is not enough to ensure its accurate performance—the observers must remember those critical elements. The second process of modeling is retention, whereby the observer transforms what was observed into symbolic codes that can be stored into memory so the skill or behavior can later be performed without repeating the demonstration. As with perceptual and attentional skills, children's use of memory strategies develops with age. For instance, labeling, rehearsal, and organization generally are not spontaneously used by primary-aged children (Gallagher et al., 2002). *Labeling* is naming a movement or part of a movement, like when the follow-through on a basketball free throw is named "gooseneck" for what the hand looks like when the shot is done correctly. *Rehearsal* is when children repeat, either aloud or to themselves, the important aspects of a motor skill (e.g., "turn, step, racket back, swing" for the forehand drive in tennis). When children use *organization,* they put the important parts of a skill in the same logical order as they try to remember them, as just illustrated with the cues for the forehand drive.

Teachers can help students of all ages remember the critical elements attended to in the attention process by helping them create either visual or verbal representations. A good visual representation of a skill can be formed when teachers use descriptive words or phrases to help students remember features of a skill; for example, "squash the bug" is a cue often used by teachers to help students visualize stepping forward as they swing a bat.

Another way to help students develop a visual representation of a skill is to mentally practice the skill after it has been demonstrated, before actual practice. Verbal representations can be formed by having students use **verbal rehearsal,** which is the act of repeating, either out loud or to oneself, the important cues. Verbal rehearsal can be used to help students remember all kinds of skills, but is especially helpful for remembering sequences, such as the steps to a dance or gymnastic routine. For instance, to help remember the steps to the electric slide line dance, students can repeat the cues "grapevine right, grapevine left, back 3, rock step, kick and turn."

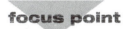

focus point

In the retention process of modeling, teachers can help students remember the critical aspects of a demonstration by using descriptive words, encouraging the students to mentally practice the skills, and having the students verbally rehearse the cues.

Behavior reproduction process

Merely attending to and remembering the critical elements of a demonstration will not guarantee that students will accurately perform the skill or behavior; the student must actually practice what was modeled. In the third modeling process, behavior reproduction, the observer transforms what was retained in memory about the movement into actual physical action. An accurate reproduction of a skill or behavior rarely happens instantly, and the teacher must help the students learn the skill by providing an appropriate progression of tasks and specific feedback. Moreover, the teacher must ensure that the learner has the prerequisite physical capabilities to actually perform the skill; without those, the modeling process does not work.

focus point

In the behavior reproduction process, teachers should ensure students have the prerequisite skills to perform the tasks, and provide an appropriate progression of tasks and feedback.

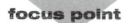

Motivation process

The final modeling process, motivation, influences the other three processes. If a student isn't motivated to pay attention to the model, or isn't motivated to commit the vital elements of the demonstration to memory, or isn't motivated to actually practice the skill, the model won't be effective in helping the student learn the skill or behavior. So it is very important that the physical educator work to increase students' motivation to attend to the model, commit the important elements to memory, and practice the modeled skill or behavior. Reinforcing task attempts, emphasizing the importance of skills, and using respected models are all strategies teachers can use to increase student motivation in the modeling process.

Applying the cognitive mediation theory to teaching

Let's use the modeling processes to determine why Mr. Todd's demonstrations may not help his students improve their motor skills. First, it is possible students aren't attending to the critical elements in Mr. Todd's demonstrations. He simply demonstrates, without pointing out the critical elements of the skill, and perhaps students aren't perceiving the important parts of the skill. It may be the students aren't attending to Mr. Todd's demonstrations because they do not respect him, or they are distracted, or they are not in a good position to see the demonstrations. Perhaps retention of the demonstration, rather than attention, is the problem. Mr. Todd doesn't instruct them to mentally imagine the demonstration, nor does he ask them to verbally rehearse any related cues. He usually only demonstrates a skill once at the start of the lesson, and it is unlikely his students remember all that is involved with a skill from one demonstration. Perhaps the students remember the model, but their physical practice (the motor reproduction process) isn't very effective: the tasks they practice are not sequenced logically, and they receive little helpful feedback from Mr. Todd. Finally, Mr. Todd's demonstrations may not be effective because students may not be motivated to attend to the model, remember the demonstration, or practice the skill.

Learning from Observing a Model

Although cognitive mediation theory explains the process of modeling, including aspects that may impact the effectiveness of a model, the theory doesn't explain what an observer actually learns when they watch a model. The most common thought is that observers learn the *pattern of coordination for a motor skill* (Magill, 1993; Magill & Schoenfelder-Zohdi, 1996; Scully & Newell, 1985; Shea, Wright, Wulf, & Whitacre, 2000)—they learn the actions various body parts perform in a motor skill, as well as when and where in space each body part acts in relation to the others. For example, a child observing demonstrations of the overhand throw learns when to step on the opposite foot of the throwing hand and when to turn the hips relative to the shoulders. One implication of this notion is that demonstrations are most effective when learners are first learning a skill or task, and not as effective after learners have the basic idea of the movement and are learning the appropriate amount of speed or force needed for a movement (e.g., throwing a softball from the out-field to second base vs. from the pitcher's mound to second base). However, there is some evidence that learning a movement's overall speed or force can also be enhanced via modeling (e.g., Blandin & Proteau, 2000; Zelaznik, Shapiro, & Newell, 1978), but probably not to the same degree as the pattern of coordination.

Another implication is that demonstrations are most helpful when teaching more complex motor skills, like the overhand throw or the tennis serve, than with relatively simple skills, like kicking a stationary ball. However, the results of some studies show that even simple tasks, like throwing darts (Kitsantas, Zimmerman, & Cleary, 2000), can be learned better when a model is observed than when one is not. All of these ideas focus on the learning of motor skills; it is likely that observing a model helps students learn the correct organizational format of a task (e.g., where to stand, how to take turns, etc.), prosocial behaviors, and psychological skills.

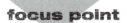

focus point

Probably the main benefit of observing a demonstration is enhanced learning of the motor skill's basic pattern of coordination, which suggests that demonstrations are most effective with complex skills and new skills.

Modeling Research

Research related to modeling and demonstrations has been conducted in the areas of pedagogy, motor learning, and sport psychology. Some researchers have examined the effectiveness of modeling on certain types of learning. Others have investigated the influence of model characteristics on the model's effectiveness, including the model's similarity with the observer, the model's skill level, and peer mastery vs. coping models. Researchers have examined how often and when demonstrations should be done to enhance their effectiveness, as well as the use of verbal cues during demonstrations, retention strategies like verbal rehearsal, and auditory modeling. Studies from each of these areas will be reviewed in this section. Although research conducted with children learning motor skills like ones they would learn in physical education will be reviewed, other studies conducted with adults learning laboratory or computer tasks will be included when necessary to enhance your knowledge about a topic.

The Effectiveness of Modeling

This section discusses the effectiveness of modeling on learning motor skills and prosocial behaviors and influencing psychological states.

Motor skills

Most studies show that children, ranging from 4 years old to 9th grade, who observe a demonstration of a skill or task perform better than those who don't see a model (Feltz, 1982; Feltz & Landers, 1977; Kitsantas et al., 2000; Lirgg & Feltz, 1991; Weiss, 1983; Weiss, McCullagh, Smith, & Berlant, 1998). A variety of skills and tasks were learned by the children in those studies, including balancing, dart throwing, swimming, and navigating an obstacle course, indicating that modeling can improve students' learning and performance of several kinds of motor tasks.

Prosocial behaviors

Other studies show that modeling can positively impact the prosocial behaviors (i.e., sportspersonship, encouraging and supporting classmates, teacher-independent conflict resolution skills) and moral reasoning of children who range from 5 years old to teenagers (Bredemeier, Weiss, Shields, & Shewchuk, 1986; Gibbons & Ebbeck, 1997; Gibbons, Ebbeck, & Weiss, 1995; Giebink & McKenzie, 1985; Sharpe, Crider, Vyhlidal, & Brown, 1996; Shields & Bredemeier, 1989). Some of these studies were conducted in actual physical education settings over a 7-month period, while others were conducted in summer motor skill instructional programs. The types of modeling used in these studies included students role-playing and demonstrating prosocial behaviors, modeling by former Olympians and the teachers, displaying posters of appropriate behaviors, and positively identifying students who display appropriate behaviors. In most studies, modeling was combined with other strategies, such as reinforcement of prosocial behaviors or discussions of moral dilemmas. These studies suggest that modeling can help students learn prosocial behaviors, especially when combined with other strategies like reinforcement.

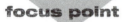

focus point

Research shows that modeling, either alone or in conjunction with other strategies, can enhance the learning of motor skills, prosocial behaviors like sportspersonship, and psychological skills like self-efficacy.

Psychological states

Some research indicates that modeling can positively influence children's psychological states like self-efficacy and anxiety, and even their feelings like satisfaction and interest (Kitsantas et al., 2000; Lirgg & Feltz, 1991; McAuley, 1985; Weiss et al., 1998). For instance, 6-year-old children learning to swim who observed a peer model had higher self-efficacy for swimming and were less fearful than children who did not see a model (Weiss et al., 1998). Similarly, high school girls who saw a model perform a dart-throwing task had higher self-efficacy, greater satisfaction in their performance, and higher interest in dart throwing than girls who did not view a model (Kitsantas et al., 2000).

Model Characteristics

According to social learning theory, models similar to the observer are more likely to have a positive impact on the learning of motor skills and prosocial behaviors and influencing psychological states than dissimilar models. Likewise, cognitive mediation theory asserts that observers are more likely to attend to a model if the model is similar to the observers. In physical education, this means that fellow students should be the most effective models. But is this true? If the student model isn't highly skilled at the task, can that person still be an effective model?

Similarity of model with observer

Researchers have examined how model similarity to the observer in terms of skill level, amount of experience with a task, and gender impacts the observer's learning, performance, self-efficacy, or self-regulation (George, Feltz, & Chase, 1992; Gould & Weiss, 1981; McCullagh, 1987; Meaney, Griffin, & Hart, 2005). For example, in an early study, Gould and Weiss (1981) found that female college students (who were not athletes or physical education majors) who viewed a similar model (i.e., female, not an athlete) did better on a leg extension task than those who viewed a dissimilar model (i.e., male, athlete). Another more recent study found that 4th grade girls learning to juggle exhibited more of the learning strategies during practice that were demonstrated by female models than when they watched male models demonstrating the same learning strategies (Meaney et al., 2005).

focus point

Using a model with similar motor skill ability and who is the same sex as the observers enhances the model's impact.

Model skill level

Although various terms are used in modeling studies to indicate the model's skill level (skilled vs. unskilled, correct vs. learning, beginner vs. advanced), basically all of the studies compare the effectiveness of a model who could correctly perform the skill with one who could not (at least initially). Although some researchers found that students who observed skilled models performed better and had higher self-efficacy than those who observed unskilled models (Lirgg & Feltz, 1991), many researchers found that observing unskilled or learning models can be just as helpful or even more helpful for learning motor skills as observing a skilled model (Blandin, Lhuisset, & Proteau, 1999; Landers & Landers, 1973; Lee & White, 1990; Martens, Burwitz, & Zuckerman, 1976; Meaney et al., 2005; Pollock & Lee, 1992).

Other researchers determined that an observer's performance of motor skills can be enhanced when the observer hears the feedback a learning model receives (Hebert & Landin, 1994; McCullagh & Caird, 1990; McCullagh & Meyer, 1997; Weir & Leavitt, 1990). For example, college students learned the tennis volley with the nondominant hand better when they observed a learning model who received corrective feedback than

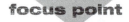

when they simply practiced the skill and received feedback about their own performance (Hebert & Landin, 1994). It seems that hearing the model's feedback helps the learner engage in the same problem solving as one does during actual physical practice, so one learns to detect errors the model makes and to correct those errors during one's own practice (Adams, 1986; Blandin & Proteau, 2000).

Peer mastery vs. peer coping models

In a few studies, researchers compared the effectiveness of mastery models to coping models. **Mastery models** are similar to a correct or skilled model because they demonstrate the skill correctly, but they also make statements during the demonstration that convey

- confidence ("I can do this"),
- ease ("This is easy"), and
- a positive attitude ("This is fun").

On the other hand, **coping models** first have trouble performing the skill but gradually show improvement until correct performance is demonstrated; also, coping models initially verbalize

- high perceptions of task difficulty ("This is hard"),
- a negative attitude ("I don't like doing this"), and
- low confidence in performing the skill ("I can't do this").

Those statements gradually change to reflect low task difficulty, a positive attitude, and high confidence.

Most investigators have found that both peer mastery and coping models can enhance motor performance, but peer coping models tend to be associated with less anxiety and greater self-efficacy (Clark & Ste-Marie, 2002; Kitsantas et al., 2000; Lewis, 1974; Weiss et al., 1998). In one study, young children (about 6 years old) in a swimming class identified as having a fear of water were assigned to one of three groups: peer mastery, peer coping, or control (Weiss et al., 1998). Although all groups improved their swimming skills from pre- to post-intervention, the two peer model groups improved slightly more. Children who observed either of the peer models saw greater increases in self-efficacy and decreases in swimming fear than the control group, and those who saw the peer coping model saw the largest changes in self-efficacy.

Instructional implications

Based on research studies such as the above, physical educators should use students of various ability levels and both genders to demonstrate skills and tasks. This will increase the likelihood that the observing students will find a model similar to them and to whom they can relate. Magill (2004) suggests skilled demonstrators be used when the skill is one students have not seen or attempted before, because the learners are trying to get the idea of the movement and learn the overall coordination pattern of the various body parts involved. But once students have the basic idea of the movement, or the task is an extension of a basic skill, learning models should also be used. In fact, Magill (2004) suggests pairing students together, as in the peer teaching instructional model (described later in this chapter), so one student observes another practicing a skill. As discussed in more detail later, either give the practicing student feedback that the observing student can hear, or give the observer a checklist of the skill's critical elements to use in giving feedback to the student practicing the skill. These feedback strategies will allow the observers to do some active problem solving related to performing the skill correctly as they watch the other student practice.

Other implications for practice can be derived from the research on peer mastery vs. coping models. McCullagh and Weiss (2002) suggest peer mastery models be used when the observers have little anxiety about a skill or task, as in bowling or golf. But for activities that may produce fear, anxiety, or low self-confidence in learners (e.g., swimming, gymnastics, diving, pole vaulting), peer coping models should be used (as discussed in more detail later). In fact, McCullagh and Weiss suggest that specific skills within particular sports, like taking a charge in basketball, diving for a ball in volleyball, or playing the goalee in team handball, can also illicit fear and anxiety in students, and these skills could also benefit from the use of coping models. Physical educators can recruit students from their class to take on such modeling roles and train them to make initial low confidence and high task difficulty statements concurrent with imperfect demonstrations of the skill, which gradually become positive statements and correct skill demonstrations.

Modeling Frequency and Timing

One question that arises with modeling is when and how often should learners observe demonstrations. Is one demonstration enough to improve performance and learning? If not, how many demonstrations should be done? The number of demonstrations performed could influence the second process of modeling, retention. Should all demonstrations take place before students begin physical practice, or should some demonstrations be interspersed throughout physical practice? Answers to the latter questions found in the research process inform us about the third process of the cognitive mediation theory, behavior reproduction.

Frequency

Researchers have found that more frequent observations of a model yield better skill learning (Feltz, 1982; Sidaway & Hand, 1993). In one study, college females who saw a demonstration of a golf skill after every task attempt learned it better than the students who only saw a demonstration after every 5 or 10 task attempts (Sidaway & Hand, 1993). Studies also indicate that observations of those skills requiring minimal motor involvement can take the place of some physical practice of those skills without hurting performance and learning (Deakin & Proteau, 2000; Shea et al., 2000). For example, college students learning a video game task who physically practiced the task for 20 trials showed poorer learning than other students who did half as many physical practice trials because they observed a partner practice the task on the other 10 trials (Shea et al., 2000). The researchers believed that cognitive processing that enhances learning occurs during the observation trials. These studies indicate that having students partner up and alternate practice attempts with observations of their partner's attempts may not hurt student learning due to decreased physical practice and could actually enhance it. This may be especially true for tasks that are highly cognitive and require minimal motor involvement.

Timing

So, when should these demonstrations take place? Recent studies conducted with adults indicate that to most positively influence actual skill learning, participants should not see all of the demonstrations before practice; rather, several demonstrations should precede physical practice, followed by more demonstrations in the early stages of practice (Shea, Wulf, & Whitacre, 1999; Weeks & Anderson, 2000). For example, in one study (Weeks & Anderson, 2000), college students learning the overhand volleyball serve were randomly placed into one of three groups, with every group observing 10 demonstrations of the skill and making 30 practice attempts. The All Pre-Practice group saw all 10 demonstrations before they began physical practice, the Interspersed group observed one demonstration before practice and then observed a demonstration after every third attempt, and the Combination group saw five demonstrations before physical practice began and then observed a demonstration after every third attempt (so modeling was completed by the middle of the practice attempts). The results showed that the Combination group learned the form for the volleyball serve the best.

Instructional implications

One implication of these studies is that the more demonstrations students observe, the better; one demonstration of a skill will not be enough. As

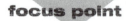

focus point

Studies suggest that more frequent observations of a model yield better skill learning, and that demonstrations can take the place of some physical practice without hurting, and may even enhance, performance. This is especially true of tasks with high cognitive and low motor involvement.

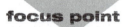

focus point

To maximize the impact of demonstrations, observers should see several demonstrations of a skill prior to physical practice, followed by more demonstrations in the early stages of practice.

discussed later in the chapter, decreasing the number of actual practice attempts students make (but not eliminating them), because students are observing skill demonstrations, will not hurt learning of the skill and may actually enhance it, especially for highly cognitive and low motor involved skills. Several demonstrations of a skill should be done before students begin practice, and then students should be periodically stopped during practice to see more demonstrations. However, these studies need to be replicated with school-aged children, because the recent studies were conducted with college students.

Use of Verbal Cues with Modeling

As mentioned previously, the attentional abilities of young children are not yet mature, so they might have difficulty attending to the most helpful aspects of a demonstration (Gallagher et al., 2002). Using verbal cues during demonstrations helps direct students' attention to critical aspects of the skill, which could improve their attention to the model. Some studies indicate that giving verbal cues while demonstrating enhances learning, especially with children younger than 7 years old (Weiss, 1983; Weiss, Ebbeck, & Rose, 1992) and non-native English speaking children (Meaney & Edwards, 1996). Verbal cues helped children improve the form of skills (McCullagh, Stiehl, & Weiss, 1990; Weiss et al., 1992) and remember the order of sequential skills (Weiss et al., 1992). Even college students learning the soccer pass for accuracy performed best when they viewed a videotape model while hearing verbal cues and seeing arrows on the video that pointed out critical skill elements (Janelle, Champenoy, Coombes, & Mousseau, 2003).

In other studies, however, adding verbal cues to a demonstration did not enhance children's motor performance (Kowalski & Sherrill, 1992; Weiss, 1983; Wiese-Bjornstal & Weiss, 1992). In fact, seeing a model that provided verbal cues actually caused the hopping form used by 6-year-olds to decline (Roberton, Halverson, & Harper, 1997). Roberton et al. believed these unexpected results were due to cognitive overload; the young children received too much information in a very short period of time and were not cognitively able to handle it, which then hurt their hopping.

Rehearsal Strategies and Modeling

Earlier you learned that children's use of memory strategies develops with age and that primary-aged children do not spontaneously use strategies like labeling, rehearsal, and organization (Gallagher et al., 2002). This would affect the retention process of modeling. This has been confirmed in several studies (e.g., Bouffard & Dunn, 1993; Ille & Cadopi, 1999), such as that conducted by Cadopi, Chatillon, and Baldy (1995), who

focus point

Providing verbal cues during demonstrations may not benefit all observers, but may be most helpful with young children and non-native English speaking children, as long as the verbal cues are very few in number.

found that 11-year-olds were better at remembering a series of ballet movements than 8-year-olds, due to the use of more advanced memory strategies like verbal self-instruction.

Even though young children do not spontaneously use more advanced memory strategies like verbal rehearsal, researchers have found that young children can learn to use such strategies (Bouffard & Dunn, 1993; McCullagh et al., 1990; Weiss et al., 1992). But does the use of such strategies enhance the model's effectiveness? After seeing a skill demonstrated, verbally rehearsing cues or the steps to performing the skill enhanced the performance of 5- to 10-year-olds learning a sequential obstacle course (Weiss & Klint, 1987), 9- to 11-year-olds learning to juggle (Meaney, 1994), 7- to 8-year-old boys with learning disabilities learning a motor sequence (Kowalski & Sherrill, 1992), and 9- to 11-year-old English speaking students (Meaney & Edwards, 1996). But verbal rehearsal had no effect on the motor performance of Spanish-speaking 9- to 11-year-olds (Meaney & Edwards, 1996) and others (McCullagh et al., 1990; Weiss, 1983; Weiss et al., 1992). Perhaps verbal rehearsal is more effective for students with learning disabilities and those whose native language is English. Because it takes little time to verbally rehearse cues, physical educators should encourage students to do so, as it may help some of them learn skills better.

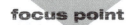

focus point

Verbal rehearsal of cues that accompany a demonstration may be more effective for students with learning disabilities and those whose native language is English.

Auditory Modeling

Normally, we think of modeling as visual—the observer watches a visual presentation of the skill or task. But many movements involve timing, and the timing of a movement can be modeled by clapping hands, hitting rhythm sticks together, or banging a drum. Researchers have discovered that **auditory modeling** can help adult listeners learn motor skills in which timing is important (e.g., sequenced dance movements or the butterfly swimming stroke; Doody, Bird, & Ross, 1985; McCullagh & Little, 1989; Wang & Hart, 2005; Wuyts & Buekers, 1995). In one study, college females who heard an auditory model of a laboratory task involving timing accuracy, either with or without a visual model, performed better than those who saw only a visual model or no model (Doody et al., 1985). Other studies show that hearing an auditory model enhances learning of relative timing (part of the overall motor coordination pattern) for laboratory tasks (e.g., Lai, Shea, Bruechert, & Little, 2002; Lai, Shea, & Little, 2000; Shea, Wulf, Park, & Gaunt, 2001). These studies suggest that when a skill involves timing (e.g., dance sequences, tinikling sequences, rope jumping, skipping), auditory modeling, either with or without a visual model, can enhance learning. Because we don't know if children react differently than adults to auditory modeling, this principle must be confirmed with children.

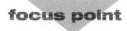

focus point

Learning skills that involve timing may be enhanced with an auditory model.

Effective Modeling in Physical Education

Demonstrations are vital to effective task presentations in physical education. Social learning theory, cognitive mediation theory, and modeling research suggest principles to follow if demonstrations are to positively impact student motor skill learning, prosocial behaviors, and psychological states.

Use a Variety of Models

According to social learning theory, models will be most effective when they are similar to the observers, and some research supports that notion. In physical education, students differ by sex, ethnic group, motor skill ability level, and so forth. To increase the possibility that each student will relate to the models, choose many types of individuals to perform demonstrations. This will help with the attention process of modeling. Ask both boys and girls as well as students of various ethnic groups to demonstrate. Although it is tempting to use only the highly skilled students as models, research suggests that isn't necessary and may not be the most effective. So use students that are typically highly successful as well as those who are not so successful in physical education. Also include students with various disabilities as models.

As suggested by Magill (2004), use skilled or accurate models (e.g., yourself, highly skilled students, DVDs of expert performers) when students are first learning a skill to help them get the basic coordination pattern of the movement. But once students have the basic idea of the skill, use learning models. When using learning models, make positive statements to go along with the demonstration, as well as clearly point out to observers what to attend to in the demonstration. For example, Kyle, a high school student who is just learning the tennis serve, has good form, so his teacher asks him to demonstrate his good form for his classmates; however, the serve doesn't go over the net or land in the service box on any of his attempts. During the demonstration, Kyle's teacher might say, "Notice Kyle's good form. He really extends his hitting arm, which is a very important aspect of good serving. It's ok that the serves didn't go in the service box right now—most people find they have trouble doing that when first learning the serve. As long as Kyle continues to practice using good form, the serve will start landing in bounds."

As an example, Janet N., an elementary physical education teacher in the southern United States, uses many different students—boys and girls, skilled and learning, various ethnic backgrounds—to be models; she rarely demonstrates herself. During a series of lessons on weight transfer with 3rd graders, the first student who modeled transferring weight from the feet to the hands was quite skilled at the task, so the students could get

focus point

To enhance the similarity between models and observers, various kinds of students should be used to demonstrate, including boys and girls, students with disabilities, students of different ethnic backgrounds, and students of varying ability levels.

a picture in their mind of how the skill should look. But Janet soon used other students as learning models; she carefully watched her students as they practiced and picked those students to demonstrate who were working hard, showed improvement at the skill, or performed parts of the skill correctly but were still working on other parts. Janet pointed out to the other students what to watch in the demonstrations by the learning models, always praised the models for something done well, and emphasized improvements the students were making. Janet's students expect to be asked to demonstrate even if they don't do the skill perfectly, as this is a regular part of her classes.

As stated previously, Mr. Todd does all demonstrations during his physical education classes. Some students cannot relate to demonstrations performed by him; some girls see a male performing skills and don't think females can do them, while some boys see a highly skilled adult performing skills that they as kids won't be able to do. Mr. Todd should start using his students to demonstrate skills and tasks. For instance, when preparing to teach the volleyball overhand serve, Mr. Todd could ask students before the lesson if they can correctly perform that serve. Then, in the first lesson on the overhead serve, those students could demonstrate. For subsequent demonstrations, Mr. Todd should choose a variety of students, including those who haven't mastered the skill yet. When learning models are used, Mr. Todd should tell the observers exactly what to watch, and praise the model for aspects done correctly, improvement, and effort.

Use Peer Coping Models

Use peer coping models when the activities or skills learned in physical education may produce fear, anxiety, or low self-confidence in children (McCullagh & Weiss, 2002); for example, swimming, diving, tumbling and gymnastic skills, martial arts, playing goalee, taking a charge in basketball, sliding in softball, heading in soccer, and diving for a ball in volleyball. Because a peer coping model initially demonstrates with words and actions the same anxieties and fears observers may have, but then gradually presents statements of confidence and ease along with successful performance, using peer coping models can enhance learners' psychological states (e.g., increased self-confidence, decreased anxiety) concurrently with their motor skills (Weiss, 1991). Students are likely to watch these models closely, which enhances the attention process of modeling.

So, how do you use a coping model in a lesson? After all, making statements out loud that describe one's fears and lack of confidence in performing a skill isn't something children are prone to do in front of others. One way to use peer coping models is by making videotapes of those students who are willing to serve as models. For instance, let's say that Mr. Todd wants to teach heading in soccer to his 6th graders. He knows that heading is a skill that can hurt (if done incorrectly) and that many students are hesitant to try it. A week before Mr. Todd is to teach this skill, he could recruit a 6th grade student who doesn't yet know how to head a ball and has some anxiety about trying it. When recruiting, Mr. Todd should explain to the student that it is perfectly normal to have anxiety about performing this skill, and that it will help other students to see this student learning the skill and not being perfect. Before or after school, or during lunch or study halls, Mr. Todd could work with the student to teach her to head the ball. These sessions then are videotaped; Mr. Todd teaches the student to verbalize out loud her initial fears about trying the skill, but being willing to try it, then gradually making more confident statements. Mr. Todd can show clips from the videotaped sessions to his classes, first showing the model's initial attempts and low confidence statements, and eventually showing the model making confident statements and successful performances. It is important to use students who really don't know how to perform the skill as coping models instead of those students who already know how to perform the skill and just fake unsuccessful attempts and lack of confidence statements so that the student's responses on the videotape are authentic and believable by the observers.

focus point

When creating a videotape of a peer coping model learning a skill, recruit a student who doesn't know how to perform a skill and has some anxiety about it to ensure the authenticity and believability of her responses.

Explain That Perfection Is Not Required

Most students believe models must demonstrate a skill perfectly. So when students who are still learning a skill are asked to be learning or coping models, they may be hesitant to do so. In addition, students observing a model purposely chosen to be a learning or coping model may expect a faultless demonstration. Make it clear to your students—those observing and those modeling—that demonstrations don't have to be perfect to be helpful. The last thing you want is for the class to laugh at a learning or coping model's imperfect efforts. In addition to regularly reminding students that demonstrations don't have to be flawless to be helpful, continually point out what to pay attention to in the learning model's demonstration (as described previously with Kyle demonstrating the tennis serve). Once students realize that learning models are regularly used in class, their hesitancy to act as models and expectancy for perfection with models should decline.

focus point

When using peer coping or learning models, emphasize to both models and observers that the models don't have to be perfect to be helpful.

Janet N., the elementary physical education teacher described earlier, consistently reminds her students that all of them will be models, even if the skills aren't mastered yet. So, Janet's students are familiar with this process, are eager to perform as models, and don't expect the demonstrations they observe to be perfect. They know that she will point out something they are doing well, even though they may not have mastered the skill.

real world

Likewise, when Mr. Todd first starts using learning or coping models in his classes, he must explain to his students that he isn't expecting perfection, and that the students can learn from watching imperfect models just as well as accurate ones. He must stop any students from laughing at learning models, and clearly point out what observers should watch and what was done well.

Demonstrate Frequently

Perhaps the most important change physical educators can make regarding their demonstrations is the frequency. It isn't unusual to demonstrate a skill or task only once in a lesson (or several lessons) and expect students to learn the skill accurately based on that one demonstration. Researchers have shown that once is not enough; students must see a skill or task modeled several times before practicing to most effectively improve their performance. Once students begin physical practice, they should periodically see the skill modeled. Demonstrate the skill to individual students or small groups during practice, or stop practice and model for the entire class. Demonstrating a skill several times is vital to the retention process of modeling, because students who see a demonstration often are more likely to remember it.

As a student teacher at a middle school in the Midwestern United States, Melissa F. did an excellent job of repeating demonstrations several times throughout lessons. For instance, in a lesson on the "give and go" in a basketball unit, Melissa demonstrated the first task five times in the first task presentation. While students practiced the task and Melissa was giving feedback to her students, she also repeated the demonstration to those students who were having trouble with the task. In a refinement task for the give and go, Melissa demonstrated the task four more times.

In contrast, presently Mr. Todd only demonstrates a skill once during a class, thinking more demonstrations waste time. He should increase the number of times skills are demonstrated. Several demonstrations during task presentations, as well as when students are practicing and receiving feedback, should help his students remember what the skill looks like.

Repeat Verbal Cues During Demonstrations

Students must receive guidance on what to look for or at when observing demonstrations. Therefore, as mentioned earlier, as a physical educator, you should tell students specifically what to pay attention to during demonstrations: "Watch Sarah's feet," "Notice what Joe's arm does after he throws the ball," "See how Quinton keeps his body between the defender and the ball to protect the ball." Also verbally repeat important cues, or refinements, for the skill during the demonstration. No more than three cues at a time should be given, otherwise students will be overloaded with information and will forget the cues. For instance, when teaching young children the locomotor movement of sliding, you might repeat these cues during the demonstration: step-together, don't cross feet, shoulder leads. In fact, elementary physical education expert George Graham and his colleagues suggest only one cue be given at a time to maximize the chance children remember the cue (Graham, Holt/Hale, & Parker, 2004). In that case, point out the most critical cue in demonstrations when the students first practice a skill, and then move on to other cues when they have mastered that cue. So the cue of step-together will be the first cue repeated during demonstrations for sliding; when children consistently use that cue as they slide, then you can repeat the cue of shoulder leads during demonstrations.

For discrete skills too short in duration to repeat cues during the demonstration (e.g., tennis volley), repeat the cues during a slow-motion demonstration, and then before and after a regular speed demonstration. These verbal cues can be even more effective if descriptive words or phrases are used to help students remember the skill's features. For example, the cue "hand in the cookie jar" is commonly used by physical educators to help students understand how to follow through after shooting a basketball. Repeating important cues helps students remember the model, which enhances the retention process of modeling.

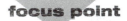

Alerting students about what to look for in a demonstration and repeating no more than three verbal cues critical to a skill during a demonstration will help students remember the model.

Students Should Verbally Rehearse Cues

Before practicing a skill or task, have your students repeat, either out loud or to themselves, the verbal cues you just gave them. This is important for all tasks, but especially for sequential tasks like dance routines or gymnastic sequences. The person modeling the task or skill can also model rehearsing the cues; for instance, if Cody is demonstrating a cartwheel, he should say out loud as he demonstrates, "Hand, hand, foot, foot." Afterward, have the entire class repeat the cues together aloud two or three times before practicing. Older students might repeat the cues to themselves several times before practicing. Even in refinement tasks, in which only one cue is focused on, the students can verbally rehearse that one cue. For example, in a refinement task to make sure students are rolling to the basket in the correct direction after a screen in basketball, the students should repeat the cue "Open away" to help them remember to turn away from the defender. Remind students as they practice to keep repeating the cues to themselves. Verbally rehearsing the cues helps students remember the model and is another way to help with the retention process of modeling.

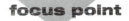

Retention can be enhanced by having students repeat, either aloud or to themselves, the cues you repeat during the demonstration.

Joe B., as a preservice teacher at an elementary school in the Midwestern United States, consistently pointed out cues to students during demonstrations; he also had the students verbally rehearse cues. During a 2nd grade lesson on throwing and catching with a beanbag, Joe first demonstrated each new task and repeated the cues "watch, reach, give" during the demonstrations. Then he asked a student to demonstrate the task, during which he repeated the cues again. Before the students began to practice, Joe asked them to repeat the cues out loud with him twice. At the start of the lesson, he even asked them to repeat the cues as they practiced.

Mr. Todd can help his students attend to the important aspects of demonstrations by pointing out important cues during demonstrations. He can help them remember the cues by repeating them aloud before they start practicing. For example, during demonstrations of the overhand volleyball serve, Mr. Todd should repeat cues like "bow and arrow, toss by shoulder, heel to target." Students then say the cues out loud as a class at least two times before starting practice. Then, students should be directed to repeat the cues, either out loud or to themselves, as they practice.

connected   CONCEPTS

Another method of enhancing retention of the model is to have students use imagery to practice the skill or task in their mind after seeing the demonstration and before physical practice (see Chapter 6 on how to teach students to use imagery).

Give the Model Feedback During Demonstrations

As discussed earlier, several studies show that the feedback a learning model, or even a skilled model, receives about a demonstration can enhance the observer's motor skill learning. During a task presentation, for example, as a physical educator, you can give the demonstrator positive, specific feedback (e.g., "Nice job of stepping on the opposite foot," "You're giving with the ball when you catch it—good") as well as corrective feedback (e.g., "Try to bring your arm back further next time," "Make sure you keep the racket flat"). This can be a method of repeating the cues verbally to students during demonstrations. While your students are practicing tasks, have some students stop their attempts and observe another student as he practices and receives feedback from you. As mentioned earlier, this helps learners engage in the same kind of problem solving as during actual physical practice; they learn to detect errors the model is making and how to correct those errors in their own practice.

Giving models feedback about their demonstrations is regularly done by Dave W., an elementary physical education teacher in the Midwestern United States. During a lesson on rope jumping with 2nd graders, Dave gave the students who modeled during task presentations feedback about their performances, especially for refinement tasks: "Sarah, nice small jumps. You also have small wrist movement, as you should. Make sure your feet stay together during the bell jump." This feedback allowed Dave to repeat the cues during the demonstrations.

This is a strategy that Mr. Todd could easily implement once he starts using students to demonstrate.

Increase Motivation

As described earlier, the fourth process of modeling, motivation, influences each of the other processes; students must be motivated to attend to the model, remember the model, and physically reproduce the model's actions if modeling is to be successful. A few of the strategies mentioned in this chapter thus far should help with this; using a variety of models increases the possibility that the students respect and attend to the models, while using peer coping models should enhance the possibility that students believe they can learn the skill.

In this section, two simple methods of increasing student motivation, often neglected by teachers, are presented: do a set induction at the beginning of class and a closure at the end of class.

Do a set induction

In a set induction, do the following (in any order):

1. tell your students what they are working on in the day's lesson (e.g., "Today we're going to work on the give and go in basketball" or "Today we're practicing self-space")

2. convey the lesson objective to your students (e.g., "Your goal for the day is to use the give and go at least three times during a modified basketball game and score at least once from it" or "By the end of the lesson, your goal is to move in general space at a medium speed for at least 1 minute without touching anyone")

3. communicate the importance of the tasks and/or skills to be learned in the lesson (e.g., "I've noticed that you've been standing around a lot as you played your modified basketball games. The give and go is a basic strategy used to score points in basketball at all levels, and it really helps players learn to keep moving" or "We do many things in physical education that require us to move in general space, so we need to be able to move safely without hurting ourselves or others")

Goals motivate students, as can knowing why skills or tasks are important. As a physical educator, don't expect your students to perform tasks without knowing why the tasks might help them.

connected   CONCEPTS

Many other means of motivating students are described in other chapters: giving appropriate reinforcement and feedback (see Chapter 2); establishing a task-involving motivational climate (see Chapter 5); increasing students' interest in and value for activities (see Chapter 8); helping students make more adaptive attributions (see Chapter 7); and enhancing students' perceptions of competence (see Chapter 6), control, and relatedness (see Chapter 9).

Do a closure

Before dismissing students at the end of the lesson, gather the class together and do a closure, in which you do the following (in any order):

1. review the cues for the skills practiced

2. ask students if they achieved the lesson objective

3. remind students, either by telling them or asking them, why the skills or tasks worked on in the lesson are important

4. inform the students about the skills they will work on in the next lesson

Asking students if they reached the goal stated during the set induction holds them accountable; when students know that you will do this, they may be more apt to try to achieve the goal. Telling students again why skills are important will increase the chances they remember the reason.

Sample set induction and closure

One physical educator who effectively uses a set induction and closure in her classes is Amy B., who teaches at an urban middle school on the East Coast. Amy's second period 7th grade class is currently in the middle of a badminton unit. At the start of a lesson, after the students have warmed up by hitting clears to each other, Amy gathers the students together for the set induction:

"Today we're going to work on two different serves in badminton—the short, low serve and the high, deep serve. (Point #1 of the set induction)

"Why would it be good to be able to do two different serves? (She gets some responses from students.) Those are good ideas. It's good to know different kinds of serves because it helps to keep your opponent off guard—she doesn't know what type of serve you're going to do. The two different serves are also good to use in different situations—use the high, deep serve to push your opponent back, as it's an offensive kind of shot. But the low, short serve is more defensive and is usually most effective to your opponent's backhand. (Point #3 of the set induction)

"Your goal for the day is to be able to perform the type of serve—low, short or high, deep—on my command when I ask you to at the end of class. (Point #2 of the set induction)

"Now let's get started with the high, deep serve. Watch Jesse as he demonstrates."

After practicing tasks for the serves, Amy gathers the students again and closes the lesson:

"Great job everyone! How many of you were able to perform the type of serve I asked you to correctly? Good! (Point #2 of the closure)

"Who remembers why we should be able to perform at least two different serves? When would you use each serve? (Point #3 of the closure)

"What were the cues for performing each serve? Excellent. (Point #1 of the closure)

"In the next class, we're going to work on serving and then recognizing which type of shot to take next based on how effective your serve was. We're also going to set up some situations so you can practice when to use each serve." (Point #4 of the closure)

No matter what Amy teaches, the set induction and closure are always included. Do those things motivate all of her students to attend to, remember, and reproduce the demonstrations? Not necessarily, but they do help some students, and these elements help establish a learning environment in her classes.

Right now, Mr. Todd doesn't tell his students why they are working on skills or give them any goals to shoot for during the lesson. His students might be more motivated to watch and remember demonstrations, as well as practice the tasks demonstrated, if he uses a set induction and a closure in each lesson. For instance, in a lesson on heading the ball in soccer, Mr. Todd could start the lesson like this: "Class, today we're going to work on heading the ball in soccer. Does anyone know what heading is? Why might you use heading? That's right—it's used when the ball comes to you at a high level and you want to gain control of it for your team. You can also use the skill to redirect the ball another direction, like when the ball is traveling toward the opponent's goal and you want to make it move toward your goal. You're going to work with a partner today, and each partner will have a checklist of four important things to do when heading the ball. Your goal for today is to try to head the ball using all four cues on the checklist at least five times." At the end of the lesson, Mr. Todd should gather the students and close the class: "Raise your hand if you were able to head the ball five times using the four cues. Good, many of you could do that. What were those four cues again? Who remembers some of the reasons why this is an important skill to learn in soccer? That's right. Next time we'll work on heading the ball in more game-like situations. Good job today, class." These easy additions to Mr. Todd's lessons may serve to increase some of his students' motivation.

Peer Teaching Instructional Model

The theme of **peer teaching** is "I teach you, then you teach me" (Metzler, 2005, p. 343). In Mosston and Ashworth's (2002) spectrum of teaching styles, it is called *reciprocal teaching*. In peer teaching, students take turns assuming the role of tutor for a partner or small group of peers. The tutors actually take on the role of teacher during the lesson, demonstrating tasks, reciting cues, giving feedback, and assessing their learner. Each lesson begins with you explaining the first task to the tutors. The tutors observe a demonstration of the skill, learn cues for the skill, learn about the organizational aspects of the task the learners will practice, and obtain

focus point

When students act as tutors in the peer teaching instructional model, the learners are essentially observing learning models, which may be beneficial to learning.

information about how to assess the learners. While the tutors receive this information, their partners, the learners, are in another part of the gym either warming up or practicing a familiar task. The tutors then teach the skill or task to their learners, complete with demonstrations by the tutors. After the learners practice the new skill or task, the partners switch roles and the new tutor learns a new task to present to the new learner, while the new learner practices the first task. Alternate the roles for the rest of the lesson. While the tutors and learners interact, move to each group and ask questions of the tutor regarding the learner's performance; do not directly interact with the learner, as that is the tutor's job. These questions ensure that the tutor demonstrates the task for the learner and that the tutor is giving the learner accurate and frequent feedback. You should create an assessment tool for the tutor to use in assessing the learner's performance; this will also help the tutor remember the cues to repeat during demonstrations and give the learner accurate feedback. Although Metzler (2005) suggests peer teaching be used with 4th graders and older, the model has been adapted and used successfully even with 2nd graders.

real world

While teaching lessons for a university methods course at a private elementary school in the Midwestern United States, Gina W. successfully used peer teaching to teach rope jumping skills to 5th graders. After the students paired themselves, Gina taught the first tutors the initial skills they would teach their learners, while the first learners warmed up by jumping rope. Each tutor received an assessment sheet that included the cues for the skills the tutors would teach (see Exhibit 3.2 for a sample assessment sheet). Gina demonstrated the skills several times while repeating the cues, had a tutor demonstrate the skills, and then had the tutors repeat the cues aloud. Before sending the tutors off to teach their learners, Gina emphasized that they must demonstrate the skills and repeat the cues several times for their learners. Because the tutors had never attempted these skills before, their demonstrations were not always perfect, but Gina encouraged them in their attempts and reminded them that demonstrations don't have to be perfect to be helpful. In one instance, where the tutor couldn't jump rope at all, much less demonstrate a new rope jumping skill, Gina had the tutor demonstrate the skill without the rope.

Mr. Todd's students could really benefit from the use of an instructional model like peer teaching. Because most students tend to pair themselves with students similar to themselves and ones they respect, the learners may actually attend to the tutors' demonstrations more closely than if Mr. Todd demonstrates. And because many of the tutors are likely to be learning models, the observers will probably engage in more active cognitive processing with those models than with accurate models, which can benefit learning. When using peer teaching, Mr. Todd must emphasize that the demonstrations don't have to be perfect in order to be helpful.

Directions: When your learner is ready, have him or her make 10 attempts at the assigned rope jumping skill. Count the number of jumps in a row the learner can make using the skill before missing (up to 10). Then, determine their ability to follow the cues by checking the appropriate response.

Skill: Skier

Learner Name _____

Tutor Name _____

Cues: Feet together, side-to-side

Number of consecutive jumps performed _____

The learner's ability to follow the cues is best described by the following (check one):

○ Followed both cues in all jumps.

○ Performed both cues in most, but not all jumps.

○ Performed both cues in a few jumps.

○ Rarely, if ever, performed both cues in jumps.

Skill: Straddle

Learner Name _____

Tutor Name _____

Cues: Feet together/apart/together/apart, side-to-side

Number of consecutive jumps performed _____

The learner's ability to follow the cues is best described by the following (check one):

○ Followed both cues in all jumps.

○ Performed both cues in most, but not all jumps.

○ Performed both cues in a few jumps.

○ Rarely, if ever, performed both cues in jumps.

Skill: Bell

Learner Name _____

Tutor Name _____

Cues: Feet together, forward and backward

Number of consecutive jumps performed _____

The learner's ability to follow the cues is best described by the following (check one):

○ Followed both cues in all jumps.

○ Performed both cues in most, but not all jumps.

○ Performed both cues in a few jumps.

○ Rarely, if ever, performed both cues in jumps.

Skill: Scissors

Learner Name _____

Tutor Name _____

Cues: Feet together/apart/together/apart, forward and backward

Number of consecutive jumps performed _____

The learner's ability to follow the cues is best described by the following (check one):

○ Followed both cues in all jumps.

○ Performed both cues in most, but not all jumps.

○ Performed both cues in a few jumps.

○ Rarely, if ever, performed both cues in jumps.

Use Auditory Modeling with Temporal Tasks

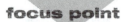

To help students learn skills or tasks that involve timing (e.g., dance sequences, rope jumping, gymnastic routines, tinikling routines, or locomotor skills like skipping, galloping, or sliding), you can use some form of auditory modeling. Auditory modeling might involve beating a drum, clapping hands, hitting rhythm sticks, or even using one's voice to speak cues using the rhythm involved. For instance, you can model the rhythm involved in skipping by clapping your hands to that rhythm, or saying the cues for skipping out loud using the appropriate rhythm: "step, hop step, hop step, hop step" with "hop" verbalized quickly and "step" held longer, as in the rhythm to a skip. A visual demonstration can accompany the auditory model. After the demonstration, students can rehearse the rhythm by clapping the rhythm or repeating verbal cues using the rhythm. Auditory modeling is something Mr. Todd has never done, but he teaches many skills activities that involve timing, and his students could really benefit from auditory models.

real world

While teaching square dancing to middle school students in the southern United States, Theresa H. noted that her students consistently performed the grand right and left too slowly, which spoiled the timing for the rest of the dance. Theresa used auditory modeling to help her students' timing of this skill. While playing the music for the square dance at the point of the grand right and left, she hit a drum stick against a cow bell each time the students should take the next student's hand. After doing this several times, she combined this auditory model with a visual model, using students who were close to the correct timing to perform the skill with the music and taking the next student's hand each time they heard the bell. This strategy helped, because when all students tried the grand right and left again, their timing was more accurate.

Combine Reinforcement with Modeling to Enhance Prosocial Behaviors

Modeling is one means of helping students acquire prosocial behaviors, but research cited earlier shows that it is most effective when combined with other strategies like reinforcement. That is consistent with social learning theory, which claims that learning occurs through the processes of modeling, reinforcement, and social comparison.

Sources for modeling prosocial behaviors

The following models can be used in physical education to model prosocial behaviors.

Physical educator. As a physical educator, you can consistently model prosocial behaviors like sharing, encouraging and helping others, controlling one's temper and other emotions, and basic manners like saying "please" and "thank you." You can model even complex prosocial behaviors like conflict resolution. Many students have not seen, or are even aware of, such basic prosocial behaviors like "please" and "thank you," so they need to see someone regularly exhibiting these behaviors before they can be expected to show them.

Other students. In physical education classes, other students can also serve as models of prosocial behaviors. According to social learning theory, these models are especially effective because the observers can see someone who is socially comparable to themselves demonstrating appropriate behavior. You can point out students who are demonstrating appropriate behaviors, while at the same time reinforcing them for their behavior; for example, point out the good behavior of a 1st grade student in the following way: "I really like the way Craig is waiting his turn in line without pushing others. That's very nice, Craig."

You can even recruit a student to role-play inappropriate and appropriate behaviors in class in a deliberate attempt to teach students about prosocial behaviors. For example, before class begins a high school physical educator might ask one student to model an appropriate response to a poor call by a referee during a game, while another student models an inappropriate response. The other students don't know that these two were asked to act this way. At the beginning of class several students, including these two, are asked to demonstrate some aspect of game play for the class—with the real intention of teaching students about responding appropriately to poor referee calls. During the demonstration, the two students role-play their respective behaviors, and the physical educator uses the opportunity to discuss appropriate responses with the class.

Famous athletes. These individuals can make good models of prosocial behaviors. As a physical educator, you will want to keep newspaper clippings, magazine articles, and videotape clips that describe instances of appropriate behaviors by high school, college, Olympic, and professional male and female athletes. Be alert for such promotions, as athletes' inappropriate behaviors are reported much more frequently than their appropriate behaviors. Prioritize the learning of prosocial behaviors for your students by taking class time to show them these videotape clips and articles of famous athletes' good behaviors.

Posters displaying prosocial behaviors. These posters can be displayed in the gym to help model desired behaviors. The newspaper clippings and articles of famous athletes described above can be used in the posters.

focus point

Sources that can model prosocial behaviors in physical education include the teacher, students, famous athletes, and posters of appropriate behaviors.

real world The posters might be used to define and illustrate sportspersonship, as done by Ashle M., an elementary physical education teacher in the southern United States. The poster included Ashle's definition of sportspersonship for her students: Follow the rules, have a positive attitude, respect others and equipment, and try your best. Pictures of individuals modeling those behaviors were placed on the poster as well.

Example of modeling combined with reinforcement

real world A teacher who does an excellent job of using a variety of individuals to model prosocial behaviors for her students is Jean R., who teaches at an inner-city elementary school in the southern United States. Jean consistently models appropriate behaviors herself, saying "please" and "thank you" to students and other teachers, always showing self-control, and never yelling at her students. She regularly reinforces students and uses students to demonstrate prosocial behaviors like encouraging and sharing equipment with each other. She also frequently points out the helping behaviors of the local professional athletes that the students admire.

Mr. Todd complains that his students argue a lot and can't control their tempers—but he is modeling lack of control and poor methods of dealing with conflict by yelling at them. So, to enhance his students' prosocial behaviors, Mr. Todd first needs to model appropriate behaviors himself; he must stop yelling, show self-control, and find other ways to deal with students' conflicts. When Mr. Todd sees students acting appropriately, especially those who are well-liked by others, he should praise them and point out their actions to the other students. Many of his students frequently discuss the local college sports teams, so he could search for information about college athletes' positive prosocial behaviors and point those out to his students.

Summary

Modeling, or demonstrating, is an important part of physical education instruction. Social learning theory holds that modeling is one of three methods by which we learn skills and behaviors. According to cognitive mediation theory, the effectiveness of a model is influenced by how well we attend to and remember the model, our attempts to physically reproduce the model, and our motivation to do those three things.

The most common belief about what observers learn when they observe a model is that they learn the pattern of coordination for a motor skill. Research shows that modeling can help individuals learn motor skills, prosocial behaviors, and psychological skills. Other research suggests ways physical educators can enhance the impact of modeling on student learning. Many of these methods are easy to follow: use a variety of models, repeat demonstrations several times before and throughout practice, repeat verbal cues and/or feedback for the model during demonstrations, have students verbally rehearse cues before practice, do a set induction and closure, and use auditory modeling for temporal skills. Other strategies require more effort on your part: create and use videotapes of peer coping models to help teach skills that students might be fearful of or anxious about, use the peer teaching instructional model, and set up a role-play by students of appropriate and inappropriate behaviors. It is important to use this common instructional tool.

Modeling	Verbal rehearsal
Demonstration	Mastery model
Observational learning	Coping model
Social learning theory	Auditory modeling
Cognitive mediation theory	Peer teaching

KEY **concepts**

application exercises

1. Imagine that in the past, many of your 6th grade physical education students had a hard time learning rhythmical activities like tinikling, creative dance, and line dancing. For each of the modeling processes described in the cognitive mediation theory, identify two methods of positively influencing the process to make your modeling more effective and enhance your students' learning. Make your examples specific to certain activities.

2. You are preparing to teach a volleyball unit in your middle school physical education classes, and you want to teach them how to dive for a ball. You know that many students will be hesitant to perform such a skill, so you decide to put together a video of a peer coping model learning the skill. Describe how you would go about recruiting a student to help you make the video, and describe how the model's statements about and performance of the skill would change in the course of creating the video.

3. You work with a first-year physical education teacher who is convinced that she need only do one demonstration of a skill or task during a lesson. She remembers that her teacher education program at the university emphasized maximizing physical activity time for children, and she doesn't want to waste class time on task presentations and demonstrations. Describe how you might convince her that many more demonstrations are needed; use the research evidence cited in this chapter.

Moral Development

Mr. Joseph's 6th grade physical education class has been working on soccer skills for the past few weeks and are now playing modified games of soccer. In this particular lesson, Mr. Joseph divides the students into four teams of six players each, with two teams playing each other on one small soccer field, and the other two teams playing on another small soccer field. Mr. Joseph spends the class period moving between one game and the other. He had originally planned to give the students feedback on their soccer skills, but has instead spent most of the time settling disputes between the two teams. The students constantly argue about who last touched the ball when it went out, illegal touches, and so on. When the students line up to leave class, those on the "winning" teams are taunting those on the "losing" teams, calling each other names, and still arguing about disputes from the game. After class, Mr. Joseph, frustrated at this lack of sportspersonship shown by his students, wonders what he can do to help them become better sports.

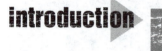

introduction

U nfortunately, scenarios like the one described are not uncommon in physical education lessons. These situations happen despite the commonly cited affective goals in physical education of developing sportspersonship, character, cooperation, self-control, and responsible behavior. Two of the six characteristics of the physically educated person described in NASPE's (2004b) *National Standards for Physical Education* depict such prosocial behaviors. But why is it so common to see unsportsmanlike behavior in physical education? What can be done to enhance moral development and prosocial behaviors? In this chapter, I will examine theories related to moral development, instructional models that can promote such prosocial behaviors as responsibility and cooperation, and research related to the theories and the models. Finally, specific strategies for enhancing sportspersonship and related behaviors in physical education will be described.

Defining Sportspersonship and Moral Reasoning

B efore discussing theories, models, research, and strategies related to moral development, it is important to clarify the two main concepts presented in this chapter: sportspersonship and moral reasoning. Being a "good sport" is often cited as a goal of physical education programs, but what does that mean? For many physical educators, **sportspersonship** encompasses prosocial behaviors, behaviors that society generally deems desirable and that help one function in and contribute to society, such as cooperation, generosity, sympathy, honesty, and helping. In fact, elementary students defined sportspersonship in terms of four types of prosocial behaviors (Entzion, 1991):

1. respect for authority and rules (e.g., be honest; don't cheat);
2. proper responses to winning and losing (e.g., don't brag when you win; don't get mad, cry, or make excuses when you lose);
3. sensitivity to others (e.g., take turns; don't hit or yell at others, or call others names); and
4. be the best you can be (e.g., try hard, don't quit).

Such prosocial behaviors are one aspect of moral development examined in this chapter.

The other aspect of moral development is **moral reasoning.** Weiss (1987) defines moral reasoning as "the rationales children use to judge the rightness or wrongness" of behaviors (p. 140). Two children may exhibit the same prosocial behavior (e.g., taking turns), but the reasoning process behind this behavior may be different for each child. For instance, one child may take turns because it is a rule that should be followed in physical education and is meant for everyone's best interest, while the other child takes turns because he wants other students to let him take turns. It is important for physical educators to learn how children's moral reasoning matures and how to help students enhance their moral reasoning.

focus point

Moral development consists of prosocial behaviors and the reasoning behind behaviors.

Moral Development Theories

Over the years, several ways of conceptualizing moral development have emerged. Two approaches, social learning theory and structural developmental views, have proven especially helpful for educators. The two approaches provide different insights into moral development and yield different yet complementary strategies that physical educators can use to enhance students' moral development.

Social Learning Theory

As described in Chapter 3, a person learns thoughts and behaviors through three processes in social learning theory (Bandura, 1977, 1986): reinforcement, modeling, and social comparison. Moral development occurs as a person internalizes or adopts society's prosocial norms. Thus, moral behaviors are those that are consistent with the norms of society. A person learns these behaviors by observing significant others and people similar to him or her (e.g., parents, family, peers, teachers, coaches) and perhaps seeing them rewarded in some way for those behaviors. Prosocial behaviors are also learned when a child himself displays prosocial behaviors and is rewarded for those behaviors. Undesirable behaviors are also learned through observation, such as when a person or significant other is not reprimanded or is even rewarded for demonstrating such behaviors. The focus of social learning theory is on overt, observable behaviors; social learning theory does not address the reasoning behind behaviors.

In physical education, the primary socializing agents available to influence a child's behaviors are his or her peers and the physical educator. Social learning theory suggests that prosocial behaviors like honesty, respect, and concern for others can be learned in physical education if the teacher models such behaviors, positively identifies those students who exhibit the behaviors, and praises students for showing the behaviors. For instance, Mr. Joseph might enhance sportspersonship in his students by demonstrating how a good sport behaves, identifying individual students (especially those who are respected and admired) who show good sportspersonship, and rewarding students for those behaviors. Conversely, dishonesty and lack of concern for others will be learned if he allows his students to demonstrate those behaviors, or even models them himself. Perhaps Mr. Joseph's students are showing poor sportspersonship because in the past he has let students get by with teasing others, gloating when they win, and complaining whenever something doesn't go their way. In addition, students might not have been rewarded when they showed prosocial behaviors.

focus point

According to social learning theory, moral development consists of adopting the prosocial norms of society and occurs through modeling, reinforcement, and comparison to similar others.

Structural Developmental Approaches

Unlike social learning theory, **structural developmental approaches** to moral development focus on the reasoning behind behaviors, rather than the behaviors themselves. A person's reasoning structure affects that person's judgments of behaviors as well as the actual behaviors the person exhibits. A key element in structural developmental theories is that moral reasoning changes, or develops, along with a person's cognitive or mental development and with various social interactions (Weiss & Smith, 2002b). Thus, a child who can think abstractly and so can take another person's point of view is able to reason differently and demonstrate a different level of moral development than a child who can only think concretely and cannot take another's point of view. For example, the first child would understand that being pushed by a friend while playing tag was probably not intentional and may have been the result of the speed at which his friend was running, so he ignores the push. The second child, however, only knows that she was pushed and, not able to take her friend's point of view to understand why she was pushed, pushes her back. Although several theorists have contributed to the structural developmental approach (e.g., Gilligan, 1977; Haan, 1977; Kohlberg, 1976), Norma Haan's model will be presented in more detail due to its extensive use in youth sport and physical education research.

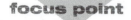

focus point

Structural developmental theories focus on moral reasoning, which is said to change along with a person's cognitive development and with various social interactions.

Haan's interactional theory of moral development

Three main concepts in Haan's **interactional theory** (Haan, 1977; Haan, Aerts, & Cooper, 1985) are moral balance, moral dialogue, and moral levels. **Moral balance** is a state of basic agreement about the rights and/or responsibilities among all involved parties. Morality emerges as people realize their interconnectedness and the need to balance the give-and-take among them. Moral imbalance results when one party gives or takes too much in a relationship, and there is disagreement about rights and responsibilities. The process through which moral balance is achieved is called **moral dialogue.** A dialogue may involve verbal negotiation of rights, or even nonverbal interactions. For instance, a child who is pushed while playing tag may feel he was unfairly treated and thus experience moral imbalance. He may then try a nonverbal moral dialogue to restore moral balance by later pushing the child who pushed him.

Haan (1977; Haan et al., 1985) described three phases and five levels of moral development through which children may progress (see Exhibit 4.1). In the three phases, a child moves from self-interests to others' interests to mutual interests as the basis of moral reasoning. Within the phases, there are five specific **levels of moral development.** Each level describes the reasoning used by someone at that level to decide whether an action is right or wrong. Weiss (1987) later explained these levels in terms of sportspersonship in movement settings.

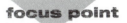

focus point

According to the interactional theory, moral development is described as levels of moral reasoning through which people progress, moving from self-interests to others' interests and then mutual interests as the basis of moral reasoning.

Assimilation phase. The first two levels comprise the **assimilation phase,** in which a child gives preference to his own needs and interests. A child in this phase is not necessarily selfish (Shields & Bredemeier, 2001), he simply cannot take on the perspectives of others due to his level of cognitive development (i.e., concrete thinking). A child in one of these two levels seeks to "take" more than "give" in a relationship as he strives for moral balance.

The development of moral reasoning (phases and levels) (adapted from Weiss, 1987).	**EXHIBIT**	**4.1**

PHASES OF MORAL REASONING	LEVELS OF MORAL REASONING
Equilibration	Level 5—Maximize interests of all
Accommodation: Priority to others ("giving")	Level 4—External rules and regulations
	Level 3—Golden Rule
Assimilation: Priority to self ("taking")	Level 2—Eye-for-an-eye
	Level 1—It's okay if I don't get caught

In Level 1, a child reasons that an action is right or wrong depending on its outcome; the action is okay if he doesn't get caught and it results in something good for him, but it's wrong if he does get caught and/or it produces something negative for him. For example, Suzan, a student in Mr. Joseph's class, might reason that teasing others is fine if she doesn't get caught. But if Mr. Joseph reprimands her for doing that, then Suzan will conclude that those actions are not acceptable. A child at Level 2 takes an "eye-for-an-eye" approach to moral reasoning. The child still wants to maximize her own self-interests, but she is capable now of seeing more than just the action's outcome. If Suzan was at Level 2, she might reason it was okay to tease others because other students have done that to her. Conversely, she might think she shouldn't tease others if she hasn't been teased.

Accommodation phase. The next two levels of moral reasoning are part of the **accommodation phase,** in which a child gives preference to the needs and interests of others. A child in these phases often will "give" more in a relationship in order to achieve moral balance than to "take." Moral reasoning at Level 3 centers on the Golden Rule; a child decides he's going to treat others the way he wants to be treated. To reason at this level, a person must be capable of abstract thinking and taking on another person's point of view. Now Suzan decides not to tease others because she does not want anyone to tease her. In Level 4, a child focuses on following external rules and regulations. The child has learned that not all people willingly adopt the altruistic perspective in the previous level, and that objective and impartial rules were created for the good of all. Thus, Suzan, when reasoning at Level 4, does not tease others because the physical education rules prohibit those actions and those rules were created in the best interest of all students.

Equilibration phase. The **equilibration phase** includes Level 5 of moral reasoning. In this phase, the child seeks a balance in the "give" and "take" (moral balance). In this final level, a person considers what would be best for all of the people involved, regardless of the rules. The person recognizes the rights and needs of everyone in the situation and seeks moral balances that maximize the mutual interests of all. Suzan, if reasoning within Level 5, will likely decide not to tease others even if there isn't a specific rule against it. She believes all students should be able to participate in activities without fear of being ridiculed, and teasing others would violate that right for all.

According to the interactional theory of moral development, children will use gradually higher levels of moral reasoning with increased cognitive development as well as guided chances to solve moral dilemmas, which will be discussed later in this chapter. Not everyone, however, reaches the highest levels of moral reasoning. Neither do they always use the highest level of reasoning of which they are capable. A child may choose to use a less advanced level of reasoning even when she is capable of higher levels. For instance, Suzan might be capable of taking on another person's perspective and reasoning at Level 3 (the Golden Rule), but may just decide to reason at Level 2 and make fun of someone just because she was teased yesterday.

Moral Development Research

Research on children's moral development has been conducted in a variety of physical activity settings, including youth sport, summer activity camps, and physical education. Because research in this area specific to physical education is limited, this section will include studies performed in all of these settings. The impact of age and gender on moral reasoning will first be examined, followed by a review of the effect traditional physical education programs have on prosocial behaviors and moral reasoning. The influence of programs based on social learning and structural developmental theories, specifically designed to affect children's moral development in movement settings like physical education, will then be considered. Finally, research on some instructional and curricular models and their influence on moral development will be explored.

Age, Gender, and Moral Reasoning

According to the structural developmental idea of moral development, children's moral reasoning should mature with age. This idea is generally supported in research (Bredemeier, 1995; Bredemeier & Shields, 1984; Jantz, 1975; Rainey, Santilli, & Fallon, 1992). In one study, Bredemeier and Shields (1984) found that college students demonstrated more mature moral reasoning than high school students for both everyday life and sport dilemmas. They also found that people reason at a lower level about sport situations than everyday life situations, and that this difference in levels of reasoning about sport and life appears to increase with age.

Gender differences have also been found in some studies regarding moral reasoning (e.g., Bredemeier & Shields, 1986a, 1986b). For instance, Bredemeier and Shields (1986a) found that college males tended to show greater divergence in life and sport reasoning than females, while high school and college male athletes showed bigger differences in life and sport reasoning than female athletes. The females showed higher levels of moral reasoning than the males.

It is likely, therefore, that older students and females will demonstrate higher levels of moral reasoning than younger students and males, and that females will display less divergence between life and sport moral reasoning than males. Physical educators, however, should keep in mind that

focus point

Evidence exists that moral reasoning will be more advanced for older students and females, and that females show less divergence between life and sport moral reasoning than males.

these differences are not guaranteed, and all students can still benefit from strategies to enhance their moral reasoning. Teachers should also be aware that students may be more apt to demonstrate inappropriate behavior in physical education than in non-physical activity settings due to possible lower levels of moral reasoning in physical activity settings.

Traditional Physical Education and Moral Development

Even while physical educators laud the sportspersonship and character-building goals of physical education, they are often frustrated by the lack of such virtues being displayed by their students, as shown in the chapter's opening scenario. But can traditional physical education programs, where mere participation is believed to promote moral development, actually enhance students' moral development? In traditional physical education, the teacher holds the authority, most activities are sport-related and competitive, students are evaluated on performance outcome, and basic drills are used to practice skills, if skills are practiced at all (Theeboom, DeKnop, & Weiss, 1995); little is done purposely to promote moral development. Although some studies support the beneficial aspects of traditional physical education for social and moral development (e.g., Emmanouel, Zervas, & Vagenas, 1992), the vast majority of research does not (e.g., Bredemeier et al., 1986; Gibbons et al., 1995; Romance, Weiss, & Bockoven, 1986). In the following sections, studies will be described in which traditional physical education was compared with programs specifically designed to promote moral development, with traditional programs showing little to no influence. Physical education has the potential to enhance moral development, but only if teachers plan and use specific strategies to teach for it (Patrick, Ward, & Crouch, 1998).

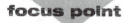

focus point

Unless specifically planned for and taught, moral development in physical education programs is unlikely to occur; it does not happen by accident.

Effectiveness of Social Learning and Structural Developmental Strategies

Researchers have examined the impact that intervention programs based on social learning and structural developmental theories can have on children's moral development. Some programs used a combination of strategies from both theories, some were based on one theory alone, while other studies compared the effectiveness of those types of strategies.

Combined programs

Instructional interventions based on a combination of social learning and structural developmental strategies have effectively enhanced the moral reasoning and behaviors of students in movement settings. Gibbons et al.

(1995) studied the impact of "Fair Play for Kids," a program that used both types of strategies, on several aspects of the moral development of upper elementary children. Over a 7-month period, some students received the Fair Play curriculum during all of their school subjects, while other students received the curriculum only during physical education or not at all. Social learning strategies included modeling of prosocial behaviors by former Olympians, role-playing, observational learning, and rewards for fair play. Structural developmental strategies used the presentation or recognition of moral dilemmas, followed by dialogue among the involved students in order to reach moral balance. For instance, one specific strategy was the "problem-solving running shoe." A big running shoe, drawn on a piece of paper, had areas marked *problem, alternatives, consequences,* and *solution.* Students involved in conflicts, such as disagreeing over a call during a game, or who lost self-control were instructed to go to the "listening bench" and fill out the running shoe areas. The shoe could also be used by peer counselors to help students in conflict come to a solution. By the end of the program, both groups receiving the intervention exhibited higher levels of moral judgment, reason, intention, and behaviors than students who did not. The two treatment groups, however, didn't differ on moral development, suggesting that employing such a program in physical education classes alone can impact students' moral development.

Social learning

Some researchers have found that strategies based on social learning theory alone can be effective in enhancing sportspersonship and prosocial behaviors in physical education (Giebink & McKenzie, 1985; Patrick et al., 1998; Sharpe et al., 1996). For example, a good behavior game used in a 20-lesson volleyball unit increased the appropriate and decreased the inappropriate behaviors of upper elementary physical education students (Patrick et al., 1998). Teams of students earned points for appropriate behaviors and lost points for inappropriate behaviors displayed during 10 minutes of game play each class period. Teams that met the criterion number of points for a day received a reward of 3 extra minutes of game play, and the two teams that met the criteria the most days received an additional activity reward at the end of the unit. The researchers also found the social learning strategies did not negatively influence the students' skill attempts, as the number of successful overhead and forearm passes did not decrease during the good behavior game. In another study, a one-semester prosocial curriculum in physical education—implemented in only one of five physical education classes per week—effectively increased student leadership behaviors (e.g., encouraging and supporting classmates) and teacher-independent conflict resolution skills in elementary students (Sharpe et al., 1996).

These studies indicate that programs using social learning strategies alone, even for as little as one class period per week, can be effective in enhancing student prosocial behaviors. Strategies such as clearly defining sportspersonship, demonstrating sportspersonship during game play, role-playing, positively identifying students demonstrating those behaviors, praising and providing tangible rewards to students for appropriate behaviors, and closing the lesson with discussions about prosocial behaviors can yield positive results in student sportspersonship.

Structural developmental

Like social learning strategies, structural developmental strategies alone have also proven effective in enhancing students' moral development. In a study by Romance et al. (1986), two intact 5th grade classes participated in daily physical education for 8 weeks. Although the same physical activities were taught to both classes during that time period, one class received instruction that integrated several structural developmental strategies, while the other did not. Some of those strategies included the following:

- student discussion of rules and behaviors that affected them and others;
- student input in establishing guidelines for moral behavior during class;
- student participation in and adjustment of games with built-in moral dilemmas;
- student creation of games that allow all students to participate, enjoy, and succeed; and
- student participation in and discussion of the merits of a game with a moral dilemma vs. the same game adapted to solve the dilemma.

In the results, the treatment group had greater gains than the control group in moral reasoning. It is interesting that although the control group had significantly greater improvement in basketball skills than the treatment group, there was no difference between the groups in fitness scores, and the treatment group improved more than the control group in gymnastics skills. Thus, a moral development program based on structural developmental strategies can improve students' moral reasoning, and this may occur without adversely affecting their motor skill development.

Comparing social learning and structural developmental strategies

Although combination and single strategy programs can positively influence students' moral development, are strategies based on one theory more effective than strategies based on the other? Brenda Bredemeier and her colleagues (Bredemeier et al., 1986) found no difference in moral reasoning improvement in 5- to 7-year-old children who participated in a social learning group vs. a structural developmental group during a 6-week summer instructional sport camp. Shields and Bredemeier (1989) later examined the impact of those instructional strategies on the children's coping and defending processes. **Coping processes** are more mature moral reasoning capabilities such as being empathetic, being able to suppress one's primitive impulses and instead display socially acceptable behavior, and conducting a logical and accurate analysis of a situation. On the other hand, **defending processes** yield an inaccurate evaluation of a situation and may include less mature moral reasoning capabilities such as the rationalization or denial of one's actions, or the projection of one's motives onto others. On these aspects of moral reasoning, the researchers found that the defending scores of both treatment groups decreased significantly over the 6 weeks, but the coping scores of the structural developmental group increased significantly more than the social learning or control groups.

In a study conducted in physical education over a longer time period, Gibbons and Ebbeck (1997) extended their previous study (Gibbons et al., 1995) and compared social learning and structural developmental strategies in the "Fair Play for Kids" curriculum. Students in the 4th, 5th, and 6th grades participated in regular physical education 4 to 5 days per week over 7 months. The three classes at each grade level were randomly assigned to a control, social learning, or structural developmental group. The specific strategies in the two treatment groups, implemented at least 1 day per week during physical education, were similar to those in Gibbons et al. (1995). By the end of the 7 months, the students in the social learning and structural developmental groups scored higher than the control group on moral judgment, moral intention, and prosocial behaviors. Moral reasoning, however, was higher in the structural developmental students than the control or social learning groups.

The results of the research indicate that programs using social learning or structural developmental strategies, either alone or in combination, can enhance children's moral development. Taking class time to implement such programs doesn't appear to negatively impact motor skill learning. In fact, Sharpe et al. (1996) found that students who participated in the prosocial curriculum during physical education had more activity time than students who did not. Moreover, the amount of time per week that moral development programs need to be effective isn't much; one class period out of five per week was effective in some programs. The program, however, should be implemented over an extended period of time (e.g., months instead of weeks, but preferably continuously) to be most effective. A program that occurs just during physical education, and not other school subjects, can impact students' moral reasoning, but it is unlikely that the positive development will transfer to other settings. Finally, there is evidence that moral

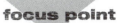

focus point

Using physical education class time to implement moral development strategies doesn't seem to negatively influence students' practice time or motor skill development.

focus point

Programs based on social learning or structural developmental strategies, either alone or in combination, can effectively enhance children's moral development. But structural developmental strategies might have a slightly stronger influence than social learning methods.

development strategies based on the structural developmental perspective have a slightly greater influence on aspects of moral reasoning than social learning strategies, although both types will yield positive results.

Instructional Models and Curricula Research

Recently, physical education specialists, recognizing that affective goals are vital to the mission of physical education, developed instructional models and curricula that either exclusively address prosocial behaviors or include such constructs as part of the instructional process. Such models include the taking personal and social responsibility model (Hellison, 2003), cooperative learning (Grineski, 1996; Metzler, 2005), sport education (Siedentop, 1994; Siedentop, Hastie, & van der Mars, 2004), and adventure-based learning (Prouty, Panicucci, & Collinson, 2006). Specific features of these models will be described later in this chapter. In this section, each model will be briefly explained, along with a presentation of research on its effectiveness to enhance prosocial behaviors.

Taking personal and social responsibility

Physical educators are faced with meeting a multitude of motor skill, fitness, cognitive, and affective goals. Yet, as Don Hellison (2003) points out, trying to accomplish so many goals often yields development in none of them. Hellison decided to focus his teaching efforts on goals within the affective domain. He created a curriculum model for physical educators and others working with youth in movement settings that specifically focuses on helping children take personal responsibility for their own actions and contribute to the welfare of others (Hellison, 2003). The primary components of the **taking personal and social responsibility** (TPSR) model include five goals or levels of student responsibility, a daily lesson format, and strategies to promote self-responsibility at each level.

Research results generally support the effectiveness of the TPSR model in developing prosocial behaviors with a wide variety of students, including elementary-aged boys who are at risk and young children with disabilities (DeBusk & Hellison, 1989; Wright, White, & Gaebler-Spira, 2004). In one study, 10 delinquency-prone 4th grade boys participated in a special 6-week noon-hour program in which the boys were taught a variety of fitness and sport activities using the TPSR model (DeBusk & Hellison, 1989). TPSR strategies included daily teacher talk, student sharing, reflection time, discussion and reflection of levels, talking bench, student juries, student choices, student contracts, cross-age teaching, modeling, and reinforcement. By the end of the program, the teacher-researcher and the teaching assistants reported positive behavioral changes in the boys during the noon-hour program, especially in self-control (Level I) and caring (Level IV).

In another study, Wright et al. (2004) found that the TPSR model effectively enhanced the prosocial behaviors of students with disabilities. Males (ages 4 to 11 years) with spastic diplegic cerebral palsy participated in a developmental martial arts program into which the TPSR model was integrated. Some of the strategies used were awareness talks, opportunities to take on responsibilities and leadership, partner work, providing help and feedback to peers, opportunities to make group decisions, and reflection time. The 13-week program was held 1 day per week for 45 minutes through a rehabilitation hospital. The case studies of five boys suggested that the program enhanced several social skills (e.g., taking turns, waiting, raising a hand to speak, not interrupting others, paying more attention to other students, being willing to participate and speak up). Other researchers have found that programs integrating the TPSR model into sport education units had positive results on student reflective abilities, problem solving, leadership skills, and conflict resolution skills (Hastie & Buchanan, 2000; Sharpe, Brown, & Crider, 1995); this research will be further explained in the section on sport education research.

focus point

The TPSR model has enhanced the prosocial behaviors of students, including boys at risk and young children with disabilities.

Cooperative learning

Group work is common in physical education; it is an integral part of more advanced motor skills. But participating in a group doesn't necessarily mean positive social behaviors are being demonstrated or learned. **Cooperative learning** is an instructional model that purposely uses partner and group work to enhance prosocial behaviors in physical education. The theme of cooperative learning, "students learning with, by, and for each other" (Metzler, 2005, p. 266), clearly describes its structure. In this model, teams of students are intentionally formed, and the teams must work together, with each team member contributing, to solve a problem or achieve goals. Cooperation, helping, sensitivity to others, personal responsibility, and giving high effort are some prosocial behaviors that may result from cooperative learning.

Researchers have examined teacher and student perspectives of cooperative learning as well as evidence regarding the impact of the model on students' prosocial behaviors and on practice time. After participating in or teaching units using cooperative learning structures, elementary students and their teachers (Dyson, 2001, 2002) and high school students (Dyson & Strachan, 2000) reported positive changes in students' prosocial behaviors: ability to work together, care for teammates, respect others' ideas, include students with disabilities, depend on each other, and accept responsibility.

Other researchers studied the impact of cooperative learning or games on children's actual prosocial behaviors (Grineski, 1989, 1997; Mender, Kerr, & Orlick, 1982; Orlick, 1981a, 1981b; Smith, Markley, & Goc Karp, 1997). These researchers found that cooperative activities can enhance the sharing, cooperative play, and helping behaviors of preschool, kindergarten, and elementary children, as well as children with learning and physical disabilities, more so than traditional, individual, free play, or competitive games. For instance, Grineski (1997) found that a cooperative games structure was more effective than free play in enhancing positive physical contact and goal-related cooperative behaviors and decreasing negative physical contact and negative verbal interactions in preschool children both with and without disabilities.

If time is spent in physical education to implement cooperative learning structures, do students then lose valuable motor skill practice time? Although more research is needed on this topic, that done so far indicates the opposite. Third and 4th grade physical education classes that used cooperative learning had low instruction time and high engaged practice time (Dyson & Harper, 1997). Students in their fourth year of experience with cooperative learning spent less time in instruction and more time in practice than students in their first year with cooperative learning (Strachan & MacCauley, 1997), suggesting as students and teachers become more familiar with the model, they are more efficient in implementing it. Specific cooperative learning strategies that have proven effective will be discussed later in this chapter.

Sport education

An instructional and curricular model that includes aspects of both peer teaching and cooperative learning is **sport education** (Metzler, 2005). The main goals of sport education are to develop competent, literate, and enthusiastic sportspeople (Siedentop, 1994; Siedentop et al., 2004). The model, devised by Daryl Siedentop, is designed to help students learn about sports from many different perspectives: player, coach, referee, statistician, manager, and scorekeeper. Students don't just learn to play a sport; they also learn about the many traditions associated with sport. In addition, students learn in all three domains: psychomotor, cognitive, and affective. In the affective domain, for instance, students can learn to work cooperatively with their teammates as they prepare for the season and make decisions about what to practice, position assignments, and so on. They can also learn leadership and responsibility as they assume the various roles.

Several researchers have found support for the positive effect that participation in sport education units can have on children's prosocial behaviors (Carlson & Hastie, 1997; Hastie & Sharpe, 1999; Pope & Grant, 1996). In one study, middle school boys considered at risk (e.g., history of discipline problems, criminal offenses, and poor grades) participated in a 20-lesson season of modified football (Hastie & Sharpe, 1999). The season consisted of a preseason, formal competition, playoffs, and an awards day. Students took on the following duties: selection of team mem-

▼ **focus point**

There is evidence that students and teachers believe cooperative learning helps children learn prosocial behaviors, and that it actually does enhance children's prosocial behaviors without decreasing practice time during physical education.

bers via a committee; and the roles of player, captain, referee, scorer, linesman, and sideline cameraman. Among the awards given was a "fair play" award for behavior during competition, as measured by compliance with referee decisions. Results showed that student compliance with referee decisions increased over the unit, as did the number of positive peer interactions, leadership behaviors, and the accuracy of the students' self-reports of their behavior; negative peer interactions decreased.

Sport education hybrids have also enhanced students' moral development. Hastie and Buchanan (2000) examined the impact of a curriculum that integrated the TPSR framework into a sport education unit with 6th grade boys. The sport education unit included a skill and team development phase, followed in turn by the preseason, formalized competition phase, and awards day. Each day, the TPSR model was incorporated into the unit via awareness talks, problem-solving tasks, opportunities to put the levels into practice, and time for reflection. By the season's end, students demonstrated a clear understanding of the goal levels, were able to accurately and honestly reflect about the levels at which they worked during class, and often solved problems in independent and effective ways. In another study that integrated TPSR with sport education (Sharpe et al., 1995), skill development time in the sportspersonship curriculum was greater than during traditional classes. In a curriculum that integrated conflict resolution skills and a sense of community with sport education ("Sport for Peace" curriculum), urban high school students' prosocial behaviors increased (Ennis et al., 1999).

focus point

Sport education, by itself or combined with other models, can enhance the prosocial behaviors of children from upper elementary age to high school.

Adventure-based learning

Adventure-based learning, or adventure education, is a curricular model that has been defined as the "deliberate use of sequenced adventure activities—particularly games, trust activities, and problem solving initiatives—for the personal and social development of participants" (Cosgriff, 2000, p. 90). The most recognized adventure-based learning programs are Outward Bound and Project Adventure, programs that most often occur outside school settings. Adventure-based learning in physical education programs could consist of a wide variety of activities: outdoor activities like hiking, canoeing, and orienteering; ropes courses and wall-climbing; team-building activities and problem-solving games (i.e., building a human pyramid, swamp crossing, group juggle); icebreakers and cooperative activities; and progressive trust activities.

Although research on the outcomes of adventure-based learning in physical education with school-aged children is limited (Brown, 2006), elementary students and physical educators do report enhanced cooperation, trust, problem-solving skills, communication, self-esteem, and responsibility (Dyson, 1995, 1996).

Enhancing Moral Development in Physical Education

If students are to actually achieve goals related to moral development in physical education, their teachers must take purposeful steps to reach those goals. In this section, strategies based on social learning theory and the instructional/curricular models that can help children learn prosocial behaviors will be presented. Means of enhancing students' moral reasoning via structural developmental strategies will also be described. Physical educators who have used the strategies will be introduced when available.

Social Learning Strategies

Several strategies based on social learning theory have enhanced students' prosocial behaviors in physical education.

Define sportspersonship

One strategy is to clearly define sportspersonship for students. Students need to understand what behaviors lead a person to be called a "good sport" and which ones result in "poor sport." Mr. Joseph, the teacher in the chapter's opening scenario, should verbally describe for his students the prosocial behaviors he wants them to exhibit. This should occur at the start of the year and frequently throughout the school year. Examples of both positive and negative behaviors should be given. These can be verbally explained to students, but they should also be modeled, just as motor skills are.

connected CONCEPTS

Prosocial behaviors can be modeled by several different sources, including the physical educator, other students, famous athletes, and posters (see Chapter 3).

Moreover, Mr. Joseph's definition of good sportspersonship should be written on a poster and placed where all students can see it every class period. Such a definition might include:

- listening when others are speaking,
- accepting officiating calls without arguing,
- trying your best, and
- congratulating others on good performances.

Compliment cards and fair play agreement

Among the social learning strategies found in the Fair Play for Kids (Gibbons & Ebbeck, 1997) program were the use of compliment cards and a fair play agreement. On an index card, students wrote examples of good sportspersonship their classmates exhibit during class, like "said 'good job' to opponent" or "apologized for running into a classmate." The compliment cards were then turned into the teacher and shared with the group once per week.

A fair play agreement is a contract that each student creates, describing several prosocial behaviors he or she will strive to demonstrate during an activity (e.g., work cooperatively with teammates, accept official's calls without complaints). The student's signature on the sheet seals the contract between that student and the other class members. Mr. Joseph could combine the fair play agreement with rewards to try to enhance his students' sportspersonship behaviors. He could help his students write their own contracts, directing individual students to behaviors they especially need to show more often. Students who keep their contracts could then be rewarded in some way.

Assess prosocial behaviors

Even though physical educators say they want to enhance students' prosocial behaviors, most don't assess their students' improvement in those behaviors. Just like with motor skills, sportspersonlike behaviors need to be specifically and clearly assessed. Good assessments can help both you and your students know if a reward was earned or if a fair play agreement was kept. Students can rate themselves on their sportspersonship during the class period—you may give them a piece of paper at the end of class that says: "On a scale of 1 to 10 (with 10 being the best sport), how would you rate your sportspersonship during class today? Why?"

Peers can assess each other on their prosocial behaviors. For instance, each student playing a game can be assigned an assessment buddy who observes game play and marks a tally on a sheet of paper each time the buddy displays a good sport behavior or a poor sport behavior. Make a list of specific social skills you are looking for in your students (e.g., offers verbal support for teammates' efforts, accepts official's call without complaint, congratulates opponents on good play, listens to instructions, takes turns, shares equipment). List the behaviors on a sheet, along with student names, and complete it during class or at the end of class to help assess students on their prosocial behaviors (see Exhibit 4.2 for a partially completed example and Appendix A.2 for a blank form). You can choose to assess a few children each class period on all behaviors on the form, or assess all children on one or two behaviors.

EXHIBIT	4.2	Sample form for assessing prosocial behaviors in physical education.

Class _5th period_

Date _10/12/08_   Lesson Content _Volleyball_

✓+ = *Consistently demonstrates*   ✓ = *Sometimes demonstrates*   ✓— = *Rarely demonstrates*

STUDENT NAME	SUPPORTS TEAMMATES	ACCEPTS OFFICIATING	PRAISES OPPONENTS	LISTENS TO INSTRUCTIONS	TAKES TURNS	SHARES EQUIPMENT
Tom	✓+	✓+	✓	✓+	✓+	✓+
Alice	✓—	✓—	✓—	✓+	✓	✓
Jon	✓	✓	✓	✓+	✓+	✓+
Kim						

real world

Ashle M., physical education teacher in a suburban elementary school in the southern United States, developed an intervention based on social learning theory to enhance her 3rd graders' sportspersonship behaviors (Meers & Blankenship, 2005). Ashle clearly defined sportspersonship for her students as the following: keeping the rules, having a positive attitude, respecting others and equipment, and trying your best. This definition was posted on the gym wall for all the students to see and was discussed with the students daily at the start of each class period. In these discussions, Ashle verbally described and demonstrated prosocial behaviors that exemplified sportspersonship, such as giving compliments, high-fives, and encouraging classmates. Negative behaviors were also discussed and demonstrated, including complaining, teasing, and being aggressive. "Teachable moments" were constantly taken advantage of, as Ashle used natural breaks in activities to discuss positive and negative behaviors that occurred. She served as a role model of good sportspersonship by complimenting and clapping for students during activities. At the close of each lesson, Ashle led a discussion with her students about the positive and negative behaviors that occurred during the lesson, seeking suggestions from them on how they could improve in the next lesson.

A major part of Ashle's social learning intervention was the "shining stars" reward system. The students were divided into two teams. A poster for each team and a "shining stars" poster were displayed in the gym. Whenever Ashle observed a student showing a positive behavior, the student was rewarded by being allowed to put a star on his or her team poster and signing the "shining stars" poster. Ashle placed a tally on a team's poster if a student performed a negative behavior. Each team's goal every class period was to have twice as many positive stars as negative tallies. Each day this happened, a team earned 5 minutes of bonus physical education time, which could eventually add up to an additional physical education period. The intervention increased the students' prosocial behaviors and decreased their negative behaviors.

Structural Developmental Strategies

The basic structural developmental strategy is to identify or create a moral dilemma for your students, and then help them discuss the dilemma and come up with a solution. Let's say several students in Mr. Joseph's class are complaining that some of their classmates aren't giving them a turn at jumping the long jump rope, and the complaining students always have to turn the rope. Mr. Joseph could stop the class, point out this naturally occurring dilemma, and help the students discuss this problem and come up with a solution. Mr. Joseph could also create dilemmas for the students themselves to identify. For instance, he could create teams for soccer in which all of the students who have lots of experience playing soccer are on one team. Mr. Joseph would let them play for a few minutes, then gather the students for a discussion of this dilemma, such as the following, helping them come up with a solution:

Mr. Joseph: "Are you having any problems with the game so far?"

Students: "That team has all the good players!"

Mr. Joseph: "What makes that a problem?"

Students: "The other team is scoring all the points—that isn't any fun and it isn't fair!"

Mr. Joseph: "But what about the team with the good players—aren't they having fun?"

Students: "It's too easy to score—we can't get better if it's too easy."

Mr. Joseph: "So what could we do to make this game more fun?"

Students: "Switch up some players so that the teams are more equal in soccer ability."

Several other structural developmental strategies are described as part of the Fair Play for Kids curriculum (Gibbons & Ebbeck, 1997; Gibbons et al., 1995). Students can participate in establishing rules for moral behavior in physical education. One strategy, the problem-solving running shoe, was described in the research section. Other strategies include the following.

Creating games that solve moral dilemmas. Students can create games that solve moral dilemmas that often occur within games, such as hogging the ball or unequal playing time. For example, let's say that Mr. Joseph's 6th graders are playing modified games of 3-on-3 basketball up to 10 points. One team complains to Mr. Joseph that Sarah isn't passing the ball to anybody and is the only one taking shots. Mr. Joseph could then get Sarah's team

focus point

Structural developmental strategies that can be used in physical education to enhance students' moral reasoning include having students dialogue about moral dilemmas in class, inviting students to participate in establishing behavior rules for class, and creating games or skits that solve moral dilemmas.

and the other team together and direct them to change some rules in their game to allow more students to participate. The students come up with two new rules: the ball must be passed to everyone on a team before anyone can shoot, and no one player can score any more than five points in a game.

Improv. In "Improv," several moral dilemmas that occur in physical education (e.g., someone breaking the rules, a student teasing someone) are written on cards. Each small group of students in a class receives one of the cards, and the students then make up skits that illustrate solutions to their dilemmas.

Our Secret Game. In "Our Secret Game," one team must follow the rules but the other team has its own set of rules that are unknown to the first team. For example, when playing basketball, the team with the secret rules might be able to run up to five steps without dribbling the ball or can start dribbling again after they've picked up their dribble. After playing the game for awhile, lead your students in discussing how playing that game made them feel, as well as the pros and cons of having the same rules for all players.

Use an Instructional or Curricular Model That Addresses Prosocial Behaviors

Physical educators like Mr. Joseph who want to positively impact students' prosocial behaviors may want to use one of the following instructional or curricular models.

Taking personal and social responsibility

As mentioned previously, the TPSR model was specifically designed to help students develop responsible behavior, both individually and in relationship to others. Key elements of the TPSR model are the five levels of responsibility, shown in Exhibit 4.3, which are goals for students to accomplish. According to Hellison (2003), human decency (social responsibility) is at the core of Levels I and IV, while Levels II and III focus on self-development (personal responsibility). The levels may be seen as progressive in that the levels will help you decide what personal and social responsibilities should be developed first before moving on to the next. For instance, help your students learn to willingly participate in and persistently work on skills even when the skills aren't mastered right away (Level II) before giving them tasks to try on their own (Level III). Be aware, however, that a student may demonstrate behaviors and attitudes at several different levels

connected CONCEPTS

Another instructional model, peer teaching, can also help students learn prosocial behaviors as they take on the roles of tutor and learner. Effective communication, concern for others' feelings, listening to and trusting peers, and accepting feedback are some of the prosocial behaviors students have the opportunity to learn in peer teaching (see Chapter 3).

	Levels of personal and social responsibility in physical education and appropriate strategies.	**EXHIBIT**	**4.3**

LEVEL	COMPONENTS	EXAMPLE STRATEGIES
I	**Respecting the rights and feelings of others**	Changing the rules of games to include all students
	Self-control	Sit-out progression
	The right to peaceful conflict resolution	Sport court
	The right to be included	Talking bench
II	**Participation and effort**	Teaching by invitation
	Self-motivation	Self-paced challenges
	Exploration of effort and new tasks	Redefining success
	Persisting when the going gets tough	
III	**Self-direction**	On-task independence
	On-task independence	Goal-setting progression
	Goal-setting progression	Personal plan
	Courage to resist peer pressure	
IV	**Helping others and leadership**	Peer teaching/coaching
	Caring and compassion	Group goals
	Sensitivity and responsiveness	Giraffe club
	Inner strength	
V	**Outside the gym**	Cross-age teaching
	Trying these ideas in other areas of life	Service projects
	Being a role model	One-on-one counseling

Source: Adapted from D. Hellison, *Teaching responsibility through physical activity,* 2nd ed., p. 17, copyright 2003 by Human Kinetics, Champaign, IL. Reprinted with permission.

within a single physical education lesson. For example, Jeff, a student in Mr. Joseph's physical education class, may demonstrate behavior at Level IV when he willingly helps and encourages a classmate during a soccer dribbling task, but later Jeff is acting at Level I when he calls his teammates losers after a small-sided soccer game.

In order to practice the true TPSR model, four elements must be present (Hellison, 2003):

1. integrating the levels into physical education lessons (the levels are not taught separate from the activity);

2. teaching for transfer of the levels from physical education into other settings;

3. empowering the students, so that power is shifted from you to your students; and

4. developing teacher–student relationships in which you recognize and respect students' individual differences, strengths, knowledge, and capacity to make good decisions.

To help integrate the levels into lessons daily, Hellison recommends using an established format for each physical education lesson (see Exhibit 4.4). Hellison (2003) further suggests that physical educators who decide to implement the TPSR model begin with one class, start with Levels I and II only, and gradually add various parts of the model (i.e., in turn, add awareness talks, reflection time, group meetings, Levels III and IV, and self-grading).

During the segment of the lesson in which TPSR is integrated with the physical activity instruction (Lesson Focus), several strategies can be used (see Exhibit 4.3). These strategies are designed to move learners to more advanced levels of responsibility, clearly promoting prosocial behaviors. One popular Level I conflict resolution strategy is the sport court, which is used when the students cannot resolve a dispute on their own. The class elects about three students to be the sport court, and they discuss the "unresolvable" dispute and come up with a solution all students must follow. A Level II strategy, redefining success, gives students the power to name success for themselves. They come up with their own criteria for grading in physical education, decide whether or not they want to participate in a tournament, or participate in a "crazy" station where creativity related to a skill is the goal. One strategy used to promote Level IV behaviors is to give students peer teaching responsibilities. After assigning peer teachers for small groups in the class, give the peer teachers note cards with task instructions and cues, and allow them to instruct their small groups. These and other strategies, as well as other aspects of the TPSR model, are described more specifically by Hellison in *Teaching Responsibility Through Physical Activity* (2003). Descriptions of after-school activities and in-school physical education programs that use the TPSR framework have been described by Hellison and his colleagues (Hellison et al., 2000; Hellison, Martinek, & Cutforth, 1996).

focus point

The focus of the TPSR model is to move students to higher levels of self-control and responsibility through a structured lesson format and strategies like the sport court, redefining success for themselves, and peer teaching opportunities.

Cooperative learning

As noted previously in this chapter, cooperative learning can help children learn to communicate effectively with, care for, respect and support each other, share, and resolve conflicts. There are five key elements in cooperative learning (Grineski, 1996; Metzler, 2005). First, groups should be

	EXHIBIT 4.4
Daily format for physical education lessons using the TPSR model (adapted from Metzler, 2005).	

LESSON SEGMENT	**CHARACTERISTICS OF THE LESSON SEGMENT**
Counseling Time	Quick, one-on-one interactions with students
	Primarily conducted before and after class, but may also occur while students practice, during recess or lunch, or during scheduled Level III time during class
	Recognize student talents, effort, improvement, or achievement
	Note facial expressions, new hairstyle, or clothing
	Comment on choices students make; ask for student opinion on problems that need to be solved
Awareness Talk	Time when the levels are taught to the students, or students are reminded of the responsibilities
	Very brief; do at the start of class, after counseling time
	Gradually increase student awareness and understanding of the levels, starting with Levels I and II, then adding Levels III and IV, and finally Level V
	When students are aware of the levels, let them conduct this section
Lesson Focus	Physical activity lesson with TPSR woven into instruction
	Use individual and group empowerment strategies, awareness talks, direct instruction, etc.
Group Meeting	Time for students to evaluate the lesson/program; students share ideas and thoughts; allows for student decision making
	Conducted near the end of the lesson, after the physical activity lesson focus
	Discuss problems and solutions, effectiveness of your instruction and leadership, and the levels
Reflection Time	Time for students to evaluate themselves on the five responsibility levels
	Conduct at the end of class
	Use "thumbs-up/down" method, journal entries, written checklists, workbooks

intentionally formed to include a variety of abilities, genders, and ethnic groups. These groups must remain together for several lessons, because continuous group membership enhances familiarity and interactions among the group members. Second, there must be positive interdependence among group members, meaning that each student must contribute in order for the group to achieve its goals. Third, students must be held individually accountable for their own learning and the learning of others. Fourth, the learning process should include opportunities for students to use and learn collaborative skills, such as listening to and supporting others, taking turns, resolving conflicts, and communicating effectively. Fifth, students should have opportunities to process or reflect on their experiences as a group.

Metzler (2005) has several suggestions for successful implementation of this instructional model. Cooperative learning can be used with children as young as 1st grade as long as the groups are small (two to three per group), tasks are short, and competition between groups is avoided. When using cooperative learning, you must first privately select teams or groups so they are equitable yet heterogeneous. Because these groups are supposed to stay together for some time, it is best that the model be used for an entire instructional unit, with group membership constant throughout the unit. Then, select tasks for the teams to complete that require all team members to contribute in order to be successful. For instance, Mr. Joseph could put his 6th graders into groups of four, and each member of the group must demonstrate the correct dribbling form on a dribbling task before moving on to the next task. Students must work together to help each other with their dribbling. Or in fitness lessons, Mr. Joseph could use the Collective Score strategy. In this strategy, each group member performs an exercise as many times as she can (e.g., push-ups, rope jumping). The scores for the group members are added up to get a collective score, with the group trying to achieve a certain goal (Grineski, 1996).

In cooperative learning, when presenting a task to the students, give them enough information about the task to successfully complete it, but do not give them ideas about how to complete it. Once the groups begin working on the task, you must actively monitor the groups and ask questions that ensure the groups are working cooperatively, not whether they are progressing on the task. You must also develop a method of assessing group performance on the task and their prosocial skills. Finally, close the lesson by helping the groups reflect on their social interactions during the tasks, again by asking questions instead of merely telling the students what was observed.

Several cooperative learning strategies can be effectively used in physical education settings. In Jigsaw, each group member is assigned to learn a part of the task and then teach that part to his or her teammates (Grineski, 1996; Metzler, 2005). Besides fitness activities, the Collective Score strategy discussed earlier can also be used for other activities such as team sports, individual sports, and basic motor skills (Grineski, 1996). In Think-Share-Perform, students are given a challenge that requires them to first individually think of possible solutions and then to share those solutions with their group (Grineski, 1996). They then try one solution

focus point

Cooperative learning uses the intentional formation of groups, positive interdependence among group members, individual accountability, collaborative skills, and group reflection.

from each group member and choose one to perform. These and other cooperative learning strategies are more specifically described by Grineski (1996) and Metzler (2005).

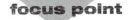

One physical education teacher who has successfully used cooperative learning to increase the prosocial behaviors of 3rd and 4th graders in the northeastern United States is Allison R. Allison placed her students in teams of four students. Upon entering the gym, each team went to its designated area and opened the folder that contained the day's task sheets and descriptions of the four roles (coach, demonstrator, recorder, equipment manager) students might play that day. The team members first had to decide among themselves who would play each role. The equipment manager then got the equipment necessary to practice the first task, the goal of which always was to demonstrate correct form on the skill for the day (e.g., kicking a soccer ball). The demonstrator showed the other team members how to perform the skill, while the coach provided feedback to the team members regarding their form. These students could get assistance from Allison if they needed help with their roles. Because all team members had to demonstrate to Allison the correct form on the skill before the team could perform any other tasks, it was to their benefit to help each other learn the skill. While students practiced this initial task as well as the other tasks, Allison moved from group to group, checking the students' form on the basic skill and giving each team stickers whenever they demonstrated a prosocial behavior (e.g., working well together, encouraging each other). At the end of the unit, the team with the most stickers had its picture taken and placed on the Wall of Fame outside the gym door. The whole process involved in these cooperative learning lessons, including the accountability system (with the stickers), helped the students learn socially desirable behaviors such as sharing, helping others, and being responsible to complete one's duties.

When using cooperative learning, following a few simple guidelines can help make group activities enjoyable for both you and your students (Metzler, 2005):

1. *Make the learning objectives for each class period clear to the students.* Allison wrote the objective for the day on the task sheets included in the groups' folders. Lesson objectives help keep the students on task and prevent aimless chatter and activity.

2. *Explain how the students will be assessed.* The students in Allison's class were assessed on their form on the skill for the day, as well as their demonstrations of prosocial behaviors. Making the assessments clear helps to focus the groups on the criteria necessary to successfully complete the task.

focus point

Effective group work in physical education should include the following: (1) clear learning objectives for the task; (2) clear criteria for assessing learning; (3) clear description of the product developed from the task; and (4) constant monitoring of the groups.

3. *Describe products that should result from the task.* In Allison's class, each group was to produce the task sheets that showed successful demonstration of the skills by each group member. This procedure will help keep the groups accountable for accomplishing the task.

4. *Provide feedback and guidance to facilitate students' group work.* Allison circulated among the groups, gave them feedback that would help them perform the task successfully, checked their form, and provided stickers for prosocial behaviors.

Sport education

Even though sport education was not designed specifically to enhance students' moral development, various aspects of the model can definitely help them learn prosocial behaviors. Sport education has six key features (Siedentop, 1994; Siedentop et al., 2004):

■ **Seasons.** Longer units, or seasons, give students the time necessary to improve their skills and knowledge of the sport, and learn the various roles within the sport. Just as in real sport, students prepare for competition during the preseason, continue practice and competition during the regular season, and then participate in a postseason competition.

■ **Affiliation.** Students become members of a team for the entire season, which provides opportunities for the development of many prosocial behaviors.

■ **Formal competition.** Teams participate in a regular schedule of competition.

■ **Culminating event.** A tournament among the teams wraps up the season.

■ **Record keeping.** Records are kept of various team and individual statistics.

■ **Festivity.** As in real sport, the seasons have a festive nature about them, which contributes to the social dimension of sport education.

Many strategies can be used to emphasize the affective domain. Students could receive daily points for encouraging others, and these points could then add up to an "Encourager" award at the end of the season for the student with the most encourager points. Each day, teams could vote on the team they believe showed the highest level of fair play, with an overall choice made at the end of the season. Students could also earn daily managerial points by acceptably completing the managerial tasks (e.g., getting out equipment, completing necessary paperwork) assigned to them for the day (thus demonstrating responsibility).

focus point

Although sport education was not designed to enhance students' moral development, the model gives students chances to learn cooperation, leadership skills, and responsible behavior, especially when you use strategies that enhance those aspects of the model.

Sport education can be used as either an entire curricular model (Siedentop, 1994) or as an instructional model for longer units (Metzler, 2005). However, sport education will not work within a traditional multiactivity curriculum, because it requires units longer than the 2- to 3-week units usually found in that kind of curriculum. The model can be used with children as young as 4th grade, as long as appropriate adaptations to the model are made (Metzler, 2005). Keep in mind that sport education requires considerable planning, such as deciding on and creating clear descriptions of student roles, creating clear assessments of student playing and role performance, deciding on the season schedule, and deciding on the award system (Metzler, 2005). See Exhibits 4.5 and 4.6 for example role descriptions and a sheet for recording when roles are performed. You can read more about sport education in books by Siedentop (1994) and his colleagues (Siedentop et al., 2004).

Description of roles in a sport education unit on team sports for physical education majors.	EXHIBIT	4.5

ROLE DESCRIPTIONS

Coach	Preparation (5 points)
10 points	Research for references on the specific skill you are about to teach
	Design a cognitive study guide (5 multiple-choice questions, 2 open-ended questions, and 2 T/F questions) for your teammates (make sure to have copies for them)
	Design an appropriate lesson plan (on the provided format) according to your lesson focus (including application task)
	Prepare additional materials (task cards, etc.) that will reinforce the skill's critical elements (optional)
	Teaching day (5 points)
	Submit a typed copy of your lesson plan and any other additional materials to the instructor and to each member on your team
	Submit a copy of your cognitive study guide to the instructor and each member on your team
	Teach 30–40-minute lesson by exhibiting effective teaching skills; make sure to reinforce the rules of the game that refer specifically to your skill

(continued)

EXHIBIT 4.5	Description of roles in a sport education unit on team sports for physical education majors, *continued*.

Fitness Trainer	**Preparation (5 points)**
10 points	Design a 10-minute warm-up activity appropriate to the lesson focus
	Submit a typed copy of the warm-up activity to the instructor and to each member of team (fitness card)
	Teaching day (5 points)
	Start the warm-up activity within your group exactly on time and keep the students active for 8 to 10 minutes
Equipment Mgr.	**Preparation (5 points)**
10 points	Ask the coach for the equipment list necessary for the lesson
	Make sure that the necessary equipment will be available by reserving it (not personal equipment)
	Come to class ahead of time and set up the equipment by the beginning of class
	After the lesson (5 points)
	Break down the equipment and return it to its designated place
Official	**Teaching day (10 points)**
10 points	Manage daily application contests
	Make calls and enforce game rules
	Record scores
Players	**Teaching day (10 points)**
10 points	Show up on time and actively participate in daily activities
	Write and submit reflection via e-mail by midnight of the teaching day
Publicist	**After the lesson (10 points)**
10 points	Summarize the day's events in a typed report of one to two paragraphs
	Read the report to the class at the beginning of the following day
	Print and provide hard copies of the report to all team members

This chart is used with permission from Rachel Gurvitch, Georgia State University, Atlanta, GA.

EXHIBIT	4.6	Sheet describing when roles are performed in a sport education unit on team sports for physical education majors.

Performance and Analysis: Team Sports
Sport Education Role Sheet

Team:

Student Name	1	2	3	4	5	6	7	8	9	10	11	12
Date	18	19	20	21	24	25	26	27	28	01	02	03
Rachel	FT	P	P	PU	O	C	EM	FT	P	P	PU	FT
Darius	EM	FT	FT	P	PU	O	O	EM	FT	P	P	EM
Deidre	C	EM	FT	P	P	PU	O	C	EM	FT	P	C
Jessamie	O	C	EM	FT	P	P	PU	O	O	EM	FT	O
Karmelina	PU	O	C	EM	FT	P	P	PU	O	C	EM	PU
Kenneth	P	PU	O	C	EM	FT	P	P	PU	O	C	P
Timothy	P	P	PU	O	C	EM	FT	P	P	PU	O	P

ROLE	RESPONSIBILITY
Official (O)	▪ Manages daily application contests ▪ Makes calls and enforces all rules ▪ Records scores
Players (P)	▪ Participates in the lesson activities ▪ Writes and submits reflection via e-mail by midnight of the teaching day
Publicist (PU)	▪ Summarizes the day events in a 1–2 paragraph typed report ▪ Reads to the class at the beginning of the following day ▪ Prints and provides hard copies of this report to all team members

Team:

Student Name	1	2	3	4	5	6	7	8	9	10	11	12
Date	18	19	20	21	24	25	26	27	28	01	02	03
Deanna	FT	P	P	P	PU	O	C	EM	FT	P	P	PU
Trenton	EM	FT	FT	P	P	PU	O	C	EM	FT	P	P
Steve	C	C	EM	FT	P	P	PU	O	C	E	EM	P
Dandre	O	O	C	EM	FT	P	P	PU	O	C	EM	FT
Christina	PU	PU	O	C	EM	FT	P	P	PU	O	C	EM
Ashley	P	P	PU	O	C	EM	FT	P	P	PU	O	C
Deter	P	P	P	PU	O	C	EM	FT	P	P	PU	O

ROLE	RESPONSIBILITY
Fitness Trainer (FT)	▪ Leads instant activity ▪ Leads stretches ▪ Develops fitness card
Equipment Manger (EM)	▪ Gets necessary equipment ▪ Sets-up BEFORE CLASS as directed by coach ▪ Collects/inventories equipment after each class ▪ Returns equipment
Coach (C)	▪ Develops coaching plan ▪ Offers positive and corrective feedback ▪ Assists with skill development ▪ Develops cognitive study guide

This chart is used used with permission from Rachel Gurvitch, Georgia State University, Atlanta, GA.

real world

One physical education teacher who has successfully used sport education as a means of enhancing students' moral development is Tony P., a professor at a university in the southern United States. Tony has implemented sport education in three different environments, including a physical education teacher education course on pedagogical content knowledge, a basic instruction physical education course, and secondary physical education. He has used the model with a variety of sports—bowling, tennis, volleyball, and golf. Two ways that Tony emphasizes the development of prosocial behaviors in sport education are through team affiliation and an accountability (award) system. About the second day of a unit, Tony places students on evenly matched teams. The students then must choose team names, colors, mascots, a cheer, and a high-five for their teams, which helps establish the affiliation aspect of the model. Some of these team affiliation behaviors and other prosocial behaviors are a major part of the accountability system for the unit. The team who wins the championship is the one with the most accumulated points at the end of the season; only a small portion of the possible points is based on motor skill performance. See Exhibit 4.7 for a daily point system for sport education units and Appendix A.3 for a scoring sheet using this system. Tony says that these two aspects helped students who are lower skilled and marginalized become an important part of the team, because they can earn points for their team in ways other than winning games. According to Tony, one high school girl, who normally didn't dress for physical education class, dressed regularly during the sport education unit so that her team would earn all of the points for daily roles, thus enhancing her sense of responsibility. College students in a bowling class showed a high level of affiliation with their team and many good sportspersonship behaviors, such as wearing team shirts with their team name on the back, doing the team cheer, and encouraging their teammates bowling on other lanes.

Adventure-based learning

Adventure-based learning, or adventure education, is a curricular model that is gaining in popularity. According to Ewert and Garvey (2006), the proposed goals of adventure-based learning include:

- moral development (e.g., enhanced moral reasoning and prosocial behaviors);
- personal growth (e.g., greater self-esteem and motivation);
- group development (developing teamwork and other ways to make groups more effective); and
- leadership development (e.g., skills needed for leadership, responsibility for one's own actions).

| Generic daily point system for sport education units. | EXHIBIT 4.7 |

POINT SYSTEM*

Behavior Displayed	Points Earned/Deducted
Team wears team colors	Add up to 5 points
Team warms up correctly	Add up to 5 points
Team performs daily roles	Add up to 5 points
Team is enthusiastic (e.g., performs team cheer)	Add up to 5 points
Obeys the instructor	Add up to 5 points
Sportspersonship behaviors noticed by instructor	Add 2 points for each occurrence
Application contests	Add 5 points for overall winner for day Add 4 points for second place Add 3 points for third place Add 2 points for fourth place Add 1 point for fifth place
Unsportsmanlike behaviors	Deduct 5 points for each occurrence

Note: A team cannot earn more than 25 points per day.

This chart is used with permission from Tony Pritchard, Georgia Southern University, Statesboro, GA.

Adventure-based learning has four key features (Cosgriff, 2000):

- *Innovative, sequenced physical activities.* The activities performed are not those typically seen in physical education; basketball is nowhere to be seen! Typical tasks are novel, fun, social, and progressive, meaning the tasks build on each other, moving from easier to more difficult.

- *Experiential learning* (Kolb, 1984). Students first perform an activity, then they spend time reflecting on what they experienced (e.g., problems, emotions, frustrations, successes) when performing the particular activity. This is followed by time to generalize this particular experience and the students' conclusions to other similar situations in other aspects of life. The students are then encouraged to describe ways to apply what they learned to different situations outside of physical education.

- *Interdependence of educational goals, curriculum, and pedagogy.* To reach the goals of adventure-based learning, the content and instructional methods must facilitate the development of those outcomes. So, tasks and activities specifically designed to enhance critical thinking and social skills, for example, are used instead of the traditional activities. Likewise, instructional methods that are more student-directed and give the students a voice in their participation are used instead of more traditional pedagogical methods like direct instruction or the command style of teaching, in which the students are told exactly what to do.

■ *Goal of developing active, committed members of schools and communities.* The end goal goes beyond physical education; all activities and instructional methods should encourage students to apply what they learned to being responsible contributors to their schools and surrounding neighborhoods.

Other critical features of adventure-based learning include challenge, risk, and the importance of process. Challenge and risk are integral to adventure-based learning; activities should challenge students and include inherent risk of some kind, which could be physical and/or emotional. For example, both physical and emotional risk is involved when a student falls backward from a height of 5 feet into the arms of fellow students (a trust fall activity). The process involved in developing solutions to a problem—the interactions among group members, who presents and decides on solutions, how to react to possible solutions—are more important than the actual solution. It is in the processes that the outcomes of adventure-based learning are achieved. More information about adventure-based learning can be obtained from *Adventure Education: Theory and Applications* (Prouty et al., 2006).

real world

An advanced physical education course based on adventure education was developed by Marlowe M. at a high school in the Midwestern United States. The "Team Concepts" course starts with 9 weeks of group initiatives, cooperative games, and trust activities designed to promote teamwork, communication, leadership, problem solving, and trust in classmates. One such activity is the T-P (telephone pole) shuffle. All students stand side-by-side on the first row of bleachers, in any order. The guidelines for the activity are that they cannot communicate verbally and they cannot step off of the bleacher row. The students are then given an order in which to arrange themselves (e.g., alphabetically, by birth date). On signal, they try arranging themselves, with Marlowe timing their efforts and counting the infractions. After the activity, discussion focuses on their experiences of touching each other, communication methods, problems encountered, and solutions developed. The students then discuss how these lessons apply to interacting with classmates outside of physical education and communication problems and solutions outside of physical education. After conquering these initial activities, the students move on to low-element challenges (at a height of 20 feet or less), such as rappelling down the gym wall, the climbing wall, and climbing a cargo net. The course concludes with two high-element challenges: high rappelling (from a height of 40 feet) and the trapeze dive. All activities take place inside the school or gymnasium. From the students' final papers for the course, Marlowe has lots of anecdotal evidence that the students develop strong peer relationships and communication skills, enhanced self-perceptions, and high enjoyment levels.

Mr. Joseph, who always uses direct instruction, might try one or more of these instructional or curricular models to enhance his students' sportspersonship behaviors in physical education. For instance, the soccer unit described at the beginning of the chapter could be taught to the 6th graders using the sport education model. Cooperative learning strategies could be used to teach content like rope jumping, creative dance, or fundamental motor skills to students of all ages. Mr. Joseph might decide to implement the TPSR or an adventure-based curricular model with his students and really focus on helping them develop personal responsibility, interpersonal skills and relationships, and leadership skills.

Summary

Enhancing student moral development is a common but often elusive goal in physical education programs. According to social learning theory, people learn prosocial behaviors, one aspect of moral development, via modeling and reinforcement by significant others and social comparison. Structural developmental approaches like Haan's interactional theory propose that moral reasoning, the other aspect of moral development, develops along with a person's cognitive development and various social interactions. Researchers have found that physical education programs in which moral development is not purposely taught are not effective in promoting either moral reasoning or prosocial behaviors. However, strategies based on social learning theory and structural developmental approaches have enhanced moral development in children. Instructional and curricular models other than direct instruction—taking personal and social responsibility, cooperative learning, sport education, and adventure-based learning—can also be effective in enhancing students' prosocial behaviors.

KEY concepts

Sportspersonship

Moral reasoning

Structural developmental approach

Interactional theory

Moral balance

Moral dialogue

Moral development levels

Assimilation phase

Accommodation phase

Equilibration phase

Coping processes

Defending processes

Taking personal and social responsibility

Cooperative learning

Sport education

Adventure-based learning

application exercises

1. Ted is a 3rd grade child who shows very poor sportspersonship during physical education class. According to social learning theory, what are some possible reasons for his poor behavior?

2. Using social learning theory, what are some strategies you could use to help Ted acquire better sportspersonship behaviors?

3. Kendra, Heather, Mary, Heidi, and Renee are 7th graders in one of your physical education classes who are participating in a volleyball tournament you set up. Each of the girls is at a different level of reasoning in the interactional theory of moral reasoning. Describe each girl's thoughts and behaviors, appropriate for her respective reasoning level, as they participate in the volleyball unit.

4. You decide to focus on helping your students learn prosocial behaviors during the upcoming basketball unit by using one of the following instructional models: TPSR, cooperative learning, or sport education. Name your specific prosocial goals for the unit. Which model would you choose and why? Describe how that unit would look different than a traditional basketball unit.

5

Achievement Goals

Mary, a high school freshman, is in the third period physical education class that is taught by Ms. Jones. She and her classmates are about to perform the progressive 20-meter aerobic fitness test. As with most tasks in physical education, Mary's main goal is to do better than the other students in her class on the test. She will perform only as fast as is necessary to do that. She doesn't care if her performance improves over prior tests.

As soon as she sees she is finishing first, she stops. However, if she sees she isn't going to finish first, she just quits and lets everyone know she wasn't trying her best. Martha, Mary's twin sister, is in the 4th period physical education class that is taught by Mr. Smith. She is also going to perform the progressive aerobic fitness test, but she approaches it, and most other tasks during her physical education class, differently than her sister. Martha's goal is to do better than she did the last time. Even if she is finishing first, she will keep going until she can't go any longer, trying to beat her previous performance. Even if she isn't finishing first, she tries as hard as she can to do her best.

introduction

hy would there be such differences in the two girls' approaches to the physical education tasks? One explanation lies in the achievement goal theory of motivation. **Achievement goal theory** (Ames, 1992b; Dweck, 1986, 1999; Nicholls, 1984, 1989) asserts that individuals do not define ability and success the same and, therefore, set different goals in achievement situations, based on their individual dispositions and on situational factors. These varying goal perspectives, in turn, influence the individuals' motivation and behaviors in achievement situations. In this chapter, the basic principles of achievement goal theory and physical education-related research will be examined. Several strategies to enhance student achievement behaviors in physical education will also be presented.

Principles of Achievement Goal Theory

everal versions of achievement goal theory have been developed to explain how goals influence a person's achievement behaviors (e.g., Ames, 1992a, 1992b; Dweck, 1986, 1999; Nicholls, 1984, 1989). Although there are commonalities among the different versions, each theorist contributed something unique. For the sake of simplicity, the discussion will focus on Nicholls's theory and terminology; Ames's and Dweck's views and works will be referred to when helpful to understanding the theory and applying it to physical education.

Goal Perspectives

According to achievement goal theory (Nicholls, 1984, 1989), a person's definition of ability in an achievement situation determines the type of **goal perspective** the person adopts in that situation. Goal perspectives refer to the type of goals a student actually adopts in any achievement situation. There are two goal perspectives that may be adopted: ego and task involvement. The two goal perspectives differ according to how success and failure are interpreted, which stems from the person's view of ability. In **ego involvement,** a person's definition of ability is "other-referenced" (Roberts, 2001) or norm-referenced, meaning that one's performance as compared to others is the main determinant of competence and success (Nicholls, 1984, 1989). A student who is ego involved in physical education wants to perform better than his classmates. He believes he is successful and has high ability if, for example, he can climb to the top of the climbing wall faster than the others. This is especially true if it can be done with low effort (Nicholls, 1984). High effort, or "trying hard," does not enhance an ego-involved person's self-perception of ability; in fact, it may diminish it. If the student has to try hard to perform as well as others, he may feel he is less competent.

In **task involvement,** ability is self-referenced; that is, improving one's own performance is the basis for perceptions of ability (Nicholls, 1984, 1989). The goal of a task-involved student in physical education is to master or perfect a task or skill. For example, climbing to the top of the climbing wall faster than previous attempts demonstrates competence and success for a task-involved student. Effort is desirable because it helps the student improve. This student doesn't concern himself with how other students perform; their performance is irrelevant to his success or ability.

focus point

Task involvement leads to high levels of effort and persistence, choosing optimally challenging tasks, and feelings of control, pleasure, and enjoyment.

Impact of goal perspectives

Goal perspectives are important because they influence how a student responds in achievement situations (Nicholls, 1984, 1989). In task involvement, high effort is common because the goal is to improve one's own performance, and that is best achieved with high effort. Task-involved students will persist at tasks even if classmates perform better because these students simply want to master the task; the performance of others does not matter. Task involvement also leads to choosing moderately difficult tasks, because challenging tasks are the ones that will most likely lead to improvement. Task-involved students typically have a heightened sense of control because they are focused on personal improvement, which is under their control more so than the performance of others. Task involvement should also lead to frequent feelings of pleasure and enjoyment because success is based on self-improvement, which all students can achieve. Martha, one of the students in the opening scenario, exhibits task involvement in her physical education class. Because her goals are self-referenced, she usually demonstrates high effort and persistence so she can improve.

Ego-involved students will demonstrate the same types of behaviors and emotions as task-involved students (e.g., persistence, sense of control, enjoyment) as long as they also believe they will show high ability (Nicholls, 1984, 1989). However, those ego-involved students who believe there is little chance of demonstrating high competence are likely to exhibit quite different behaviors (Nicholls, 1989). Instead of choosing optimally difficult tasks, these students are likely to choose either very simple or very difficult tasks, both of which protect their self-worth. With very easy tasks, they have no chance of failing, and with very difficult tasks, no one expects them to succeed anyway. Students with high ego involvement and low perceived ability are likely to experience more negative affect (e.g., lower confidence, more self-doubt) than task-involved students because their success depends on performing better than others, which won't always happen. Ego involvement can lead to a decreased sense of control because the students' demonstration of competence depends on the performance of others, which they cannot control. In addition, effort and persistence commonly diminish with ego involvement. These students believe that if they give high effort and still don't perform as good as or better than others, they have revealed their low ability. They believe they have higher ability if they can perform better than others without much effort. Ego-involved students who face failure are likely to quit trying, so their high effort doesn't reveal their lack of ability. Mary, Martha's sister, is clearly demonstrating ego involvement in her physical education class, as evidenced by her focus on performing better than others and her decreased effort and persistence when she does not.

You can see that task involvement is the goal perspective a physical education teacher wants students to employ during class because it tends to result in behaviors that enhance learning. The goal perspective a student adopts is the result of both personal (dispositional goal orientation) and situational (motivational climate) factors (Nicholls, 1989). Dispositions are part of a person's character or outlook; they refer to a person's tendencies or preferences. Thus, **dispositional goal orientations** are a person's tendency to pick one type of goal (e.g., self-referenced or other-referenced) over another in an achievement situation. The **motivational climate** (Ames, 1992a, 1992b) set up by the physical educator and others, emphasizing one type of goal over another, can also influence the goal perspective adopted. Dispositional goal orientations and motivational climates will be now be further explained.

Dispositional Goal Orientations

A student who prefers to define success as performing better than others is exhibiting an **ego orientation** (Nicholls, 1984, 1989). A person high in ego orientation uses the norm-referenced definition of success and failure. Mary may be ego involved in part because she has a high ego orientation to achievement situations such as physical education. Her primary goal is to perform better than others, and when she cannot do that, she typically lacks persistence and decreases her effort. However, one reason Mary's sister, Martha, is task involved is because she has a high **task orientation** in physical education. Her constant desire to improve her performance, as well as her consistently high effort and persistence, are very typical of high task-orientation students.

Note that these dispositional goal orientations are independent constructs (Nicholls, 1989). That is, a person is not just ego oriented or task oriented; rather, a person is both ego and task oriented, each goal orientation at a specific level, at the same time. So, a student could be high in both orientations, or low in both, or low in one and high in the other. The notion that task and ego orientation are independent constructs has been confirmed with students in physical education (Walling & Duda, 1995). Therefore, a student could have equally strong, or weak, inclinations to set self-referenced and other-referenced goals in physical education. The goals the student actually sets will be influenced by the motivational climate, which will be discussed shortly. It is important to note, though, that most high school students tend to be higher in task orientation than ego orientation in physical education (Spray, 2000; Walling & Duda, 1995).

focus point

Task and ego goal orientations are independent constructs, such that everyone has both goal orientations, with each orientation at its own level.

The development of goal orientations

According to Nicholls (1989), we do not develop both dispositional goal orientations until about the age of 12. That is because goal orientations are inextricably linked to our conceptions of ability, which change throughout childhood. Nicholls (1978) found that until the age of about 7, children cannot distinguish between the concepts of ability and effort. This is called an **undifferentiated view of ability.** Ability is self-referenced, and children under 7 believe that people who try harder have higher ability. Thus, young children tend to be task oriented because they believe that if they try hard, they have high ability, and it doesn't matter to them how their peers perform the task. They are actually incapable of being ego oriented due to their beliefs about ability and effort. Thus, if you ask preschool or kindergarten students how good they are at motor skills or tasks in physical education class, most will answer that they are very good, simply because they try hard. They don't even compare themselves to their peers.

focus point

Most children below the age of 7 can only be task oriented because they hold an undifferentiated view of ability and cannot distinguish between effort and ability.

Between the ages of 7 and 12, this undifferentiated view of ability and effort starts to change, and by about the age of 12, children have developed a completely **differentiated view of ability** (Nicholls, 1978; Nicholls & Miller, 1984). Children then understand that ability is separate from effort, and that ability is highest when someone performs better than their peers with minimal effort, which is consistent with an ego orientation. So, if you ask 6th grade children if they are good at motor skills and physical education tasks, most will be able to compare their performance and effort with others, and make judgments based on those comparisons. Thus, young adolescents, like Mary and Martha, are capable of both the task-oriented and ego-oriented dispositional goal orientations.

The development of conceptions of ability and goal orientations was confirmed in a physical education study with 4th, 8th, and 11th graders (Xiang & Lee, 1998). Even though high school students tend to be higher on task than ego orientation (Spray, 2000; Walling & Duda, 1995), Xiang and Lee found that students in physical education tend to become more ego oriented as they grow older. This change is at least partially related to their changing view of ability. As students become more ego oriented, they are more likely to view ability as stable and to judge ability in terms of their classmates, which is the differentiated view of ability. In contrast, children high in task orientation in physical education tend to have an undifferentiated view of ability and judge ability according to their own effort and achievements, not their classmates'.

Based on this information, physical educators can expect young children (e.g., pre-kindergarten to 2nd grade) to exhibit strong task orientations due to their undifferentiated views of ability. Asking children in this age group to compare their performance at physical education tasks to their peers should be avoided, because most haven't developed that capability yet. Beyond 2nd grade, it becomes especially important for teachers to promote task involvement in physical education. This is because task involvement is associated with more desirable learning behaviors than ego involvement, and ego involvement is a stronger potential with older children due to their developing capacity for an ego orientation. Teachers can promote task involvement through the motivational climate they create.

Motivational Climate

In addition to a student's dispositional goal orientation, the other determinant of the actual goal perspective adopted by the student in an achievement situation is the motivational climate in the environment (Ames, 1992a, 1992b; Nicholls, 1989). The motivational climate is the social climate that leads a student to perceive that one goal perspective is more important than the other. It is in part established by those actions taken by the instructor that, knowingly or unknowingly, emphasize a particular goal perspective over the other. When a physical educator focuses on each student's improvement and stresses a self-referenced definition of success, a **task-involving climate** is created. A physical educator who constantly compares students to each other, encourages them to perform better than their peers, and stresses a normative definition of success establishes an **ego-involving climate.** This type of climate can threaten a student's self-esteem because he can only be successful by performing better than others. These two motivational climates are believed to influence students' cognitions, emotions, and behaviors in the same way as the different goal orientations. For instance, in addition to her high task orientation, Martha probably focuses on personal improvement and gives high effort during physical education class because her teacher, Mr. Smith, tries to establish a task-involving climate. Conversely, the type of climate produced by Mary's teacher, Ms. Jones, is much more ego-involving, and so contributes to Mary's focus on doing better than others in class and frequent low effort. So, to enhance student effort, persistence, and enjoyment in physical education, a task-involving climate should be created whenever possible.

Structures in the learning environment

Epstein (1988, 1989) identified six aspects in an achievement situation like physical education that can be altered to foster task involvement. The six elements are identified with the acronym **TARGET,** which refers to the *task, authority, reward, grouping, evaluation,* and *time* structures in the learning environment. Ames (1992a) described strategies that can be used within each structure to motivate students by creating a task-involving climate. Todorovich and Curtner-Smith (2002) identified strategies within each structure that promote task involvement versus those that promote ego involvement. Following are descriptions of each structure and what each structure might look like in a task-involving climate and in an ego-involving climate (see Exhibit 5.1 for a summary). For each structure, the actions taken by Mr. Smith and Ms. Jones that contribute to their respective task-involving and ego-involving climates are described.

Task. The task structure refers to "what students are asked to learn and what assignments they are given to do" (Epstein, 1988, p. 93). In physical education, students perform movement tasks, which are "motor activities that are related to the content of the lesson" (Rink, 2002, p. 15). Examples of movement tasks include running a mile, playing a 3-on-3 volleyball game, creating an aerobic fitness dance, using the foot to dribble the ball across the field, or balancing on three body parts. In addition to the task's content, its sequence, design, and difficulty level influence the type of climate created (Epstein, 1988).

EXHIBIT 5.1	Instructional climate structures and characteristics of task- and ego-involving climates.	
STRUCTURE	**TASK-INVOLVING CLIMATE**	**EGO-INVOLVING CLIMATE**
Task—what students are asked to do; content, sequence, design, difficulty of tasks	▪ Variety of tasks offered ▪ Students perform different tasks at the same time ▪ Students set short-term goals ▪ Importance of tasks conveyed to students ▪ Novel, higher-order thinking and creative tasks are common ▪ Tasks progress logically	▪ Tasks are uniform ▪ Students perform the same tasks ▪ Teacher sets goals for class ▪ Tasks can lack meaning and importance for students ▪ Tasks often lack progression; do not build on previous tasks
Authority—degree of participation and decision making students are allowed	▪ Students given many choices and opportunities to make decisions about instruction ▪ Students have leadership roles ▪ Students conduct assessments	▪ Teacher makes most decisions about instruction; students get few choices ▪ Teacher conducts assessments
Reward—how students are recognized for progress and achievement; purpose, types, criteria, and opportunities for rewards	▪ Rewards given for improving performance ▪ Students have equal opportunities for rewards ▪ Recognition is private between teacher and student	▪ Rewards typically given for performing better than other students ▪ Usually only highly skilled students obtain rewards ▪ Recognition tends to be public
Grouping—how students are grouped; distribution of student diversity	▪ Individual tasks used when possible ▪ Other tasks use partners or small groups working cooperatively ▪ Groups are heterogeneous and flexible	▪ Large group tasks are frequently used ▪ Groups are usually homogeneous and inflexible
Evaluation—type of standards used in evaluation; means of evaluating; use of evaluation information	▪ Standards are usually objective and self-referenced ▪ Evaluation usually gives students information on how to improve ▪ Evaluation is private, often conducted by students	▪ Standards are often subjective and other-referenced ▪ Evaluation frequently doesn't help students improve ▪ Evaluation is usually public and conducted by the teacher
Time—pace of instruction; amount and flexibility of time for student practice	▪ Amount of time to complete tasks/improve usually varies by student ▪ Students typically set own time for task completion	▪ Students are typically given the same amount of time to complete tasks/improve ▪ Teacher usually sets time for task completion

Adapted with permission from J. R. Todorovich & M. D. Curtner-Smith, "Influence of the Motivational Climate in Physical Education on Sixth Grade Pupils' Goal Orientations," in *European Physical Education Review, 8*(2), 119–138. Copyright © 2002, Sage Publications and North West Counties Physical Education Association, 2002.

In a task-involving climate, students are usually offered a variety of tasks to perform and receive help with setting personal short-term goals, both of which allow them to work on tasks that are suitable to their ability levels (Ames, 1992a). Students often perform different tasks or assignments at the same time, which helps them do more self-comparison instead of comparing their performance to others (Rosenholtz & Simpson, 1984). Students are consistently challenged in a task-involving climate by being presented with novel tasks, higher-order thinking tasks, or creative tasks. Tasks in a task-involving climate have a logical progression, gradually become more difficult, and build on previous tasks (Epstein, 1988). Teachers in this type of climate help students understand the importance and personal meaningfulness of tasks (Ames, 1992b). Martha's physical education teacher, Mr. Smith, helps his students set individual goals for the progressive aerobic fitness test based on their previous performance on the test. When conducting the fitness tests, Mr. Smith establishes several stations around the gym, and the students perform a different fitness test at each station. This helps the students focus on their own performance, not the performances of others. Mr. Smith also makes sure his students understand that the purpose of fitness testing is to use the information to improve their own fitness levels. As with other skills taught, Mr. Smith helps his students improve their performance on the progressive aerobic run by gradually increasing the duration and intensity of their workouts.

Conversely, in an ego-involving climate, tasks are mostly uniform, and students usually attempt the same tasks at the same time (Todorovich & Curtner-Smith, 2002). The teacher sets the goals for the class as a whole rather than individualizing them for individual students (Todorovich & Curtner-Smith, 2002). So, students may not be challenged to personally improve the way they are in a task-involving climate. Tasks in an ego-involving climate can lack importance and meaning for students; teachers often do not help students understand those things. When Ms. Jones's class participates in fitness tests like the progressive aerobic run, students are either performing the test or watching others perform, which makes it easy for them to compare their performances. Ms. Jones encourages the students to do better than their classmates because she thinks that motivates them to try harder. The purpose for fitness testing that is emphasized to the students is that it will contribute to their grade in physical education. Moreover, little is done to help students improve their fitness levels during the year.

Authority. The authority structure refers to the types and degree of participation and decision making in the instructional process students are allowed (Epstein, 1988). Questions like the following help identify the authority structure:

- Do teachers give students an opportunity to make any decisions about how instruction will occur or how tasks are practiced?

- Are students actively involved in the instructional process beyond simply answering questions and doing what the teacher tells them?

In a task-involving climate, students get chances to make decisions and take on leadership roles (Ames, 1992a). Students might be given choices about the tasks they will practice (Treasure & Roberts, 1995), how long to practice, criteria for successful performance, their partner or group members, or type of equipment to use. Teachers in a task-involving climate help students develop self-direction and self-management by having them set up their own equipment or assess their own performance and perhaps a partner's performance (Treasure & Roberts, 1995). The students in Mr. Smith's class, for instance, work with him to develop a program to improve their fitness levels. They get to choose the types of exercises and activities they use to improve their fitness. In addition, they conduct their own fitness assessments at the various stations. In an ego-involving climate, the students are usually given little authority. The teacher makes most of the decisions about the tasks students will perform, what equipment is used, how students are assessed, and group membership (Todorovich & Curtner-Smith, 2002). The teacher also conducts the assessments of student performance. In Ms. Jones's class, the students are all tested at the same time on a fitness component, with Ms. Jones in control. Ms. Jones makes all of the decisions about the activities and the difficulty level at which tasks are performed.

Reward. The reward structure addresses how students are recognized for their progress and achievement (Epstein, 1988). Questions such as the following help identify the reward structure:

- What are the purposes for giving rewards?
- What types of rewards are given?
- How are the rewards presented?
- What are the criteria for receiving rewards?
- What opportunities do the students have to be rewarded?

In a task-involving climate, students are usually given rewards and recognition for improving their individual performance and skills, with all students having an equal opportunity to receive rewards (Ames, 1992a). Moreover, recognition for progress in a task-involving climate is regarded as private between the teacher and the student, which helps focus students on their own performance and not concern themselves with other students' performances (Treasure & Roberts, 1995). In Mr. Smith's class, any student who follows the individualized workout as designed by Mr. Smith and the student, or who improves their performance on a fitness test, is rewarded privately by Mr. Smith.

In an ego-involving climate, rewards and recognition are typically given publicly for performing better than other students (Todorovich &

Curtner-Smith, 2002), encouraging students to engage in social comparison (Treasure & Roberts, 1995). It also can lead to unequal opportunities for students to receive recognition because only the higher-skilled students will be able to achieve the criteria of performing better than others. For instance, in Ms. Jones's class, only students who have one of the top three performances for the particular student's gender and age receive rewards for the fitness tests. Ms. Jones gives those rewards out to the students publicly at an assembly at the end of the school year.

Grouping. The grouping structure deals with the placement of students into instructional groups and the distribution of student diversity (e.g., ethnicity, gender, ability level) within those groups (Epstein, 1988). Questions like the following are relevant for this structure:

- Who are the members of an instructional group?
- Are they all alike or different?
- Do these memberships change?
- How are the group members asked to interact with each other?

Grouping is important because teachers have been known to treat one group different than another (Epstein, 1988).

In a task-involving climate, students perform individual tasks whenever possible because students are less likely to engage in social comparison when working alone than when working in groups (Treasure & Roberts, 1995). When that isn't appropriate for the task or skills, partners or small groups requiring cooperation among group members typically are used (Treasure & Roberts, 1995). Teachers promoting a task-involving climate try to keep the group membership heterogeneous, ensuring that groups contain students of both genders and various ability levels, ethnic groups, and so on (Ames, 1992a). Group membership is usually flexible, meaning that the groups in which students work change frequently, allowing them to interact with a variety of students (Ames, 1992a). Mr. Smith tries to use individual tasks or cooperative groups whenever possible, such as assigning students a different "workout buddy" each day; workout buddies are to exercise together and help each other accomplish their daily workout.

In an ego-involving climate, students in a class often work on the same task as one large group (Todorovich & Curtner, 2002). This makes it easy for the students to engage in social comparison. Even if smaller groups are used, membership tends to be homogeneous, static, and inflexible because students are often grouped according to their ability (Todorovich & Curtner-Smith, 2002). As mentioned previously, most of the tasks performed during Ms. Jones's class are performed by all students at the same time (e.g., everyone does all of their curl-ups at the same time).

Evaluation. The evaluation structure refers to the standards established for student learning and behavior, the means by which achievement of those standards is determined, and whether students receive information about their performance in order to improve (Epstein, 1988). The evaluation structure of a learning environment is closely related to the reward structure because students are rewarded or punished based on whether they reach the standards (Epstein, 1988).

In a task-involving climate, the criteria or standards by which student achievement is judged are usually objective and made clear and explicit to the students (Epstein, 1988). The standards are typically self-referenced for each student, based on individual effort, participation, improvement, and progress toward personal goals (Treasure & Roberts, 1995). The self-referenced standards make the process of evaluation meaningful to students because it provides them with specific information about what they did correctly or incorrectly and how to improve (Epstein, 1988). A task-involving climate usually uses private evaluations, and students often conduct self-tests or partner checks (Treasure & Roberts, 1995; Valentini, Rudisill, & Goodway, 1999). As mentioned earlier, students in Mr. Smith's class evaluate each other on the fitness tests, and they then use that information to create a personalized workout plan. They are evaluated on their effort in completing their workout plan and whether they improved their performance on the fitness tests.

In an ego-involving climate, the criteria by which students are evaluated may be somewhat subjective and may not be clearly explained to students (Epstein, 1988). Evaluation frequently involves social comparison, is based on performing better than other students and the attainment of whole group objectives, and is closely linked to each student's ability (Todorovich & Curtner-Smith, 2002; Treasure & Roberts, 1995). Evaluation in an ego-involving climate is frequently done publicly, with the teacher usually conducting any evaluations (Todorovich & Curtner-Smith, 2002). The process of evaluation may not be meaningful to students because they receive little information about how to improve in the future. In Ms. Jones's class, the students' performances on fitness tests are conducted publicly by Ms. Jones. Students are never clear about the level at which they need to perform on a test because grades are awarded based on how well each student performs in relationship to the others. And, as mentioned previously, the fitness tests aren't very meaningful to the students because the information isn't used to help them improve.

Time. The time structure refers to the pace of instruction, including the amount and flexibility of time allocated for student practice, task completion, and student learning (Epstein, 1988).

In task-involving climates, students are usually given plenty of time to work on tasks and improve their skills (Ames, 1992a). In fact, the time allocated for task completion is frequently flexible, based on each student's needs (Biddle, 2001; Todorovich & Curtner-Smith, 2002). So, the amount of time that students work on tasks varies. Often, teachers promoting a task-involving climate help students establish their own timeline for goal achievement (Ames, 1992a; Todorovich & Curtner-Smith, 2002). Mr. Smith does just that when he helps his students establish short-term goals and a personalized fitness improvement plan. Each student sets his or her own time frame for reaching their goals.

In an ego-involving climate, students usually have the same amount of time to complete tasks and learn skills (Biddle, 2001). In addition, the teacher most often sets the time limits (Todorovich & Curtner-Smith, 2002). In Ms. Jones's class, all students perform the same exercises for the same amount of time, regardless of the level at which they performed on the fitness test. So, students who need more work on flexibility, for example, have the same amount of time to improve as students who are already highly flexible.

Approach and Avoidance Goals

Recently, an extension of achievement goals was proposed in academics, and it is just starting to be applied to physical education. In this modification, task and ego involvement are each divided into approach and avoidance goals. With an **approach goal,** a student strives to achieve a positive outcome, while with an **avoidance goal,** a student works to avoid a negative outcome (Elliot & McGregor, 2001). A student with a task-involved approach goal desires to master a task or learn the content; conversely, a student with a task-involved avoidance goal attempts to avoid not mastering a task or learning the content. Similarly, a student wants to perform better than others with an ego-involved approach goal, whereas a student desires to avoid performing poorly compared to others with an ego-involved avoidance goal.

The approach and avoidance goal distinction is important because persistence and performance are believed to be influenced by these goals; striving for a positive outcome should result in higher effort and persistence than striving to avoid a negative outcome. Thus, task-involved approach goals are predicted to yield greater persistence and effort and higher levels of performance than task-involved avoidance goals, and ego-involved approach goals are expected to result in more positive behaviors than ego-involved avoidance goals. Therefore, Martha, who exhibits task involvement in her physical education class, should display higher levels of effort and persistence if she is trying to learn and improve herself (a positive outcome) than if she is trying to avoid not improving her performance (a negative outcome). Likewise, Mary, who exhibits ego involvement, should show higher effort and persistence if she strives to perform better than others (a positive outcome) than if she tries to avoid getting beat by others (a negative outcome).

focus point

Approach goals, striving for a positive outcome, should result in higher effort and persistence than avoidance goals, striving to avoid a negative outcome.

Achievement Goal Research

Research on goal orientations and motivational climates with children in physical activity settings such as youth sport and physical education has flourished. Because of the large amount of research conducted in physical education or physical education-like settings, most of the research presented here will be from those areas. However, when research on a particular topic is lacking in physical education but was conducted in related settings like youth sport, that research is included.

First, the research on the ability of physical educators to actually create a particular motivational climate will be presented, as well as research on the effectiveness of a motivational climate to change students' goal orientations. Then, studies on the impact of goal perspectives on students' intrinsic motivation and related outcomes, perceptions of success and ability, attributions, perceptions of the purpose of physical education, perceptions of teacher behaviors, and participation in voluntary physical education will be examined. Finally, research on the relationships between gender and goal perspectives, and the impact of approach and avoidance goals on motivated behaviors will be reviewed.

Manipulating the Motivational Climate

One reason the concept of the motivational climate is so appealing is because it seems more likely that teachers can actually influence and establish a particular motivational climate in their classes, versus changing a student's dispositional goal orientation. As mentioned earlier, the type of climate believed to be most desirable for teachers to promote is a task-involving climate (Ames, 1992a, 1992b) due to its ability to enhance student behaviors conducive to learning. But can physical educators actually create a particular climate in their classrooms that can be detected by students? The results of two studies suggest that they can (Papaioannou & Kouli, 1999; Solmon, 1996). For example, Solmon (1996) assigned small groups of middle school physical education students to either a task-involving or ego-involving climate group during juggling lessons. The task-involving lessons were taught using several TARGET (Epstein, 1988, 1989) strategies, such as an emphasis on individual challenge and improvement, the use of short-term goals and self-referenced criteria for success, rewards for effort and improvement, and encouragement to work with others and at the students' own pace. The ego-involving lessons used a competition ladder and focused on performance, moving up the ladder, being superior to classmates by winning contests, and being the best juggler. The results showed that students could perceive the differences in climates between the two groups. Specifically, students in the task-involving lessons perceived a higher level of task involvement than students in the ego-involving lessons. Conversely, students in the ego-involving

focus point

Students can detect the difference between a task-involving motivational climate and an ego-involving one, so it is important that physical educators find ways to promote a task-involving climate.

lessons perceived a higher level of ego-involvement than did students in the task-involving lessons.

Changing Goal Orientations

If a teacher can establish a particular motivational climate, can that climate then impact students' goal orientations? Roberts (2001) contends that goal orientations are inclinations and not traits, so they may be amenable to change, and research (e.g., Lloyd & Fox, 1992; Todorovich & Curtner-Smith, 2002, 2003) confirms this. For instance, Todorovich and Curtner-Smith (2002, 2003) found that manipulating the motivational climate (using the TARGET strategies) in a 10-lesson modified field hockey unit seemed to change the goal orientations of 3rd and 6th grade students. Specifically, the students' task orientation levels in the task-involving climate and their ego orientation levels in the ego-involving climate moderately increased.

focus point

The motivational climate established by the teacher may impact the students' dispositional goal orientations.

Positive Affect

Positive affect in physical education might include high interest, enjoyment, satisfaction, and fun, and low levels of pressure, anxiety, and boredom. **Flow,** in which a person has total concentration, a sense of control, loss of self-consciousness, and a merging of action and awareness (Csikszentmihalyi, 1975), is another positive affect that students could experience. Researchers have mostly found that students with high task orientation in physical education and physical activity tend to experience these positive affective outcomes (e.g., Cury et al., 1996; Spray, Biddle, & Fox, 1999; Williams & Gill, 1995), including flow in physical education (Papaioannou & Kouli, 1999).

Other researchers found that students with high perceptions of their performance or ability experience positive affect whether they are high in task or ego orientation; conversely, students with low perceptions of ability experience positive affect if they are high task orientation, but experience negative affect if they are high ego orientation (Vlachopoulos & Biddle, 1997; Vlachopoulos, Biddle, & Fox, 1996). In one study, a positive relationship between task orientation and positive affect in physical education (confidence, satisfaction, pleasure, happiness, pride) was found for students ages 11 to 16 who had either high or low perceived ability (Vlachopoulos & Biddle, 1997). However, students with low perceived ability and high ego orientation were likely to experience low levels of positive affect but higher levels of negative affect (depression, shame, disappointment, embarrassment) in physical education.

The impact of the motivational climate on students' affect during physical education appears similar to that of goal orientations, with high perceptions of a task-involving climate resulting in positive affect, and high perceptions of an ego-involving climate producing more negative affect (Carpenter & Morgan, 1999; Cury et al., 1996; Papaioannou, 1994; Papaioannou & Kouli, 1999; Treasure, 1997). For instance, adolescent students' perceptions of a task-involving climate were positively related to their flow states, but negatively related to their somatic anxiety (i.e., heart rate, sweating, blood pressure, breathing rate) experienced in lessons (Papaioannou & Kouli, 1999). Moreover, as students' perceptions of an ego-involving climate rose, so did their somatic anxiety. Interestingly, other researchers found that adolescent girls' perceptions of the motivational climate predicted their interest in physical education better than their dispositional goal orientations (Cury et al., 1996).

Student Behaviors

focus point

Research shows that task involvement is more beneficial to students' affect, effort, and persistence in physical education than ego involvement, especially for children who have low perceptions of their ability.

Task persistence and effort are vital to student achievement in physical education. There is evidence that high task involvement, whether due to one's task orientation or a task-involving climate, is associated with high task persistence and effort (Martinek & Williams, 1997; Rudisill, 1990; Solmon, 1996; Williams & Gill, 1995), especially among boys with low perceived ability (Sarrazin, Roberts, Cury, Biddle, & Famose, 2002). For example, middle school students' level of task orientation helped predict their perceived effort in physical activities, so that higher levels of task orientation resulted in higher levels of perceived effort (Williams & Gill, 1995). In another study, Solmon (1996) found that junior high students who participated in task-involving lessons on juggling did significantly more difficult trials per minute (i.e., higher persistence) than students who participated in ego-involving lessons. Thus, teachers should promote a task-involving climate as much as possible in physical education.

Self-Perceptions

The results of many studies clearly indicate that task-involvement (due to task orientation, or participating in or perceiving a task-involving climate) is related to high self-perceptions in children participating in physical activity settings (e.g., Carpenter & Morgan, 1999; Dunn, 2000; Ferrer-Caja & Weiss, 2000; Guinn, Vincent, Semper, & Jorgensen, 2000; Papaioannou & Kouli, 1999; Rudisill, 1990; Stephens, 1998; Treasure, 1997; Vlachopoulos & Biddle, 1997; Wang & Biddle, 2001; Wang, Chatzisarantis, Spray, & Biddle, 2002; Williams & Gill, 1995; Xiang & Lee, 1998). For example, Dunn (2000) discovered that perceptions of a task-involving climate positively influenced the perceptions of competence in children with movement difficulties, while the children's perceptions of an ego-involving climate negatively influenced their perceptions of competence. Of interest is that Papaioannou and Kouli (1999) found that even when junior high students participated in lessons designed to be ego-involving, as long as the students still perceived that their teacher emphasized learning (e.g., a task-involving climate), they were likely to have high self-confidence levels. Vlachopoulos and Biddle (1997) proposed that high task involvement leads to higher beliefs of success because task-oriented people can achieve their goals (which involve personal improvement) even without performing better than others.

The relationship between ego-involvement and self-perceptions is less clear. Although some researchers have discovered positive relationships between ego orientations and perceptions of competence (Wang & Biddle, 2001; Wang et al., 2002; Xiang & Lee, 1998), other researchers found that ego orientations were not related to perceptions of competence (Williams & Gill, 1995) or were even negatively related (Dunn, 2000).

These studies suggest that to help students feel confident and successful and to expect success in physical education, teachers should establish a task-involving climate. However, although the actual climate is important, students' perceptions of the climate may be even more important. So, a teacher should also casually point out to her students various aspects of the task-involving climate she tried to produce (e.g., choices they are getting, types of goals they are setting, etc.). More information on how ego orientations and an ego-involving climate affects self-perceptions is needed before teachers are encouraged to create that kind of climate.

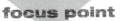

focus point

Task involvement, or even the mere perception of a task-involving climate, can enhance students' perceptions of their success and ability in physical education.

Attributions

Researchers have studied how goal perspectives may influence students' beliefs about the causes of their level of success or performance (i.e., their **attributions**) in physical education. Adolescents with high task orientation, regardless of their perceived ability, tend to make attributions for outcomes that are personally controllable (Vlachopoulos & Biddle, 1997). Therefore, they tend to believe that success in physical education is achieved through

- exhibiting high effort (Spray et al., 1999; Walling & Duda, 1995),
- having an intrinsic interest in the class,
- enjoying participation in class, and
- cooperating with their peers (Walling & Duda, 1995).

Conversely, students with high ego orientation tend to believe that high ability (Spray et al., 1999; Walling & Duda, 1995) and deceptive tactics (e.g., pretending to like the teacher; Spray et al., 1999) are what lead to success in physical education. Vlachopoulos and Biddle (1997) further found that the attributions for performance made by students with high ego orientation may be influenced by their perceived ability level. So, students with high ego orientation who have high perceptions of their ability may make personally controllable attributions, like students high in task orientation. But students high in ego orientation with low perceptions of ability tend to make attributions for performance that they cannot control, particularly their low ability. When they do poorly on a task in physical education, they attribute that poor performance to their belief that they "just aren't very good at sports" and thus believe there is little chance for improvement.

Research on the motivational climate and attributions has produced similar results as goal orientations. Students who participate in or simply perceive a highly ego-involving climate in physical education tend to believe that success in class is the result of ability (Solmon, 1996; Treasure, 1997) and deception (e.g., cheating, fooling the teacher; Carpenter & Morgan, 1999), while students who perceive a highly task-involving climate tend to see effort (Carpenter & Morgan, 1999; Treasure, 1997) and ability as the causes of success (Treasure, 1997). Solmon (1996) further found that student perceptions of the motivational climate are more important determinants of student attributions than the actual motivational climate.

Attributions made to personally controllable factors (e.g., effort, interest, enjoyment, and cooperating with others) are likely to produce behaviors conducive to learning (e.g., effort, persistence) because students believe they can control and change these behaviors to produce the outcome they want. The studies reviewed in this section indicate that task involvement yields more positive, controllable attributions than ego involvement, especially for students with low perceived ability. As with the impact of the climate on perceptions of ability, the students' perceptions of the climate seem more important to producing these adaptive attributions than the actual climate. Thus, besides working to enhance the task-involving aspects in their physical education classes, teachers should help students see those aspects in their daily lessons.

Beliefs About the Purpose of Physical Education

Although more research is needed on this topic, studies indicate that encouraging task involvement in physical education will help students appreciate the value of physical education and view physical education as a means of developing positive attributes (Papaioannou & Macdonald, 1993; Walling & Duda, 1995). Walling and Duda (1995), for example, discovered that high school students with high task/low ego orientations were less likely than other students to believe that the purpose of physical education is to provide an easy class. Students high in task orientation also rated having fun, cooperating with peers, and appreciating the value of mastering skills as important purposes of physical education.

Participation in Physical Education

Researchers have examined whether goal orientations and perceived motivational climates influence students' intentions to participate in physical education/activity when it is no longer a requirement. Most studies indicate that high task orientation and perceptions of a task-involving climate positively influence students' intended or actual future participation in physical activities (Biddle et al., 1995; Papaioannou & Theodorakis, 1996; Spray, 2000; Spray & Biddle, 1997). For instance, in one study students who chose to participate in structured physical activity in college were higher in task orientation than students who did not participate (Spray & Biddle, 1997), while in another study student perceptions of a task-involving climate positively predicted voluntary participation in physical education when it was not required (Spray, 2000).

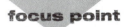

focus point

Students' intention to participate or their actual participation in physical activities in the future appears to be positively influenced by a high task orientation and the perception of a task-involving climate.

Student Perceptions of Teacher Behavior

One interesting area of research in goal achievement theory deals with the relationship of students' goal orientations and perceived motivational climate with students' perceptions of the teacher's behaviors, including discipline. Studies show that middle and high school students who perceive a high ego-involving climate in physical education believe that the teacher favors high achievers (Papaioannou, 1995) and treats boys and girls differently (Papaioannou, 1998b). Conversely, students who perceive a high task-involving climate are less likely to have those perceptions (Papaioannou, 1995, 1998b). Papaioannou (1998a) found that 10-, 12-, and 15-year-old students with high task orientation believed discipline is important to helping all students learn; those students felt ashamed and bad about themselves when they got disciplined. Students high in ego orientation, however, did not know why they were disciplined and stated that discipline wastes time. In another study, students who perceived a task-involving climate in physical education were likely to believe that their teacher used intrinsic strategies to maintain discipline, such as making the lessons more interesting, teaching new games and skills, making the lesson funny and exciting, making students responsible for their actions, and encouraging cooperation among students (Papaioannou, 1998a). Students who perceived a highly ego-involving climate, however, were likely to believe the teacher used introjected means of disciplining (e.g., tries to make students feel bad about themselves if disciplined) as well as extrin-

focus point

Enhance students' perceptions that the teacher treats boys and girls and students of different skill levels fairly by promoting a task-involving climate.

sic means (e.g., threatens students that they'll get in trouble if they misbehave, yells at those who are misbehaving, reminds students of the rules).

The results of these studies suggest that promoting task involvement in physical education could help the teacher maintain discipline and help the students perceive equality in their classes. Specific strategies physical educators can use include helping students understand the reasons for good behavior in class and why students are being disciplined, helping students accept responsibility for their own actions, helping all students improve their own skills, teaching new activities and skills, and promoting cooperation among students.

Gender

Some researchers have found that males have a higher ego orientation (Kavussanu & Roberts, 1996, 2001; Papaioannou & Kouli, 1999; Spray, 2000; Walling & Duda, 1995), lower task orientation (Kavussanu & Roberts, 1996, 2001), and tend to perceive physical education lessons as higher in ego-involvement (Goudas & Biddle, 1994; Kavussanu & Roberts, 1996; Papaioannou & Kouli, 1999; Solmon, 1996) than females. Other researchers, however, found no difference between males and females in goal orientations (Spray & Biddle, 1997; Spray et al., 1999; Williams & Gill, 1995) or in their perceptions of the motivational climate in physical education (e.g., Mitchell, 1996; Solmon, 1996; Spray, 2000; Todorovich & Curtner-Smith, 2002, 2003). Physical educators should be aware that boys may have higher ego orientations and lower task orientations, and may be more likely to perceive an ego-involving climate than a task-involving climate, than girls, but also should be aware that this is not guaranteed. When trying to establish a task-involving climate, they should more strongly emphasize the task-involving aspects of a lesson for boys to help them clearly perceive those aspects.

Approach and Avoidance Goals in Physical Education

Approach and avoidance goals have only started to be examined in physical education. For instance, a study of high school students and their achievement goals found that task-involved/approach, task-involved/avoidance, and ego-involved/approach goals all positively predicted their self-reports of effort and persistence in class (Guan, Xiang, McBride, & Bruene, 2006). But ego-involved/avoidance goals did not positively impact the students' reported effort and persistence. Thus, task involvement, whether accompanied with a desire to learn and improve or a desire to avoid not learning and improving, can positively affect students' motivated behaviors. Ego involvement, when accompanied by an approach goal

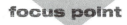

focus point

Task involvement in physical education could help students perceive discipline by the teacher more positively than ego involvement.

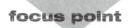

focus point

Be aware that males may have higher ego orientations than females, and that males may perceive higher ego-involving climates than females.

focus point

If a physical educator suspects a student of being ego-involved in a situation, the student should be encouraged to focus on approach goals instead of avoidance goals.

of performing better than others, will have a more positive impact on students' motivated behaviors than ego involvement with a desire to avoid losing to others. Although more research in physical education is needed on these goals, this study suggests that physical education teachers should encourage students who may be ego-involved to focus on approach goals over avoidance goals.

Means of Enhancing Task Involvement in Physical Education

Ego involvement, in the form of competition with others, is a natural part of sport. Because sport is a major content area in physical education, it is easy for an ego-involving climate to exist in physical education. Although some studies indicate that moderate or high ego involvement can still result in positive achievement behaviors in students, this generally occurs only if the students have high perceptions of success or ability (Vlachopoulos & Biddle, 1997; Vlachopoulos et al., 1996) or there is also high task involvement (Goudas & Biddle, 1994; Treasure, 1997). Because most researchers have found more positive benefits for task involvement than ego involvement, and because physical educators can produce a particular motivational climate that students can perceive, several means of establishing a task-involving climate in physical education will now be presented. Many of these ideas are based on the six learning environment structures (TARGET) proposed by Epstein (1988, 1989). It should be noted that even though you strive to produce a task-involving climate, due to the natural competition inherent in many physical education activities, elements of ego involvement will still exist that are capable of enhancing the motivation and enjoyment of ego-oriented, high perceived ability students.

Use Stations

In the task structure of a task-involving climate, students perform several different tasks at the same time, preventing them from comparing their

connected **CONCEPTS**

Instructional models can also help establish a task-involving climate in physical education. Many TARGET structures are a natural part of sport education: students form small teams/groups that work together to improve their skills (grouping); students take on various roles and responsibilities (authority); the tasks students work on will vary from team to team (task); the time students have to practice skills varies from team to team because each team works as long as they need to in order to improve (time); statistics are gathered by statisticians to help the team decide which skills to work on (evaluation); and rewards are often given at the culminating event (rewards; see Chapter 4). The peer teaching model can help create a task-involving climate by transferring the instructional (leadership) roles from the teacher to the students (the authority structure; see Chapter 3). In the cooperative learning model, the teacher intentionally forms diverse groups or teams that help each other learn motor skills and movement concepts (the grouping structure; see Chapter 4). The personalized system of instruction allows students flexibility in the time they work on various skills, allowing them to work at their own pace (the time structure; see Chapter 2).

connected CONCEPTS

Doing a set induction at the start and a closure at the end of each lesson can help students understand the importance of tasks (as part of the task structure; see Chapter 3).

performance to others. One way to do that is to create stations. Several different tasks related to the same skill or activity are created, with a different section of the gym or playing area designated for each separate task. Place students into small groups, with each group beginning practice at a different station. After spending several minutes at the station, the students rotate around to each of the stations. In a middle school basketball unit, for example, stations on rebounding, one-on-one defense, zone defense, setting a screen and roll, and shooting against a defender might be created.

real world

Rosa E., an elementary physical educator in the southern United States, frequently used stations with her students. In one lesson with 1st graders, Rosa created stations for the following activities to help her students work on various aspects of fitness:

- shuttle run
- rope climbing
- bench step-ups
- rope jumping

- jogging around the gym
- push-ups
- curl-ups.

The students were alternately placed at various stations at the start of class. They spent several minutes at each station before moving to the next station on Rosa's signal. Performing several different tasks at the same time made it difficult for the children to compare their performance to the other children's, thus creating a more task-involving task structure.

focus point

Using stations during physical education classes decreases students' opportunities to compare their performance to others.

Mary is the highly ego-involved twin you met at the beginning of the chapter. Her teacher, Ms. Jones, might help her be more task-involved, and thus enhance her effort and persistence, by creating stations so Mary and her classmates can work on skills without comparing themselves to each other. This is an instructional tool frequently used by Mr. Smith, Martha's physical education teacher, and it helps Martha focus on what she is doing, not what her classmates are doing.

Use the Games Stages

Tasks that gradually become more difficult by building on previous tasks are characteristic of the task structure in a task-involving climate. Tasks that gradually develop game skills allow students to be successful at games, regardless of their initial ability level. This logical progression can be accomplished by using four games stages (Rink, 2002). See Exhibit 5.2.

Four games stages (Rink, 2002).	EXHIBIT 5.2

Stage One. Tasks help students gain control of individual skills in an activity. Examples include dribbling a ball while moving and changing hands, serving a shuttle in badminton to the desired place on the court, or batting a pitched ball in the direction desired.

Stage Two. Skills are practiced in combinations or in preparation for another skill. This might include receiving a pass in basketball and then shooting the ball, serving a ball in tennis and then moving to home position on the court for the return shot, or batting a ball and then running to first base.

Stage Three. When a student can control the skill and combine it with others, he is now is ready to practice simple offensive and defensive strategies. For example, a Stage Three task in basketball might be to work two against two, with the offense working on making sharp cuts to get open for a pass. In badminton, a Stage Three task might be to have a partner toss the shuttle over the net to a hitter, after which the tosser moves to one of four positions: close to the net on the right or left side of the court, or to the back of the court to the right or left side. The hitter's task is to hit the shuttle to one of the open spaces on the court.

Stage Four. Tasks are modified games and the full game.

According to Rink (2002), teachers often skip stages two and three when teaching game skills. A typical basketball unit, for example, might begin with students practicing the bounce, chest, and overhead passes with a partner while stationary, and then move right into regulation basketball games. In that abbreviated progression, students do not practice the skills in game-like situations, or combinations of passes with other skills, or strategies using the passing skills. Understandably, students fail to see the meaningfulness of isolated tasks. Big jumps in task progressions are more likely avoided when the games stages are used to plan those task progressions for a unit, allowing students to gradually build up to a full game.

focus point

Use the games stages to develop tasks that gradually become more difficult and build on previous tasks, which are characteristics of the task structure in a task-involving climate.

real world

Marie D. and her colleagues, who teach at an urban middle school in the southern United States, use the games stages to develop units and lesson plans for all of their activity units. In a volleyball unit, for instance, the students start with Stage One tasks, which include learning the basic form of the forearm pass, overhead pass, underhand and overhand serve, and hit (spike). The students first practice each skill using shadow drills (i.e., without a ball). Stage One tasks following this initial practice for the forearm pass, for example, progress from a self-bump (one bump and catch, then two and catch, then continuous) to passing a ball tossed by a partner (direct tosses, then tosses making the passer move to pass, then more forceful tosses, then over a rope) to continuous cooperative passing with a partner (eventually adding boundaries and a rope).

After practicing the other skills in Stage One similarly, Marie and her students progress to Stage Two tasks, which include combining the forearm pass and overhand pass, the overhand pass and spike, the serve and forearm pass, and three or more hits (e.g., serve/forearm pass/overhand pass, serve/forearm pass/overhand pass/spike). Tasks that combine the forearm pass and overhand pass, for instance, begin with students alternating the two passes to themselves (varying the height and trajectory), move to alternating the passes with a partner (eventually using boundaries, passing over a rope, and varying the height of passes to make the partner choose the correct pass), and then add other students to the group in alternating passes.

In Marie's game stage progression, Stage Three tasks begin with 1 with 1 cooperative passing games, move to 1 vs. 1 competitive passing games, followed by 2 with 2 cooperative passing games, 2 vs. 2 competitive passing games, and continue adding people, changing from cooperative to competitive. Within each major task, the difficulty changes by varying elements like allowing a bounce if necessary, limiting space, hitting over a rope, changing the position of team members (i.e., side by side, up and back), increasing rope height, or requiring the three-hit sequence of bump-set-spike. Students are working on tactics such as returning to home base, hitting to open spaces, communicating, and sharing space. After practicing these tasks, students are ready for Stage Four activities, including modified to official volleyball games. Modifications might include allowing a bounce, increasing or decreasing space, or making pass requirements. Such gradual progressions from Stage One to Stage Four clearly help establish a task structure that is representative of a task-involving climate.

Mary's teacher, Ms. Jones, rarely has her students practice Stage Two or Three tasks during physical education class; they usually go from a brief period of simple skill practice straight into full games. The students do not get to practice the skills in the ways the skills are used in the game, which contributes to Mary's lack of motivation and effort in activities at which she isn't very skilled. Ms. Jones could develop a progression of tasks for activities using the game stages. In a team handball unit, for example, Ms. Jones' students could start by practicing the different types of passes while stationary (Stage One), then practice combinations of a dribble to a pass or a catch to a pass (Stage Two). This could then be followed by Stage Three activities, such as passing to a teammate being guarded or passing while being guarded. All of these activities eventually lead to Stage Four activities, including small-sided team handball games and regulation games. Such a progression would help Mary experience success early in practice and enhance the possibility she will keep trying when tasks become more complex and difficult.

Help Students Set Individual, Short-Term Goals

Another way to influence the task structure and help create a task-involving climate is to help students set goals. Individualized, short-term goals help students work at tasks appropriate for their ability levels, thus giving them more success. Such goals can also influence other TARGET structures of the learning environment and help produce a task-involving climate, such as the evaluation, reward, and time structures. Short-term goals, for instance, should include clear, objective criteria for accomplishing those goals (related to the evaluation structure). Base evaluation and rewards on each individual student's accomplishment of their personal self-improvement goals, so that all children have the chance to be successful and obtain rewards. Short-term goals can also help evaluation become more meaningful to students because the accomplishment of these short-term goals can be assessed throughout the unit; the results become part of the instructional unit and help you and your student determine the next practice tasks. The time structure in the learning environment is also addressed because each student should have their own timeline for improvement based on the goals that were set.

focus point

Helping students set short-term, individualized goals can influence the task, reward, evaluation, and time structures of a task-involving climate.

As a high school teacher at a rural school in the Midwest, Carole D. helped her students set individualized fitness goals. At the start of the school year, 9th graders assessed themselves on a series of health-related fitness tests. Based on the test results, each student set two fitness goals to reach by the end of the first 9-week period. Each student was also required to write strategies for reaching the goals. See Exhibit 5.3 for an example goal-setting sheet completed by one of Carole D.'s students and Appendix A.4 for a blank sheet. Carole helped students set appropriate goals, making sure they were setting goals for areas in which they needed to improve and that the goals weren't too easy or too hard, and helped them come up with good strategies. The students were then tested at the end of each 9-week period, after which they could set new goals.

real world

Individual goal setting would be very effective in helping Mary become more task involved. For the progressive 20-meter aerobic fitness test, for example, Ms. Jones could help Mary set a series of short-term goals over the school year to help her improve her performance from her first attempt in the fall. This would help Mary focus on her own performance and help her persist in the test, regardless of whether she finishes first in the class or otherwise.

Use Alternative Assessments

Using alternative assessments in physical education can help you establish a task-involving climate by addressing the authority and evaluation structures of TARGET. Many types of alternative assessments (e.g., port-

EXHIBIT   5.3   Goal-setting sheet.

GOAL-SETTING SHEET

Name: Janelle   Class: 4th period

Contract set date: September 15th   Target date: November 17th

GOALS DEFINED:

Goal 1:   To improve my upper body strength so I can do three more push-ups

Goal 2:

STRATEGIES TO ACHIEVE GOALS:

Strategies for goal 1:   Do 3 different upper weight lifting exercises 3 days each week,
performing 3 sets of repetitions each day.

Strategies for goal 2:

WEEKLY PROGRESS NOTES:

Week 1, September 22nd. I exercised on Monday, Wednesday, and Friday with no
change yet in the number of push-ups I am able to do.

Week 2, September 29th. I exercised on Tuesday, Thursday, and Saturday. Still no
change in the number of push-ups I am able to do, but I wasn't as sore as I was
last week.

Week 3, October 6th. I exercised on Monday, Thursday, and Saturday. Hooray! I am able
to do one more push-up! I am one-third of the way toward my goal.

folios, journals, group projects, peer and self-observations with performance checklists) allow students to assess themselves or their peers, thereby putting the students in leadership roles and helping them develop self-management and self-direction (the authority structure). Alternative assessments usually have objective criteria, which are characteristic of the evaluation structure, that can be clearly explained to your students, often in the form of a rubric. Furthermore, alternative assessments are meaningful to students because such assessments are usually conducted throughout the instructional unit, not just at the end, as a means of providing information to both you and your students to help them improve.

One physical education teacher who regularly uses alternative assessments is Larry S., who teaches at a suburban elementary school in the southern United States. Larry uses what he calls "seamless assessment," in which the lines between instruction and assessment are blurred—a single task may be performed by students for both instructional and assessment purposes; students learn as a result of such tasks. Some of the alternative assessments Larry uses are teacher assessments of student performance that he completes, while others are student peer assessments of a partner's performance or student self-assessments. Regardless of who performs the assessment, the results are used to help students improve their skills. For instance, in a 3rd grade 5-lesson unit on striking with hockey sticks, Larry assessed his students using a skills check during task practice and game play, a peer assessment, and a self-assessment of skills during task practice. In the unit's first lesson, students dribbled a puck or ball in general space. During that task, Larry quickly did an informal assessment of his students' initial striking/dribbling skills by making notes related to the striking cues on a generic class roster page (see Exhibit 5.4). Larry used this information to help him design refinement tasks that needed to be performed, or extensions for which students may be ready. In the second or third lesson, students conducted peer assessments of their partner's ability in one of three components of passing a puck: holding the stick, body positioning, or the swing (see Exhibit 5.5). In the third or fourth lesson, students conducted a self-assessment of how good they believed they were at dribbling and passing skills (see Exhibit 5.6). Each assessment includes objective criteria that are made clear to the students. The assessments give Larry and his students valuable information about their current ability levels and aspects of the skills that need work.

Mary would greatly benefit from alternative assessments. For example, Mary and a partner could regularly test each other on the number of push-ups they can do to help them and Ms. Jones see how they are improving throughout the year and to make needed adjustments to their

EXHIBIT 5.4 Form for skill assessment.

SKILL ASSESSMENT SHEET
MS. TURNER'S CLASS

Skill or concept: Passing a hockey puck

Date: January 24, 2008

Student Names	Comments
Sarah	Holds stick correctly; get body further from the puck when passing
Tom	Contacts puck consistently; brings stick back above waist
Rich	Doesn't follow through to his partner
Chris	
Alyse	
Erin	
John	
Patty	
Tiffany	
Shereka	
Collin	
Tariq	
Deanna	
Marjorie	
Frank	
Pete	

This chart is used with permission from Larry Satchwell, Shiloh Elementary School, Snellville, GA.

| Form for peer-assessment of hockey skills. | **EXHIBIT** | **5.5** |

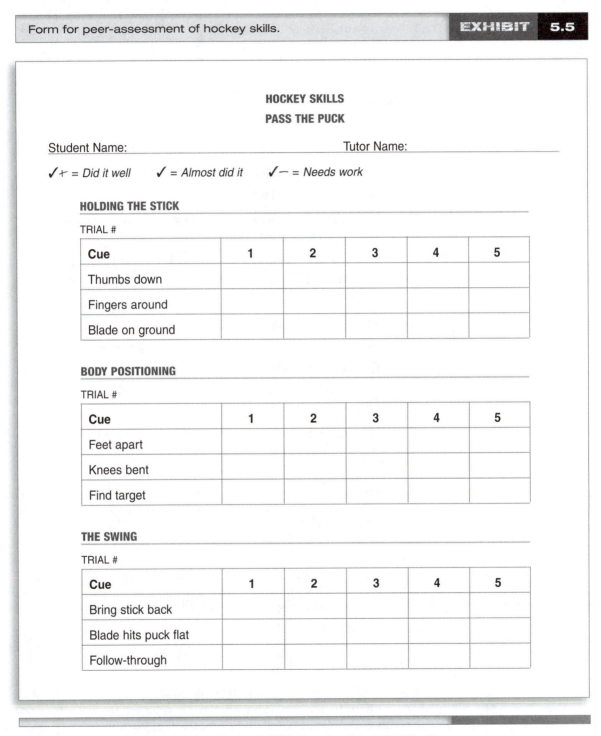

HOCKEY SKILLS

PASS THE PUCK

Student Name: _____   Tutor Name: _____

✓+ = *Did it well*   ✓ = *Almost did it*   ✓— = *Needs work*

HOLDING THE STICK

TRIAL #

Cue	1	2	3	4	5
Thumbs down					
Fingers around					
Blade on ground					

BODY POSITIONING

TRIAL #

Cue	1	2	3	4	5
Feet apart					
Knees bent					
Find target					

THE SWING

TRIAL #

Cue	1	2	3	4	5
Bring stick back					
Blade hits puck flat					
Follow-through					

This chart is used with permission from Larry Satchwell, Shiloh Elementary School, Snellville, GA.

EXHIBIT   5.6   Form for self-assessment of hockey skills.

Name: _____

Class: _____   Date: _____

✓+ = a skill you can do very well

✓ = a skill you can do sometimes but still needs work

✓− = a skill you cannot do most of the time

☐ I can dribble a puck with a hockey stick in a straight pathway, keeping the puck close to the stick.

☐ I can dribble a puck with a hockey stick in a curved pathway, keeping the puck close to the stick.

☐ I can dribble a puck with a hockey stick in a zig-zag pathway, keeping the puck close to the stick.

☐ I can dribble a puck around two cones in a figure eight, keeping the puck close to the stick.

☐ I can dribble a puck while running, keeping the puck close to the stick.

☐ I can pass a puck between two cones (one hockey stick apart) from 20 feet at least 3 out of 5 times.

This chart is used with permission from Larry Satchwell, Shiloh Elementary School, Snellville, GA.

exercise programs. In a golf unit, Ms. Jones could create a rubric designed to help students assess each other on the key elements of the golf swing. This puts the students in leadership roles, helping establish a task-involving climate in the authority structure.

Offer Students Choices

One way the authority structure can be influenced to help establish a task-involving climate in physical education is by offering students choices. Students can make choices on many elements in physical education, such as the type of equipment used, their partners or group members, the tasks they will work on, the competitive level at which they will play, the activities/sports they will participate in during class, the time allotted to practice various tasks, or even the criteria for successful performance.

As part of a Jump Rope for Heart event, Jana P., who teaches at an urban elementary school in the southern United States, let her students choose how they would jump during the event: with an individual rope, with a long rope and a small group of students, swinging an individual rope on a side swing without jumping over the rope, or jumping over a line without a rope. This kind of choice allowed all of her students, regardless of their rope jumping skill level, to participate successfully in Jump Rope for Heart.

Ms. Jones makes nearly all the decisions in Mary's physical education class. To help develop a task-involving climate, Ms. Jones could start by giving the students some simple choices, like whether to practice volleyball skills using a trainer volleyball or a regulation volleyball. She might also let students choose whether to work on serving or on setting the ball up for a spike. Once students are used to making decisions and are making appropriate decisions, Ms. Jones might try teaching a sport using the sport education model, which would allow students decisions on things like team members, the skills and drills to practice each day, and even rule modifications for game play. These kinds of decisions would give students like Mary a sense of authority in physical education and work to enhance their task involvement.

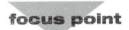

real world

focus point

When students are given choices in physical education, a task-involving climate is enhanced by influencing the authority structure.

Summary

The way students define ability and success in physical education can vary. Some students define success as being able to perform better than others (ego involvement), while others believe they are successful when they improve their own performance (task involvement). The goal perspective adopted in a particular situation is influenced by a person's personal disposition (goal orientation) and the context in which she is performing (motivational climate). Physical educators should work at producing a task-involving climate because research shows that task involvement positively influences intrinsic motivation, enjoyment, effort, persistence, perceptions of success and ability, attributions, beliefs about the purpose of physical education, long-term participation in physical activity, and perceptions of discipline. Some of the ways you can enhance your students' task involvement in physical education include the following: using stations, preparing a progression of tasks using the games stages, helping students set individual goals, using alternative assessments, and offering students choices.

Although some of the ideas for enhancing task involvement can be quite simple (e.g., giving students a choice of equipment), many of them take a lot more work than traditional physical education teaching. For instance, creating five stations with a different task at each station takes more preparation than having all students practice the same task at the same time. The long-term impact, however, on students' task involvement, effort, persistence, and enjoyment will be well worth your time and effort.

KEY concepts

Achievement goal theory

Goal perspective

Ego involvement

Task involvement

Dispositional goal orientations

Motivational climate

Ego orientation

Task orientation

Undifferentiated view of ability

Differentiated view of ability

Task-involving climate

Ego-involving climate

TARGET

Approach goal

Avoidance goal

Flow

Attribution

application exercises

1. Choose an activity to teach to middle school or high school students. Describe one thing you could do in each of the six TARGET structures to establish a task-involving motivational climate in physical education for that activity.

2. Besides enhancing student motivation, what are some of the other benefits of promoting a task-involving climate in physical education?

3. Mr. Crace and Mr. Childes are each preparing to teach a ropes climbing unit in their middle school physical education classes. Mr. Crace is preparing a task-involving motivational climate, while Mr. Childes is promoting an ego-involving climate. Describe some of the differences between the two units.

4. After teaching a fitness unit for several weeks, you suspect that Carrie has a strong ego orientation. Describe evidence from the fitness unit that leads you to believe that. What could you do to help Carrie be more task-involved in the fitness unit?

Self-Perceptions

Mr. Barry is a first-year middle school physical education teacher. One of his goals for his students is the development of positive self-esteem, something he often hears from the school administrators and other teachers. He also believes that his students' confidence levels affect their effort and willingness to try new skills and activities in physical education. For instance, Josie, a 6th grade girl in his first period class, refused to try the climbing wall or tinikling with jump bands, which were new activities for her. But her friend, Carole, tried hard at both new activities, even when she had trouble with the skills at first. Aaron, an 8th grade boy in fifth period who Mr. Barry feels has pretty high athletic ability, gave up quickly when he wasn't successful right away during the lacrosse unit. Conversely, his friend, John, kept working at the skills and eventually experienced success. Although Josie and Aaron's lack of effort could be due to several different factors, Mr. Barry suspects a lack of confidence in their motor skills is a key because he has heard both students comment on their low motor ability. Mr. Barry wonders what more he could do to help these students and others develop more positive self-perceptions.

introduction

any teachers want to help students "feel good about themselves." Positive perceptions of self are one important goal of education systems and are even part of the national standards for physical education (NASPE, 2004b). Moreover, students' self-perceptions can have a major impact on their motivation and performance in physical education. In this chapter, students' self-perceptions will be explored, first clarifying the various terms that are used when referring to self-perceptions. Then two theories, proven helpful in movement and education settings in understanding the role of self-perceptions in learning and how to enhance self-perceptions, will be described. Next will be an examination of the research related to self-perceptions, children, and movement situations. The chapter concludes with a description of various instructional methods to enhance self-perceptions, based on the two theories and current research.

Self-Perception Terms

elf-concept, self-esteem, perceived competence, self-confidence, and self-efficacy are all terms that educators may use when they talk about helping students "feel good about themselves." All of these terms fall into the general category of self-perceptions. **Self-perceptions** are the "thoughts and feelings by individuals about themselves as persons, in general, or their abilities in a particular achievement domain such as sports, academics, or social activities" (Weiss & Ebbeck, 1996, p. 364). Each of the other terms refers to a slightly different aspect of a person's self-perceptions. **Self-concept** is your relatively stable, global description of yourself (James, 1892; Weiss & Ebbeck, 1996)—your abilities, activities, qualities, traits, personal beliefs, morals, values (Fox, 1988)—without any evaluation of worth. Your self-concept is multidimensional, meaning it consists of many different elements or domains. Although it is primarily stable, it is also somewhat dynamic, meaning elements of it change with time. For example, Mr. Barry may see himself as an intelligent, hard-working, and creative physical educator and coach who is a regular exerciser. Though many of those self-concept elements have remained stable over the years, 10 years ago his self-concept included being a college student and athlete instead of a teacher and coach, and being a competitive marathoner instead of an exerciser.

Another term commonly used when referring to self-perceptions is **self-esteem** (or self-worth), which is the "evaluative component of the self" (Horn, 2004, p. 102; James, 1892). This global construct is one's personal assessment or judgment of her value or worth, based on the self-concept elements. Whereas self-concept can be separated into various domains (e.g., social self-concept, motor self-concept), one's self-esteem is more global and is based on the domain-specific self-conceptions (Harter, 1987). However, self-esteem is not simply the additive value of the various self-concept domains because self-esteem is in part determined by the importance someone places on the various self-concept domains (Harter, 1987). For instance, a person's self-concept of himself in the musical domain may not be high, but if that domain is not important to him, it will not negatively impact his self-esteem. Self-esteem is also influenced by one's mastery in a domain and his beliefs of how others view him, or perceived social regard (Harter, 1987). So, if someone experiences success and believes others view him as highly competent in a domain and that domain is important to him, it will probably positively impact his self-esteem.

Perceptions of competence, or **perceived ability,** refers to a person's domain-specific self-conceptions (Weiss & Ebbeck, 1996), or her description of and evaluation of her abilities in a specific domain or subdomain. These perceptions of competence are less global than one's self-concept or self-esteem, and less stable, because they can change over time and vary with the achievement domain (Harter, 1987; Horn, 2004). Aaron, from the opening scenario, may have had high perceptions of his academic competence and physical competence at the start of middle school; however, he may have experienced much less success during physical education class in middle school than he did during elementary school due to the changes in his body. His middle school experience could then contribute to his lower physical perceptions of competence.

Like perceptions of competence, one's **self-confidence** is specific to various domains. Self-confidence is the strength of a person's belief that he will be successful in that domain or context (Horn, 2004). High perceptions of competence usually relate to high self-confidence, so a student with high perceptions of competence in physical education is likely to believe he will be successful during physical education. There may be exceptions, however, such as a student with high perceived competence in physical education overall but who does not believe he will be successful in physical education this semester because he thinks the teacher does not like him.

A closely related concept is **self-efficacy,** which is situation-specific self-confidence (Bandura, 1986). Self-efficacy is a person's beliefs about what she can accomplish, or the level of performance she can achieve, with the skills she has (Bandura, 1986, 1997). In other words, self-efficacy is one's degree of confidence in her capability to achieve a specific performance level or outcome in a particular situation. A student may strongly believe that she can bench press 50 pounds for 10 repetitions during weight lifting class today, but have much lower self-efficacy in her ability to bench press 80 pounds for 10 reps today.

Although it is important to understand the distinctions among these self-perception terms for research purposes, for practical purposes (e.g., for physical educators), the subtle differences among the terms are not as crucial. The terms are clearly related, as each describes a slightly different aspect of a person's self-perceptions. All of the concepts have something to do with children's views of and feelings about themselves, and so all are likely to have some kind of influence on their motivation and eventual performance in physical education. In this chapter, when referring to a particular theory or a specific research study, the self-perception term that is the actual focus of the theory or study will be used. But when summarizing the results of several studies that examined different self-perception concepts, or when discussing the practical application of self-perception theories and studies, the term "self-perceptions" will be used.

Self-Perception Theories

In the next section, two self-perception theories will be described: Susan Harter's **competence motivation theory** (1978, 1981) and Albert Bandura's (1986, 1997) **self-efficacy theory.** These two theories, one that focuses on perceptions of competence and the other on self-efficacy, have often been used in research with children in educational and movement settings.

Competence Motivation Theory

Harter (1978, 1981) asserts that an individual's domain-specific perceptions of competence have a major influence on that person's emotions and competence motivation in achievement situations related to that domain. **Competence motivation** is one's desire to show mastery and make task attempts—one's motivation and effort. A person's **perceptions of control,** beliefs about who or what controls one's performance or learning, are also proposed to affect that person's emotions and competence motivation. Specifically, high perceptions of competence and internal perceptions of control (believing that factors influencing my performance are within my control, like my effort) in a domain yield positive emotions and high competence motivation. Conversely, low perceived competence and external perceptions of control (believing that the causes of my performance are outside of my control, like the weather, other students, the teacher) produce negative emotions and low motivation.

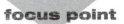

According to competence motivation theory, high perceptions of competence and internal perceptions of control in a domain yield positive emotions and high competence motivation.

Factors influencing perceptions of competence and control

According to this theory, several factors can affect one's perceptions of competence and control, including performance outcomes, feedback and reinforcement from significant others, and one's motivational and goal orientations.

Performance outcomes. Experiencing success on **optimally challenging tasks,** those that are not too hard or too easy for an individual, will enhance the person's emotions and perceptions of competence and lead to more internal perceptions of control. But failure on mastery attempts (attempts to learn and be successful at a task) can result in negative emotions, low perceptions of competence, and external perceptions of control. Most important, this theory predicts that success on very easy tasks may not positively affect perceived competence, and could actually decrease it, especially if the person receives excessive praise for that success.

Success on optimally challenging tasks should enhance a person's perceived competence and lead to more internal perceptions of control.

Feedback and reinforcement from significant others. Perceptions of competence and control are also influenced by the type of feedback and reinforcement significant others (e.g., parents, teachers, peers) give for task attempts. Harter asserts that perceptions of competence and internal perceptions of control are enhanced when someone receives positive reinforcement or praise for making task attempts. The person is then encouraged to make more task attempts. However, when someone's task attempts are ignored or even criticized excessively, perceptions of competence and internal control can be harmed.

As mentioned earlier, excessive praise can also hurt perceived competence if given for success on very easy tasks. Praise should be contingent—it should match the student's performance level. Conversely, specific, corrective feedback that conveys information about how to improve one's performance, when accompanied by positive feedback, can enhance perceptions of competence and control. Excessive praise subtly implies that the significant other doesn't believe the student can perform any better, while corrective information implies that the significant other believes the person can get better if adjustments are made.

Motivational and goal orientations. Harter (1978, 1981) further proposes that the type of feedback and reinforcement received from significant others can influence a person's motivational and goal orientations, which in turn affect perceptions of competence and control. Praise and encouragement for mastery task attempts, along with contingent corrective feedback, are believed to help a child develop an **intrinsic motivational orientation** (performing activities to seek challenges, or for one's own curiosity or interest) and a task goal orientation (a self-referenced definition of ability and tendency to set goals to improve oneself and master a task). Conversely, lack of reinforcement, noncontingent feedback, and/or excessive criticism from significant others for task attempts contribute to an **extrinsic motivational orientation** (performing activities to receive external rewards such as trophies or praise from others) and an ego goal orientation (an other-referenced definition of ability and a desire to perform better than others). Perceptions of competence and an internal sense of control are enhanced in children who have an intrinsic motivational orientation and are high in task goal orientation because success for them doesn't depend on others' performances. On the other hand, children with low task orientation, high ego orientation, and high extrinsic motivation are more likely to experience decreased perceptions of competence and control because they focus on how they perform compared to others, which is outside of their control.

The process of competence motivation theory

The process by which perceptions of competence are formed and eventually influence motivation and effort is shown in Exhibit 6.1. Very simply, here is how competence motivation theory would explain the differences in Aaron and John's motivation and effort during the lacrosse unit. Aaron's first few attempts at lacrosse skills are unsuccessful, but Mr. Barry just praises Aaron for his attempts without giving him feedback on how to perform the skills correctly. This inappropriate reinforcement strengthens Aaron's ego goal orientation, along with his extrinsic motivational orientation. All of these things contribute to external perceptions of control and low perceived competence for Aaron in lacrosse, which then leads

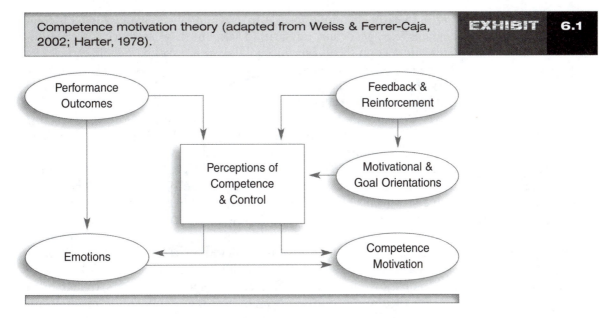

EXHIBIT   6.1

Competence motivation theory (adapted from Weiss & Ferrer-Caja, 2002; Harter, 1978).

to his low motivation and effort and negative affect. If this process happens frequently for Aaron during physical education, it could negatively impact his perceived competence and motivation. Conversely, John experiences early success on the lacrosse skills, even though the tasks are somewhat difficult for him. Mr. Barry praises John for his attempts, while still giving him some feedback on how to do even better. Mr. Barry's actions reinforce John's task goal orientation and intrinsic motivational orientation. All of these factors contribute to internal perceptions of control and high perceptions of competence for John, and thus, high motivation and effort and positive affect.

Multidimensional and developmental nature of competence motivation

Because perceptions of competence are specific to various domains (e.g., physical, social, cognitive), Harter (1978, 1981) predicts that children's competence motivation will vary with the achievement domain. So, although Aaron may have low perceptions of competence, an external perception of control, and low motivation in physical education, he may have high perceived competence, an internal perception of control, and high motivation in music or science.

Harter further proposes that certain constructs in the competence motivation model, like perceptions of competence, vary according to age. For instance, as children become older, they are able to distinguish their perceptions of competence among an increasing number of domains (Harter,

focus point

Perceived competence levels can vary in different achievement domains.

1999). In early childhood (ages 4 to 7), children can identify five different domains (e.g., academic, physical, social), but they cannot consistently differentiate among them. But during adolescence, young people can clearly distinguish their competence in nine different domains. In addition, their perceptions of competence, at least in the academic domain, tend to decline and become more accurate with age (Stipek & MacIver, 1989).

Two major factors are believed to contribute to these age-related changes in perceived competence. First, as children become older, they develop the cognitive capacity to distinguish between ability and effort as the causes of their performances (Fry & Duda, 1997). So, young children tend to have high perceptions of competence because they believe that high effort means high ability, while older children's perceived competence levels may be lower because they know that high effort sometimes means low ability. Second, the sources that children rely on to provide information about their competence are believed to change as they get older (Stipek & MacIver, 1989). Young children tend to rely on task mastery and feedback from adults, without comparison to their peers, to help them develop their perceptions of competence; older children compare themselves to their peers and use less task mastery and adult feedback. This results in young children developing higher and less accurate perceptions of competence.

Thus, competence motivation theory provides valuable information about various influences on perceptions of competence, how perceptions of competence affect motivation and performance in different domains, and the developmental nature of perceived competence. Conversely, self-efficacy theory helps us understand more situation-specific confidence and the particular factors that can affect self-efficacy.

Self-Efficacy Theory

According to Albert Bandura (1986, 1997), self-efficacy judgments are important because they influence a person's behaviors, thought patterns, and emotional reactions. High self-efficacy will then positively influence a person's eventual performance when she has the necessary skills and is motivated, or has the incentive, to perform well. Specifically, one's level of self-efficacy is believed to influence behaviors such as choice of tasks, effort on those tasks, and level of persistence when things become difficult. Thought patterns that may be affected by self-efficacy include the types of attributions a person makes, the types and levels of goals that are set, and the degree of worry in which a person engages. Pride, shame, happiness, and sadness are among the emotional reactions that are affected by a person's self-efficacy. See Exhibit 6.2.

It is likely that Josie, from the opening scenario, has low self-efficacy for her ability to perform a particular task on the climbing wall. Her low self-

focus point

Developmental changes in perceptions of competence are probably due to children's changing cognitive abilities and changes in their sources of competence information.

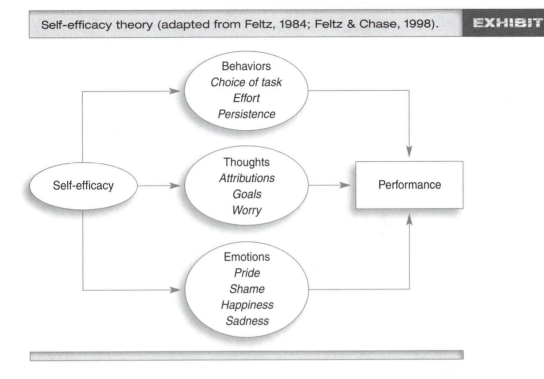

Self-efficacy theory (adapted from Feltz, 1984; Feltz & Chase, 1998).   **EXHIBIT   6.2**

efficacy has obviously affected her behaviors because she refuses to attempt the task; even if she did, she likely would give little effort and give up quickly if she wasn't successful right away. She worries about other students' reactions if she tries climbing the wall and is unsuccessful, but at the same time, she feels shame and sadness for not even trying the task. She attributes her projected failure on the wall to her low ability, leading to even more feelings of shame and sadness. In contrast, Carole has high self-efficacy for climbing the wall. She eagerly makes many attempts at climbing, even after she is initially unsuccessful. Carole attributes her performance on the wall to her high ability, setting new and more challenging goals each time she achieves one goal. She feels a pride and happiness in what she has accomplished. If Carole has the skills needed to climb the wall and is motivated to do well, it is likely she will experience success at climbing the wall.

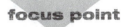

focus point

In self-efficacy theory, self-efficacy judgments can influence a person's choice of tasks, effort, persistence, attributions, goals, worry, emotions, and even performance.

Sources of efficacy information

Individuals are thought to form their self-efficacy beliefs from six sources of information (Bandura, 1986, 1997; Maddux, 1995; Schunk, 1995; see Exhibit 6.3):

- Performance accomplishments
- Vicarious experiences

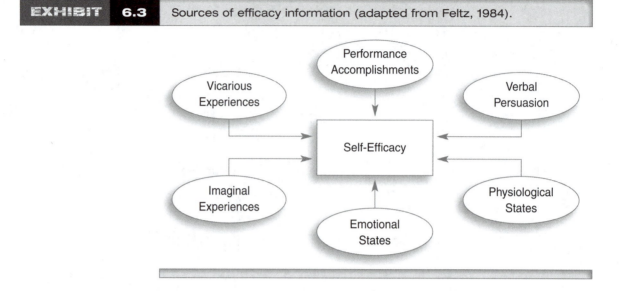

Sources of efficacy information (adapted from Feltz, 1984).

- Verbal persuasion
- Physiological states
- Emotional states
- Imagery

Performance accomplishments. The most influential source of efficacy information is a person's **performance accomplishments** (Bandura, 1986, 1997). Basically, past successes increase self-efficacy, while repeated failures lower it, especially if failures occur early in learning and are not due to low effort or difficult external conditions. Aaron may have low self-efficacy related to lacrosse due to past unsuccessful experiences with activities requiring other long-handled implements (e.g., floor hockey, golf) and his lack of immediate success on the lacrosse skills. Conversely, his buddy, John, may have higher self-efficacy for learning lacrosse because he had past successes on similar tasks and has initial success at the lacrosse tasks.

Vicarious experiences. Another influence on an individual's self-efficacy are **vicarious experiences,** or modeling (Bandura, 1986, 1997). Observing someone similar to oneself perform a task or skill successfully can enhance self-efficacy, while seeing a similar person perform unsuccessfully can decrease self-efficacy. Although not as powerful an influence on self-efficacy as one's own performances, vicarious experiences can have a big impact with younger students and students who lack experience with a task because they lack prior performance accomplishments by which to judge their ability. Vicarious experiences can also sway a person's self-efficacy if

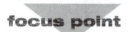

focus point

Of the six sources of information that help form self-efficacy beliefs, performance accomplishments are the most influential.

the results of past experiences with a task or skill have been mixed, with some successes and some failures. Essentially, the idea is "If Susie can do this skill, and she's like me, I should be able to do it, too!" In physical education, one way modeling is used is in the demonstrations of skills or tasks during task presentations. According to self-efficacy theory, these demonstrations would positively affect self-efficacy if successful and performed by students similar to the ones observing. Perhaps Aaron's self-efficacy related to lacrosse skills is low in part because Mr. Barry himself demonstrated all of the lacrosse skills and tasks and Aaron cannot relate to him.

Verbal persuasion. Another source of self-efficacy information is **verbal persuasion,** in which significant others like teachers, parents, and peers try to convince students that they have the ability to be successful at a task (Bandura, 1986, 1997). This persuasion may be either motivational statements ("Come on and try it. I know you can do it!") or informational feedback about how to perform a task or skill ("Remember to keep your wrist stiff"; Standage & Duda, 2004). Although not as strong an influence as one's performance accomplishments, verbal persuasion can increase effort and is most effective with students who have reason to believe that they can be successful. In fact, Bandura cautions against raising unrealistically high self-efficacy beliefs in individuals through verbal persuasion because subsequent failure will discredit the persuader (e.g., teacher) and negatively impact self-efficacy. Verbal persuasion is also a stronger influence if the significant other is an expert, genuine, and trustworthy. Mr. Barry does not try to convince Aaron that he can be successful at lacrosse, or give him helpful feedback on how to improve his skills, which may contribute to the boy's low self-efficacy.

Physiological states. A fourth source of efficacy information are one's **physiological states,** which refers to how a person views the body's responses (e.g., increased heart rate, being out of breath, muscle fatigue and soreness) to task attempts or stressful situations (Bandura, 1986, 1997). If a student perceives these responses as signs of physical inadequacy, her self-efficacy will likely decrease. However, if these physiological states are perceived as normal responses to physical challenges, her self-efficacy will increase, or at least not be harmed. Josie interprets the "butterflies" in her stomach and the sweaty palms she experiences when faced with the wall climbing tasks as signs that she isn't physically capable of climbing the wall, which contributes to her low self-efficacy. Viewing those states as the body's normal way of preparing for a new challenge, responses everyone experiences, will help prevent those physiological states from negatively impacting Josie's self-efficacy. As a person trains and the body adapts to the physical challenge, she should perceive different physiological states, which can affect her self-efficacy. For example, a stu-

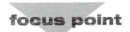

focus point

Vicarious experiences are more powerful sources of efficacy information for students who lack experience on a skill (e.g., young children) or who had mixed past performance outcomes.

focus point

Verbal persuasion should only be used with students the teacher truly believes can master a task because failure will harm the teacher's credibility and the student's self-efficacy.

focus point

Help students perceive physiological responses to task attempts (e.g., increased heart rate, sweating, and breathing) as normal, not as signs of inadequacy.

dent may perceive less effort in running a 10-minute mile at the end of the year than at the start of the year, which should enhance her self-efficacy.

Emotional states. A person's **emotional state,** or mood, can also influence her self-efficacy (Maddux, 1995; Schunk, 1995). Positive emotional states like happiness, exhilaration, and tranquility are more likely to enhance self-efficacy than negative affect such as sadness, anxiety, and depression (Maddux & Meier, 1995). As with physiological states, negative emotions are probably interpreted by a person as a sign she is not capable of performing the task. Along with Josie's regular feelings of anxiety during physical education, on the first day of wall climbing she had earned an unexpected low score on a spelling test in the previous class period. One can see how her negative mood might contribute to low self-efficacy for climbing the wall.

Imaginal experiences. Using **imagery** to see oneself or similar others performing successfully or unsuccessfully on a task one is about to perform is one more source of efficacy information (Maddux, 1995). Simply speaking, imagery is "using all the senses to create or re-create an experience mentally" (Gill, 2000, p. 181). A positive image is likely to enhance self-efficacy, while a negative image will decrease it. Perhaps Mr. Barry could help Josie and Aaron feel more confident in their abilities if he helped them use imagery to mentally experience success on their respective tasks before they actually tried the tasks.

Although these sources of competence information were presented individually, they likely do not act in isolation from each other. A student's bad mood might lead her to interpret her increased heart rate negatively; a teacher's verbal persuasion in the form of informational feedback may result in a student's successful performance. According to self-efficacy theory, the more sources teachers can positively influence, the greater the impact on student self-efficacy.

Self-Perceptions Research

Numerous studies have been conducted with children that examine the principles of competence motivation and self-efficacy theories, along with other self-perception concepts. This section reviews this research, giving special attention to studies conducted with children in physical education. Research with children conducted in other movement settings like youth sport will also be described when it furthers your understanding of children's self-perceptions and how they might be enhanced.

One area of research deals with how the different characteristics of children might influence the various self-perceptions, while another area is concerned with the accuracy of children's perceptions of competence.

focus point

Promoting positive emotions or moods during physical education class might positively impact students' self-efficacy.

focus point

Using imagery to see oneself accomplish a task could enhance a student's self-efficacy.

Researchers have examined the sources of information children use to decide on their competence levels, along with all of the factors that might affect the sources used. The relationships among various psychological factors (attributions, emotions, perceived importance, dispositional ability conceptions) and self-perceptions are explored, as well as how self-perceptions are related to motivated behaviors and physical activity participation. The impact of various instructional models on student self-perceptions and performance accomplishments is another area of research examined.

Student Characteristics

One primary area of research focuses on how various student characteristics relate to self-perceptions. Children's age, gender, race, and disabilities have all been examined to see how these variables might influence self-perceptions.

Age

Developmental differences in perceptions of competence are predicted by competence motivation theory, and researchers have found that perceptions of academic competence decline with age (Stipek & MacIver, 1989). But research regarding physical perceptions of competence and related constructs shows mixed results. Although some studies in non-physical education settings show that physical self-confidence and perceptions of competence decline with age (Marsh, 1989; Ulrich, 1987; Yun & Ulrich, 1997), other studies failed to reveal such decreases (Eccles, Wigfield, Harold, & Blumenfeld, 1993; Feltz & Brown, 1984; Marsh, 1998; Rudisill, Mahar, & Meaney, 1993) or even document increases (Duncan & Duncan, 1991). In physical education, Lirgg (1993) found that middle school students were more confident than high school students in their ability to learn basketball skills during class. Other research specific to physical education, however, shows that children's perceptions of their general ability in physical education do not differ by age (Dunn, 2000; Xiang & Lee, 1998; Xiang, Lee, & Williamson, 2001). Perhaps the less competitive, more inclusive nature of physical education settings (i.e., all children participate) results in stable perceptions of competence in this domain over the years. Until we have more definitive information, physical educators should at least be aware that the physical perceived competence levels of some students might decline as they get older, which might contribute to older students' decreased effort in class.

Gender

Most studies show that boys have higher physical self-perceptions than girls (e.g., Biddle et al., 1993; Black & Weiss, 1992; Eccles et al., 1993; Marsh, 1989; Williams & Gill, 1995). This has been found in children as early as 1st grade (Eccles et al., 1993), in children of different ethnic groups (Hagger, Ashford, & Stambulova, 1998; Morgan et al., 2003; Van Dongen-Melman, Koot, & Verhulst, 1993), in physically awkward children (Dunn & Watkinson, 1994), in children with developmental coordination disorder (Cairney, Hay, Faught, Mandigo, & Flouris, 2005), and with play, informal recreational, and formal competitive activities (Mullan, Albinson, & Markland, 1997). In children with intellectual disabilities, girls showed lower perceptions of competence than boys, but not until 12 years of age (Yun & Ulrich, 1997).

Some studies indicate that one reason for this gender difference in perceptions of competence might be the children's actual motor skill levels (Marsh, 1998; Rudisill et al., 1993). For instance, Rudisill et al. (1993) found that although upper elementary boys had higher motor skill perceptions of competence than girls that age, the boys also performed better on the actual motor skill tests. So, it makes sense that the boys had higher perceived competence levels than the girls.

focus point

Some research shows that students' self-perceptions in physical education decline with age, and girls have lower self-perceptions than boys.

As with age differences, some research indicates that there may be something about the physical education setting that results in smaller gender differences in perceptions of competence than in other settings (e.g., Dunn, 2000; Shapiro & Ulrich, 2002; Xiang et al., 2001). This is most clearly illustrated in a study by Shapiro and Ulrich (2002), who found that 10- to 13-year-old boys, some with and some without learning disabilities, had higher physical perceptions of competence than similar girls at recess and at home, but not in physical education classes. Physical educators should be aware that girls might have lower self-perceptions related to motor skills than boys, but that ensuring that girls improve their skill levels could help with this.

Ethnicity

Research on possible ethnic group differences in physical self-perceptions is limited. Hagger et al. (1998) found few differences between the physical self-perceptions of Russian and British 13- to 14-year-olds, while Morgan et al. (2003) discovered that Mexican American adolescents had lower physical self-perceptions than European Americans. Obviously, more research is needed on this topic, and at this point, physical educators should simply look for any students, regardless of ethnic group, who might need a boost in their confidence in class.

Children with disabilities or other difficulties

The self-perceptions of children with various disabilities have been examined, including learning disabilities and several types of motor coordination difficulties and obesity. When comparing children who have learning disabilities with those who do not, no differences in 3rd and 4th graders' perceptions of athletic competence (Smith & Nagle, 1995) or in 10- to 13-year-olds' perceptions of physical competence (Shapiro & Ulrich, 2001, 2002) have been found.

Children with motor coordination difficulties (Cairney et al., 2005; Rose, Larkin, & Berger, 1997) and obesity (Southall, Okely, & Steele, 2004) have been shown to have lower physical self-perceptions than children without those difficulties. Of interest, Southall et al. (2004) found that although overweight children did score lower on locomotor skills tests, they performed equally well on the object control motor skills, so actual motor competence did not account for all of the perceived competence differences. Dunn and Watkinson (1994) further found that perceptions of physical competence decreased in 3rd graders as physical awkwardness increased; but in 5th and 6th graders, perceived competence actually increased along with awkwardness severity. The researchers believed that the older children who were physically awkward had developed strategies to protect their perceptions of competence, such as only comparing their physical abilities to those of other physically awkward children and using self-information (e.g., their effort and attitude) to decide on their competence levels.

Perhaps physical educators can enhance the self-perceptions of overweight children and children with movement difficulties by helping them use more self-information to decide on their competence levels (as suggested by Dunn & Watkinson, 1994) and helping them set goals, focusing on their own improvement and effort. More research, conducted with a greater age range of children and with other disabilities, is definitely needed before fully understanding the self-perceptions of children with difficulties in physical education.

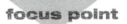

focus point

Current research shows that although the self-perceptions of students with learning disabilities do not differ from students without those disabilities, obese and poorly coordinated students tend to have lower self-perceptions.

Accuracy of Self-Perceptions

Some researchers compared children's perceptions of their motor competence with their actual motor competence, assessed either through teacher/coach ratings of their ability or the children's performance on a motor skill test. Most studies show that positive correlations between measures of perceived and actual physical competence get stronger as children become older, meaning they become more accurate in judging their competence (e.g., Feltz & Brown, 1984; Horn & Weiss, 1991; McKiddie & Maynard, 1997; Xiang & Lee, 1998; Yun & Ulrich, 1997).

Besides age, other factors that may be related to the accuracy of children's competency judgments are gender and various psychological characteristics. Several researchers have found no gender differences in children's accuracy of judging their competence (Goodway & Rudisill, 1997; Horn & Weiss, 1991; McKiddie & Maynard, 1997). But in another study, 8- to 9-year-old boys in physical education overestimated their abilities more than girls that age, while 13- to 14-year-old girls overestimated their abilities more than their male cohorts (Chase, 2001a). McKiddie and Maynard (1997) further found that 14- to 15-year-old boys—but not 11- to 12-year-old boys—were more accurate than girls in judging their competence in physical education. In another study with 8- to 13-year-old children participating in a summer motor skill instructional program, gender differences were found in the relationships between some psychological characteristics and the accuracy of the children's ability judgments (Weiss & Horn, 1990). Girls who underestimated their motor skill competence level preferred less challenging skills, experienced higher anxiety, and perceived higher levels of external control over their performances than accurate or overestimating girls. Boys who underestimated their ability, however, perceived higher levels of unknown control (i.e., could not identify the factors controlling their performance outcomes) than their accurate or overestimating male peers, but were similar on perceived external control.

The results of these studies indicate teachers can expect students to become more accurate in judging their competence in physical education as they get older. Boys and girls may differ in their accuracy based on their age, with younger elementary-aged girls being more accurate and older elementary boys being more accurate. Physical educators should be alert to children who underestimate their competence; they should help underestimating girls reduce their anxiety and choose challenging tasks, and help underestimating boys and girls focus on internal factors like effort that may affect their performance.

Sources of Competence Information

Both the competence motivation and self-efficacy theories propose that people use a variety of sources when judging their competence levels, and the research in youth sport and physical education settings has found support for four of the proposed sources: past performances, vicarious experiences, emotional states, and verbal persuasion. The effects of age, gender, perceived competence accuracy, various psychological characteristics, skill or experience level, perceived motivational climate, and perceived parent beliefs have all been examined to determine how they might affect the sources of competence information used.

Age

Many researchers in both youth sport and physical education settings have found that the age-related increases in perceived competence accuracy could be influenced by age-related differences in the sources of information children use to determine their competence. The results of several

focus point

Children tend to become more accurate in judging their physical competence as they get older—lower elementary girls may be more accurate than their male peers, while upper elementary boys may be more accurate than their female peers.

studies indicate that elementary children and high school juniors and seniors tend to use past performances to judge their competence level in sport and physical education more than early adolescents (e.g., Chase, 1998; Horn, Glenn, & Wentzell, 1993; Horn & Hasbrook, 1986; Horn & Weiss, 1991). But the elementary children and late adolescents used different forms of past performances. Elementary children used game outcomes, effort, simple participation in activities, and even their behavior in physical education class (e.g., "I am good at skills because I listen to the teacher and follow directions") to determine their competence (Chase, 1998; Horn & Hasbrook, 1986; Horn & Weiss, 1991; Xiang et al., 2001), while older high school students tended to use more self-referenced information like skill improvement, their perceptions of their own natural ability, and effort (Horn et al., 1993; Xiang et al., 2001).

Vicarious experiences, mostly by children comparing themselves to their peers, are another source of competence information supported by research whose use tends to vary by age. Most researchers have found that early adolescents tend to use peer comparison more than younger children to judge their ability in physical activity settings (Chase, 1998; Horn & Hasbrook, 1986; Horn & Weiss, 1991; McKiddie & Maynard, 1997).

Another source of competence information supported by research is children's emotional states, and the use of this source also appears to be age-related. Studies indicate that elementary children and older high school students will use their level of attraction to an activity and enjoyment more than early adolescents to determine their competence in physical activities (Horn et al., 1993; Horn & Hasbrook, 1986; Horn & Weiss, 1991; McKiddie & Maynard, 1997).

Two sources of competence information proposed by self-efficacy theory have not been mentioned by children in research thus far: physiological states and imaginal experiences. Either children do not use these sources or they are not aware they are using them. For instance, when a child remembers past performances in deciding his competence level, he may be visualizing those performances as he remembers. Although imagined experiences have not been mentioned by children in past research as an important source of competence information, several studies show that imagery can positively affect children's motor skill performance (Li-Wei, Qi-Wei, Orlick, & Zitzelsberger, 1992; Porretta & Surburg, 1995; Screws & Surburg, 1997; Wrisberg & Anshel, 1989),

connected | **CONCEPTS**

Verbal persuasion is another source of competence information found by researchers to be used by children and to have age-related differences (see Chapter 2). Specifically, elementary children have a stronger preference for feedback from significant adults than older children. Early adolescents (e.g., middle school students) preferred to use information from their peers more so than older and younger children; they would also use the teacher's behaviors to determine their competence. This means that physical educators must ensure that their behaviors do not implicitly convey a belief that students have low ability (e.g., only using high-skilled students to do demonstrations or be coaches in sport education).

 **focus point**

Research shows children use four of the six proposed sources of information in deciding their physical competence: past performances, verbal persuasion, vicarious experiences, and emotional states.

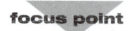

which may then influence their self-perceptions. In addition, even though they do not name imagined experiences or physiological states as sources, children could still learn to use these sources to enhance their perceptions of competence. A physical educator could teach her students that an increased heart rate and sweaty palms are evidence they are ready to perform a task and not a sign they cannot do the task. Similarly, children might be taught how to use positive imagery (e.g., imagining a past successful performance) to enhance their self-efficacy.

One conclusion that can be made from the research conducted thus far is that children start relying heavily on information from peers to judge their competence while in middle school. This is different than elementary children, who use evidence like their class behaviors, game outcome, participation, attraction to sport, and effort, and upper high school students, who seem to use more self-referenced information (e.g., improvement, effort, and enjoyment). In physical education, this means that early adolescents compare their performance to their classmates and rely on feedback from their classmates. Although this can enhance a highly skilled student's self-perceptions, it can be detrimental to many students' self-perceptions because there will almost always be someone better than them in something. Physical educators can help students of all ages, but especially middle school students, focus on their own performance instead of comparing themselves to their peers in several ways. Decreasing the time spent waiting in line for a task attempt and arranging tasks so everyone is practicing at the same time decreases the possibility of peer comparison. Peer comparison can be decreased by helping students set individual goals for skill improvement and praising such improvement, not just praising students when they win games or do better than others.

Gender

In studies with children below age 14, no gender differences were found in the sources children used to judge their competence in movement settings (Horn & Hasbrook, 1986; Horn & Weiss, 1991; McKiddie & Maynard, 1997). Older females, however, have been shown to use self-comparison, internal information, and feedback from important adults more than males, while males used more competitive outcomes (e.g., win/loss records and performance statistics) as well as their perceived ease of learning new skills to judge their competence (Horn et al., 1993; McKiddie & Maynard, 1997). Perhaps children need to reach a certain age before males and females use different sources. High school physical educators should be aware that boys and girls might use different types of information to decide on their ability level in class. Boys especially should be encouraged to use more self-referenced information, and to rely less on game outcomes, as the basis for their perceived competence.

Accuracy of self-perceptions

The degree of accuracy with which children judge their competence level could be related to the information sources they use. Some researchers found that children who accurately estimate their motor skill ability levels tend to use peer comparison and evaluation to determine their ability, while under- or overestimators use self-comparison information (e.g., skill improvement over time and speed in learning new skills) and feedback from important adults like their teacher (Horn & Weiss, 1991; McKiddie & Maynard, 1997). Conversely, Weiss and Amorose (2005) discovered that children who are inaccurate estimators of their competence use primarily external information (e.g., game outcome, peer comparison and evaluation), while the accurate estimators use a variety of sources, both external and self-referenced criteria.

Comparisons to others and other external criteria are likely to decrease motivation and effort in lower skilled students because the comparisons are unlikely to be favorable. Because most physical educators value high student motivation and effort, it is probably more desirable to encourage students to use self-information and teacher feedback than to promote peer comparison.

Psychological characteristics

Some researchers have examined whether the sources of competence information children use vary with their levels of perceived competence and control and anxiety. These researchers discovered that children with high perceptions of competence and low competitive trait anxiety (one's predisposition to experience low anxiety in competitive situations) prefer to use internal, self-criteria (e.g., effort, skill improvement, and ease of learning) over other sources to decide their competence (Horn & Hasbrook, 1987; Weiss, Ebbeck, & Horn, 1997). Conversely, children with an external perception of control tend to use game outcome and children with high anxiety usually use their level of pregame anxiety to judge their competence.

These findings suggest that physical educators should help children with higher levels of anxiety and external perceptions of control use more internal, self-related criteria like effort and skill improvement to decide on their competence level, rather than game outcome or their perception of anxiety. Students can also be taught some simple relaxation techniques (e.g., taking deep breaths, using positive self-statements) to help them control their anxiety.

Experience level

Children's level of experience with activities appears to affect the sources of competence information they use, at least in youth sport settings.

Among 7- to 10- and 12- to 14-year-old female softball players, those with at least one season of previous experience playing softball relied more on a player's actual swing technique and less on the coaches' feedback than girls with no previous playing experience when deciding on the ability level of girls they watched on video batting a ball (Amorose & Smith, 2003). Physical educators need to be aware that students with less experience in a motor skill or physical activity are likely to place high importance on the teachers' feedback; thus, teachers should be especially careful with that feedback.

Perceptions of the motivational climate

Halliburton and Weiss (2002) found that the sources of competence information preferred by 12- to 14-year-old competitive gymnasts were related to their perceptions of the motivational climate. Specifically, perceptions of a task-involving climate (focus on individual improvement, using a self-referenced definition of success) were associated with the use of self-referenced sources of information like effort and enjoyment, but negatively related to the use of peer comparison, performance during competition, and learning/improvement of skills. Gymnasts with high perceptions of an ego-involving climate (focus on performing better than others and a normative definition of success) tended to use peer comparison, performance in competition, and learning or improvement to judge their competence, but rarely used their own enjoyment and effort. These results indicate that promoting a task-involving climate in physical education, in which children are encouraged to improve their own performance and avoid comparison to peers, encourages children to use more self-referenced criteria to decide on their ability level.

Perceptions of parent beliefs

In an interesting study by Babkes and Weiss (1999), children's perceptions of their parents' beliefs and actions were related to the sources of competence information used by the children. Youth soccer players (about 9–12 years old) who perceived their parents were positive role models of exercise participation and who believed their parents had positive perceptions of and responses to the child's soccer ability, had higher perceptions of their competence and used more internal, self-referenced sources of competence information than children with less positive perceptions of their parents' actions and beliefs. Physical educators can encourage parents—via physical education newsletters, regular reports of physical education activities, e-mails, phone calls, or conferences—to participate with their children in physical activities, because parents' perceived degree of participation can influence their children's self-perceptions and the sources of competence information children use.

focus point

Research shows the sources of information children use to determine their physical competence vary depending on the children's accuracy of their judgments, perceptions of control, perceived competence and anxiety levels, experience in an activity, perceived motivational climate, and perceptions of their parents' beliefs regarding physical activity.

Psychological Factors Related to Self-Perceptions

Researchers have identified several psychological factors that are associated with various self-perceptions. Among them are children's attributions, emotions, perceived importance of skills and activities, and beliefs about the nature of motor skill ability.

Attributions

The reasons children give for their performance outcomes, or their attributions, have been shown to be related to their self-perceptions. In general, children with high perceptions of competence or success tend to identify more internal, stable, and personally controllable reasons for their performances than children with lower perceptions of competence (Chase, 2001b; Fielstein et al., 1985; Robinson & Howe, 1989; Vlachopoulos & Biddle, 1997; Weigand & Broadhurst, 1998; Weiss, McAuley, Ebbeck, & Wiese, 1990). For example, Chase (2001b) found that 3rd, 5th, and 8th grade children with low self-efficacy on a physical education task tended to attribute their failure to low ability, while children with high self-efficacy attributed their failure to lack of effort. Help children with low self-perceptions attribute their performance outcomes to factors they can control, like their level of effort or the strategies they use to practice.

connected   CONCEPTS

Research reviewed in Chapter 5 indicates that high task orientation is associated with high self-perceptions, while the relationship between ego orientation and self-perceptions is unclear. So, establishing a task-involving physical education climate could enhance students' self-perceptions.

Emotions and perceptions of importance

Other researchers have examined how children's emotions and their perceptions of the importance of motor skills and physical ability are related to their self-perceptions. The results of these studies show that high self-perceptions tend to be associated with high levels of positive affect and enjoyment, low levels of negative affect, as well as high perceptions of usefulness, importance, and value placed on skills and activities (Ebbeck & Stuart, 1993; Ebbeck & Weiss, 1998; Shapiro & Ulrich, 2002; Stephens, 1998; Vlachopoulos & Biddle, 1997).

Physical educators can help all children experience success by using strategies like developmentally appropriate tasks and individual goal setting. But teachers can also help children recognize when they are successful in physical education by clearly defining success, because some children may not believe they were successful even if the teacher thinks so. For instance, a student who improves the number of laps she completes in the PACER cardiovascular fitness test from 21 to 27 might not believe she was successful because she compares herself to her friend who completed 45 laps, so the teacher must emphasize that such an improvement is quite significant and demonstrates success. Experiencing and recognizing success can help children have positive emotional experiences in physical education, and should enhance their self-perceptions.

Children must be taught the usefulness and importance of motor skills that are practiced in physical education. At times, physical educators have students practice skills and tasks without any explanation of how the skills will help them in life or simply how the skill will help their game playing ability. The importance can be explained during the set induction at the start of class, before students begin practicing individual tasks, or at the end of class during the closure. When children perceive they have been successful at skills they value and believe are important, their self-perceptions may be enhanced.

Dispositional ability conceptions

Individuals can hold different beliefs about the nature of motor ability, referred to as dispositional ability conceptions (Dweck, 1999, 2002). One belief is that ability is fixed and unchangeable (an **entity conception**), while another belief is that ability is changeable and can be improved with effort and practice (an **incremental conception**).

The type of dispositional ability conceptions students hold can influence their self-perceptions. Students with an incremental view of ability, for instance, should have higher self-perceptions than students with an entity view because those with the incremental view believe that even if they cannot do a skill right now, they might master it in the future with practice. In fact, 11- to 15-year-olds' perceptions of physical competence have been shown to be positively related to their incremental beliefs about ability (Wang & Biddle, 2001; Wang et al., 2002) and negatively related to their entity beliefs (Wang & Biddle, 2001). Similarly, college males and females with incremental views of ability had higher perceptions of competence than those with entity views (Solmon, Lee, Belcher, Harrison, & Wells, 2003).

Because the incremental view of ability appears more likely to enhance self-perceptions than the entity view, emphasize the positive impact effort and practice can have on students' motor skills. Even though students may not become the best in their class in an activity, they need help understanding that they can always improve their skill level.

focus point

Children with high physical self-perceptions often exhibit the following attributes: make personally controllable attributions, believe motor activities are valuable, experience positive emotions, and hold an incremental view of ability.

connected   CONCEPTS

Research reviewed in Chapter 9 shows that high self-perceptions are associated with high levels of intrinsic motivation and low levels of amotivation.

Self-Perceptions and Motivated Behaviors

According to the competence motivation and self-efficacy theories, self-perceptions should positively influence a person's motivated behaviors (choice of tasks, effort, and persistence) in achievement situations like physical education, and several studies support this (Chase, 2001b; Ferrer-Caja & Weiss, 2000; Sarrazin, Roberts et al., 2002). For example, high school students with high perceptions of competence in physical education had higher levels of effort and persistence than students with low perceptions of competence (Ferrer-Caja & Weiss, 2000). Thus, one important reason to strive to enhance students' self-perceptions in physical education is the positive impact it could have on their motivated behaviors and possibly learning.

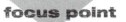

focus point

Students with high self-perceptions in physical education are more likely to show high effort and persistence in class, as well as choose more difficult tasks.

Self-Perceptions and Physical Activity Participation

One goal of physical education programs is to help children value and become regularly physically active. There is considerable evidence that students with high self-perceptions are more physically active than those with low self-perceptions (e.g., Biddle, Whitehead, O'Donovan, & Nevill, 2005; Dishman, Motl, Saunders et al., 2005; Dunton, Jamner, & Cooper, 2003; Guinn et al., 2000; Hagger et al., 1998; Morgan et al., 2003; Parish & Treasure, 2003; Raudsepp, Liblik, & Hannus, 2002; Sallis, Prochaska, & Taylor, 2000; Tremblay, Inman, & Williams, 2000; Wang & Biddle, 2001; Watkinson, Dwyer, & Nielsen, 2005; Welk, 1999; Welk & Schaben, 2004). For instance, various types of self-concept increased as teenaged girls' physical activity increased (Dunton et al., 2003), and 12- to 15-year-olds who were considered poorly motivated toward physical activity exhibited low perceptions of competence (Wang & Biddle, 2001). Other researchers found that adolescents with greater confidence in their ability to continue with an exercise program (self-efficacy toward exercise) tended to be more consistent exercisers than adolescents with lower confidence (Maddison & Prapavessis, 2006; Nigg & Courneya, 1998; Prapavessis, Maddison, & Brading, 2004). Similarly, 6th graders' self-efficacy in overcoming barriers to physical activity was positively related to their physical activity during the summer and winter months (Loucaides, Chedzoy, Bennett, & Walshe, 2004). Recently, Marsh and his colleagues found a reciprocal relationship between school-aged (primary, middle, and secondary) students' self-perceptions and their physical activity levels (Marsh, Papaioannou, & Theodorakis, 2006). Specifically, high physical self-concepts at the beginning of a school year were associated with high exercise levels at the end of the year, and high exercise levels at the start of the school year led to higher physical self-concepts at the end of the school year.

Other researchers found that self-perceptions are positively related to other psychological factors, which in turn predict students' physical activity. For example, 9- to 14-year-olds' perceptions of competence did not directly account for their activity levels; rather, perceived competence positively influenced the students' attraction to physical activity, which in turn had a positive effect on their activity levels (Paxton, Estabrooks, &

Dzewaltowski, 2004). Sixth and 8th grade girls' self-efficacy about physical activity positively influenced their use of self-management strategies like positive self-talk regarding exercise and finding ways to make exercise more enjoyable; the use of those self-management strategies then positively influenced the girls' activity levels (Dishman, Motl, Sallis et al., 2005).

The research indicates that students' self-perceptions may impact their physical activity participation, even if indirectly, by affecting other psychological or behavioral factors. The opposite also appears to be true; high levels of physical activity can lead to high self-perceptions. It is vital to students' activity levels that physical educators create an environment to enhance students' self-perceptions. Help students believe they can overcome obstacles to being physically active by describing various options for physical activity participation and working with students to develop strategies for being active when barriers arise.

focus point

Children with higher self-perceptions are more likely to be physically active than children with lower self-perceptions.

Self-Perceptions and Instructional Models

The impact of various instructional models on school-aged children's self-efficacy and motor skill performance has been examined in several studies. Some researchers examined the impact of the "Team Building Through Physical Challenges" (TBPC) program, consisting of cooperative activities, on the self-conceptions of 6th and 7th grade students in physical education (Ebbeck & Gibbons, 1998). Shortly after the start of the school year, students in four physical education classes were randomly assigned to either a TBPC group (one 6th and one 7th grade class) or control group (the other 6th and 7th grade classes). The TBPC classes received regular physical education, except that on every other Friday, team-building activities were performed. An example of such a physical challenge, which could be one of three difficulty levels, was "Try to balance your entire group on an automobile tire." The control group participated in regular physical education without any team building. The TBPC had a positive impact on the students' self-perceptions—before the intervention, the control and TBPC groups did not differ on any of six self-perception scores, but after the intervention, males in the TBPC group scored higher than males in the control group in four self-perception areas, while TBPC females scored higher than control females in all six self-perception areas. The results of other studies also show that cooperative activities, either alone or combined with peer teaching, can positively impact students' success, which may then enhance their self-perceptions (Barrett, 2005; Dyson, 2001; Johnson & Ward, 2001; Mender et al., 1982).

In a review of research on peer-assisted learning strategies, Ward and Lee (2005) report that peer teaching enhanced various measures of student performance, which may help students feel more competent; some of the studies included in the review involved students with disabilities in inclusive physical education settings. When the personal and social responsibility model was applied in an adapted martial arts program, the therapists and parents of five young boys with spastic diplegic cerebral palsy believed the program increased the boys' sense of ability (Wright et al., 2004). Other studies indicate sport education, whether implemented alone or in combination with conflict resolution and personal responsibility strategies (e.g., the Sport for Peace model), may enhance teachers' and students' perceptions of success (Alexander, Taggart, & Thorpe, 1996; Ennis, 1999; Ennis et al., 1999).

Working with others to achieve results and giving students independence and various responsibilities are elements common among the cooperative learning, peer teaching, sport education, and taking personal and social responsibility models. The fact that these models appear to enhance self-perceptions and performance of a wide variety of students (i.e., students with disabilities, urban students, elementary and high school, males and females) makes their use even more valuable.

Means of Enhancing Self-Perceptions in Physical Education

Competence motivation theory, self-efficacy theory, and related research suggest several ways physical educators can enhance student self-perceptions in physical education.

Help Students Experience Success

A crucial premise in both competence motivation theory and self-efficacy theory is that past performance outcomes have a powerful impact on students' self-perceptions. As a physical educator, you can use several strategies to help students be successful and hopefully enhance their self-perceptions: modify equipment, maximize practice opportunities, provide additional motor skill instruction, and help students perceive success.

Modify equipment

One way to help students be successful is to modify the equipment used in tasks. A study with 9- to 12-year-old recreational basketball players found that lowering the basket improved the children's shooting performance and self-efficacy, while using a smaller basketball enhanced their self-efficacy (Chase, Ewing, Lirgg, & George, 1994). Those aspects of equipment that can be modified include the height of baskets, nets, or balance beams; the size of targets, balls, and rackets; and the material the equipment is made of (e.g., foam paddles, trainer volleyballs, plastic bats).

How do you know whether you should adjust equipment for students? Rink (2002) states that if the equipment being used causes the student to

focus point

There is evidence that instructional models like cooperative learning, peer teaching, personal and social responsibility, sport education, and Sport for Peace enhance students' motor skill performance and self-perceptions.

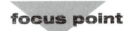

focus point

The use of developmentally appropriate equipment in physical education can enhance children's performance as well as their self-perceptions.

use inappropriate form, the equipment should be modified. For instance, if most 7th graders are having trouble serving the volleyball over the net, lower the net. Of if a 3rd grader is having trouble dribbling a basketball, he can dribble a playground ball. Help your students understand that it is better to use "unofficial" equipment and use proper form than to use "official equipment" and use incorrect form. And just as students might perform slightly different tasks during a class period, you can also help your students to understand that they might use different equipment during class.

Several physical educators are very good at adjusting the equipment to fit the needs of the students.

real world

For example, Barbara P., who taught at an urban elementary school in the southeastern United States, had her lower elementary students use short, foam paddles when working on striking, but her upper elementary students used longer handled, plastic (heavier) rackets when they worked on striking. She also readily changed rackets for students if one type of racket caused them to use poor form. So, lower elementary students who were very skilled at striking and who had the strength were given the longer, plastic rackets to use, while students who had trouble striking with the bigger rackets were given foam paddles. Because this modification of equipment was a regular occurrence in her program and because Barbara continually emphasized to students it was normal for them to use different equipment in the same lesson, they accepted these changes.

Mr. Barry can readily adapt equipment for students like Aaron, perhaps by using whiffle balls instead of official lacrosse balls to practice throwing and shooting, to enhance Aaron's chances for success.

Maximize practice opportunities

Most people know that the best way to improve motor skills is to practice. The more practice attempts students get with a skill, the greater their success. Unfortunately, some physical educators don't maximize practice time for their students. Students wait in line for a turn or participate in large group activities where most of the students stand around and seldom get a chance to make a task attempt for one reason or another. Some may think it is necessary for them to observe every task attempt made by every student in order for the students to improve, but actually student learning can be enhanced when they do not receive feedback about every attempt (Schmidt & Wrisberg, 2000). Other physical educators may prefer a setting where participation is not maximized because they seem more in control of the situation—knowing exactly what every student is doing at any particular time. But with good management techniques, you can set up a classroom that maximizes participation, and thus practice opportunities, while still maintaining order.

One way to maximize student practice opportunities is to use the minimum number of students needed for a group task. For example, a common task in a volleyball unit to work on the pass or set is to put five to six students into the form of a circle and they try to keep the ball in the air. In reality, several students may spend lots of time watching others hit because they are less aggressive than others and allow them to take over. A better task is for students to get a partner and try to keep the ball in the air between the two of them. If there isn't enough of the "official" equipment, substitute other types of equipment—if there aren't enough volleyballs, use foam balls or beach balls. Groups can switch equipment for different tasks so everyone has a chance to use the "official" equipment.

There might also be situations where every student has a ball, but they are still waiting in line. For instance, students might practice dribbling by standing in several lines of six students, and each student dribbles to the other end of the floor and back before the next student in line can dribble. Lines should be avoided whenever possible; that includes "relay lines," which supposedly are designed for students to practice dribbling fast while making it "fun." When all students have a ball, they can simultaneously practice dribbling by moving in general space.

When games are played in physical education, modify the game to make sure participation is meaningful. The fact that official volleyball consists of six players and official basketball consists of five players does not mean that number of players has to be used.

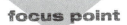

focus point

Students may experience more success in physical education, and thus higher self-perceptions, if you ensure maximum and meaningful participation.

real world

For instance, throughout most of a volleyball unit in a 7th grade volleyball unit taught by Bonnie T., students played 3-on-3 volleyball using half of a volleyball court during the game play portion at the end of each class period. Most of the time, they were required to get three hits on a side before hitting it over. This forced those students who normally would allow more aggressive players to take over the game to actually hit the ball, and such practice helped them to improve their game play (as seen in 6-on-6 volleyball play during the last week). Conversely, using more than the official number in a game, as in playing volleyball with 12 students on each side, severely limits practice opportunities during game play. Students get very few practice opportunities in that setting, so avoid such activities whenever possible.

As a student teacher at an urban middle school in the Midwest, Zach M. did an excellent job of maximizing practice opportunities for his students during a basketball unit. He always tried to use the minimum number of students needed for tasks. For example, during warm-up, each student worked on individual dribbling with his own ball, which in one large class of 45 students may have been a playground ball. During this warm-up, all students simultaneously practiced dribbling in general space; students never waited in line for a turn. And when students worked on dribbling against a defender and passing to a partner who was being guarded, no more than four students were in each group. All game play consisted of 3-on-3 half-court games, and all 6 baskets in the gym were used. Students whose teams weren't assigned to play a game either substituted for absent students on other teams or kept track of the number of shot attempts taken by team members. Students had to pass the ball to all team members before shooting, and no one team member was allowed to take more than 50 percent of their team's shots during a game. Zach designed these rules so that all students were meaningfully involved in the games.

One aspect of Mr. Barry's physical education class that he can change to help Josie and Aaron experience success is to maximize their practice opportunities. Currently, students usually only get a few opportunities to practice a skill during class because Mr. Barry puts the students in lines to wait for a turn; he likes the appearance of order in his classes. He must move past that perception and realize he can still have order when his students aren't waiting in line for a turn. He also must adapt the games, putting smaller numbers of students on teams and having more games occurring at once so all children get a chance to participate meaningfully.

Provide additional motor skill instruction

As stated previously, it takes a great deal of practice for motor skills to improve. Unfortunately, many physical education classes do not meet often enough or long enough to positively affect student skill levels; more practice time is needed. Research on motor skill instructional programs that supplement physical education shows that such programs can positively influence preschool children's (Goodway & Rudisill, 1996) and teenage girls' self-perceptions (Daley & Buchanan, 1999). However, intensive involvement in one activity may not be beneficial; Bar-Eli, Pie, and Chait (1995) found that the physical self-perceptions of children who participated in an after-school program that focused on mastery of one sport and intense competition were not any higher than children who just participated in regular physical education. Moreover, children in the supplemental instructional program actually had lower perceptions of their social competence and self-worth.

One way to provide additional motor skill practice time for students is to offer a before- or after-school physical activity club. The activities offered in such a club should correspond with the current activity units in physical education whenever possible, so students get more practice at the skills. The club should be open to students of all skill levels, but you must ensure that the higher skilled students do not dominate practices and games. Promote an instructional atmosphere, not a competitive one.

For students who really struggle with certain motor skills, offer them additional motor skill instruction during non-class time (e.g., before or

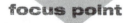

focus point

Additional motor skill practice time can positively affect children's physical self-perceptions; however, intensive involvement in one sport may not further enhance those self-perceptions and may hinder their perceptions of social competence.

after school, lunch, study halls, etc.). Make the invitation to participate in such sessions privately, so negative attention isn't drawn to the student. The sessions may be conducted individually or with small groups who are working on the same skills. You can help the students with any motor skills with which they have a particularly hard time, but especially those activities currently being practiced during physical education class.

A teacher who has successfully implemented a physical education club at his middle school in the Midwestern United States is John G. Any students can come into the gym during the 30 minutes before school to participate in tasks related to the current units in physical education; these tasks are highly organized, so it is not just an "open-gym" time. The tasks range from Stage One to Stage Three activities (refer back to Exhibit 5.2 on page 139), thus providing a challenge for students at all skill levels. Although the club is open to all students, John makes special invitations to students with low skill levels in activities, which gives him the opportunity to help them improve their skills. The club is very popular with the boys, and John admits he has trouble getting many of the girls to join.

Because Mr. Barry coaches after school and must care for his own children before school, he is unable to run a before- or after-school physical activity club. However, he could invite Josie and her friends into the gym during lunch to practice wall climbing or use the jump bands without fear of ridicule from other students.

Help students perceive success

It is not unusual for a physical educator to believe a student is doing well, but the student does not feel he has been successful. Do not assume that students know when they are doing well; help them perceive success when they experience it. Make sure that students know the criteria you are using to define success on a task. For instance, students tend to focus on the outcome of a performance (e.g., did they make the basket) rather than the process (e.g., did they use correct form in shooting the ball). When students are supposed to be working on form instead of outcome, make that clear to them: "As you work on your shooting today, remember I am looking only at your form—Is your shooting hand under the ball? Is your guide hand properly beside the ball? Do you 'put your hand in the cookie jar' on the follow-through? You shouldn't be thinking or talking about the number of baskets you did or did not make because it doesn't matter right now."

Sometimes students have unrealistic expectations for their performance, so they rarely perceive they have been successful. Help your students understand realistic levels of success for their ability level. For example, a student who is just learning tennis should not expect to get 80 percent of her serves in the service box; a more appropriate level of success might be 50 percent. As another example, explain to your students in

focus point

Help your students perceive success by making the criteria for success clear to them and by helping them understand realistic levels of success.

connected   CONCEPTS

Other ways of helping students experience success include using a content development (see Chapter 8) and/or the games stages (see Chapter 5), and helping students set individual goals (see Chapter 5). According to competence motivation theory, students will have higher perceived competence if they are successful on tasks that are neither too hard nor too easy for them—use tasks that are developmentally appropriate for them using a content development and the games stages. Appropriate goals help students focus on their own performance, while improving their performance by gradually increasing task challenges.

a softball unit that professional baseball players are considered very good if they can get a hit 4 times out of 10 at bats; beginning batters shouldn't expect to hit the ball every time!

Teach Students to Use Imagery

Even though imagined experiences have not been named by children in past research as an important source of competence information, imagery can still be an effective way of enhancing students' self-perceptions in physical education. All of us use imagery regularly, whether we realize it or not. If you've ever "relived" in your mind a sport performance like a race you've run or basketball game you've played, you've used imagery. If you've mentally reviewed a physical education lesson you're about to teach, like how to do transitions, you've used imagery. Students automatically use imagery in physical education as well, mostly without being aware of it. Unfortunately, their images may not enhance their self-efficacy and may actually harm them. Teach your students to use imagery purposefully so those images help students feel better about themselves.

Principles of effective imagery

Imagery can be done from two different perspectives: internal and external (Gould & Damarjian, 1996). The *external* perspective is the observer's view; it's like watching a videotape of your own performance. The *internal* perspective is a personal view; with this kind, you're inside your own head, experiencing your performance as you would from inside your body. Although some people prefer one type over another, others switch back and forth between internal and external. Imagery experts tend to agree that the type of perspective used in imagery is less important to its effectiveness than other aspects of images.

Gould and Damarjian (1996) outlined several key principles of effective imagery; images should be

1. *Vivid, using all of the senses.* It is not enough for a student to see himself doing a motor skill using the visual sense; rather, the student must also hear the sounds, smell the aromas, feel using the tactile and kinesthetic senses, and even experience the emotions that he might when actually performing the skill.

2. *Controllable.* Students must be able to make the image do what they want, such as make the basket or roll a strike.

3. *Positive.* This can either mean imaging success right away or creating a coping image in which one imagines having difficulty performing a skill but ultimately overcomes that difficulty and experiences success.

4. *Time accurate.* Although there may be some benefit to imagining a skill slower or faster than it actually takes, it is important to imagine the skill in the time it takes to really perform it (e.g., imagining a 1-minute dance routine for 1 minute instead of 30 seconds).

5. *Practiced regularly.* Imagery is a skill just like a motor skill, and if you want your students to use imagery to enhance their self-perceptions, you need to help them regularly practice creating effective images.

Phases of imagery training

Although imagery ability usually starts to decline once children enter elementary school (Martens, 1987), you can help students of all ages redevelop imagery skills with guided practice. In fact, it will probably be easier and take less time for elementary children to learn imagery than older students because young children often use imagination in their play. Imagery practice should include three phases: (1) sensory awareness training, (2) vividness training, and (3) controllability training (Martens, 1987; Tjeerdsma, 1991).

Sensory awareness training. In the first phase, students become aware of what they experience through all of the senses when they move in order to eventually reproduce those experiences in an image. Ask your students to slow down and note what they see, hear, smell, and touch, as well as their body positions, timing, force, and emotions as they perform a well-learned skill.

Vividness training. In the next phase, vividness training, the students use all of the senses to practice making sharp, detailed images. A good initial exercise is for students to place a piece of familiar equipment in front of them (e.g., a basketball). The students then close their eyes and imagine all of the ball's physical features (e.g., color, size, texture, bounciness, weight). Next, they imagine themselves using the equipment, first just touching it, tossing it up and down, and eventually dribbling it, moving from simple to more complex dribbling (depending on the children's skill levels). Remind the children periodically to make sure they are using all of the senses in their images.

Controllability training. During the third phase, controllability training, the students practice making the images do what they want. Simple control should be imagined first, like making the ball bounce to the height desired. More difficult control, like dribbling successfully around a defender, can be imagined in later sessions. Exhibit 6.4 contains a scenario of how Ms. Tyler goes through the imagery training phases with elementary physical education students.

EXHIBIT   6.4   Illustration of the imagery training phases.

Ms. Tyler, who teaches K–5th grade physical education, uses imagery consistently as a competitive rower to help her in practices and competitions. She also uses imagery to help her improve her motor skills in the recreational activities in which she participates, like bowling and rock climbing. After learning about the phases of imagery training from one of her professional physical education journals, she decided to go through the phases with her students and then use it during class to help their confidence and performance.

Ms. Tyler introduced imagery to each of her K–5th grade classes at the start of one school year by explaining what imagery is and how it can be used to help her students inside and outside of physical education class. Next, Ms. Tyler worked with her students for 3 class periods, about 10 minutes in each period, on sensory awareness. In each session, the students slowly performed a well-learned motor skill while Ms. Tyler cued them to pay attention to each sense, giving them time to notice each sense before cuing the next sense. For instance, as the students walked slowly around the gym in the first session, Ms. Tyler said, "As you walk, notice the things and people you see—their shapes, colors, places. How do those things change as you move? Now as you walk, pay attention to the sounds you hear—can you hear footsteps? Coughing? Building noises?" Smells and emotions were cued, followed by the tactile and kinesthetic

senses: "As you walk, notice what you are feeling in your feet. How does the floor feel? What does it feel like when you turn? Notice the air against your skin as you move. What do you feel in your hips? Your arms? What happens to these things if you walk faster? If you walk slower? If you walk with heavier steps?" Ms. Tyler gave her students plenty of time between questions to let them experience the sensation she was cuing.

Ms. Tyler next worked with her students for parts of three class periods on making vivid images, the second imagery training phase. In each period, every student had two pieces of equipment (all students had the same equipment), and Ms. Tyler guided them through creating vivid images of each piece: "Think first about the playground ball. Close your eyes. Think about the color of the ball and its size. Does it have a smell? How heavy is it? If you have trouble imagining any of those things, open your eyes and look at it. When you can make a good image with your eyes closed, try to imagine holding the ball. What is its texture? What does it feel like? How heavy is it? What do your hands, arms, and muscles feel like as you do that? If you are having trouble imagining that, open your eyes and pick it up. Then put the ball down, close your eyes, and imagine holding it again. Next, try imagining gently tossing the ball up and down. Pay attention to the light force you are using, the feel of the ball, what your arms and muscles do as you

EXHIBIT 6.4 Illustration of the imagery training phases, *continued.*

toss it up and then catch it, as well as the sounds, color, size, and texture. If you need to, actually pick the ball up and toss it up and catch it a few times." Ms. Tyler went on to have her students imagine bouncing the ball to the ground once and then catching it; older students also imaged dribbling the ball continuously. As during sensory awareness, Ms. Tyler gave the students time to develop the image she cued before moving onto the next cue.

The final phase of imagery training, controlling images, was worked on during parts of three class periods. Ms. Tyler first worked with her students on controlling the images of simple skills performed by oneself, like tossing or bouncing a playground ball to the height desired, moving in the direction or speed desired, or catching a yarn ball tossed gently up to oneself. "Boys and girls, when your eyes are closed and you are still and quiet, I want you to imagine you are jogging slowing around the gym floor. Once that image is very clear, try to imagine yourself jogging faster. Gradually make yourself jog faster and faster in your image. Now try to gradually jog slower in your image." Younger students (K–1st grade) continued to work on controlling images of motor skills performed alone, while 2nd graders and older students worked on controlling images of skills performed cooperatively with a partner, like catching a ball tossed by a partner from various heights and directions or hitting a ball with a foam paddle continuously with a part-

ner. Older students (4th–5th graders) practiced controlling images of even more complex motor skills, strategies, and competitive tasks with a partner or small group of students (e.g., imaging where to throw a ball if playing the outfield in various softball situations, or dribbling against a defender trying to steal the ball and passing it to an open teammate).

Ms. Tyler now felt comfortable having her students use imagery in various ways during physical education. Sometimes she asked the whole class to create an image, like when she asked one 1st grade class to imagine themselves performing the movement sequence, "jump off a box, roll in some way, then balance on three body parts" to help them remember the sequence. Although Ms. Tyler tried to avoid having students wait in line for a turn, it still happened sometimes due to space and equipment limitations (e.g., during bowling with 5th graders); at those times, she directed students to imagine themselves performing the skill while they were waiting. Students who couldn't participate for some reason were asked to imagine themselves performing the skills as they sat at the side. If individual students seemed to be having trouble with a skill, Ms. Tyler asked them to use imagery to practice the skill at home. For students who seemed to lack confidence and were hesitant to try a skill, she reminded them to imagine a skill they previously had trouble with and eventually learned, to enhance their confidence.

Ways to use imagery to enhance self-perceptions

Imagery can be used in various ways during physical education class to enhance students' self-perceptions. Students can imagine previous successful motor performances they have experienced in physical education to directly affect their confidence. When students are not able to physically practice a skill, imagery can be used as a means of additional practice for motor skills to enhance actual performance, which in turn positively affects their confidence. For example, students can use imagery to review a skill while waiting in line for a turn to perform that skill. While waiting on the sidelines to get into a game, students can imagine their motor responses to various game situations. Students who are injured or cannot participate for some reason can practice skills with imagery during class, thus enhancing their success when they can participate. Students having trouble with a motor skill can be asked to practice the skill using imagery while at home. The sequences of dance or gymnastic routines can be imagined either during class or outside of class to enhance the memory of the sequence order. It can also be used as a relaxation technique, to help ease some children's anxiety about performing skills in physical education (discussed in the next section). You must remember, however, that imagery should not replace physical practice of skills; if students can physically practice skills, they should do so. Imagery can be used if students cannot practice, to supplement practice, to increase confidence, and decrease anxiety.

Mr. Barry may decide to take all of his students through the phases of imagery training. Once the training is complete, Mr. Barry considers how imagery can be used to help Aaron and Josie with their self-perceptions. Because Aaron has actually experienced success quite often in physical education class, Mr. Barry asks him to imagine some of those successes, particularly those skills that he had trouble with initially but mastered after practice when he gets frustrated as he learns new skills. Mr. Barry thinks Josie could benefit most from practicing skills using imagery when she cannot practice those skills physically. For instance, during the wall climbing unit, Mr. Barry gave Josie an index card with the main cues for climbing and asked her to imagine climbing the wall using those cues while in class and waiting for a turn, as well as at home five times the night before each physical education class.

Teach Students Arousal Regulation Techniques

According to self-efficacy theory, student emotions such as anxiety and how students interpret their physiological states can influence their self-perceptions. Teaching students arousal regulation techniques will help them regulate their physiological and emotional states, which may enhance their self-perceptions. Students like Josie can be taught to inter-

focus point

Physical education students can use imagery if they cannot practice skills physically, to supplement physical practice, to increase their confidence, and to decrease anxiety; however, imagery should not replace physical practice of skills.

pret increased heart rate and breathing, butterflies in the stomach, and sweaty palms as signs of being ready to physically perform and necessary for good performance, not as indications of inadequacy. At the very least, students should learn that these feelings are normal when attempting new skills, and that even the most highly skilled students have those same phys-iological reactions in new situations. Students can be taught to use imagery (e.g., imaging past success, being successful on this attempt, or the cues for a skill) as a way to help calm their feelings of anxiety when they get ready to try a new skill or perform in front of others. Another arousal regulation technique students can use is positive self-talk—they learn to recognize negative thoughts that lead to feelings of anxiety, stop those thoughts, and replace them with positive, performance-related thoughts. This technique and others are described more fully in the article "The Stress Process in Physical Education" (Blankenship, 2007).

focus point

Teaching students in physical education to use arousal regulation techniques can enhance their self-perceptions by regulating their emotional and physiological states.

Offer Students a Choice of Coed or Same-Sex Classes/Units

With the passage of Title IX, many schools switched to coeducational physical education classes. But how do such classes influence students' self-perceptions? Research shows that some students (especially boys and high school students) are more comfortable and confident in coeducation-al classes, while other students (especially low-skilled girls and middle school students) prefer same-sex classes (Lirgg, 1993; Treanor, Graber, Housner, & Wiegand, 1998).

Lirgg (1993) suggests offering middle and high school students a choice of coeducational or same-sex classes, if possible, to allow students to par-ticipate in the type of class they feel most relaxed and secure as this may positively affect their self-perceptions in physical education. For instance, a high school program with several teachers might offer the required 9th grade fitness class several times throughout the day: first period might have one coed class and one boys only class; second period would offer a coed class and a girls-only class; third period, a boys-only and a girls-only class, and so forth. Or perhaps this required 9th grade fitness class is offered only two periods a day: each period three different classes (a coed, boys-only, and girls-only) could be offered and the students choose one.

focus point

If possible, offer students a choice of participating in coeducational or same-sex physical education classes because the type of class that enhances students' self-perceptions varies with the individual student.

Even if a program can't have separate classes and all classes must be coeducational, individual units within classes might offer same-sex and coed options if another teacher is teaching the same unit at the same time. For example, perhaps two 7th grade physical education classes are offered in the same time period, and they are both in a soccer unit. The students can choose to participate in a coed class taught by one teacher or a same-sex class taught by the other. Whether such choices are offered at the course or unit level, the same educational experiences must be offered in

connected   CONCEPTS

Physical educators can also enhance student self-perceptions by giving appropriate feedback (see Chapter 2), establishing a task-involving climate (see Chapter 5), using effective models/demonstrations (see Chapter 3), and using a variety of instructional/curricular models like sport education, cooperative learning, TPSR, adventure-based learning (see Chapter 4), peer teaching (see Chapter 3), and PSI (see Chapter 2).

both the coed and same-sex classes, as this is required by Title IX. So, a high school aerobic fitness class that is for boys only should not include activities that differ from those in a girls-only or coed class.

Obviously, in order to offer students such choices, the physical education program must have the space and personnel available. A middle school program, for example, might have three 8th grade classes during the same time period, but each class must be in a different unit at any particular time because of space limitations (e.g., Class A does basketball in the gym, Class B does aerobic dance in the multipurpose room, Class C does bowling at the local bowling alley). At the very least, in those situations students can still be given some choices in their type of participation; for instance, during a basketball unit, students can have the choice of competing on and against coed or same-sex teams. This is something Mr. Barry could easily implement in his coeducational classes and would be especially beneficial for Josie, who is very intimidated and uncomfortable performing in front of and competing against boys.

Summary

Competence motivation theory proposes that students' self-perceptions in physical education will be affected by their performance outcomes, feedback and reinforcement from significant others like their teacher, and their motivational and goal orientations. Self-efficacy theory also asserts that students' performance accomplishments and feedback from the teacher (i.e., verbal persuasion) will affect their self-perceptions, along with demonstrations and modeling of tasks by others, the students' physiological and emotional states, and imagery. Much research has been conducted on students' self-perceptions in movement situations, showing that the factors influencing self-perceptions are quite complex. For instance, research shows that students' age, gender, ethnicity, disabilities, and various psychological factors may be related to their self-perceptions. Studies have also found that the accuracy with which students judge their competence level, as well as the sources of information students prefer to use to decide their competence level, are affected by several factors. So, although enhancing student self-perceptions is complex, researchers have identified several methods that will help: modifying equipment, offering them a choice of coeducational or same-sex classes, offering supplemental motor instruction sessions, and using imagery.

Positively influencing student self-perceptions is a difficult and complex task because many factors outside of your control affect students' self-perceptions. However, it is an important task, as researchers have found that students with high self-perceptions tend to have higher motivation, effort and persistence in movement situations, and show higher levels of physical activity participation overall. With focus and purposely designed strategies, you can help your students feel more confident and positive about their movement skills in physical education.

KEY concepts

Self-perceptions

Self-concept

Self-esteem

Perceptions of competence/
   perceived ability

Self-confidence

Self-efficacy

Competence motivation theory

Self-efficacy theory

Competence motivation

Perceptions of control

Optimally challenging tasks

Intrinsic motivational orientation

Extrinsic motivational orientation

Performance accomplishments

Vicarious experiences

Verbal persuasion

Physiological state

Emotional state

Imagery

Entity conception of ability

Incremental conception of ability

application exercises

1. Marcus is a 5th grade boy who seems to have low perceptions of his ability in physical education. According to competence motivation theory, what are some possible reasons for and consequences of his low self-perceptions in physical education?

2. Chloe is a low-skilled 7th grader who seems to enjoy physical education, is always working hard during class, and even pushes herself to try new, more difficult skills. How might self-efficacy theory explain Chloe's behavior?

3. Ambrose, a 9th grade boy, is a student in the required physical fitness class, in which students learn about principles of fitness while creating and implementing a conditioning plan of their own. He has very low motor ability and rarely experiences any success on tasks during class. Describe three specific ways you will help Ambrose experience success during this class.

4. You are teaching physical education in an elementary school that has very little money, so you have very little equipment. In addition, students only have physical education during one 30-minute class period per week. Students generally seem to have low self-perceptions and tend to give up easily when they cannot do the task correctly right away. How could imagery be used to improve this situation?

Attributions

Caleb and Joshua are two 7th grade students in Ms. Harper's second-period physical education class. Both students are having trouble learning a new activity, wall climbing. Ms. Harper notices that Joshua and Caleb are each reacting differently to these difficulties. Joshua says to Ms. Harper, "I think I'm trying to use my arms too much to climb the wall. If I use my legs more, I should be able to do this." Throughout the rest of the lesson, Joshua makes as many attempts as he can at the new skill and eventually succeeds in learning it. Caleb, however, doubts his ability to learn wall climbing. When Ms. Harper asks Caleb about the task, he says, "I can't do things like this. I'm better at things like basketball and baseball. I'm just not built for this kind of activity. I'll never be as good as guys like Joshua." Ms. Harper notices that Caleb avoids wall climbing the rest of the class period and doesn't learn the new skill. Even though Ms. Harper doesn't expect Caleb to perform at the same level as Joshua, she still wants him to try hard and wonders, "Why do the two boys react so differently to the difficulty they experienced? What can I do to enhance Caleb's motivation and help him keep trying new skills when he doesn't learn them right away?"

introduction ▶

focus point

Attributions can influence a person's motivation and eventual achievement.

I n this scenario, two students responded very differently to failure in physical education. Students can also show different emotions and behaviors following success in class. One reason for these different reactions might be the attributions the students make. An **attribution** is a perceived cause of a performance outcome, or how a student explains her successes and failures. The attributions a student makes are important because they influence the student's motivation and eventual performance. In this chapter, attributions and how they influence student motivation and achievement will be explored. The related concept of learned helplessness and the influence of teacher expectations on the attribution process will also be examined. Research on those constructs will be described, along with practical implications for physical educators.

Attribution Theory

T he **theory of attributions** most commonly used in physical activity research was formulated by Bernard Weiner (1985, 1986) (see Exhibit 7.1). According to Weiner, upon experiencing a performance outcome (especially if the outcome is unexpected, negative, or important), a person will search for a reason why that outcome occurred. Joshua (from the opening scenario) ascribed his initial failure at wall climbing to using

The attribution process (adapted from Weiner, 1986).   **EXHIBIT** | **7.1**

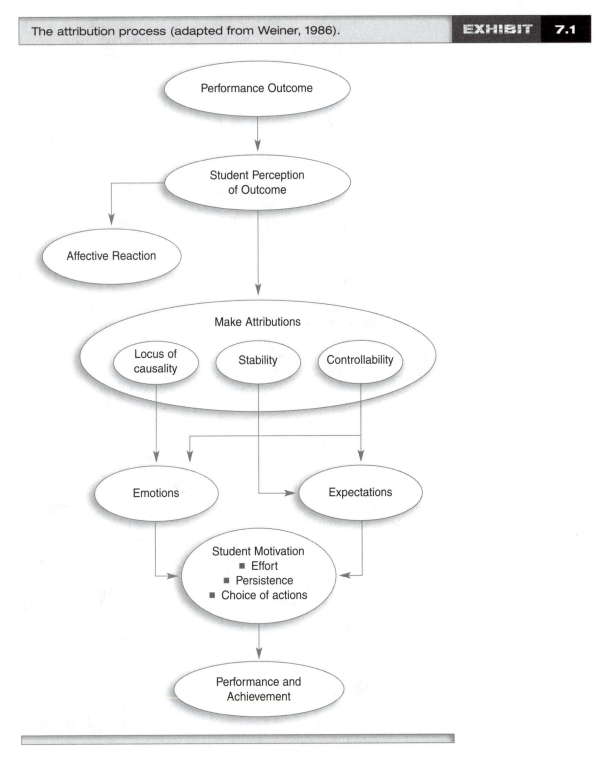

an incorrect technique, while Caleb believed that his inability to do the task was due to his lack of ability and having the wrong body build. There are literally thousands of different causes to which students can attribute their performance outcomes in physical education class (Weiner et al., 1972). A student might attribute her good performance while bowling to a lucky ball, the type of bowling lane, a new approach to the release, the teacher's help, her high athletic ability, or practice. Another student might attribute his poor bowling performance to using the wrong ball, bad luck, the distractions caused by other students, lack of teacher assistance, his lack of athletic ability, or the fact that he's never bowled before. Even though there are many specific attributions that can be used to explain performance outcomes, Weiner et al. (1972) assert there are four most commonly used attributions: (1) ability, (2) effort, (3) luck, and (4) task difficulty.

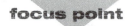

focus point

The four most common attributions are ability, effort, luck, and task difficulty.

Classifications of Attributions

Central to Weiner's (1985, 1986) theory of attributions is the idea that the actual attribution given is less important to future motivation and behavior than the characteristics or properties of those attributions. There are three ways of characterizing or classifying attributions: by locus of causality, by stability, and by controllability. **Locus of causality** refers to whether the cause of the performance outcome is internal or external to the person. Internal attributions are such causes as ability and effort, while task difficulty and luck are external to the person. With the **stability** dimension of attributions, causes can be seen as stable and permanent (meaning you can expect the same outcome in the future) or unstable and temporary (meaning a different outcome is possible in the future). Ability is generally viewed as a stable attribution, particularly when an entity (innate) view of ability is adopted (see Chapter 6), while effort and luck are usually seen as unstable. The **controllability** characteristic of attributions refers to whether the person believes he has the power to change the cause or not. Ability and luck are usually seen as uncontrollable causes, while effort is viewed as a controllable cause. Task difficulty may be perceived as being either unstable and controllable (if one believes he can adjust the difficulty of the task) or stable and uncontrollable (if a person believes that the task is entirely under the control of others and he cannot make changes to a task). Joshua attributed his initially poor performance on wall climbing to his inappropriate technique, which is an external (not inherent to Joshua), unstable (it can be changed), and controllable (Joshua can change it) cause. Caleb's attributions for his poor performance, a lack of ability and an inappropriate body build, are internal (Caleb was born with these), stable (these are permanent in Caleb's eyes), and uncontrollable (he cannot change these).

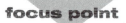

focus point

Attributions can be classified by their locus of causality (internal or external), stability, and controllability.

Consequences of Attribution Classifications

According to Weiner (1985, 1986), these attribution types are important because they influence a person's expectations and emotions, which in turn affect the person's motivation, behaviors, and eventual performance.

Influencing expectations

The stability dimension tends to influence a person's future performance expectations (Weiner, 1985, 1986). Stable attributions for a performance outcome lead a person to expect the same outcome in the future. With unstable attributions, however, the same outcome cannot necessarily be expected again in future attempts. So, stable attributions for success (e.g., high ability) would yield expectations for success in the future and higher levels of effort on the task, while unstable attributions for success (e.g., good luck) would result in lower expectations for future success and lower levels of motivated behaviors. Conversely, stable attributions for failure (e.g., low ability) would lead a person to expect failure again in the future and result in low levels of motivated behaviors, while unstable attributions for failure (e.g., low effort) would yield an expectation for change in the future and produce higher levels of motivated behaviors.

Some theorists (Abramson, Seligman, & Teasdale, 1978; Bandura, 1986) believe that controllability also relates to expectancy. If an outcome's cause is perceived as personally controllable, a person might expect a positive outcome in the future and show high effort. But if the cause is perceived as uncontrollable by oneself, there is no reason to expect future success and no reason to try hard.

Influencing emotions

The locus of causality and controllability dimensions are believed to affect a person's emotional response to an outcome. Just experiencing success or failure will result in an initial emotional reaction (e.g., happiness and pride with success, shame or disappointment with failure). But internal attributions serve to strengthen or weaken those emotions and influence self-worth. Specifically, if a person attributes a perceived success to an internal cause (like high ability or effort), feelings of pride and satisfaction increase and self-esteem is enhanced. But if success is attributed to an external cause (like an easy task or luck), the positive feelings will decrease and self-esteem is not affected. Similarly, attributing a perceived failure to internal causes (e.g., lack of ability) will have a negative impact on self-esteem and result in greater levels of shame or disappointment than if the failure was attributed to an external cause (such as a lack of teacher assistance). Simply put, you feel better about yourself (e.g., higher self-esteem) if a perceived success is due to internal rather than external causes, but you

focus point

The stability and controllability of attributions influence a person's expectations, while the locus of causality and controllability of attributions influence a person's emotions.

feel worse about yourself (e.g., lower self-esteem) if a perceived failure is due to internal rather than external causes. You will more likely continue an activity when you feel good about yourself than when you don't.

Regarding controllability, if a negative outcome is viewed as personally controllable (e.g., low effort), one may feel guilty for that cause but also feel hope for a better future outcome because that cause can be changed. These emotions can then trigger higher effort. Hopelessness is often felt if an outcome, particularly negative, is attributed to personally uncontrollable causes (e.g., bad luck, low ability), which usually yields low motivated behaviors.

Attributions and Motivation

Attribution theory would thus propose that students who show high levels of motivated behavior in physical education class would attribute their successes to controllable, internal, and stable causes, while negative outcomes are ascribed to external, controllable, and unstable causes. In contrast, physical education students who show low motivation tend to attribute success to external, unstable factors outside their control, while failure is believed to be the result of internal, stable factors they cannot control (see Exhibit 7.2). The characteristics of attributions help explain why Joshua continued to work hard at wall climbing and eventually learned the skill, while Caleb stopped trying to learn the skill. Joshua attributed his failure to an unstable but personally controllable cause (poor technique), which led him to expect success in the future by changing his technique, thus enhancing his motivation and effort. Caleb, however, attributed his initial failure to stable, internal causes that he could not change (lack of ability and wrong body build), which strengthened his shame, further decreased his self-esteem, and gave him little hope for success in the future. Hence Caleb displayed low motivation and gave up.

EXHIBIT 7.2	Attributions for success and failure of students with high versus low motivation.

HIGH-MOTIVATION STUDENTS		LOW-MOTIVATION STUDENTS	
Success	**Failure**	**Success**	**Failure**
Internal	External	External	Internal
Stable	Unstable	Unstable	Stable
Controllable	Controllable	Uncontrollable	Uncontrollable

The Attribution Process

Exhibit 7.1 on page 189 summarized the attribution process. A task is attempted by a student in physical education, such as a new jump rope skill. The young person perceives that he was either successful or unsuccessful at the skill, which then triggers an immediate emotional response to that perceived outcome (e.g., happy or sad). If performing well on that task is important to the student, or the outcome was unexpected or negative, he searches for a reason for that outcome (e.g., makes an attribution). The characteristics of the attribution (i.e., locus of causality, stability, controllability) then influence the student's expectations for future success and emotions, which then impact his future behaviors such as effort and persistence, and eventual performance.

The Developmental Nature of Attributions

According to John Nicholls's (1989) theory of achievement motivation, children's cognitive development influences the types of attributions they make. Nicholls proposed that young people do not develop a mature understanding of ability, or the related concepts of effort, luck, and task difficulty, until about 12 years of age. Students are thought to progress through various levels of understanding of these primary attributions in the academic domain, although the age when individual children develop these understandings can vary greatly. At the earliest, least mature level of understanding, children cannot distinguish tasks of varying difficulty, or those that require luck to perform well versus those requiring skill. Task difficulty is based only on whether the young person believes he or she can perform the task, without considering the performance of others. Children believe that everyone could perform equally well on any type of task, as long as they try hard. So, showing high effort is equivalent to high ability and everyone who shows high effort also is highly skilled. At intermediate levels of understanding, youngsters understand that it is harder to be successful on tasks requiring luck than those requiring skill and that people vary in ability. But this thinking is inconsistent, and they still often believe that anyone who tries hard will be successful at any task. Task difficulty is based on objective information related to the task (e.g., how far away is a target you're trying to hit), still without considering the performance of others. At mature levels of understanding, the concepts of effort and ability are clearly distinguished, and children understand that a person who gives little effort on a task but is successful has high ability. Moreover, they understand that effort will help performance on tasks requiring skill but not help on tasks involving luck. These young people also understand that in order to judge a task's difficulty, you must know how other children performed on the task.

Such developmental differences can have important implications for physical educators. Young children are likely to attribute their performance outcomes to effort, which to them is equivalent to ability. In addition, because they do not clearly distinguish tasks requiring luck from those that require ability or tasks of varying difficulty, they are likely to expect success in the future because they believe high effort will produce that success. Such attributions and beliefs contribute to the high effort and persistence seen in most early elementary students in physical education. However, as children continue through elementary school and become adolescents, they become more vulnerable to making attributions for their performances that inhibit their effort and persistence. Because they can distinguish tasks of varying difficulty and tasks requiring luck, and because they understand the difference between effort and ability, adolescents know that showing high effort on an easy task indicates low ability and that some students are better at performing motor skills than others. Even prior to adolescence, some children may start making attributions for failures in physical education to their low ability, which can then lead to low expectations for future success and low effort and persistence. As teenagers, Caleb and Joshua likely have mature understandings of ability and effort, which allowed Caleb to attribute his poor performance to his low ability. Physical educators must be aware of these developmental changes and help students like Caleb attribute their poor performances to factors they can control and change, like a new practice plan or strategy.

For some students, this attribution process serves to reinforce their belief that they cannot be successful at anything they try in an achievement situation. No matter what task is tried in physical education, these students have an "I can't" attitude and often refuse to try. Physical educators can become very frustrated as they attempt to assist these children. These students may suffer from a phenomenon called learned helplessness, which can have a severe negative impact on effort and achievement. The following section explores this condition.

focus point

Because children do not develop mature understandings of ability, effort, luck, and task difficulty until around age 12, young children tend to make different attributions than adolescents that lead to higher expectations for future success and greater effort and persistence in young children than adolescents.

Learned Helplessness

earned helplessness is the belief there is no relationship between one's actions and an outcome (Dweck, 1980). A person with this condition believes he is doomed to fail regardless of the task. The controllability characteristic of attributions is thought to play a big part, as the person thinks he has no control over negative or positive outcomes. Students who display learned helplessness usually attribute failure to low ability, which they see as a stable, uncontrollable cause (Diener & Dweck, 1978, 1980; Robinson, 1990). Because they believe nothing they do will change their ability and thus the outcome, they tend to avoid challenges and give up easily when they aren't immediately successful. Successful outcomes are also attributed to uncontrollable but external factors, so they have trouble accepting their own successes. Caleb's consistent attributions for his poor performances in physical education to his low ability and other uncontrollable factors, attributions for any successes he experiences to uncontrollable factors, and low persistence on tasks are signs he may exhibit learned helplessness in this setting.

The learned helpless student can be contrasted with the mastery- or success-oriented student, who continues to persist and seek challenges after initial failures (Diener & Dweck, 1978, 1980; Robinson, 1990). Mastery-oriented students often attribute their negative outcomes to an inappropriate strategy or low effort, which are unstable, controllable causes. They view failure as temporary and expect a more positive outcome in the future. These individuals actually enjoy working on difficult tasks. If Joshua reacts as positively to other challenges in physical education as he did to the rock climbing task, he is likely a mastery-oriented student.

Pervasiveness and Permanence of Learned Helplessness

The degree to which a person becomes learned helpless depends in part on the stability and specificity of the attributions made for negative outcomes (Abramson et al., 1978). If failures are attributed to stable causes, such as low ability, learned helplessness tends to be more permanent or chronic than if failures are attributed to unstable causes, such as low effort. Furthermore, when in certain situations only negative outcomes are attributed to stable, uncontrollable causes (e.g., low ability), the results are a permanent but situation-specific form of learned helplessness. For example, a student may consistently attribute her poor performance in physical education to her low ability and exhibit learned helplessness there, but exhibit more mastery-oriented behaviors (e.g., persistence) after negative outcomes in band, where she believes she has high ability and just needs to practice more. If stable and uncontrollable attributions for failure are consistent across many situations, however, learned helplessness is both permanent and pervasive. A child who consistently attributes her negative outcomes in every school subject to her low ability is demonstrating this global form of learned helplessness. Although the global form of learned helplessness is more serious and probably requires more extensive intervention to alleviate, the situation-specific condition can also have negative consequences for learning in that particular domain. Physical educators who suspect a student of learned helplessness will need to determine if it is specific to physical education or global. If Caleb frequently makes stable and uncontrollable attributions for performing poorly in physical education but not in other achievement situations, his learned helplessness is specific to physical education.

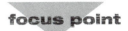

focus point

Learned helplessness leads to expectations of failure, avoidance of challenging tasks, and extreme lack of effort.

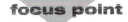

focus point

Learned helplessness can be temporary and specific to a situation, permanent and specific to a situation, or permanent and pervasive across many situations, depending on the stability and specificity of attributions for failures.

Mediators of Controllability

As mentioned earlier, a perceived lack of control is a key condition of learned helplessness. Early in life, most children generally believe they can control their outcomes. Around 8 years of age, however, doubts about this control emerge (Ziglar, 1985). Tom Martinek (1996) proposed that to determine whether these doubts dominate from this age on or if confidence about control over outcomes prevails, three mediators of controllability exist: (1) parental behavior, (2) expectations of significant others, and (3) the social context surrounding the child.

Parental behavior

One mediator is the behavior of such caregivers as parents or guardians. Children observe how their parents react to positive and negative events in their own lives to learn possible causes for events. For example, a mother is talking to a friend in the presence of her daughter about an exercise class the mother began several weeks ago and has since stopped attending: "You know, that's just the way I am. I always start things and never finish them. I'll never be disciplined enough to get in shape!" If the daughter regularly hears the mother using such internal, stable, and uncontrollable attributions for the mother's failures, the daughter will eventually learn that these are the types of attributions to make for negative events, especially related to physical activity, and that there is little hope for controlling such negative outcomes. It may be that Caleb has regularly heard his mother or father making uncontrollable attributions for situations in their lives, and he has learned that this is the way to respond.

Teacher expectations

A second mediator of control are the expectations of significant others, such as teachers, for the child's performance or achievement (Martinek, 1996). **Teacher expectations** can serve as self-fulfilling prophecies (Rosenthal & Jacobson, 1968), impacting student perceptions of control and eventual achievement through the following process (Horn, Lox, & Labrador, 2001; see Exhibit 7.3). A physical educator forms expectations about a student's future performance via person cues (e.g., gender, race, siblings, body type, physical attractiveness, socioeconomic group, physical appearance) and prior performance cues (e.g., observing the student's motor skills while on the playground, scores on a fitness test). These expectations then may influence the teacher's behaviors toward the student (e.g., the quality and amount of teacher feedback) and further impact the student's perceptions of control over outcomes, motivation, and eventual motor performance. For example, a physical educator may give a student for whom she has low expectations noncontingent praise, meaning the stu-

| Teacher expectancy—student performance process. | **EXHIBIT** | **7.3** |

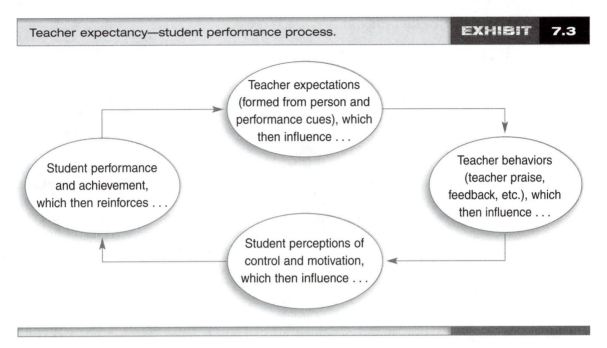

dent was praised even though he didn't perform well. Because this praise wasn't based on any student accomplishment, the student may assume he has no control over whether or not he receives the praise. Other teacher actions may convey to the low-expectancy student that the teacher doesn't believe the student can achieve at a high level, such as giving the low-expectancy student easier tasks, less encouragement, less technical information, and less contact time than the high-expectancy student. Such teacher behaviors can have a direct negative impact on student performance because students who receive less technical information and are encouraged to practice easier tasks will probably achieve less. But these teacher behaviors also negatively impact the student's sense of control or hope for future outcomes and result in less persistence, effort, and achievement.

Perhaps Ms. Harper is unknowingly contributing to the maladaptive attributions Caleb is making through the expectations she has for him. For example, based on his poor performance on adventure activities in the past, she may have low expectations for his possibility for success on this wall climbing task. She then may fail to give him specific information on how to improve his performance when he attempts wall climbing, and instead may just encourage him to keep trying. Caleb in turn may perceive this lack of help as a sign that Ms. Harper doesn't believe he can learn the task, and thus gives up. His lack of effort, along with the lack of technical information, may lead him to perform and achieve at the level Ms. Harper expected of him in the first place.

Social context

A third mediator of perceived control is the social context surrounding a child (Martinek, 1996). One important part of a child's social context is the type of achievement climate present in the school. In many schools, a competitive environment, where students are compared to each other in terms of achievement, dominates; success is performing better than others. Students who believe they have low intellectual or motor skill ability will have little hope for and control over success in this environment. Such a learning climate is especially harmful in physical education, where the demonstration of skill is very public (Martinek, 1996). School situations having an individual learning climate, where students try to improve their own past performance, are more likely to enhance a child's sense of control because their success is based on their own former achievements and not the achievements of others over whom they have no control. Perhaps the learning climate in Ms. Harper's physical education class is more competitive, so Caleb feels like he has no chance of being successful (performing better than others) in that situation.

Physical education teachers can influence a student's perceptions of control, and in turn their attributions and the degree to which a child becomes learned helpless, via the expectations they hold for the student and the type of learning climate established in physical education class. In the next section, research related to attributions, learned helplessness, attribution retraining, and teacher expectations will be presented. Though the main focus of this review is research conducted with children in such movement settings as physical education and youth sport, research conducted with young adults will be described when helpful to further our understanding.

focus point

Perceptions of control that are key to learned helplessness can be influenced by the reactions of parents to negative outcomes, the expectations of significant others like teachers, and the social context in which a child lives.

Attribution Research

Some attribution researchers have examined how student characteristics, such as age, gender, ethnicity, and disabilities, influence the types of attributions made. Other investigators examined the consequences of various attribution types, which include task persistence, performance, and emotional reactions.

Student Characteristics

Age

The proposed developmental nature of children's understanding of the main attributions in the physical domain has been confirmed by Mary Fry's research (Fry, 2000a, 2000b; Fry & Duda, 1997). In one study designed to distinguish children's levels of understanding of ability and effort, 5- to 13-year-olds were shown films of two children showing unequal effort on a motor skill task (Fry & Duda, 1997). In one film, the two young people performed equally well, and in the other film, the child giving the least effort performed the best. In a second study, designed to determine children's understanding of luck and ability, individuals with the same ages were shown two similar motor skill games they could play, one game requiring luck to be successful and the other requiring ability (Fry, 2000a). In the third study, children were presented with three situations, each situation displaying tasks of various difficulty levels (Fry, 2000b). The youngsters were asked questions to determine their levels of understanding of task difficulty and personal preference for task difficulty. Generally, the researchers found that 5- to 6-year-olds tend to exhibit the least mature level of understanding of ability, effort, task difficulty, and luck in the physical domain. However, as early as 7 years old, children start to comprehend those concepts, and by the age of 12 years, most have reached the mature levels of understanding. The results of other studies lend support to the idea of developmental differences in students' attributions (Bird & Williams, 1980; White, 1993).

Physical education teachers should be aware that the attributions children make may change as they age, primarily due to their level of cognitive development. Kindergarten and 1st grade children can be expected to make mostly effort attributions, which to them is equal to ability. Part of the reason physical educators can expect these young children to show high effort during class is because they believe that giving high effort will result in success on any task. However, some 2nd graders begin to understand that giving high effort doesn't mean you have high ability, people differ in motor skill ability, tasks can vary in difficulty, and the role luck plays in task performance. Most 6th graders will already have developed mature understandings of these concepts. These older children are at greater risk of utilizing **maladaptive attributions** (attributions that inhibit their motivation and effort and produce negative emotions) because they realize that students differ in motor skill ability and that giving high effort but performing poorly on an easy task indicates low ability. Because of these realizations, some students may start attributing their failures to internal, stable, uncontrollable factors like ability, which can inhibit their effort and persistence.

Gender

Some researchers found that males and females make similar attributions for performances in movement settings (Morgan, Griffin, & Heyward, 1996; Robinson & Howe, 1989; Weiss et al., 1990), whereas other researchers have discovered differences, especially by later adolescence (Bird & Williams, 1980; White, 1993). Bird and Williams (1980), for

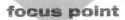

focus point

Maladaptive attributions become possible around 2nd grade but are more likely in adolescence; physical educators should be ready to help these students make more functional attributions.

focus point

Because female adolescents may make attributions that are less adaptive than males, physical educators should be sure to help girls attribute their performance outcomes to controllable factors.

example, found that boys and girls younger than 16 years of age made similar attributions, while older children attributed the performance outcomes of males to effort (under their control) and females to luck (controlled by external forces). Recognizing that boys and girls, especially in adolescence, may attribute performance outcomes to different causes will result in different strategies to address dysfunctional attributions. Particularly, girls should be helped to attribute their performances to controllable factors like their effort, so they can expect a different outcome when they fail and expect a similar outcome in the future when they succeed.

Ethnicity

focus point

Determine how students of different cultural backgrounds define success and failure, because these definitions can influence students' attributions.

Few researchers have compared ethnic groups on the attributions made in physical performance situations. Morgan et al. (1996) found that Anglo American high school athletes attributed their success to more internal and controllable factors than African Americans or Native Americans. Anglo Americans attributed their failures to more controllable factors than Native Americans and African Americans, and further made more internal but less stable attributions than Native Americans. Hispanic athletes did not differ with any of the other groups. The researchers suggested that ethnic minorities differ from Anglo Americans in family, interpersonal, and traditional values. These differences can then lead to differences in definitions of success and failure, which may produce different attributions. Be alert, therefore, to possible differences in attributions among students of different ethnic backgrounds.

connected   CONCEPTS

Research on self-perceptions suggests students with high self-perceptions tend to make more internal, stable, and personally controllable attributions than students with lower self-perceptions (see Chapter 6). Therefore, teachers should help students with low self-perceptions change their attributions to factors they can control, like their level of effort or the strategies they use. Research reviewed in Chapter 5 indicates that students with high task involvement, whether due to high task orientation or a high task-involving climate, tend to make more positive, controllable attributions than high ego involvement, especially for students with low perceived ability. So establishing a task-involving climate in physical education should help students make more adaptive attributions.

Students with disabilities

The expectations, persistence, and post-task attributions of 5th grade children with and without intellectual disabilities were compared as they participated in a novel task (Kozub, 2002). Each child was individually shown a novel game on video, then asked how they thought they would perform on the task (to elicit their expectations). After giving them 20 minutes to work on the task, they were interviewed after watching their play on video to determine their attributions. Although the students did not differ on their expectations for performance, the students without intellectual disabilities persisted longer on the task than the students with those disabilities. The two groups of students did not differ on the attributions they made for perceived success or failure. Although more studies of students with disabilities and their attributions are needed, early evidence indicates physical educators can expect those students to make similar attributions to students without disabilities.

Consequences of Attribution Types

In another area of attribution research, the possible influence that attributions may have on achievement-related variables is examined. Researchers have explored the impact of various types of attributions on student persistence and performance on tasks, as well as the students' emotional reactions in movement settings.

Persistence and performance

Several researchers have investigated the influence of various types of attributions on a person's persistence and performance on tasks. In an experiment designed to test that proposal, middle school students were led to believe that their performance on a balancing task was due to (1) controllable, unstable factors; (2) uncontrollable, stable factors; or (3) nothing in particular (Rudisill & Singer, 1988). Students assigned to the controllable, unstable group persisted longer at the task than the students in the other two groups. They also improved their performance more than the students in the uncontrollable, stable group. Other studies indicate that, when performance is low, persistence is enhanced when students believe they need to use different strategies or give greater effort in addition to strategies (Singer, Grove, Cauraugh, & Rudisill, 1985), but persistence decreases with internal attributions (Gernigon, Fleurance, & Reine, 2000).

Emotions

Other researchers have examined whether various types of attributions influence students' emotions or affective reactions in movement settings (Robinson & Howe, 1989; Vlachopoulos, Biddle, & Fox, 1997). In one study, high school students (average age 14) participated in a six-week competitive team sport program and were graded on their performance (Robinson & Howe, 1989). The researchers found internal and stable attributions predicted the students' positive affective reactions to perceived success in the program, while the students' negative affective reactions to perceived failure were predicted by the use of uncontrollable attributions. Other factors, however, such as perceived performance, were stronger predictors of the students' affective reactions. Other researchers found only a weak link between attributions and emotions in younger children (ages 11 to 14 years) in physical education (Vlachopoulos et al., 1997).

As a physical education teacher, you can enhance student persistence and eventual performance on tasks by helping students attribute their per-

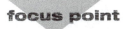

focus point

Research thus far suggests that students with intellectual disabilities will make attributions for their performance outcomes that are similar to students without intellectual disabilities.

focus point

Student persistence and performance can be enhanced by helping them attribute their performance to controllable, unstable factors.

formance to controllable, unstable factors like the students' effort or a practice strategy. However, the type of attribution does not appear to have as strong an impact on students' emotions as originally believed. Nonetheless, physical educators may slightly enhance students' positive feelings by helping them attribute perceived successes to internal, stable factors, and decrease negative feelings after perceived failure by helping them attribute that outcome to unstable, controllable factors.

Learned Helplessness Research

Unfortunately the research on learned helplessness in physical education and other movement-related achievement situations with school-age children is limited. The studies that have been conducted provide valuable information about the types of attributions learned helpless students make, how age influences learned helplessness and attributions, and the task persistence and goal orientations of learned helpless students.

Types of Attributions

The results of several studies confirm the idea that learned helpless students attribute their performance outcomes to uncontrollable factors, especially lack of ability (Gernigon et al., 2000; Martinek & Griffith, 1994; Portman, 1995; Walling & Martinek, 1995). For example, Portman (1995) found that 6th grade low-skilled students, all of whom showed clear signs of learned helplessness in physical education, directly attributed their failures in class to a lack of ability. Interestingly, they also attributed their lack of success in physical education to another uncontrollable cause: the teacher. The students claimed that the teacher did not and could not help them, and that the teacher treated boys and girls differently. So, attributing performance outcomes to factors beyond one's control, such as ability level and teacher behaviors, does appear to contribute to the development of learned helplessness, at least for middle school and high school students. Physical educators should help learned helpless students attribute their performances, especially failures, to controllable factors like the students' efforts and strategies used.

Age

Martinek and Griffith (1994) compared the attributions of 2nd and 3rd graders with 6th and 7th graders who were participating in a university physical activity class once per week. Some of the students at each age level were considered learned helpless while others were mastery oriented (who persist when initially unsuccessful). Although the younger learned helpless and mastery-oriented students did not differ in the attributions they made for success and failure, the older learned helpless students attributed failures to a lack of ability while the older mastery-oriented students attributed failures to a lack of effort. The fact that the younger learned helpless and mastery-oriented students did not differ on their attributions but the older ones did is probably related to the developmental nature of children's understanding of the primary attributions. Fry (2000a, 2000b; Fry & Duda, 1997) suggests that younger children cannot distinguish among ability, effort, luck, and task difficulty, thus resulting in the similar attributions for the learned helpless and mastery-oriented students. By adolescence, however, many children have developed a mature understanding of those attributions, which results in different attributions for failures for the learned helpless and mastery-oriented students. So, be aware that learned helpless adolescents are especially vulnerable to attributing their failures to uncontrollable causes such as ability, and help them find more controllable causes (such as effort and strategy) for their failures.

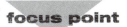

Learned helpless students, especially adolescents, tend to attribute their performances to uncontrollable factors, so physical educators should help them make controllable attributions.

Task Persistence

The results of other research confirm that learned helpless students show low levels of persistence at motor tasks (Martinek & Griffith, 1994; Martinek & Williams, 1997; Portman, 1995; Walling & Martinek, 1995). For example, Portman (1995) found that low-skilled students in physical education who showed clear signs of learned helplessness stopped trying if they were not immediately successful at a task. Interestingly, the students believed physical education was a place to demonstrate competence, not a place to learn new skills. So one clear sign of learned helplessness physical educators should be aware of is low persistence at tasks. Teachers should find ways to help learned helpless students experience immediate success at tasks. A reminder to all students that physical education is a place to try new things and learn new skills helps them accept that it is normal to experience less success when first trying a new skill.

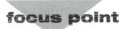

Because learned helpless students show low persistence on tasks especially if they are not immediately successful, physical educators should help them experience immediate success.

Goal Orientations

One personal characteristic that might be related to a student's level of persistence and degree of learned helplessness in physical education is the child's goal orientation. Martinek and Williams (1997) found that learned helpless middle school students were significantly higher on ego orientation and lower on task orientation than mastery-oriented students. In addition to the types of attributions they make, this might help explain the low persistence of learned helpless students. Establishing a task-involving climate in physical education is especially important for helping learned helpless students make more appropriate attributions and give greater effort.

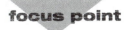

Learned helpless students tend to have high ego orientation and low task orientation, so physical educators should try to establish a task-involving climate in their classes.

Attribution Retraining

I f children are making maladaptive attributions for their performance outcomes, can they learn to make more adaptive attributions? Researchers provide evidence that college-age adults in recreational activity settings can learn to make more controllable, unstable attributions (e.g., effort and strategy) for their performances (Orbach, Singer, & Murphey, 1997; Orbach, Singer, & Price, 1999). **Attribution retraining** has also been effective with school-age children in movement settings (Miserandino, 1998; Sinnott & Biddle, 1998). In a study with 11- to 12-year-olds, children who thought they did poorly on a dribbling task and made maladaptive attributions for their performance received 20 minutes of attribution retraining to help them attribute failure to their strategy (Sinnott & Biddle, 1998). Other children who thought they were successful were not trained. At the end of the intervention, the children who received the attribution retraining were making more adaptive attributions than before. They also had higher success perceptions and intrinsic motivation than children who were not trained, whose attributions did not change.

These studies indicate that attribution retraining can be effective with children who make maladaptive attributions for their performance outcomes in physical education. Believing certain students are making maladaptive attributions and consciously helping them change their attributions can aid those students in attributing their successes to their ability or high effort and failures to low effort or poor strategies—things they can control and change.

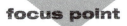

focus point

Attribution retraining can help children make more adaptive attributions in physical education.

Research on Teacher Expectations

M ost research examining physical educator expectations was conducted in the 1980s by Tom Martinek and Bill Karper. Much of their research was conducted within a special after-school physical education program for children in grades K–3 and explored the teachers' expectations for students in four areas:

1. Performance of motor skills
2. Social relations with classmates
3. Cooperative behavior
4. Ability to reason

These researchers examined several person cues (i.e., presence or absence of a disability, student physical attractiveness) and performance cues (i.e., student motor ability and effort levels) that might influence a teacher's expectations for students in physical education. The impact of teacher expectations on variables such as teacher interactions with students and student academic learning time were also examined.

Performance Cues

Student motor ability

A student's actual motor ability is a performance cue upon which physical educators could base their expectations for students. A couple of studies found that teachers' expectations for students' physical performance were positively related to the students' scores on a gross motor skill test, or their motor ability (Karper & Martinek, 1983; Martinek & Karper, 1982). Either the teachers accurately based their expectations for student performance on the performance cue of student motor ability, or the expectancy process was operating; in other words, the teachers' expectations led them to interact differently with high- and low-expectancy students, which then contributed to student performance that was consistent with the teachers' expectations. Although actual motor performance is one of the most desirable cues upon which to base expectations for student motor performance, those expectations should not lead to interactions with students that inhibit motor skill learning.

Perception of student effort

Another performance cue upon which expectations are formed is student effort. In some studies, students for whom the teachers had high expectations in all four areas were perceived by the teacher to give more effort during class than low-expectancy students (Martinek & Karper, 1982, 1984a, 1984b). Effort, especially the teacher's perception of student effort, is often used to grade students in physical education (Lund & Kirk, 2002; Matanin & Tannehill, 1994). In such settings, high-expectancy students are likely to receive higher grades than low-expectancy students. Being aware of this possible bias can lead to more objective ways of measuring student effort in physical education.

Person Cues

Disabilities

A person cue that could influence teacher expectations for students in physical education is the presence or absence of disabilities. Students with mild disabilities (e.g., hyperactivity, learning disabilities, seizure disorders, cardiac problems, visual impairments) were among the students included in the after-school physical education programs examined in several studies. The teachers in this program had similar expectations for students with and without disabilities on their motor skill performance, cooperative behavior, and reasoning ability. While the teachers did have lower expectations at the start of the program for the social relations of students with disabilities than students without disabilities, these lower expectations vanished by the end of the 24-week program (Karper & Martinek, 1985; Martinek & Karper, 1981). The researchers believed that the teachers' interactions with the students with disabilities throughout the program led to their revised expectations. Because this research was limited to young students with mild disabilities in a special physical education program, more research is needed to determine if teachers in regular programs have different expectations for older students who have disabilities or for students with different disabilities.

Physical attractiveness

A couple of studies show that teacher expectations tend to be higher for highly attractive elementary children than less attractive children (Martinek, 1981; Martinek & Karper, 1984b). Understanding that personal expectations may be affected by this unrelated person cue is the first step to avoid such a situation.

Variables Affected by Teacher Expectations

Teacher behaviors

The fact that physical educators form different expectations for different students isn't necessarily negative, especially if the expectations are accurately based on performance cues. But these differing expectations become negative if they then lead to the expectancy process described earlier in this chapter (see Exhibit 7.3 on page 197), where teachers interact differently with students based on the teachers' expectations and these differential behaviors negatively impact learning for some students. Several researchers found that teacher expectations can influence their interactions with students. For instance, physical educators tend to give high-expectancy children more technique instruction (Martinek & Karper, 1983, 1986), more contact time with teachers (Martinek & Johnson, 1979), more praise and encouragement (Martinek & Johnson, 1979; Martinek & Karper, 1982), and more corrective behavioral feedback (Martinek, 1988; Martinek & Karper, 1982) than low-expectancy children. In addition, physical educators tend to show greater acceptance of and use of high-expectancy students' ideas (Martinek & Johnson, 1979; Martinek & Karper, 1982). Conversely, other researchers found that low-expectancy students and athletes are the ones who receive greater praise, encouragement, and empathy from their physical education teachers and coaches (Horn, 1984; Martinek, 1988; Martinek & Karper, 1984a). These contrasting results may be due to the quality of the praise given to low-expectancy students (Horn et al., 2001). These students may be praised for success at a very easy task, for moderate performance, or for simply attempting a task without success. Thus,

focus point

Physical educators' expectations for students can vary according to students' motor skill abilities, physical attractiveness, and perceived effort, but teachers' expectations for students with and without mild disabilities appear similar.

some teachers might give low-expectancy students less praise than high-expectancy students while other teachers give low-expectancy students more praise, but inappropriate, noncontingent praise.

Let's consider a scenario in a 9th grade physical education class where the expectancy process is occurring. In this example, you will find that the teacher has different expectations for different students, which then cause him to behave differently with them. These behaviors then result in different perceptions of control, motivation, and achievement by the students. The class is in the middle of a team handball unit, a sport none of the students have played before or are even familiar with. They are practicing taking off from one foot behind the 6 meter line and shooting at the goal while they are in the air before they land on the floor. Mr. Taylor has high expectations for Chenee's performance but low expectations for Betty. After Chenee makes some unsuccessful attempts, Mr. Taylor says to her, "Chenee, you're not getting high enough in the air. Make sure you really lift up on that last step." When Betty is unsuccessful at the skill, however, Mr. Taylor says to her, "Good try, Betty. You're doing good. You'll get it. Just keep working at it." Throughout the class period and the unit, Mr. Taylor consistently gives Chenee more specific technique instruction while Betty is just encouraged to keep trying without specific information about how to improve. Such specific information is bound to help Chenee improve at the skill more than Betty, so Chenee ends up achieving more than Betty. But the different interactions also subtly convey to Chenee that Mr. Taylor is giving her specific information about the skill because he believes she can improve, which then increases her motivation. On the other hand, Betty sees she isn't receiving the specific information about the skill other students are getting, which conveys to her that Mr. Taylor doesn't think she'd ever learn the skill anyway.

focus point

Physical educators tend to interact differently with high-expectancy students than low-expectancy students, with most studies showing that the behaviors displayed with high-expectancy students were more helpful to learning than the behaviors displayed with low-expectancy students.

Academic learning time

The reason differing teacher expectations and behaviors are important to investigate is their possible impact on the learning process for students in physical education. One learning process variable that has been explored in relation to teacher expectations in physical education is **academic learning time (ALT)**. ALT is the amount of time a student spends in class engaged in learning activities at an appropriate level of difficulty (Rink, 2002). Cousineau and Luke (1990) found that high-expectancy 6th grade students had higher ALT than middle-expectancy students, who exhibited higher ALT than low-expectancy students. These results were confirmed in case studies of a low-expectancy student and a high-expectancy student (Martinek & Karper, 1983). So, different teacher expectations can influence teacher behaviors and, in turn, the degree of appropriate learning activities students experience in physical education.

focus point

High-expectancy students tend to experience greater ALT in physical education than low-expectancy students.

Expectancy Process Reminders

Before moving on, several issues about the expectancy process should be clarified. First, it is not necessary for physical education teachers to treat all their students in the same way (Horn et al., 2001). Students differ in their skill levels, prior experiences, and personalities; teachers should consider these things when interacting with students and use that information to help individualize instruction. So, if a teacher displays different behaviors with different students, it doesn't necessarily mean the expectancy process is occurring. Different behaviors might be necessary to help each student learn and achieve at the highest level. But if a teacher consistently interacts with students differently and in ways that impede the learning process for some, such behaviors are inappropriate and suggest the expectancy process is in effect.

Second, not all physical educators allow their expectations to negatively influence their behaviors with students or what students achieve (Horn et al., 2001). These teachers are careful to provide all students with the information and opportunities they need to learn, regardless of the teachers' initial expectations for the students.

Third, even if teachers do treat high- and low-expectancy students differently, not all students allow the differential behaviors to negatively impact their learning and perceptions of control (Horn et al., 2001). Martinek (1989) proposed that students may perceive the teacher behaviors differently than the behaviors were exhibited. In fact, Martinek (1988) found that high-expectancy students believed they received more praise than reprimands from their physical educator when they actually received more corrective behavior feedback than praise. Such students may be distracted and not hear or see some teacher behaviors directed toward them, or they may perceive the teacher's praise as more meaningful than the reprimands and attend to and remember the praise while ignoring and forgetting the corrective feedback. Therefore, differential treatment of students may not have negative consequences, although every attempt should be made to interact with all students in ways that enhance learning.

Practical Implications for Physical Education

Clearly, students' inappropriate attributions, as well as inappropriate teacher expectations and behaviors, can have a devastating impact on students' perceptions of control and motivation, with the most extreme negative result being learned helplessness. This section presents strategies physical educators can use to avoid these negative outcomes, based on the theories and research related to attributions, learned helplessness, and teacher expectations.

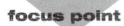

focus point

Just because a physical educator interacts differently with different students doesn't mean the expectancy process is occurring; the teacher may be appropriately individualizing instruction to maximize student learning.

focus point

Just as some physical educators don't allow their differing expectations for students to influence their interactions with students, some students don't allow differential teacher behaviors to negatively influence their learning and performance.

Become Aware of Students' Attributions

One strategy you can adopt as a physical educator is to become aware of the causes to which students attribute their performance outcomes. There are several ways to do this. Informally ask students questions related to their perceived causes of outcomes as they practice: "Why do you think you were successful on that try?" "Can you think of any reasons you might be having trouble with this skill?" Also, consider having students complete an exit slip at the end of class. Each student receives a paper with questions related to the student's perceived causes of their performance level for that day, for a particular content over several days, or in physical education in general. The exit slip can include either open-ended questions or closed-response questions with specific choices of performance causes (see Exhibit 7.4 for an example and Appendix A.5 for a blank closed-response form).

Once the attributions students make have been determined, the physical educator should now categorize those attributions by locus of causality, controllability, and stability. Some attributions students might give, and how they would be categorized, are as follows:

- "I'm usually pretty good at dancing." (ability—internal, uncontrollable, stable)
- "This is easy—anybody could do it." (task difficulty—external, uncontrollable, stable)
- "I changed my grip, and that helped." (technique—internal, controllable, unstable)
- "Dancing just isn't my thing." (ability—internal, uncontrollable, stable)
- "There isn't enough gym space for this." (facilities—external, uncontrollable, stable)
- "Those guys never pass me the ball." (other people—external, uncontrollable, stable)
- "I'm not working hard today—I have a speech to make next period and I don't want to get all sweaty." (effort—internal, controllable, unstable)
- "I practiced each part until I could do it really well, and then I put it all together." (strategy—internal, controllable, unstable)

Attributions likely to harm students' motivation in physical education include external, unstable, and uncontrollable attributions for success (e.g., luck, weather), and internal, stable, and uncontrollable attributions for failure (e.g., ability). Uncontrollable attributions, for successes or failures, are most damaging, because they make a child feel like they have no control over their performances. Although the attribution categories of all students should be determined, research suggests that the teacher should be especially alert to maladaptive attributions by adolescents, females, and students with low per-

EXHIBIT	7.4	Example exit slips for discovering students' attributions.

OPEN-RESPONSE EXIT SLIP

9TH GRADE WALL CLIMBING

Name: _____   Date: _____

Would you describe your performance in class today as successful or unsuccessful?

_____

What are some possible reasons you were successful or unsuccessful today?

_____

CLOSED-RESPONSE EXIT SLIP

9TH GRADE WALL CLIMBING

Name: _Tyler Fuentes_____   Date: _Oct. 10_____

On a scale of 1 to 5, with 5 being very successful and 1 being not successful at all, how would you rate your performance in class today? *(circle the number)*

1	2	3	(4)	5
Not successful at all				*Very successful*

What are some possible reasons for your level of success today? *(put a check beside all that apply)*

✓ I have lots of athletic ability.   _____ I have little athletic ability.

✓ I tried hard today.   _____ I didn't try hard today.

✓ Rock climbing is an easy skill.   _____ Rock climbing is hard.

_____ I had good luck.   _____ I had bad luck.

✓ I used a good practice strategy.   _____ I used a poor practice strategy.

_____ Others (please name)   _____ I like rock climbing a lot.

_I like rock climbing_____

_a lot._____

---

ceptions of ability. The attributions of students with different ethnic backgrounds should also be noted, as research suggests these may vary.

Based on Ms. Harper's concerns about Caleb's low effort in physical education, she determined the types of attributions her 9th grade students were making during several classes. For instance, after the students completed several fitness assessments, she privately asked several students (including Caleb) why they did well or had trouble with the assessments. She also gave all of her students exit slips at the end of several lessons in various units, such as wall climbing, badminton, and bowling. After categorizing Caleb's attributions, she found that he tends to make uncontrollable attributions for his unsuccessful performances as well as his more successful ones, citing factors like his low ability for his failures and luck or easy tasks for his successes.

Identify Learned Helpless Students

Once you have some ideas about the types of attributions your students make, you can use that information to help identify possible learned helpless students.

Look for signs of learned helplessness

One sign of learned helplessness is the tendency to attribute both success and failure outcomes to uncontrollable causes. The techniques described in the previous section for determining student attributions will help you identify students exhibiting this sign.

Another sign of learned helplessness is very low task persistence. Learned helpless students may try a task a couple of times and if they aren't successful, stop making task attempts. In fact, learned helpless students often make no task attempts at all and play the role of **"competent bystander"** (Tousignant & Siedentop, 1983), finding ways to avoid participating while still looking like they are busy. For example, a student may wait in line for a turn but keep slipping to the end of the line as her turn approaches. In game play, competent bystanders avoid major roles in the game (e.g., the pitcher or catcher in a softball game), stand in less involved areas (e.g., right field), or stand close to skilled students who cover for them (e.g., in volleyball).

To assess task persistence, you could simply observe the student suspected of learned helplessness during class and note his task attempts. But that will either keep you from working with other students, or cause you to miss some of the observed student's behaviors when you do help other students. It is better to ask another teacher or staff member to observe lessons live or to videotape lessons for completing the observations later. Simple forms like the ones in Exhibits 7.5a and 7.5b can document student persistence. Exhibit 7.5a is a form used to record the number of task attempts made on discrete tasks, tasks that have a definite beginning and ending and can be easily counted, like throwing. The form in Exhibit 7.5b is used to record the amount of time students spend practicing continuous tasks, tasks that have no definite beginning and ending, such as dribbling or skipping. As you can see, several students, not just the students of interest, are observed, so the task persistence of students not suspected of being learned helpless can be compared to those students you do suspect. If a lesson is videotaped, make sure the student suspected of learned helplessness is included in the picture throughout the lesson. The task persistence of several students can be obtained when recording task persistence via videotapes (see Exhibit 7.5a). But if observations are conducted live, the assistant will need to observe fewer students and alternate between students for each task, because it is hard to observe more than one student at once (see Exhibit 7.5b).

After determining that Caleb makes uncontrollable attributions for his performance outcomes in physical education, Ms. Harper decided to record his task persistence over several lessons: one lesson each in team handball (see Exhibit 7.5a), wall climbing (see Exhibit 7.5b), weight training, and basketball. The team handball lesson was videotaped, and Ms. Harper recorded the task attempts made by Caleb, Joshua, Patty, and Deanna. An assistant observed the wall climbing lesson live, alternately recording the time Caleb and Joshua spent practicing each task. The forms

EXHIBIT	7.5a	Example form for recording the number of practice attempts for discrete tasks.

Date: February 12   Grade Level: 7th

Class Period: 2nd   Content: Team handball, shooting to goal

Lesson # in unit: 5

	Task #1	Task #2	Task #3	Task #4
Student Name	Shoot to goal, standing	Shoot to goal, walking	Shoot to goal, jogging	Shoot to goal, different angles
Caleb	2	0	0	1
Joshua	12	10	14	12
Patty	1	0	1	0
Deanna	10	5	2	6

EXHIBIT	7.5b

Example form for recording length of practice attempts (in seconds) for continuous tasks.

Date: April 21   Grade Level: 7th

Class Period: 2nd   Content: Wall climbing

Lesson # in unit: 1

Student Name	Task #1 Moving up the wall	Task #2 Moving across the wall	Task #3 Combined-up and across	Task #4
Caleb	:10, :05		No attempts made	
Joshua		:20, :25, :20, :45, :15, :30, :20, :25		

show that Caleb made very few attempts during any of the lessons, especially compared with most other students. In fact, Ms. Harper noticed that Caleb displays several competent bystander behaviors (e.g., moving to the end of the line during wall climbing to avoid the task, letting more skilled students play his position in addition to theirs in basketball). These data support the idea that Caleb may be learned helpless in physical education. While Patty also had very low task persistence during team handball, this wasn't consistent across the observed lessons.

Determine pervasiveness of learned helplessness

If a child is believed to be learned helpless in physical education, try to determine the pervasiveness of the learned helplessness: is it specific to physical education, or is it more global and occurring in other subject areas or activities? If it is pervasive, but attempts to abate the condition only occur in physical education, the attempts will fail. One way to determine the extent of learned helplessness is to talk with the student. Before or after class, consider informally asking the student how she is doing in her other classes. Start with questions about how things are going for the student in school in general, and then ask about her performance in specific subject areas or activities, such as science, reading, or band. Do this with several students to avoid singling out the suspected learned helpless student.

Another means of determining if a student's learned helplessness is pervasive or specific to physical education is to have students complete "Getting to Know You" (GTKY) surveys. The purpose of the surveys is to learn more about all of your students, not just the ones you suspect of learned helplessness, in areas other than physical education. For instance, a GTKY survey might include questions about students' favorite meals at school, where they would most want to visit, and their best and worst subjects at school (see Exhibit 7.6, also reproduced in Appendix A.6). Another question that would help ascertain attributions for performance outcomes would be as follows: "Think back to last week. In what school subject did you do your best/worst? Why do you think that was your best/worst school subject last week?" Students should also be asked to give reasons for their responses, to help determine their attributions. Avoid extremely personal questions, and give students the option of not completing the survey or certain questions. As their physical educator, you could complete the survey, too, answering questions about subjects in terms of how you performed when you were in school. Beyond learning more about students outside of class, utilizing these surveys will help determine whether a particular student attributes her successes and failures to uncontrollable causes in other areas as well as physical education.

The pervasiveness of learned helplessness can also be determined by talking to teachers of other subjects the student is taking or activities in which the student is involved. Does the student exhibit low task persistence in those subjects as well? Consider meeting privately with other teachers to discuss this; this is not a topic for the faculty lounge. If other teachers also note low task persistence, the student may have a pervasive form of learned helplessness; an intervention to alleviate this will require the assistance of all the student's teachers and other personnel. If the student displays signs of learned helplessness in physical education only, work on this with the school counselor's help.

real world

While teaching physical education part-time at a middle school in the South, Mary W. got to know LuAnn, a 13-year-old girl, whom Mary eventually identified as being learned helpless (Walling & Martinek, 1995). Even though Mary believed LuAnn had average ability in physical education, LuAnn clearly attributed her lack of success in class to low ability, as heard in comments she made during class: "I can't throw too good" (p. 464); and "I can't do sit-ups too good" (p. 465). Although Mary did not complete a form like Exhibits 7.5a and 7.5b to record LuAnn's task persistence, Mary's field notes showed that LuAnn refused to try a relay involving a

An example "Getting to Know You" survey.   **EXHIBIT   7.6**

"GETTING TO KNOW YOU" SURVEY

Your Name: _____

Class Period: _____

Date: _____

The purpose of this survey is to help your teacher get to know more about you outside of physical education class. You may choose not to complete this survey if you want, or choose not to answer specific questions if you want. Your teacher will not share your responses with any other students or school faculty/staff.

1. What is your favorite meal at school? Why is that your favorite meal?

_____

_____

2. If you could take a vacation anywhere in the world (and had the money to do that), where would you go? Why do you want to go there?

_____

_____

3. What do you think is your best subject at school? Why do you think it is your best subject?

_____

_____

4. What do you think is your worst subject at school? Why do you think it is your worst subject?

_____

_____

5. Think back to last week. In what school subject did you do your best/worst? Why do you think that was your best/worst school subject last week?

_____

_____

new skill for fear of failure and being laughed at by her peers. She also waited for the teacher to prompt her before attempting tasks. To determine the pervasiveness of LuAnn's learned helplessness, Mary talked to LuAnn and other teachers about her performance in other subjects and her relationships with her peers, and observed her in other classrooms and in the lunch room. Because the data gathered from all of these different sources were quite consistent, Mary concluded that LuAnn was learned helpless and that her learned helplessness was pervasive.

Based on conversations with Caleb and other teachers, as well as Caleb's responses on the GTKY surveys, Ms. Harper believes Caleb's learned helplessness is limited to physical education. While he comments that other subjects are "boring," his attributions for outcomes in those subjects aren't as uncontrollable as in physical education. Likewise, other teachers noted that Caleb doesn't exhibit the same low persistence on tasks as he does in physical education.

Involve the school counselor

It is important that the physical educator contact the school counselor when the teacher believes a student is learned helpless. School counselors are trained to deal with psychologically debilitating conditions such as learned helplessness. Although several means of alleviating learned helplessness are presented in this chapter, check with the counselor before proceeding with any of them. If a child's learned helplessness is pervasive, the counselor should organize the intervention with other school personnel. If the learned helplessness is specific to physical education, the counselor will be able to give more ideas for abating the condition. Moreover, the school counselor will also know how to involve parents or guardians in an intervention, which is vital in dealing with learned helplessness.

Conduct Attribution Retraining Sessions

If a student is found to make maladaptive attributions in physical education, whether to the extreme of learned helplessness or not, the teacher can help the student change those attributions to more adaptive ones. The purpose of an attribution retraining program is to help students change the uncontrollable attributions they usually make for unsuccessful outcomes, especially attributions to lack of ability, to more controllable ones. Following is an attribution retraining program based on the program used by Sinnott and Biddle (1998) in their experiment with 11- to 12-year-olds. In the program, the physical educator meets outside of class (e.g., before or after school, during lunch hour or study halls) with a small group of students who make maladaptive attributions and takes them through four steps.

Step One: Provide consensus and consistency information

In the first step, the students are given "consensus" and "consistency" information about a task or skill. This means the children are informed that "in general, many children of your age find this task hard and feel unsuccessful at it" (consensus information), and that "given time, they are able to overcome this and begin to find the task easier and feel more successful" (consistency information; Sinnott & Biddle, 1998, p. 139). This helps the students realize it is normal to have trouble with a task at first, and that other children who initially found a task difficult later learned it, trying to establish some hope for improvement.

Step Two: Present strategy as attribution for failure

In the second step, lack of a suitable strategy is presented as an appropriate attribution for failures. Although lack of effort is also a controllable attribution, the strategy attribution is preferred over or in addition to effort attributions in attribution retraining, because students may have tried hard in the past and still were not successful (Martinek, 1996; Sinnott & Biddle, 1998). In step two, the word "STRATEGY" is written in large letters on a poster and shown to the students. The teacher informs the students that children who eventually succeed at a task, as described in step one, use certain strategies to help them learn the task. Students are told to break a task down and try different strategies to overcome difficulties with each part of the task. Students who are unsuccessful may not have found the appropriate strategy yet. But students who keep trying different strategies are likely to find one that works and improve their performance. The teacher should provide examples of strategies that can enhance learning tasks in other areas, such as math, history, and art (e.g., look in the book for similar types of math problems, use acronyms to help remember lists, slow down and take their time). The students should then be asked to provide examples of times they tried different strategies to learn things or solve problems and were successful (e.g., when they got locked out of the house, when their purchases exceeded the money they had).

Step Three: Model the strategy attribution process

In the third step, the physical educator models the process of breaking down a motor task or skill and attempting different strategies. For instance, the teacher could pretend to be someone having trouble dribbling a basketball. In breaking down the task, the teacher shows that dribbling can be done while standing still, walking, jogging, guarding, and combined with other skills (e.g., catch a pass then dribble, dribble then shoot). The teacher figures out the types of dribbling that he can do and the ones with which he is having trouble. Let's say he figures out he has trouble dribbling while walking. He then verbalizes various strategies he might use to improve this aspect of dribbling (e.g., keep the ball to the side, slow down, focus on the basketball and don't be distracted by others). Each strategy is demonstrated as it is verbalized. The teacher then selects one and practices dribbling while moving, using that strategy. When the teacher experiences success, he verbalizes crediting his success to the strategy used.

Step Four: Practice strategy attribution process with students

In step four of attribution retraining, the students are guided through the process of attributing failure to a lack of correct strategy using another skill, preferably one they will learn in an upcoming physical education lesson. For example, if the students will soon work on rope jumping skills, the teacher could show them one skill he believes will give most students trouble (e.g., the crossover) but can eventually be learned, give them cues, and explain that some kids find this skill hard at first but they usually learn it once they find the correct strategy. The students then try the skill; after they aren't successful they work together to break the skill down and come up with strategies they might use to improve their performance (e.g., start with arms crossed, make a big cross with the arms, keep arms crossed, slow down). The students choose and try a strategy several times; if that strategy doesn't work, they try another one until they find one that does. The teacher makes sure students verbally attribute success to the strategy used.

Tips in attribution retraining

A scenario illustrating the attribution retraining steps is found in Exhibit 7.7. It would be helpful to place the "STRATEGY" poster discussed in step two on a gym wall so the students can see it and be reminded of what they learned. Some general strategies should also be on the poster so students can refer to this for ideas when searching for strategies to try, for example:

- Keep your eyes on what you are doing.
- Take your time.
- Watch/ask successful students or the teacher for tips.
- Make at least 20 tries.
- Focus on one cue at a time.
- Practice one part of the skill only before adding other parts.

Strive to help your students create strategies more specific to individual skills, especially when the students are first learning the process. Although one 20-minute attribution retraining session produced dramatic

EXHIBIT   7.7

Illustration of the steps in attribution retraining.

Ms. Harper has discovered that three of her 7th grade students—Caleb, Jenny, and Tenille—tend to make uncontrollable attributions for their performance outcomes in physical education. When those students are unsuccessful in class, they usually attribute their failure to their low ability and show low task persistence. Ms. Harper has decided to meet with these students before school and go through the attribution retraining steps with them.

"Good morning, everyone. In a little bit, we're going to work on some rope jumping skills we'll be doing in class next week. But first, let's talk about batting a softball. Batting is a skill that many kids your age find hard, and they often feel unsuccessful at first. But given time, they are able to overcome this and start to find batting easier and feel more successful. Do you see this poster on the wall here? What word is on the poster? Right, STRATEGY. The kids who first found a skill hard, and then later were successful at the skill, used certain strategies to help them learn the skill. They broke the skill down, figured out what they were having trouble with, and then tried different strategies to overcome their trouble. When kids are unsuccessful, it simply means they haven't yet found the right strategy to help them learn the skill. The key is to keep trying different strategies until you find the one that works and helps you improve at the skill. And remember that our goal in physical education isn't to become perfect at a skill, but just to improve our own individual performance. We'll talk about some specific strategies for batting in a second, but let's think first about some strategies you might try in other classes. If you have a math problem that you can't figure out, a strategy you might try is to look in your book for some other similar problems and use that as a guide to figure out how to solve that math problem. Or let's say in history class, if you're supposed to memorize the presidents of the United States in order, you might use several acronyms to help you remember them. So instead of trying to remember 'Washington, Adams, Jefferson, Madison, Monroe, Adams' as the first six presidents, you just remember 'WAJMMA'— the first letters of their last names. Can you think of any times you tried different strategies to help you learn something or remember something?"

Jenny: "I got locked out of the house once, and I went to the hiding place where the extra key is supposed to be, and it wasn't there! So I thought a little bit, and then went to Mrs. Greene's house across the street. I used her phone to call Mom at work and ask where the key was. She told me it was in a different spot, so then I went back and found it and got in."

(continued)

Ms. Harper: "That was good problem solving, Jenny. The first thing you tried didn't work, so you thought of another thing, and it did work. That's what I want you all to do in class when we're working on activities—try different strategies to help you learn the skills. Let me show you how it's done. Let's pretend that I'm a student who's trying to learn softball batting. I first break the skill of batting down, thinking of the parts of the skill and ways it can be done. It includes the stance, grip, swing, step, and follow-through. Batting can be done from a tee, a slow-pitch ball, or a fast-pitch ball. I know I can bat okay off of a tee, but I have trouble batting a slow-pitch ball and a fast-pitch ball, so I want to work on hitting a slow-pitch first. I'm having trouble actually contacting the ball—I always swing and miss. One strategy I can use is to have my teacher watch me and tell me why she thinks I am missing the ball. So I do that, and my teacher says it is because I am swinging too soon. The next strategy I try is to wait longer before I swing the bat. I ask someone to slow-pitch the ball to me 10 times, and I really try waiting longer before I swing. *(Ms. Harper demonstrates someone pitching to her 10 times and her batting attempts.)* This doesn't work, because I still miss the ball every time. I then try batting the pitched ball ten times, this time trying a new strategy I thought of—swinging harder. *(Ms. Harper demonstrates this.)* This strategy doesn't work either. The next strategy I try is to ask Johnny, who's very good at batting, to watch me bat to see what he thinks I need to do. Johnny says he thinks I'm not watching where the ball is going, and I'm just swinging anywhere. So the next strategy I try is to really watch the ball and swing at the ball—I do this ten times. *(Ms. Harper demonstrates this.)* And it works! I hit the ball four times in those ten tries, which is better than most major league batters. So I was finally able to improve my batting because I tried different strategies, and eventually found that focusing on the ball helped me improve."

Ms. Harper continued: "Now let's all try the STRATEGY approach to learning a new skill. We're going to be learning some rope jumping skills next week in physical education class, so let's try the STRATEGY approach while learning one of those skills. The skill is called the forward 180—let me show it to you now. *(Ms. Harper demonstrates and states the cues for the forward 180.)* Many kids your age find the forward 180 difficult and feel unsuccessful at first. But over time, they try different strategies, eventually finding one that works and helps them learn the forward 180. They then find the skill easier and are more successful. Now it's your turn. Here's a jump rope for each of you. Warm up first by doing some straight rope jumping for a couple of minutes, and then try the forward 180."

Each of the three children gets a rope, warms up, and then tries the forward 180. After several unsuccessful attempts by each of them, Ms. Harper stops them and continues the attribution retraining process.

"Each of you is having trouble with this skill. That's normal—remember that many children do have trouble with it at first. Let's break the skill down together and try to come up with some strategies you can try to help you improve. When you break a skill down into its parts, try to remember the cues. What were the cues for the forward 180?"

Caleb: "It started with a sideswing, but I can't remember after that. That's the part I'm having trouble with. I can't do a sideswing."

Ms. Harper: "Tenille or Jenny, do you remember any of the other cues? All right, let me show you and tell you the cues again: sideswing, turn, open, jump. *(Ms. Harper repeats these and demonstrates the skill several times.)* Caleb has already figured out which part he's having trouble with—Tenille and Jenny, now you do the same. *(The girls make that determination.)* Now let's come up with some strategies you might try to improve your performance. Any ideas?"

Tenille: "The first strategy you used is to ask the teacher to watch and give you help."

Jenny: "The poster says to slow down. That might work—it's too fast right now."

Caleb: "I think a good strategy would be to just start with the sideswing—don't do regular jumps before it."

Ms. Harper: "Those are all really good ideas for strategies! Here are some others you might not think of: turn to the same side that you make the sideswing; first practice the sideswing and turn only and get that down before adding the open and jump; be sure to open your hands wide after the turn. Now, each of you choose a strategy and try that several times. Remember, it's okay if it doesn't help you; you'll just pick another strategy to try."

The students go through the process of trying strategies until they find one that helps them learn the sideswing. Ms. Harper works with the students, making sure that when they do learn the skill, they attribute their success to the strategy that they used and the fact that they kept trying strategies until they found one that worked.

improvements in children's intrinsic motivation, types of attributions, and perceptions of success in the Sinnott and Biddle (1998) study, those elements were only measured 24 hours after the retraining session. We don't know if the children still made appropriate attributions days, weeks, months, or years later. It is probably best to repeat attribution retraining sessions with children several times throughout the year to obtain maximum and long-lasting results.

Develop Accurate, Realistic, and Flexible Expectations for Students

Because teacher expectations for students in physical education may affect the teacher's interactions with students, teachers should make sure their expectations are as accurate as possible. Performance instead of person cues should be used to develop teachers' expectations in physical education (Horn et al., 2001). Avoid using person cues like student gender, ethnic group, or physical appearance when forming expectations. Information about students' prior motor performances tends to be more accurate than person cues. When possible, use objective measures of students' motor performances (e.g., results from skills tests, motor skill assessments, or fitness tests) to form expectations. Objective measures tend to be more accurate than subjective assessments such as informal observations of students on the playground or secondhand information from other teachers.

As a physical educator, strive to form realistic expectations for students in physical education. Although teachers should be optimistic about students' potential to improve, do not expect all students to perform at the same level. Even some 2nd grade children can distinguish effort and ability and understand that some of them have higher motor skill ability than others. Besides ability, previous experience and body build can also impact student performance. For example, it would be unrealistic for a golf instructor to expect a middle-aged person who has never played golf before to eventually perform at a professional level, due to that person's lack of previous experience and time to practice. But the instructor should expect that person to improve and convey that belief to the learner.

Physical educators should also be prepared to modify their initial expectations (Horn et al., 2001). Your early assessment of a student's expected achievement level may be inaccurate, even if objective performance measures were used. Perhaps your initial expectations were accurate, but with time a child changed physically since performing the skill test used to form your expectations. Or perhaps you used performance information about a student in one type of motor activity (e.g., basketball or team handball) to form your expectations for their performance in another kind of activity (e.g., rock climbing or gymnastics).

Hopefully students improve motor skills as they practice. Initial expectations may be incorrect or students' skill levels may have changed, so be ready to adjust your expectations.

Ms. Harper wanted to ensure her expectations for her students' wall climbing skills were accurate, realistic, and flexible. She couldn't have her students do a pre-unit assessment of their wall climbing skills because none of them had seen the activity before. But she could use the results from other skill tests that used motor abilities similar to wall climbing (e.g., balancing, weight lifting). Ms. Harper discovered that her initial expectations for Joshua and Caleb's skill levels on wall climbing were pretty consistent with those previous skill tests; Joshua performed at a higher level than Caleb on weight lifting and balancing tests. She did, however, make a concerted effort to expect both students to improve their wall climbing skills. Ms. Harper also had her students complete a wall climbing assessment at the end of the second wall climbing lesson, and was ready to change her initial expectations. She found Joshua had improved more and performed at a higher level than Caleb on wall climbing, confirming her initial expectations. Later we'll look at Ms. Harper's interactions with those students and how those behaviors (influenced by her expectations) may have contributed to the boys' performance levels.

Monitor Your Attributions for Student Performance Outcomes

Because the attributions teachers make for student performance outcomes in physical education can influence their interactions with students, it is important that teachers become aware of these attributions. One way to do that is to complete the "Reasons for Outcomes" form (see Exhibit 7.8 for a sample and Appendix A.6 for a blank form). In the first column, the names of all the students in a class are listed. In the other two columns, the teacher's beliefs about the causes of those performance outcomes are recorded. One way to use the form is simply to write each student's name in a space and as you think about that student, write down the first reason that comes to mind when you think about why that student is successful and unsuccessful during class. Another way to use the form is to carry it with you one day during class and as you observe students being successful or unsuccessful, record the first reason that you think of for that outcome. B.J., a graduate student teaching tennis to college students in the Midwestern United States, used that method to determine his attributions for his students' performance levels. Most of his attributions for his students' failures were about the strategy they used (e.g., "doesn't turn body," "folds elbow"), while his attributions for their successes were a combination of strategy (e.g., "hits ball on racket center") and ability (e.g., "very good athlete"). These are the kinds of attributions that are

| EXHIBIT | 7.8 | "Reasons for Outcomes" form. |

REASONS FOR OUTCOMES

Class: Team Handball—dribbling & passing

Time/Period: 3rd period—10:15

Grade Level: 8th grade

Date: 12-10

Student Name	Successful Outcomes	Unsuccessful Outcomes
1. Jackson Pauley	Tends to be good at most sports	Not trying; just messing around
2. Teesha Jones	Experience playing basketball	Tends to carry the ball as in basketball
3. Rudy Robles	Stayed focused on the task	Doesn't like sports
4. Alex Wincek	Partner really helped her	Better at individual sports
5.		
6.		
7.		

most likely to enhance student motivation, so B.J. should continue to make these kinds.

The attributions teachers make for student performance outcomes are often conveyed in the feedback teachers give to students. So it is important as a physical educator to scrutinize your feedback and determine the attributions you may be conveying to students. One way to do this is to have a fellow teacher come into your class several times and record any statements you make to students that express your attributions for their performance level. The observer should listen for statements like the following:

- "It looks like it comes naturally to you! You're just a natural athlete!" (ability)

- "You only gave it a couple of tries. You'll get it if you just keep practicing." (effort)

- "I think you haven't gotten it yet because you are only making one attempt before giving someone else a try. Why don't you try it about ten times in a row?" (strategy)

- "That ball looks flat. Try this one and see if it helps with your dribbling." (equipment)
- "That's okay. I know that gymnastics isn't your thing." (ability)

Consider having someone videotape several classes, or wear a portable audiotape recorder in your pocket. Then you could watch or listen to your tape later on and record your attributions yourself. If available, use a remote microphone and receiver when your lessons are videotaped so you will be able to hear everything you say during class. If you are observed live, a remote microphone and receiver could also be used, because that would allow the observer to hear everything you say without having to follow you closely and possibly be disruptive.

The first times you are observed, videotaped, or audiotaped, you will most likely be self-conscious and may not convey the same attributions in your feedback you usually do. Although this is not necessarily bad, several observations, videotapes, or audiotapes should be made to become used to the observer's presence or recording device. This way, you will forget you are being observed or recorded and interact naturally with students.

Ms. Harper asked colleagues to videotape several lessons with her 7th graders, then later recorded her attributions for students' performances, especially Joshua's and Caleb's. She found that, in later lessons when she was comfortable being taped, she attributed Joshua's successes mostly to his effort and ability and attributed his failures to poor technique and low effort. Ms. Harper attributed Caleb's successes to high effort and low task difficulty (e.g., "I told you this was something anyone could do"); however, no ability attributions were made. Caleb's failures were met with requests to try harder; he did not get technical advice like Joshua.

Make Adaptive Attributions for Student Performance Outcomes

A teacher may discover she is conveying maladaptive attributions for some students' performance outcomes in her feedback to the students. Once a teacher knows this, she can then work to revise those attributions and her feedback. Monitoring feedback, using the techniques just described, can determine if more adaptive attributions are being communicated. As with student attributions, the teacher attributions that are most helpful for student motivation are controllable ones for both successful and unsuccessful outcomes.

Teacher feedback about student successes

Feedback to students about successes should convey attributions for those successes to effort, strategies, or ability. Teacher feedback about student successes should communicate attributions to high effort (e.g., "Your serve is getting better, Chris. That hard work is paying off"). Students may need help understanding that effort and persistence can help them improve their skills. Again, it is important to be honest; if it looks like the task was easy for a student and he didn't have to try hard, then attribute his success to high ability. Effort is important to stress in feedback for success because it is something students can control, and if they worked hard on this task and had success, they might also experience success on other tasks if they try hard.

The use of an appropriate strategy is another attribution you should convey to students in feedback about success (e.g., "Good serve, Chris. Working on the toss by itself really paid off"). Although this attribution can be communicated to all students, it is especially important to express to students who have participated in attribution retraining sessions. Students can control the strategies they use to learn motor skills, thus attributing their successes to using appropriate strategies will help them expect success in the future, given they keep trying different strategies.

If you believe a student has the ability, success should be attributed to high ability (e.g., "Nice serve, Chris. You look like a natural tennis player. Keep working hard and you could become a very good tennis player"). Be honest, however; don't attribute success to high ability if you don't believe students have high ability. Most upper elementary and older students understand their motor abilities; you will lose credibility if you tell students they're highly skilled when you don't believe it. Although ability is an uncontrollable attribution, it is also internal and stable, thus it can help students feel good and expect success on future attempts.

Sometimes physical educators believe the more they praise students, the better students will feel about themselves and the more effort they will give. However, this is not necessarily the case. Avoid excessively praising students for marginal levels of success (Horn et al., 2001; Robinson, 1990). As described earlier, teacher praise that doesn't match the student's performance level (e.g., excessive praise for a very easy task or praise for low success levels) can convey to the student that the teacher doesn't believe he can perform any better. That kind of praise can have the opposite effect the teacher wanted; the student gives up because he believes the teacher thinks the student has achieved all he can.

Teacher feedback about student failures

When students experience unsuccessful outcomes in physical education, provide feedback that attributes those failures to low effort or a poor strategy while avoiding attributing failures to low ability. Even though there may be good evidence from objective performance assessments that a student has low ability in a skill, low ability attributions for failures (e.g., "That's okay, Chris. You're really not a tennis player, anyway") should not be made. Ability is an internal and uncontrollable attribution, and attributing unsuccessful outcomes to low ability can negatively affect student self-esteem and expectations for future performances.

One attribution to convey in feedback to students following failure is the need for greater effort ("Come on, Chris. You can't try the overhand serve once and expect to learn it. Your serve will improve if you keep working on it"). Strive to consistently emphasize that skills can be mastered or at least improved with effort, and that success rarely comes right away. Be careful using low effort as a reason for failure however; if the student believes he already gave maximum effort and was still unsuccessful, he won't believe that he can give any greater effort or that it would produce a different result anyway.

Perhaps the safest attribution for student failure to convey in teacher feedback to students is the use of an inappropriate strategy ("That's all right, Chris. The strategy to work on the toss alone didn't seem to help much; let's see if we can come up with another strategy"). As with strategy attributions for successes, this is especially important to communicate to students who have participated in attribution retraining sessions, although it is good feedback to give to all students. When students understand that their lack of success isn't personal (as implied in feedback attributing failure to low ability or effort), they will feel better about themselves and understand that eventually they will find a strategy to help them improve their skill.

When a student experiences low success on a physical education task, you must give the student technical information about how to improve performance on that task (Horn et al., 2001). Teachers often convey their expectations and attributions for student performance by what they don't say as well as what they do say in their feedback. When you simply tell a student who is being unsuccessful to keep trying without giving specific information about how to improve, you are subtly expressing your belief that this student cannot improve and has low ability. Giving all students specific information about how to correctly perform a skill when errors or failures occur conveys a belief in students' potential for improvement.

real world

One teacher who conveys adaptive attributions for student outcomes in her feedback is Myra A., who teaches elementary physical education in an urban community in the southern United States. After student successes, Myra might say: "Wow, you are really good at striking!" "I knew you would learn that because you always work so hard in class." "See how good you do when you work at it—way to go!" Most of her feedback for success attributes the outcomes to high ability and effort, while an inappropriate strategy is the attribution most commonly used for lack of student success: "Malaysia, you're not hitting the headpin because you're twisting your wrist as you release it. Try keeping your wrist straight—that should help." "This group—going slower will help you get more beanbags in your

buckets. When you go too fast, you can't aim the way you should."
Myra's students are known for giving high effort in physical education.

After learning she gave different types of feedback to Joshua and Caleb, Ms. Harper consciously tried to give Caleb more adaptive feedback. Because Caleb was learning strategy attributions in attribution retraining sessions, her feedback to him focused on attributing his successes to finding a strategy that helped him improve, while feedback about his failures centered on the need to keep trying different strategies as well as giving him specific information about how to improve. After a couple of weeks, Ms. Harper asked her colleagues to videotape her several more times, and she found that her feedback to Caleb had changed as she had desired.

Provide Equal Opportunities for Students

In addition to verbal feedback, another way physical educators can convey their expectations for student performance levels to students is in the amount of practice opportunities provided for students. Tasks should be set up that give all students equal practice time (Horn et al., 2001). This procedure suggests to students that the teacher believes all of them can improve. Exhibits 7.5a and 7.5b can be used to monitor the amount of practice time or number of practice opportunities for students. A colleague can either conduct live observations, or the physical educator can observe videotapes that have been made of several lessons. Both high- and low-expectation students should be observed, so the amount of practice each gets can be compared.

It is also helpful to monitor the time students spend in non-skill-related activities during practice time (Horn et al., 2001). In other words, how much time do high- and low-expectancy students spend doing things like shagging balls, waiting in line, or sitting out during game play? If tasks are set up that include large amounts of non-skill-related activities, low-expectancy students often spend a disproportionate amount of time doing these activities, compared to the higher-expectancy students. This suggests to students that the teacher thinks it is okay for some students (i.e., high-skilled) to get lots of practice or activity time, and that other students (i.e., low-skilled) don't need to practice because they won't learn the skills anyway. A form like the one in Exhibit 7.9 can be used to monitor time students spend in non-skill-related activities.

Let's say a low-expectancy student is found to get little practice time and is spending more time waiting in line or shagging balls than other students. How does the teacher know if this is because she didn't provide equal practice opportunities for the students, or if the student is demonstrating low task persistence, as is common in learned helpless students? The key is to determine the cause of the low amount of practice; is it the result of how the task is set up, or is it the result of behaviors by the student? For example, Exhibit 7.5b showed that Caleb had very little practice

	EXHIBIT	7.9
Example form for monitoring time students spend in non–skill-related activity.		

Grade Level: 7th	Class Period: Second	
	Date: January 15	**Date: February 12**	**Date: April 21**
Student Name	**Content: BB game**	**Content: Team handball, goal shooting**	**Content: Wall climbing**
Caleb	15:30	17:15	21:45
Joshua	2:30	5:00	7:15

time during a wall climbing lesson. This was partially because there was only one climbing wall in the gym, so students had to wait in line for a turn. But the videotape showed that Caleb also contributed to his low practice time because he would frequently slip to the end of the line when it was his turn and ended up with less practice time. In addition, the low number of attempts made by Caleb during the team handball lesson (see Exhibit 7.5a) was clearly the result of his low task persistence, because every student had a ball and there were several goals around the gym to maximize participation. Similarly, Exhibit 7.9 shows that Caleb spent much more time than Joshua in non-skill-related activities during several lessons. In the basketball lesson, this was mostly because the students were playing a basketball game using only one court, so only a few students could play at once and Joshua's group got to play more than Caleb's. Thus it is important to carefully look at the task structure and each student's actions when determining if low practice time is due to the teacher's actions or the student's.

connected CONCEPTS

Various instructional models are designed to give students leadership roles and take more responsibility in physical education, like sport education, cooperative learning (see Chapter 4), peer teaching (see Chapter 3), and the personalized system of instruction (see Chapter 2).

Create Leadership and Responsibility Roles for Students

One strategy proposed by Walling and Martinek (1995) to abate learned helplessness is to create leadership and responsibility roles for students. Perceived lack of control over outcomes is a key characteristic of learned helpless students. Giving them small tasks to perform can help them feel important and more in control. Asking such students to set the equipment out for class, collect assignments, take care of the heart monitors or pedometers, or assist with a demonstration are just a few tasks they can do to enhance their sense of responsibility and control.

Develop Realistic but Optimistic Expectations for Attribution Change

As a physical educator, you must understand that even if all the strategies described here for changing students' attributions are used, students may still make maladaptive attributions. Many factors outside of physical education influence students, and students are in physical education only a short time. The types of attributions students make have been learned and reinforced over many years and so can be difficult to change. So, be optimistic about the possibility of altering student attributions and abating learned helplessness, but be realistic and understand that such changes will not happen quickly and may not happen at all. Especially for students who are believed to be learned helpless, it will take an extended period of time, maybe even years, of consistent application of these strategies to help students change the types of attributions they make for their performance outcomes.

connected CONCEPTS

Physical educators should decrease the competitive orientation (an ego-involving climate) in class because learned helpless students tend to give up in those kinds of climates; they compare their performance to others and don't believe they can ever perform better than them. Moreover, attributions to ability are common in an ego-involving climate, because ability is a major factor determining which students perform the best. Therefore, strive to establish a task-involving climate in your classes (see Chapter 5).

Summary

According to attribution theory, the types of attributions students give for performance outcomes can influence students' expectations, emotions, motivation, and even performance in physical education. Research shows that children's attributions may be influenced by a number of factors, including their age, gender, and ethnic group. Students who consistently make uncontrollable attributions may develop learned helplessness, a debilitating condition in which students perceive no relationship between their actions and performance outcomes. Learned helpless students display extremely low persistence and effort, which then negatively affects their achievements.

Teacher expectations for students' performance can influence their interactions with students, which can then affect the students' performance levels, perceived control, attributions, and the development of learned helplessness. However, teachers can help students make adaptive attributions and help abate the negative impact of learned helplessness through several strategies: identifying poor student attributions and learned helplessness; conducting attribution retraining sessions with students who make maladaptive attributions; monitoring their own expectations and attributions for students and ensuring those expectations are accurate, realistic, and flexible; ensuring that the feedback they give to students reflects adaptive attributions; providing equal practice opportunities for students; and creating leadership and responsibility roles for students.

Attribution	Teacher expectations
Attribution theory	Maladaptive attributions
Locus of causality	Attribution retraining
Stability	Academic learning time (ALT)
Controllability	Competent bystander
Learned helplessness	

KEY concepts

application exercises

1. Using Exhibit 7.1 of the attribution theory and process as a guide, explain why Laurie displays high effort and persistence during her 5th grade physical education class, but Annie shows low effort and persistence in the same class.

2. Let's say you are Annie's physical educator. What steps could you take to determine if Annie is learned helpless, and if so, the pervasiveness of the learned helplessness?

3. You are a physical educator who understands the impact your expectations for students can have on their effort and performance. What strategies would you use to determine your expectations, ensure those expectations are accurate, and ensure your expectations don't negatively influence your interactions with students and their attributions?

4. You have identified several students in your freshman physical education classes that make maladaptive attributions, and you want to take them through the attribution retraining steps. Describe what the first before-school session with these students would be like, using bowling as the activity used in the session.

5. Besides attribution retraining sessions, describe three specific strategies you would use to help Annie (from question 2) make more adaptive attributions.

Interest and Value

Jamal, a high school sophomore, enjoys all kinds of physical activity. He plays on the soccer and tennis teams at school, plays golf with his grandparents, and plays in the basketball league at his church. But Jamal rarely participates in physical education class. When he does participate, he doesn't try hard. When asked about this, he says, "PE is boring. I'm just not interested in what we do in class. It's not important to me. It's always the same thing over and over again. If I didn't have to take PE, I wouldn't take it at all. It's a waste of time." Ms. Clark, Jamal's physical education teacher, wonders what she can do to increase his interest in class.

introduction ▶

Unfortunately, Jamal sounds like many students for whom physical education just isn't very interesting or valuable. Interest and value play important roles in influencing student participation and effort in physical education. Webster's dictionary defines **interest** as "a feeling of concern, curiosity, etc., about something" (Guralnik, 1979, p. 251). **Value** is "the desirability or worth of a thing" (p. 528). This chapter explores the concepts of interest and value, their relationships to motivation and performance in physical education, and ways that teachers can enhance student interest in and value for physical education classes.

Types of Interest

Interest has been conceptualized as being two distinct but related concepts: personal interest and situational interest (Hidi, 2000; Krapp, Hidi, & Renninger, 1992).

Personal Interest

Personal interest is an individual's unique disposition to participate in and seek out certain activities, events, and objects (Hidi, 2000; Krapp et al., 1992). Personal interests are relatively stable preferences that are "developed slowly over time during constant and consistent interactions with certain activities in a particular environment" (Chen, 2001, p. 46). Repeated interactions with an activity, if positive, build knowledge about the activity and enhance the participant's interest in the activity. For example, a personal interest of Ms. Clark's is running, probably because of the exposure she had to running as a child (her father, brothers, and sister were runners) and the many positive experiences she had running (e.g., July 4 picnic races as a child, high school and college track and cross-country).

Through those interactions, Ms. Clark's knowledge about running as a sport grew and she began to appreciate and enjoy running. She dislikes swimming, however, probably because of her lack of exposure to and limited experience with swimming. Although she did learn to swim as a child, she has not had many opportunities over the years to practice and improve her swimming skills. Ms. Clark's knowledge about swimming is limited, and she is not interested in swimming to the same degree she is in running.

Situational Interest

Situational interest has been defined as an individual's perception of the appealing characteristics of an activity (Chen, 1996; Hidi & Anderson, 1992). Situational interest is "interest that is generated primarily by certain conditions and/or concrete objects . . . in the environment" (Krapp et al., 1992, p. 8). It helps to focus attention and is often shared among the people in that setting (Hidi, 2000; Hidi & Anderson, 1992). Situational interest often yields a temporary affective (emotional) reaction (e.g., temporary motivation and effort) because it is tied to a particular situation. If situational interest in an activity can be sustained over an extended period of time, however, personal interest in the activity may result (Hidi, 2000). For example, when Ms. Clark was in graduate school she enrolled in a beginning fencing class because it was an activity that few people knew about (e.g., there was a "mystique" to it) and she liked the instructor. This initial situational interest soon waned, however, and she dropped the class. On the other hand, Ms. Clark began attending hockey games simply to spend time with her husband, but this situational interest was maintained due to the excitement and entertainment experienced while at the games. If this situational interest continues, it could develop into a personal interest.

There are two aspects of situational interest: catching interest and holding interest (Mitchell, 1993). **Catching interest** refers to those aspects of the environment or activity that initially attract a person to an activity. Catching interest is short-lived; a teacher must do more to maintain a person's situational interest. Methods proposed in classroom settings to enhance catching interest include puzzles, group work/socialization, and computers/technology (Mitchell, 1993). For example, Kendra, who rarely participates in physical education class but loves to play with computers, started participating and increased her effort in a kick boxing unit when she learned the students would be using videocameras and computers to analyze their kick boxing skills.

Holding interest, on the other hand, is the student's continued attraction to the activity that remains after catching interest declines. Within situational interest, holding interest factors are meant to empower students to reach personal goals, which remain for extended periods of time.

Because personal goals are the focus in holding interest, it tends to be more long-lasting than catching interest. Two means of enhancing holding interest in the classroom include

1. Increasing the personal meaning in activities for students.
2. Increasing student involvement in the learning process. (Mitchell, 1993)

Personal meaning refers to a perception that what is being learned is important for students in their lives today (Mitchell, 1993). For Kendra, holding interest may develop if she discovers her clothes are fitting better and she likes the way she looks (personal meaning) after participating in the kick boxing class for the semester. Kendra's holding interest in kick boxing may also be enhanced if her teacher uses problem-solving activities during class as a means of involving the students more in the learning process.

Value

Value is a concept closely related to interest; we are often interested in activities that we find valuable. And, just like interest, value for tasks and activities has been proposed to influence student participation and effort in physical education. One theory in which value plays an important role is **expectancy-value theory,** which was originally posited by Atkinson (1964) and expanded upon by Eccles and her colleagues (Eccles et al., 1983). According to this theory, an individual's behavior in a situation like physical education is based on two factors: the degree to which the person expects to be successful and the subjective value the person places on success in that situation. High expectations and value for success in a domain should lead someone to participate, give high effort, and have good performance. One's expectations for success are largely grounded in self-perceptions; high self-perceptions in a domain (e.g., physical education) should lead to high expectations for success on many tasks in that domain. Since self-perceptions are explored in Chapter 6, this chapter will focus on the second factor, value.

Subjective task value refers to the importance of being successful on a task or in a domain and consists of four components: attainment value, intrinsic value, utility value, and cost (Eccles et al., 1983). **Attainment value** is the personal importance a person places on a task because accomplishment of the task would confirm aspects of the person's identity. Perhaps Jamal works hard as part of the soccer and tennis teams at school and the basketball league at church because those activities define him as a competitive athlete, whereas his effort is low in physical education because it is traditionally less competitive and success in class would not enhance that part of his identity. The sheer enjoyment or pleasure a person derives from participating in an activity for its own sake is **intrinsic value**. This component is similar to the construct of interest as previously defined in this chapter (Eccles & Wigfield, 2002). A task has **utility value** for someone if it helps the person achieve current and future goals. Jamal might not really enjoy golf (so it has no intrinsic value for him), but he plays it because he believes it will be important to his future career in business. Similar to holding interest, emphasizing the personal meaning of activities will probably enhance the attainment and/or utility values of activities. **Cost** refers to the negative aspects of participating in an activity (e.g., anxiety, fear of failure or success, loss of time and energy, giving up one activity for another). Jamal might resist participating in physical education because he believes his time would be better spent on doing his homework for other courses.

The value placed on a domain is proposed to be influenced by the affect (positive and negative) experienced with past attempts in that domain, perceptions of significant others' beliefs and behaviors, and perceptions of gender-role stereotypes (Eccles et al., 1983). Unlike his experiences in physical education, Jamal has high value for playing in the basketball league and playing golf with his grandfather because he experiences positive emotions in those situations. Jamal also believes that his parents place higher importance on his doing well on the soccer and tennis teams than in physical education, which his father says "everyone should get an A in." And Jamal views some of the activities done in physical education (e.g., dance, gymnastics, softball) as "girls'" activities, so he doesn't care about performing them well.

connected CONCEPTS

Intrinsic value is similar to intrinsic motivation (Eccles & Wigfield, 2002), whereas utility value is similar to introjected motivation, a form of extrinsic motivation (Eccles, 2005) (both are described in Chapter 9). Many of the barriers presented in Chapter 10 as negatively influencing students' physical activity involvement are costs that influence subjective task value.

focus point

Students are likely to place high subjective task value on physical education activities if they have had positive affective experiences in class in the past, if significant others value and encourage high performance in physical education, and if they view physical education activities as appropriate for both genders.

Research on Interest and Value

Researchers have only recently begun to examine interest and value in order to discover how best to enhance student interest in and value for physical education. In this section, the research that has been conducted on personal interest, situational interest, and subjective task value will be presented, as well as variables that seem related to these constructs, such as achievement, performance, and motivated behaviors. Student characteristics that appear to be associated with interest and value will also be explored. Finally, research on the potential sources of subjective task value and the different dimensions of situational interest will be described.

Relationships to Achievement and Performance

Some researchers have examined the relationship between student personal interest in school subjects or content within those subjects and achievement or learning in school. Achievement has been related to personal interest in subjects from mathematics to chemistry to foreign language (Schiefele, Krapp, & Winteler, 1992). Similar results have been found in physical education, at least for some activities. For example, students' achievement in dance (Shen, Chen, Scrabis, & Tolley, 2003), softball (Shen & Chen, 2007b), and rhythmic activities (Chen & Shen, 2004) increases as their personal interest in those activities increases. But that relationship was not found for students' personal interest in contact sports (e.g., team handball, rugby, basketball, soccer, self-defense), alternative games (e.g., speedball, table tennis, archery, pickleball), or other activities (e.g., juggling, flag football) (Chen & Shen, 2004).

Most research indicates that situational interest doesn't have the same impact on achievement in physical education as personal interest (Shen & Chen, 2006, 2007b; Shen et al., 2003). For example, Shen et al. (2003) measured middle school students' situational interest in three different dance lessons during an instructional unit, but found no relationship between their situational interest levels in those lessons and their skill and knowledge test grades. Similarly, situational interest was not a significant predictor of knowledge and skill gain during a 6th grade softball unit (Shen & Chen, 2007b), and 6th graders' situational interest in volleyball did not predict their gain in knowledge about volleyball during a unit (Shen & Chen, 2006).

Even though expectancy-value theory predicts high subjective task value should lead to high performance, researchers have not yet confirmed this relationship with school-age children. For example, in physical education running programs, elementary students' subjective task value for running did not predict their mile run performance (Xiang et al., 2005; Xiang, McBride, & Bruene, 2004). Subjective task value appears to be a better predictor of task choice, persistence, and intention to be active than of actual performance (Eccles & Wigfield, 2002; Weiss & Williams, 2004; Wigfield & Eccles, 2000).

At this point, there is stronger evidence that achievement or performance in physical education can be influenced by personal interest rather than situational interest or value. Students with high personal interest in certain activities in physical education can be expected to achieve more in those activities than students who show low personal interest.

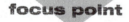

focus point

Achievement and performance in physical education seem affected by personal interest, but not situational interest or value. Therefore, physical educators can expect students with high personal interest in activities to achieve more in those activities than students with low personal interest.

Relationships to Motivated Learning Behaviors and Intentions

Motivated learning behaviors are those behaviors that suggest a student is engaged in the content, is making a high effort to learn the content, and is persistent in doing so. Intentions to continue a task or an activity should lead to greater persistence. In physical education, motivated behaviors can be seen in physical activity and intensity levels, as well as students' use of learning strategies. The results of several studies indicate that situational interest has a positive impact on such motivated behaviors (Shen & Chen, 2006, 2007a; Shen et al., 2003; Simons, Dewitte, & Lens, 2003). In one of those studies (Shen et al., 2003), middle school students' effort and persistence during class (as measured by the number of steps they took during class) increased as their situational interest in physical education increased. Other researchers have found that as situational interest increased, so did students' self-reported use of learning strategies (e.g., imagery, self-talk, physical practice; Shen & Chen, 2006, 2007a).

The research examining personal interest and motivated behaviors is less clear. Some studies show that physical activity levels in physical education increase as personal interest in class increases (Chen & Shen, 2004; Shen et al., 2003). Personal interest was weakly related to students' reported use of learning strategies (Shen & Chen, 2006, 2007a). But other studies show no relationship between personal interest and physical activity (Shen & Chen, 2006, 2007a, 2007b).

Several researchers found an association between high subjective value for sport and children's and adolescents' participation and persistence in sport (Eccles & Harold, 1991; Fredricks & Eccles, 2005; Guillet, Sarrazin, Fontayne, & Brustad, 2006). Similarly, in a qualitative study, elementary students identified all four components of value as influencing their engagement during recess (Watkinson et al., 2005). Other researchers discovered that children's and adolescents' intentions for future participation were positively affected by high subjective task value for an activity (Guillet et al., 2006; Papaioannou & Theodorakis, 1996; Xiang et al., 2005; Xiang, McBride, & Bruene, 2004, 2006; Xiang, McBride, & Guan, 2004; Xiang, McBride, Guan, & Solmon, 2003). For example, subjective task value for physical education was one positive predictor of elementary children's intentions to participate in physical education in high school (Xiang, McBride, & Guan, 2004; Xiang, McBride, Guan, & Solmon, 2003), whereas high intrinsic and utility value for physical education influenced Greek adolescents' intentions to attend and participate in physical education lessons (Papaioannou & Theodorakis, 1996).

Overall, these studies suggest a teacher's attempts to enhance situational interest in tasks during physical education class will positively affect student effort, persistence, and use of learning strategies, student responses that are highly desirable in physical education. Similarly, strategies to enhance the value of physical education for students should positively impact their participation in physical activities and intentions for future participation. Personal interest appears to more strongly impact learning and achievement than motivated learning behaviors.

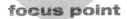

focus point

Teachers should try to increase students' situational interest in and value for physical education tasks, because those factors are related to their effort, persistence, and future intentions.

Student Characteristics
Related to Interest and Value

Researchers have found that several student characteristics are related to their personal interest, situational interest, and/or subjective task value: skill level, stage of learning, age, gender, race, self-perceptions, and goal orientations.

Skill level

Students with higher skill levels in an activity have higher personal interest in the activity. So, increasing student skill level may enhance their personal interest.

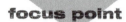

Because skill level doesn't seem to influence students' situational interest, teachers can expect any efforts to increase situational interest to be effective for students of all skill levels.

Several studies show that personal interest, but not situational interest, is positively related to students' skill level in an activity (Chen & Darst, 2001, 2002; Shen & Chen, 2006, 2007a). For example, middle school students with higher levels of skill in basketball had higher levels of personal interest in that sport than students of lower skill levels (Chen & Darst, 2002). However, the students' basketball skill level did not seem to be related to situational interest (Chen & Darst, 2001, 2002). Although more research is needed to examine skill level and interests in other activities, these studies indicate that physical educators can expect the students who have higher levels of skill in an activity to have a higher degree of personal interest in it. One way to help students develop personal interest in an activity is to make sure students experience success in physical education and actually improve their skill levels.

The finding that situational interest is not related to student skill level suggests that any efforts teachers make to enhance situational interest should help the interest levels of all students, regardless of the students' skill level. So, efforts to increase situational interest in an activity can be effective for students who have lower skill levels in an activity as well as higher skill levels.

Stage of learning

Students in the beginning stage of learning an activity can be motivated by enhancing their situational interest in the tasks, while students in more advanced stages of learning are more motivated by their personal interest in the activity.

Alexander and her colleagues (Alexander, Jetton, & Kulikowich, 1995) proposed that students in the beginning stage of learning a subject, who have little knowledge of or skill in that subject, will be more motivated by situational interest to put forth effort and persist in learning that subject. As students consistently interact with the subject, increase their knowledge of the subject, and experience success, personal interest develops. Those same processes move them from the beginning stage of learning to later stages of learning. Alexander et al. (1995) propose that students who are in the proficiency stage of learning for an activity, and in the process have developed personal interest in that activity, do not need situational factors to motivate them.

The change from situational interest to personal interest as the primary motivators as students move to more advanced stages of learning has also been suggested by researchers in physical education (Shen et al., 2003).

In fact, Shen and Chen (2006) suggest that personal interest increases as knowledge increases; they found that 6th graders' gain in knowledge about volleyball was associated with an increase in the students' personal interest in volleyball. So, attempts to enhance situational interest will most likely work with students in the beginning stage of learning, while focusing on personal interests is more relevant for advanced learners.

Age

Student situational interest in physical activities seems to decline as students get older (Chen & Darst, 2001), and girls' personal interest in physical education appears to decrease with age (Van Wersch, Trew, & Turner, 1992). Similarly, personal interest in other school subjects also seems to decline with age (Krapp et al., 1992). Likewise, subjective task value for physical education activities and sport appears to diminish with age (Fredricks & Eccles, 2002; Lirgg, 1993; Wigfield, Eccles, MacIver, Reuman, & Midgley, 1991; Wigfield et al., 1997; Xiang, McBride, & Guan, 2004; Xiang, McBride, Guan, & Solmon, 2003). But that may occur only with some components of subjective task value, because attainment and utility values for sport and physical education activities have been found to decline across elementary and middle school years but not intrinsic value (Lirgg, 1993; Wigfield et al., 1991, 1997).

It is common to see elementary children exhibit great excitement when entering the gym for physical education class, while high school students commonly show low enthusiasm. Thus, even though teachers of students of any age group can try to enhance student interest and value, it seems even more important for teachers of middle school and high school students. Moreover, emphasizing the importance and usefulness of physical education tasks for students might be especially helpful because older students still seem to enjoy physical activity.

Gender

Personal interest. Boys and girls appear to differ in their personal interest in physical education (Browne, 1992; Van Wersch et al., 1992). For example, Van Wersch and her colleagues surveyed more than 3,000 students between the ages of 11 and 18 years about their interest in physical education. The researchers found that girls' personal interest in physical education as a subject in general decreases as they get older, especially after age 14. In contrast, boys' personal interest in physical education over that same age span tends to remain stable. In fact, females at ages 11 and 12 years of age have higher levels of interest in physical education than males; but males have higher interest in the subject than females by age 15. For females, the decline is because they don't view physical education as important as other subjects (Browne, 1992; Van Wersch et al., 1992). Males, on the other hand,

focus point

Because student personal and situational interest in and value for physical education activities likely decline as students get older, teachers of middle school and high school students need to work especially hard to increase student interest and subjective task value.

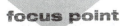

focus point

It is important to enhance adolescent girls' personal interest in physical education, because girls' personal interest in the class decreases in their teenage years, while boys' personal interest in physical education remains stable.

still consider physical education an important subject, mostly due to the social status a physically skilled boy acquires (Van Wersch et al., 1992). Physical educators can therefore probably expect high school girls to be less interested in physical education than boys and may have to do more to enhance girls' personal interest in class, especially at the high school level.

Males and females have similar personal interests in some specific activities offered in physical education, but different personal interest levels in other activities. Luke and Sinclair (1991) found that both genders highly supported the inclusion of team games, individual games, and dual activities in a physical education curriculum, and both males and females have expressed high personal interest in basketball (Fleming, Mitchell, Coleman, & Gorecki, 1997; Mitchell, Fleming, Coleman, & Gorecki, 1997) and softball (Shen & Chen, 2007b). But girls have shown higher personal interest than boys in square dance (Shen et al., 2003), volleyball (Fleming et al., 1997; Tannehill & Zakrajsek, 1993), and aquatics (Luke & Sinclair, 1991). Males seem to have higher personal interest in flag football (Fleming et al., 1997; Mitchell et al., 1997). Some of these differences may be due to gender-role stereotypes, which will be discussed later in this chapter. The different personal interests of boys and girls support the need for teachers to offer a variety of activities from which students, especially high school students, can choose, to ensure their personal interests are met.

Situational interest. When we look at research comparing males and females on situational interest, it is unclear whether there are differences. Boys and girls have exhibited similar situational interest in specific square dance tasks (Shen et al., 2003), but females have shown higher situational interest than males for softball (Shen & Chen, 2007b) and on a specific basketball task (Chen & Darst, 2002). The researchers in the latter study believed the difference was due to the students' skill levels. Remember that Alexander et al. (1995) proposed students in the early stage of learning would be primarily motivated by situational interest factors. In the basketball task, it is possible females had a higher situational interest in the task because they were at the beginning stage of learning (Chen & Darst, 2002). Because males were at a more advanced stage of learning, they relied less on situational factors to motivate them and more on personal interest. So, the boys' situational interest in specific activities wasn't as high as the females', suggesting males and females may not be differentially affected by physical educators' attempts to enhance situational interest, given they are at a similar stage of learning.

Personal meaning, an important aspect of holding interest, appears to differ for boys and girls. For high school females, meaningfulness of physical education activities stems from the development of physical fitness, the opportunity for self-expression, and the release of tension (Chen, 1996, 1998). Males that age tend to experience meaningfulness in activi-

focus point

Because boys and girls have different personal interests in specific physical activities, physical educators, especially at the high school level, should offer a variety of activities from which students may choose to participate.

focus point

As long as boys and girls are at the same stage of learning in an activity, they should be similarly influenced by a physical educator's attempts to increase their situational interest.

ties when they have opportunities for social bonding, to learn about physical activities in other cultures, and to experience challenge and variety in activities (Chen, 1996, 1998). Gender differences in the personal meaning of physical education also could be affected by race. More than African American females and Caucasian students, African American males thought participating in physical education was important for its impact on their appearance and size (i.e., stay slim and fit, stay in shape), whereas African American students and Caucasian males placed higher value than Caucasian females on participating in class for its effect on their academics (Azzarito & Solmon, 2006b). For males and females alike, meaningfulness crossed activities (Chen, 1996, 1998). In other words, a girl with fitness as her primary personal meaning for participating in activities will find an activity personally meaningful if that activity does something to improve her fitness. Activities that don't make her more fit will not hold her interest. Likewise, a boy who has socialization as his primary personal meaning for activity will likely find activities valuable if they provide opportunities to socialize. Regardless of gender or race, it seems important for physical educators to find out students' primary personal meanings for physical activity, and to then convey to students the different meanings associated with activities (Chen, 1996).

focus point

Because boys and girls differ on what they find personally meaningful about physical activities, and because race may affect these differences, teachers should clearly convey to students the various meanings associated with activities so that students find activities personally meaningful.

Subjective task value. There is considerable evidence that boys have higher subjective task value for physical activities than girls (Brustad, 1993, 1996; Eccles & Harold, 1991; Fredricks & Eccles, 2005; Lirgg, 1993; Shapiro & Ulrich, 2002), during elementary school as well as adolescence. For example, in 10- to 13-year-old children, both with and without learning disabilities, boys indicated higher attainment and intrinsic value for physical education than girls (Shapiro & Ulrich, 2002). And upper elementary boys liked physical exertion and exercise (i.e., intrinsic value) more than girls (Brustad, 1996).

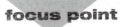

focus point

Boys seem to have higher subjective value for physical activities than girls.

Race

Although little research exists on racial differences in students' interests in physical education, the research that has been done shows that students of different races probably differ in their level of personal interest in specific activities. Both Caucasian and African American students had high personal interest in swimming, but Caucasian students had higher personal interest in bowling and cycling while African Americans preferred track and field (Fleming et al., 1997; Mitchell et al., 1997). Caucasian kindergarten children were found to be more intuitively interested in physical activity in general than minority children (Chen & Zhu, 2005). This finding further demonstrates the need to offer a variety of activities in physical education and to determine student preferences in activities.

focus point

Students should be offered several activities during physical education from which they choose to participate because of possible racial differences in students' personal interests.

Self-perceptions and goal orientations

Researchers are starting to examine how interests and subjective task values are related to students' other psychological characteristics, such as their self-perceptions and goal orientations. Several researchers have found that higher self-perceptions are related to higher subjective task values for physical education, physical activities, and sport, in elementary, middle school, and high school students (e.g., Brustad, 1993; Cury, Biddle, Sarrazin, & Famose, 1997; Dishman, Motl, Sallis, et al., 2005; Fredricks & Eccles, 2005; Lirgg, 1993; Papaioannou & Theodorakis, 1996; Shapiro & Ulrich, 2002; Xiang, McBride, Guan, & Solmon, 2003). For instance, Cury et al. (1997) found that adolescent boys learning a basketball dribbling task with low perceived ability at the task attached less value to the task than those with high perceived ability. Similarly, higher subjective task value for physical education was related to higher perceived ability in physical education in elementary children (Xiang, McBride, Guan, & Solmon, 2003).

Task involvement is another psychological characteristic that seems related to subjective task values in school-age students (e.g., Papaioannou & Theodorakis, 1996; Xiang, McBride, & Bruene, 2004, 2006; Xiang, McBride, & Guan, 2004). For example, 4th graders' task involvement in a yearlong physical education running program was positively related to their attainment, intrinsic, and utility values for running (Xiang, McBride, & Bruene, 2004, 2006). Task involvement also seems positively related to personal and situational interest. In one study, middle school students' personal interests in contact sports and alternative games (e.g., pickleball, archery, table tennis) were moderately related to their self-improvement goals (task orientation) (Chen & Shen, 2004), while in another study 6th graders with higher task orientation had higher situational interest in softball tasks (Shen & Chen, 2007b). In the latter study, goals to perform better than others in order to avoid looking bad in front of others (ego-involved/avoidance goals) were also associated with high situational interest.

Perhaps some students do not value physical education activities because they have low ability in those activities. Lessons that focus on student improvement in skills, and not just game play that displays current ability level, might enhance students' subjective task value in physical education. Similarly, these studies suggest teachers might increase student interest and value for physical education activities by establishing an environment that focuses on self-improvement, which is a task-involving climate, instead of comparing students to each other.

Sources of Subjective Task Value

Several researchers have investigated the sources of students' subjective task values in physical activity domains: positive and negative affective experiences, perceptions of significant others' beliefs and behaviors, and perceived gender roles and activity stereotypes. Eighth graders with low or

▼ **focus point**

High self-perceptions in a domain are associated with high subjective task values, while task involvement seems related to high subjective task values and personal and situational interest.

medium subjective task value for sport said that negative emotions about sport were common, but those with high value for sport claimed mostly positive emotions with sport (Stuart, 1997). Girls in that same study, but not boys, identified gender-role stereotypes as influencing the value they placed on sport (i.e., girls not allowed to play baseball or football, grandmother stating that sports weren't for girls). It is likely that gender-role stereotyping contributes to the gender differences in subjective task value for physical activity. Eccles and Harold (1991) found that elementary-age boys and girls believe it is more important that boys have high ability in sports than girls. Even specific activities are viewed as more appropriate for boys or girls; for example, activities viewed as masculine (e.g., baseball, boxing, football, weight lifting) are perceived as "boys'" activities, whereas activities characterized as feminine (e.g., aerobics, dance, gymnastics, ballet) are seen as "girls'" activities (Klomsten, Marsh, & Skaalvik, 2005).

One major source of these gender-role stereotypes and subjective task values for physical activity are significant others' beliefs and behaviors, particularly parents. Parents' self-reports reveal that they more highly value physical activity participation for their sons than daughters (e.g., Fredricks & Eccles, 2005; Xiang, McBride, & Bruene, 2003), and they provide more support and encouragement for their sons' participation than their daughters' (Brustad, 1993; Fredricks & Eccles, 2005). Parents' stereotypical beliefs and behaviors, in turn, influenced their children's value for physical activity (Brustad, 1993; Fredricks & Eccles, 2005) or their children's performance and persistence (Xiang, McBride, & Breune, 2003). In fact, Fredricks and Eccles (2005) found that children's value for sport increased along with the number of sport promotive factors reported by parents (i.e., purchasing them equipment, parent involvement in and value for sport, coaching a team, encouragement). Other researchers found that children's perceptions of their parents' beliefs and behaviors influence their subjective task value for physical activity (e.g., Brustad, 1996; Kimiecik, Horn, & Shurin, 1996; Stuart, 1997). For example, children's perceptions of the encouragement they received from their parents for physical activity and the intrinsic value parents had for physical activity positively affected upper elementary students' value for physical activity (Brustad, 1996). Children do perceive gender stereotyping in their parents' value for their physical activity, as elementary boys believed it was more important to their parents that they do well in sports than girls (Eccles & Harold, 1991).

These studies suggest physical educators can influence students' value for physical activity by providing enjoyable, positive experiences in class. Since parents' beliefs and behaviors have a strong impact on children's value for physical activity, information about this influence might encourage parents to promote physical activity for their daughters as well as their sons. Physical education teachers should also verbalize to students the importance of physical activity for all students and encourage all students' efforts.

focus point

Negative affect, gender-role stereotypes, and parents' lack of support and value for physical activity can negatively impact students' value for physical activity, especially girls'.

Dimensions of Situational Interest

In their research with middle school students, Chen and his colleagues (Chen, Darst, & Pangrazi, 1999, 2001) identified five dimensions of situational interest in physical education. These dimensions represent characteristics of the setting that might contribute to situational interest. The five dimensions are as follows:

1. *Novelty.* Novel (new and unusual) activities can produce interest in an activity because there is a gap between what the student knows and doesn't know. For example, a tae-kwan-do unit might yield high situational interest in students because it is new to them.

2. *Challenge.* Physically challenging tasks (based on complexity and difficulty) may produce situational interest if students are encouraged to move beyond what they could previously do. For example, while other students are working on regular layups during a basketball unit, a teacher could challenge a highly skilled 7th grade girl to work on a reverse layup, which could increase her situational interest in the lesson.

3. *Attention demand.* Tasks that demand a high level of thought or attention can enhance situational interest because students are forced to concentrate and become absorbed in the activity. Rock climbing is an activity that requires high concentration, and thus inherently can yield high situational interest.

4. *Exploration intention.* Students who want to find out more about and discover all the different aspects of an activity are exhibiting the **exploration intention** dimension of situational interest. A teacher who asks her 9th grade class to describe all the tactical similarities between tennis and volleyball is trying to enhance the exploratory dimension of situational interest.

5. *Instant enjoyment.* Tasks that are instantly enjoyable because they are exciting or fascinating, or because students experience immediate success and just have fun, can also yield situational interest. Bowling is one sport that can produce instant enjoyment, and thus high situational interest, in students of all ages due to the likelihood of quick success, especially if the bumpers are used!

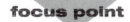

focus point

Enhancing student enjoyment of and intention to explore activities can increase student situational interest, along with offering novel activities and cognitively challenging tasks.

The dimensions that seem to have the strongest impact on situational interest in physical education are exploration intention and instant enjoyment, with novelty and attention demand having moderate impact (Chen et al., 1999, 2001). Chen and Darst (2001) also found that tasks with high cognitive demand (i.e., the attention demand dimension) produce higher situational interest than tasks with high physical demand (i.e., the challenge dimension). So far, research indicates that the challenge dimension seems to have less influence on situational interest than other dimensions.

That doesn't mean teachers should never increase the difficulty of tasks for students. Rather, Chen and his colleagues suggest physical challenge should be minimal when introducing new activities (Chen et al., 2001). Exploration intention, enjoyment, attention demand, and novelty should be considered when trying to enhance student situational interest.

Means of Enhancing Interest in and Value for Physical Education

The literature and research just reviewed suggest several strategies teachers can use to enhance student interest in and value for physical education activities; those strategies are described in this section. Higher interest in and value for physical education should have a positive impact on students' participation, effort, performance, and achievement, as well as create a more pleasant classroom climate. Since there is considerable overlap between the two types of interest and the components of subjective task value, most of the techniques are organized around the types of interest, with the related value components described when appropriate.

Personal versus Situational Interest

Educational researchers recommend teachers focus on situational interest rather than personal interest when attempting to motivate students (Renninger, Hidi, & Krapp, 1992), for several reasons:

1. Personal interest is difficult to change because it tends to be quite stable and takes time to develop. Teachers have no control over the personal interests with which students enter physical education (Mitchell, 1993).
2. Individuals differ greatly in personal interests (Hidi & Anderson, 1992). It would be difficult for a physical education program to meet all students' personal interests.
3. Situational interest, by its nature, is elicited by conditions in the environment. Thus it has the possibility of being affected by the way physical educators arrange tasks and settings.

The recommendation that teachers focus on situational interest, however, does not mean they should ignore personal interest. Studies show students' personal interests are related to achievement in physical education (Shen et al., 2003). Personal interests could also be related to attainment value, if the activity is connected to the students' self-identity, or to intrinsic value, if the student simply enjoys participating in an activity for its own sake. These ideas support the need for teachers to address students' personal interests.

focus point

Although it is important to address student personal interests, a teacher is more likely to enhance student interest in physical education by influencing situational interest.

Meet Students' Personal Interests

One characteristic of a physically educated person is a physically active lifestyle (NASPE, 2004b). Adults who exhibit a physically active lifestyle are likely participating in activities they enjoy and which reflect their personal interests. In addition, these activities undoubtedly have attainment and/or intrinsic value to students. In addition, middle school and high school students may already have developed some strong personal physical activity interests. We've already seen how the personal interests of students in physical education can vary according to their stage of learning, gender, and race. Because older students are likely to have a wide variety of personal activity interests, physical education programs should attempt to discover those interests, especially at the high school level. Once those personal interests are understood, programs can offer a wide variety of activities from which students choose. This variety will allow the students to participate in activities they value and ones that match their personal interests.

One way to identify students' personal activity interests in physical education is to give them a paper-and-pencil survey to complete. Several different types of surveys could be used. One type of survey asks students to make up their own lists of activities (see Exhibit 8.1 and Appendix A.7;

> **focus point**
>
> To meet the personal interests of many students, physical educators should survey students to determine their personal activity interests, then offer several activities from which students choose to participate.

EXHIBIT 8.1 Unlimited-choice survey to identify students' personal activity interests.

Class Period: _____   Date: _____

Directions: Please respond to the following questions.

1. Age as of last birthday in years *(please circle)*

    9   10   11   12   13   14   15

2. Gender

    Male   Female

3. List the five physical activities in which you would most like to participate.

    1. _____   4. _____
    2. _____   5. _____
    3. _____

From D. S. Fleming, M. Mitchell, J. J. Gorecki, & M. M. Coleman, "Students change and so do good programs: Addressing the interests of multicultural secondary students," in *Journal of Physical Education, Recreation, and Dance, 70* (2), 79–83. Copyright 1999, American Alliance for Health, Physical Education, Recreation, and Dance, Reston, VA. Reprinted with permission.

Fleming, Mitchell, Gorecki, & Coleman, 1999). While this type of survey gives students plenty of freedom in listing activities, students may not be able to come up with names of activities (Fleming et al., 1999) or even know that some activities exist. Another type of survey is the forced choice survey (see Exhibit 8.2 and Appendix A.8; Fleming et al., 1999), in which specific activities are named and students simply check the activities in which they are interested. A third type of survey is the ranked-choice survey (see Exhibit 8.3 and Appendix A.9; Fleming et al., 1999), which allows students to rank activities according to their preferences of participation. These surveys are best completed anonymously by students at the

| Limited-choice survey to identify students' personal activity interests. | **EXHIBIT** | **8.2** |

Class Period: _____   Date: _____

Directions: Please respond to the following questions.

1. Age as of last birthday in years *(please circle)*

   9   10   11   12   13   14   15

2. Gender

   Male   Female

3. Check all of the activities in which you would enjoy participating.

   Aerobics   Rackets (tennis/badminton)

   Basketball   Rugby

   Bowling   Soccer

   Cycling   Softball

   Dance   Swimming

   Football   Team handball

   Golf   Ultimate Frisbee

   Gymnastics   Volleyball

   Hockey (field or floor)   Weight/strength training

   Outdoor pursuits (archery, orienteering, canoeing, hiking)

   Other _____ (fill in)

EXHIBIT	8.3	Ranked-choice survey to identify students' personal activity interests.

Class Period: _____   Date: _____

Directions: Please respond to the following questions.

1. Age as of last birthday in years *(please circle)*

    9   10   11   12   13   14   15

2. Gender

    Male   Female

3. Below is a list of different activities. Read the entire list, then use the following scale to rank the top four in which you would like to participate.

    0 = I know what this activity is, but it is not one of my top 4 choices

    1 = My first choice (please choose only one activity)

    2 = My second choice (please choose only one activity)

    3 = My third choice (please choose only one activity)

    4 = My fourth choice (please choose only one activity)

    5 = I don't know what this activity is

TEAM SPORTS

___ Basketball   ___ Hockey (field or floor)

___ Football   ___ Team handball

___ Softball   ___ Ultimate Frisbee

___ Rugby   ___ Volleyball

___ Soccer   ___ Other team sport *(fill in: _____)*

Below is another list of different activities. Again, read the entire list, then use the previous scale to rank the top four activities in which you would like to participate.

OTHER ACTIVITIES

___ Aerobics   ___ Outdoor pursuits (archery, orienteering, canoeing, hiking)

___ Bowling   ___ Rackets (tennis/badminton)

___ Cycling   ___ Swimming

___ Dance   ___ Weight/strength training

___ Golf   ___ Wrestling

___ Gymnastics   ___ Other activity *(fill in: _____)*

From D. S. Fleming, M. Mitchell, J. J. Gorecki, & M. M. Coleman, "Students change and so do good programs: Addressing the interests of multicultural secondary students," in *Journal of Physical Education, Recreation, and Dance, 70* (2), 79–83. Copyright 1999, American Alliance for Health, Physical Education, Recreation, and Dance, Reston, VA. Reprinted with permission.

beginning of the school year. Any one of these surveys will give physical educators information about students' personal interests and help teachers offer activities that match those interests.

Let's consider Jamal, the student in the chapter's opening scenario. Outside of physical education, Jamal values and has personal interests in soccer, tennis, golf, and basketball. But basketball is the only personal interest of Jamal's that is offered in his physical education program. Other activities offered are flag football, softball, and volleyball, in which Jamal has low personal interest. Thus it is not surprising that he doesn't give much effort during class. Jamal's physical educators might discover his (and his classmates') personal activity interests in physical education by giving them a survey. The teachers can then use that information to offer a wider variety of activities from which students choose, making it more likely that Jamal and his classmates will participate in activities they value and in which they have higher personal interest, increasing the likelihood they give higher effort during class.

Catch Interest with Technology

Students of all ages love to use technological gadgets; having students use different technologies can initially catch their situational interest (Mitchell, 1993). Some students may find intrinsic value in working with technology, while for other students, working with technology confirms part of their identity (i.e., attainment value). Computers can be used in several ways, for example, students can enter their own fitness, skill, or knowledge scores using the computer. Teachers who use the Fitnessgram® (The Cooper Institute, 2006) health-related fitness tests can have students enter their own scores using the Fitnessgram® software. Similarly, students could enter their own daily physical activity using the Activitygram® software (The Cooper Institute, 2006). Such software packages help students learn important concepts while using the computer to enter their data, which can catch their interest.

Videocameras are another form of technology useful for recording student skill and game performance. Once students have practiced skills or game strategies, they can be recorded performing the skill or playing the game. The students can then watch the video and use checklists to determine their success at learning those skills or strategies. For example, students in a basketball unit who have been practicing how to move to receive a ball from a teammate, defend an opponent who may or may not have the ball, and make a quick transition from offense to defense and vice versa can be recorded while playing the game. They can then watch the video and assess their own performance using a rubric that includes those three tactical elements. Video recordings of performances allow students to objectively see their performance and detect the elements they do well or which need to be improved.

real world

Other technologies that catch student interest quickly and that students might find valuable are heart monitors and pedometers. At an urban middle school in the southern United States, students use heart monitors to assess their activity level during class. Because of a limited physical education budget, there are only about 30 heart monitors available during a class period. Because each period may have up to three different classes of 30 students each, the classes alternate weeks during which they use the heart monitors. For instance, three 6th grade classes meet during the same class period. Melissa G.'s 6th grade class uses the heart monitors during the first three weeks, Michelle H.'s 6th grade class uses them the second three weeks, and Mr. H.'s class uses them the third three weeks. Their students record their results by hand each day, but if computers are available, the students can download their results into a computer using a heart monitor program.

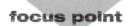

focus point

Physical educators can catch student situational interest in and value for activities by using technology (e.g., computers, computer programs, videocameras, heart monitors, pedometers).

Pedometers can also catch student interest. For example, as part of a rhythms course at a university in the midwestern United States, physical education majors teach children rhythmical activities at a local elementary school. The children wear university pedometers to teach the children the importance of physical activity. At the end of each lesson, the university student who is closing the lesson discusses with the children the number of steps they took during the lesson and what that means to their fitness levels. Ideas for using pedometers in physical education can be found in the book *Pedometer Power: 67 Lessons for K–12* (Pangrazi, Beighle, & Sidman, 2003). Such gadgets as heart monitors and pedometers are great for catching student interest, while at the same time teaching important fitness concepts.

Technology is never used in Jamal's physical education program, so this could be one way to enhance his situational interest in and value for physical education. Simply recording Jamal while practicing a skill, such as batting a softball, and having him watch the video and analyze his form for certain critical elements could increase his situational interest in softball.

Hold Interest with Personal Meaning

Students holding interest in a physical activity, as well as attainment and/or utility value, can be enhanced by increasing the personal meaning of that activity for students. To do that, you as a physical educator must first discover students' primary personal meanings for participating in activities. Do they participate to develop their fitness? Bond with others? Release tension? Be physically challenged? As with identifying personal interests, paper-and-pencil surveys can uncover students' personal meanings for activities. Students can be asked to identify their 5 favorite activities and then explain why those are their favorite activities. Or students may check their 5 favorite activities from a list of 30 and explain why those are their favorite activities.

In each type of survey, the explanations given for choosing activities will expose the students' primary personal meanings. For example, a student who chooses basketball, flag football, volleyball, team handball, and soccer as her favorite activities might write "they help me get in shape," which suggests a personal meaning of developing her fitness, while the reason "I like to play on a team" suggests a personal meaning of bonding with others.

Once students' personal meanings are revealed, strive to find ways to communicate to students the various meanings associated with activities (Chen, 1996, 2001). For example, weight lifting can develop students' fitness levels, but it can also help them bond with others, release tension, and physically challenge one's self. One way alternative meanings can be conveyed to students is to discuss the meanings individually with students. Knowing beforehand that a student's primary personal meaning is to release tension can serve as an opening to casually discuss with the student during or after class how the activity meets the student's meaning.

An activity's alternative meanings can also be presented to the whole class. One time to do this is at the start of the lesson, during the set induction. Students need to know why they are learning an activity, and these reasons should be presented to the students at the beginning of a class or unit. Reasons for participating in an activity should relate to the various meanings attached to an activity and could impact utility value. For example, at the start of a wall climbing unit, wall climbing could be presented as a new type of activity that

- Few students know (for students with a variety of activity primary meaning)
- Helps develop muscular strength (physical fitness personal meaning or utility value)
- Can be adjusted to meet students' individual abilities (the challenge meaning)

The alternative meanings of a task can also be presented to the class in task presentations throughout a lesson. So, while presenting a particular wall climbing task later in the lesson, again remind students how the activity will develop their muscular strength.

Jamal's primary personal meaning for participating in physical activities is to be physically challenged; he enjoys tasks that improve his skill level, even if the task is difficult. Unfortunately, many tasks students are required to do in Jamal's physical education classes are easy and not much challenge for him. That is why Jamal often gets bored in class. If Jamal's teachers knew that he finds personal meaning in activities that physically challenge him, they could design tasks that do that. For example, Jamal is often bored during his basketball unit, even though bas-

focus point

Surveys can reveal students' personal meanings for activities, after which the teacher can convey to students the various meanings associated with activities via individual discussions, the set induction, and task presentations.

connected   CONCEPTS

More information about the set induction can be found in Chapter 3.

ketball is one of his personal interests. He lacks interest in it during physical education because the tasks are not challenging to him; tasks are simple, like shooting alone from different spots around the court or standing in a circle and passing to classmates. Jamal's interest in and attainment value for basketball during class would probably increase if he were challenged with learning new skills, such as a reverse layup or how to defend against a screen. He could even challenge himself by setting goals, like making 7 of 10 shots at each shooting spot.

Offer Novel Activities

One way to enhance situational interest is to offer activities students have not participated in before (Chen et al., 1999, 2001).

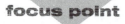

For example, Bonnie T., a physical educator at a rural elementary school in the midwestern United States, taught her 5th and 6th grade students the novel activity of juggling. Student interest was usually high for this unique activity. Similarly, team handball is a novel activity that has become part of the physical education curriculum for a suburban school district in the southern United States. One reason students in that district show high interest in this activity is because it is new for all students when they first encounter the activity during middle school; all students begin on the same level because none of them have previous experience with the sport.

In Jamal's school, the same familiar activities are always offered: basketball, flag football, volleyball, and softball. Jamal and his classmates would be interested if new activities were offered during class, such as team handball or kick boxing.

Keep in mind two principles when presenting novel activities to students. First, keep the physical challenge to a minimum when the activity is introduced to the students (Chen et al., 2001). Students will not find new activities enjoyable or interesting if the tasks are physically too difficult; find ways to simplify the initial tasks. For example, when Bonnie T. taught her students to juggle, they first used scarves and beanbags, and gradually moved from one piece of equipment to three. Second, don't offer an activity simply because it is new; make sure it contributes to your program's accomplishment of the NASPE content standards (2004b) and your state and local curricular goals. It does your program no good to offer a novel activity that does not help your students meet the national, state, or local standards.

focus point

When offering novel activities, keep the physical challenge minimal at first, and make sure the activity helps your students meet curricular goals and standards in physical education.

Challenge Students Cognitively

Another way to enhance interest in and possibly intrinsic value for a physical activity is to increase the cognitive demand within tasks (Chen & Darst, 2001). In Chen and Darst's (2001) study with middle school students, basketball tasks with high cognitive demands, regardless of the physical challenge, were more situationally interesting to students than tasks with low cognitive demands. Such tasks might also have intrinsic value for students who find pleasure in such cognitive challenges. One highly cognitive task was a skill identification task, in which students watched a video of skilled basketball players and identified the various basketball skills used by players. The task included virtually no physical demand, but high cognitive demand. The other task with high cognitive demand also had high physical demand—a pass-shoot task that required six students to pass, dribble, move, and shoot in a complex pattern. The two tasks in which students had low situational interest also had low cognitive demand. One was a simple stationary chest-pass task, in which partners stood 15 feet apart and passed the ball back and forth. The other task was a defensive footwork drill, a task that had high physical demand but low cognitive demand.

The results of this study suggest that physical educators should avoid simple rote physical drills in which students stand and mindlessly complete tasks (like the stationary chest-pass task), especially when students are already familiar with those skills. More complex tasks require students to think about what they are doing and therefore engage them cognitively. For example, a low cognitive task in a basketball unit would be shooting jump shots at five different spots (A, B, C, D, E) around the basket. The student shoots 15 shots at each spot before moving to the next spot; a partner rebounds the ball for the student. A more cognitively challenging task is for the shooter to start at spot A and shoot the ball. While the ball is on its way to the basket, the partner/rebounder calls out the next spot from which the student must shoot. The spots are called out in random order. The student shooting must think about where the spot is and move to that spot in time to receive the pass from her partner. The cognitive challenge can be increased by having the partner call out a move the shooter must make before shooting, such as a fake to the right or a pump fake shot. Students could also use imagery to imagine themselves shooting against an opponent. As mentioned before, most tasks in Jamal's basketball unit were simple tasks that required very little thought. Tasks with more cognitive involvement, like those just described, would prove helpful in enhancing Jamal's interest level.

Puzzles or brain teasers are cognitively challenging tasks that can help catch student interest (Mitchell, 1993). At the start of a lesson, a physical educator can use puzzles or word finds to help students review concepts from previous classes or discover what they will be working on today. At the end of a lesson, the teacher can provide a crossword puzzle to review the concepts learned in the day's lesson. When teaching an individual sports course for physical education majors at a university in the southern United States, Bonnie T. frequently provided students with a crossword

focus point

Tasks that require high cognitive involvement work increase student interest in and intrinsic value for physical education.

puzzle to help familiarize them with the important terms related to an activity, which was much more interesting than other forms of review.

Students also face cognitive challenges when they are trying to learn novel activities. This occurs because in the beginning stage of learning a new skill or activity, we must think carefully about the task at hand, often repeating important elements of the task to ourselves as we practice. For example, when students first learn to juggle, they have to think carefully about the steps, and could repeat to themselves, "toss, toss, catch, catch" as they practice juggling. Such cognitive involvement when learning new skills or activities can work to enhance interest in the activity.

focus point

Using puzzles, brain teasers, and novel activities can enhance student cognitive involvement in physical education.

Arouse Students' Intention to Explore

A strong intent to explore and discover all the different aspects of an activity is a good predictor of student interest in the activity (Chen et al., 2001). One way physical educators can elicit students' exploration behavior is to use a **movement analysis curriculum** (Jewett, Bain, & Ennis, 1995). These types of curricula encourage students to find new and different ways of moving and applying principles of movement. Such curricula could have high intrinsic value for students who find pleasure in discovering new things. An example of one such elementary-level curriculum is the movement education curriculum (Logsdon et al., 1984). In this curriculum, tasks are designed to let children experiment with a movement concept and think about movement in new ways.

focus point

Using a movement analysis curriculum, such as movement education, can arouse students' intentions to explore.

real world

For example, Carolyn J., physical educator at an urban elementary school in Virginia, lets her 5th grade students explore various ways of producing countertension balances with a partner. After students have created several different countertension balances, they are then instructed to choose their favorite balance and use it in a movement sequence.

Another way to enhance students' exploratory intentions is to ask them to look for any similar elements between a new skill they are learning and a skill they have already learned. Three types of elements in skills should be examined for similarities: movement, perceptual, and conceptual (Schmidt & Wrisberg, 2000).

1. **Movement elements** deal with the form or movement patterns used to perform the skill. For example, the legs extend in a volleyball forearm pass similar to the leg extension in a basketball free throw.

2. **Perceptual elements** are environmental stimuli produced during a skill performance that a person needs to detect and correctly interpret in order to have a successful performance. For example, passing to a moving teammate in both basketball and soccer requires a person to be able to detect the direction and speed a teammate is moving and then use the correct force and direction to pass it to

where the person is moving. Likewise, a solid hit in softball and golf each elicit a characteristic sound.

3. **Conceptual elements** refer to similar strategies, rules, or concepts between activities. For example, in both tennis and volleyball, you try to hit the ball away from your opponents.

Jamal's teachers could enhance his interest in class by asking him and the other students to look for skill elements in an activity that are similar to elements in another activity. For example, during a volleyball unit, the students could be asked to come up with any elements in volleyball that are similar to elements in basketball (e.g., a set to a hitter at the net needs to be accurately placed in volleyball, just like a pass from one player to another player going in for a slam in basketball needs to be accurately placed).

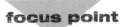

focus point

Students' exploratory intentions in physical education can be stimulated by asking them to look for similarities between skills in movement, perceptual, and conceptual elements.

Use a Different Instructional Model

Several characteristics of the environment that catch and hold student interest include group work, student involvement and empowerment, success and enjoyment, opportunities to explore, and cognitive demand. Such characteristics can also enhance various value components. Unfortunately, many of these characteristics are lacking in direct instruction, the most commonly used instructional model in physical education (Metzler, 2005). In direct instruction, the teacher makes nearly all the decisions about content, management, student engagement, pacing, and task progression; little student input or involvement is allowed. Often only highly skilled students get involved; lower skilled students manage to avoid participating to avoid embarrassment. Group work is not common in such a model, and students are expected to just do what they're told without any exploration or cognitive challenge. Although student success and enjoyment can occur with direct instruction, other instructional models—like the inquiry and tactical games models—can yield those positive outcomes while at the same time utilizing environmental characteristics that more readily enhance student situational interest and value.

focus point

Direct instruction often lacks many of the contextual characteristics (e.g., group work, student involvement and empowerment, opportunities to explore, cognitive demand) that can enhance students' situational interest and subjective task value.

connected CONCEPTS

Other instructional models that have characteristics proposed to enhance student situational interest as well as value include sport education, cooperative learning, and adventure-based learning (see Chapter 4). Each of those models employ group work, student involvement and empowerment, chances to explore, and cognitive demand.

Inquiry

One instructional model that requires a lot of student involvement is the **inquiry model** (Metzler, 2005). This model has many similarities to the guided discovery teaching style (Mosston & Ashworth, 2002). The major theme of the inquiry model is the "learner as problem solver," so cognitive challenge is an intimate part. In fact, the cognitive domain is often the primary focus of student learning in this model. The inquiry model also provides students with many opportunities to explore all different aspects of movements, which is another way of enhancing situational interest and intrinsic value. In addition, student interest undoubtedly will intensify because many different solutions are possible, allowing many students to experience success.

In the inquiry model, the teacher presents a learning problem to students (e.g., use your jump rope to create a circle on the floor, then find all the ways you can travel into and out of the circle without touching it). The teacher then helps the students solve the problem in various ways and at different levels by asking them a series of questions (e.g., "How can you move more quietly?" "Can you combine a low movement with a high movement and still go in and out of the rope?" "What would happen if you tried to hold a ball in your hands as you move in and out?"). After hearing a movement problem or a question, the students are encouraged to "think and move," attempting to find various solutions to the problem (Metzler, 2005).

Metzler (2005) gives several tips for the successful implementation of the inquiry model:

1. *Plan your questions ahead of time,* especially when first learning to use this model. As a result, you can plan for progression and move students from simple to more complex motor skills, as well as from lower levels of cognitive understanding to higher levels.

2. *Avoid giving students answers to problems;* let them create solutions on their own. If they are having trouble coming up with solutions, you can simplify the problem, ask more questions, or give them hints to help them develop solutions.

3. *Give students plenty of time to try out different solutions;* don't rush. Remember, students are to "think first, then move."

4. *Clearly frame the learning problem.* Students need clear directions on the space and equipment available to solve the movement problem, any restrictions, etc. For example, instructions to "create a movement sequence consisting of a jump, a roll, and a balance" provide a much clearer learning problem than "come up with a sequence of three movements."

5. *Feedback to students as they work should primarily take the form of questions:* "Did you think of different ways to move before you tried that?" "How does that sequence meet the requirements?" "Can you think of another way to roll that might make your sequence smoother?"

According to Metzler (2005), the inquiry instructional model can be used with any grade level. It can also be used with any content, but is especially good with the following: movement concepts, educational

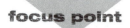
focus point

The high cognitive demand, inherent opportunities to explore, and high success that characterize the inquiry model can enhance students' situational interest and value.

gymnastics, educational games, dance, personal fitness concepts, sport and activity concepts, and skill themes. Read more about the inquiry model in *Instructional Models for Physical Education* (Metzler, 2005).

The inquiry instructional model has been used successfully by pre-service physical educators from an urban university in the southern United States. For example, in a practicum at an urban elementary school, pre-service teacher Jennifer T. used a series of questions to help 1st graders discover various ways of rolling across a mat without getting hurt. In the same practicum, another pre-service teacher, Dion C., asked his 3rd graders questions to help them determine good ways of balancing while moving. Both teachers saw greater involvement in the lesson than what may have been seen in a direct instruction lesson.

real world

Tactical games

In a traditional physical education sport or games unit, discrete motor skills are practiced to develop correct technical performance of those skills before the actual game is played. For example, the chest-pass is practiced in basketball—often with stationary partners throwing back and forth to each other—to make sure the students step toward their partner and release with the thumbs down. Students might also practice dribbling around cones, while the teacher emphasizes head up, fingerpads, ball outside the cone, and so forth. Although there is nothing wrong with wanting good technical performance of skills, students often fail to see the relevance of such tasks for actual game play. Students are interested in playing "the game"—they are not motivated to practice isolated, repetitive drills. Yet often when students do play the game, they cannot perform these skills sufficiently to enjoy the game. Such are the problems of a traditional sport or games unit.

An instructional model that takes advantage of students' inherent interest in playing "the game" is the **tactical games model** (Griffin, Mitchell, & Oslin, 1997; Metzler, 2005; Mitchell, Oslin, & Griffin, 2003). This model's main goal is to help students learn the tactical aspects of games, while at the same time enhancing their execution of skills. This goal is accomplished through the practice of modified game forms, tasks that students often find more interesting and relevant to the game than stand-alone technical practice of skills. Such tasks could also enhance students' attainment value (if being good at sports is part of the student's identity), utility value (as the tasks actually contribute to helping students become good games players), or intrinsic value (if students find skillful game playing inherently pleasurable). Each class period includes the following sequential segments (Griffin et al., 1997; Metzler, 2005):

- Game form
- Teaching for understanding

- Drills for skill development
- Return to game form
- Closure

Each class period begins with the students playing a game form—so the students get to "play the game" right away, which creates instant enjoyment. The game form is a modified game (e.g., 3-on-3 basketball, no dribbling, must pass to every person before shooting) that the teacher uses to initially assess students' skills and tactical knowledge. After playing the game form for several minutes, the teacher gathers the students and asks them questions about their success or problems on the task, and ways to improve their performance. The key component during the "teaching for understanding" segment is to question the students so they come up with some solutions, not for the teacher to simply tell the students how they can improve. This strategy enhances student involvement in the lesson and cognitive demand, which are ways to increase student interest. After the students identify possible solutions, the teacher then explains and demonstrates one or two drills for the students to practice that could solve the problem. For example, if students have trouble getting passes to their teammates in the 3-on-3 game form described above, the teacher will want to show and have students practice the backdoor move. After practicing the drill/s to develop skill, the students return to the original game form and try to incorporate the skill or tactic just practiced. The teacher stresses the use of the new technique by giving a team a point each time they catch a backdoor pass, in addition to the points for scoring a basket. The class period ends with a closure in which the teacher reviews the new tactic or skill with the students.

In order to successfully use the tactical games model, physical educators must be able to identify tactics used in games. This can be difficult for teachers who are used to teaching skills in isolation from game play. In the tactical games approach, games are classified according to tactical similarities among them: net/wall, invasion, target, and fielding-run scoring games (Griffin et al., 1997; Metzler, 2005). Net/wall games—such as volleyball, tennis, badminton, and racquetball—have some similar tactics: a need to return to base position after hitting an object, trying to hit the ball where the opponent isn't, or trying to hit the ball so hard the opponent cannot return it. These are the conceptual elements described earlier that can be similar among games. Once a teacher identifies the game category, basic tactics to teach to students can be identified. Students should be encouraged to look for these similarities among games, which can enhance student interest and intrinsic value by increasing their exploration.

The tactical games model can be used with elementary through high school students, although simple games and tactics must be used with young children (Metzler, 2005; Mitchell et al., 2003). Extensive explana-

focus point

Because lessons in the tactical games instructional model begin with a game form, students usually experience instant enjoyment, which can increase situational interest and intrinsic value.

tions of the model, along with progressions of tactical problems within game categories and example lessons, can be found in the following books: *Teaching Sport Concepts and Skills: A Tactical Games Approach* (Griffin et al., 1997) and *Sport Foundations for Elementary Physical Education: A Tactical Games Approach* (Mitchell et al., 2003).

real world

The tactical games model has been used successfully by many teachers, including a group of pre-service physical education majors from a midwestern university. These students taught a flag football unit to 8th grade boys at a private school. One lesson began with a game form in which the boys played 3-on-3. The offense had four downs to score a touchdown on a smaller than regulation field, and they could only score by catching a pass from the quarterback. The defense had to play person-to-person defense and could not rush the quarterback. After playing this game form for several minutes, the teachers brought the boys together and asked them these kinds of questions: "What things worked well on offense?" "Defense?" "When the defense wasn't successful in stopping the offense, why did that happen?" "Where was the defensive person positioned in relation to the offensive person?" "What would work better?" The pre-service teachers then showed the boys how to keep the receiver in front when playing defense and how to knock the ball down without getting a penalty. Next, the boys did a drill in which two defenders went against two receivers off the scrimmage line, with the receivers trying to get open and the defenders trying to get in the right position. The second drill was just like the first, except one of the pre-service teachers tried throwing the ball to one of the receivers so the defenders could work on knocking the ball down. The lesson ended with the boys playing the same 3-on-3 game form they played at the beginning of the lesson. The boys, who participated in units taught with other instructional models over the semester, commented that they enjoyed the flag football unit taught with the tactical games model the most because they got to play right away.

Jamal's interest in and value for physical education might increase with either of these instructional models. For example, the tactical games model might be interesting for Jamal in a basketball unit because he is ready to learn more complex strategies involved in the activity.

Create a Content Development

Tasks that are physically challenging for students, pushing them beyond what they could previously do, are proposed to increase students' situational interest (Chen et al., 1999, 2001). Such tasks might also carry attainment or intrinsic value for students. Yet in many physical education programs, the same simple skills (e.g., stationary passing and receiving in basketball, dribbling between cones) are practiced by students year after year. Students who can perform such skills become bored with physical education. But there are also students who still have problems with such skills, and so do not enjoy and are not interested in class because they do not experience success. You can spark student interest in and enhance value for physical education if the tasks you ask the students to do are developmentally appropriate; tasks are more difficult for some students (so they are challenged) but easier for other students (so they can experience success and enjoyment). One way to create tasks that are at the appropriate level of challenge for all students is to create and use a **content development** (Rink, 2002), which is a progression of tasks designed to move students from one skill level to the next. A content development consists of three types of tasks: *extensions, refinements,* and *applications.*

Extensions

Extensions are those tasks that gradually become more difficult or more complex (Rink, 2002). This result can be accomplished in various ways: changing equipment, adding movement, changing the spatial requirements for the task, changing the number of people involved, combining skills, or changing the rules or conditions of performance. For example, the simplest way to dribble is to stand and use your favorite hand. Extensions of this method include using your non-favorite hand, switching hands, walking, jogging, gradually decreasing the space in which dribbling occurs, catching a pass and then dribbling, and dribbling against a defender. The key to a good progression of extending tasks is to have small steps between tasks; difficulty should only be increased slightly with each consecutive extending task, to ensure that students are successful at more difficult tasks. For example, if students have only practiced the basketball chest pass to a partner while stationary, they might next practice passing to each other while walking up the court; practicing the "3-person-weave" after stationary passing with a partner is too big of a step. When using a list of many extension tasks for a lesson, from very simple to complex, choose an easier task from the list if the class is not being successful on an initial task, or a harder task if the students are being successful. Likewise, make adjustments for individual students; a student having difficulty can be given an easier extending task, while a student who is not being challenged can be given a harder extension.

Refinements

Refinements are used to help students achieve quality performance (Rink, 2002) and include the cues or critical elements to performing a skill correctly. For example, "watch," "reach," and "pull it in" are all good refinements for catching a beanbag. Refinements help develop quality of

focus point

A comprehensive list of extending tasks allows a teacher to adjust a task, making it more challenging or easier, for the class as well as individual students.

movement and ensure the task is performed with good form. Physical educators should have a comprehensive list of refinements or cues for each task in the lesson that can be used to help individual students be successful as well as the class. For example, a student in bowling who turns her wrist as she releases the ball and so is not being successful may be helped if you say, "Shake hands as you release." Likewise, if many 2nd graders are having trouble catching a ball in their scoop, consider stopping the class and say, "Do the same task again, but this time make sure you give with your scoop. That will help you catch the ball."

A key to developing good refinements is to make sure refinements change with the extension tasks. Students who are dribbling well enough to start practicing dribbling against a defender don't need to be told anymore to use their "fingerpads" or to "look forward"; instead, tell them to keep their "body between the ball and the defender."

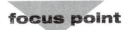

Refinements that correspond with the difficulty of the related extending tasks can help ensure student success and enjoyment.

Applications

Application tasks give students the chance to apply or use the skills they have practiced in extension tasks (Rink, 2002). Games (modified and full), self- and group challenges, and performances are all types of application tasks. Application tasks tend to be quite interesting for students; such tasks could also help students demonstrate high ability, which can have attainment value for students for whom being highly skilled in physical activities is part of their identity. Examples of application tasks include playing "Simon Says," playing 3-on-3 volleyball to 5 points, trying to get 8 of 10 badminton serves into the target box, seeing if you and your partner can keep the badminton going continuously for 30 seconds, and performing a dance or gymnastic routine for the rest of the class. Good application tasks relate directly to the extending tasks that were just performed. So, a good application task after stationary passing a basketball back and forth with a partner might be to see how many passes you and your partner can get in a row without dropping the ball, *not* playing 3-on-3 basketball.

Application tasks are most interesting and valuable when they relate directly to the extending tasks just practiced.

Written content development versus content development in action

There are two kinds of content developments: the written content development and the one actually implemented. An example of a short written content development is seen in Exhibit 8.4. A written content development is best prepared for an entire unit, covering all of the possible tasks one might present to students in that unit. Having all of these tasks written and available allows you to individualize for students and adapt for the entire class more readily.

EXHIBIT	8.4	Portions of a content development for floor hockey, game stages one and two.

EXTENSIONS	REFINEMENTS	APPLICATIONS

Stage One

Major task: Stick handling

1. Dribbling in self-space
   - forehand
   - backhand
   - alternating

   Refinements:
   - Keep the puck close
   - Keep your head up—feel the puck

   Applications:
   + Dribble the puck for 10 seconds and see if you can dribble without looking down at the puck more than once while staying in control (puck close)

2. Dribbling in general space
   - forehand
   - backhand
   - alternating
   - different directions (forward, backward, side to side)
   - increase speed
   - decrease the space
   - add obstacles (e.g., cones)

   Refinements:
   - Keep the puck close
   - Keep your head up—feel the puck
   - Use small taps to change direction
   - Use small taps to go backward
   - Use large taps if increasing speed
   - Keep body between obstacles and the puck

   Applications:
   + Red light, green light dribbling (on green, students dribble puck toward to the light; on red, students stop with puck in control. Goal is to reach the light first)

Major task: Shooting

1. Form and body position
   - hold the stick
   - foot movement
   - head movement

   Refinements:
   - One hand high, one low
   - Step with lead foot
   - Keep head steady

2. Stationary shooting
   A. Forehand shot/wrist shot
   - shooting low and high
   - shooting to a stationary target
   - shooting to a larger, then smaller goal
   - change distances to target
   - shoot from different spots on the floor
   - shoot at targets in the goal
   - shoot from different angles, close and far

   Refinements:
   - Ready position: knees bent, eyes forward, back straight, arms holding stick in position, feet shoulder width apart
   - Eyes on puck on contact
   - Position body toward target
   - Extend arms toward target (for high and low shots, too) on follow through
   - Stick flat on floor
   - Stick below waist on follow through
   - Hands together on stick
   - For longer shots, bring stick back farther on backswing (but not above waist)
   - Pretend you are hitting with the palm of your favorite hand

   Applications:
   + See if you can shoot at goal and make 7 out of 10 shots with correct form

This chart created by Jocelyn Cavalier, Victoria Gatlin, Brandon House, and Jorge Valdez, undergraduate students at Purdue University. Used with permission.

	EXHIBIT	8.4
Portions of a content development for floor hockey, game stages one and two, continued.		

EXTENSIONS	REFINEMENTS	APPLICATIONS

Stage Two

B. Backhand shot ■ shooting low and high ■ shooting to a stationary target ■ shooting to a larger, then smaller goal ■ change distances to target ■ shoot from different spots on the floor ■ shoot at targets in the goal ■ shoot from different angles, close and far	Same as above, except: ■ Pretend you are hitting with the back of your favorite hand	+ See if you can shoot and make 7 out of 10 shots with correct form

Major task: Dribbling and shooting

1. Stationary dribbling and shooting *A. Forehand shot* ■ dribble slow and fast ■ soft and hard shots ■ high and low shots ■ different distances (e.g., 10 feet vs. 20 feet) ■ different angles (e.g., straight vs. right vs. left)	■ Ready position: knees bent, eyes forward, back straight, arms holding stick in position, feet shoulder width apart ■ Eyes on puck on contact ■ Position body toward target ■ Extend arms toward target (for high and low shots, too) on follow through ■ Stick flat on floor ■ Stick below waist on follow through ■ Hands together on stick ■ For longer shots, bring stick back farther on backswing (but not above waist) ■ Pretend you are hitting with the palm of your favorite hand ■ Make sure you have control of the puck before you shoot	+ See if you can make shots from 5 different spots within 30 seconds
B. Backhand shot ■ dribble slow and fast ■ soft and hard shots ■ high and low shots ■ different distances (e.g., 10 feet vs. 20 feet) ■ different angles (e.g., straight vs. right vs. left)	Same as above, except: ■ Pretend you are hitting with the back of your favorite hand	+ Play Horse with a partner; dribble stationary from different spots and backhand shoot into the goal

(continued)

EXHIBIT   8.4   Portions of a content development for floor hockey, game stages one and two, continued.

EXTENSIONS	REFINEMENTS	APPLICATIONS
2. Moving dribbling and shooting	■ Keep the puck close	+ Play Challenger with a partner: partner calls out 5 types of dribbling and shots (of the ones practiced so far); see how many out of the 5 you can make; then challenge your partner in the same way
A. Forehand shot	■ Keep your head up—feel the puck	
■ dribble slow and fast	■ Use small taps to change direction	
■ soft and hard shots	■ Eyes on puck on contact	
■ high and low shots	■ Position body toward target	
■ dribble and shoot from different distances (e.g., 10 feet vs. 20 feet)	■ Extend arms toward target (for high and low shots, too) on follow through	
■ dribble and shoot from different angles (e.g., straight vs. right vs. left)	■ Stick flat on floor	
	■ Stick below waist on follow through	
	■ Hands together on stick	
	■ For longer shots, bring stick back farther on backswing (but not above waist)	
	■ Pretend you are hitting with the palm of your favorite hand	
	■ Make sure you have control of the puck before you shoot	
B. Backhand shot	■ Keep the puck close	+ Play Challenger
■ dribble slow and fast	■ Keep your head up—feel the puck	
■ soft and hard shots	■ Use small taps to change direction	
■ high and low shots	■ Eyes on puck on contact	
■ dribble and shoot from different distances (e.g., 10 feet vs. 20 feet)	■ Position body toward target	
■ dribble and shoot from different angles (e.g., straight vs. right vs. left)	■ Extend arms toward target (for high and low shots, too) on follow through	
	■ Stick flat on floor	
	■ Stick below waist on follow through	
	■ Hands together on stick	
	■ For longer shots, bring stick back farther on backswing (but not above waist)	
	■ Pretend you are hitting with the back of your favorite hand	
	■ Make sure you have control of the puck before you shoot	

Note: This content development does not include all the skills or tasks for floor hockey. For instance, all passing, receiving, and goal-tending skills have been excluded, as well as all tasks at game stages three and four. This was done to save space.

But not all of these tasks will actually be used in the physical education lessons. The tasks actually used are called the content development in action. A good content development in action consists of all three types of tasks: extensions, refinements, and applications. The task most likely to be underutilized by teachers is the refinement task. Physical educators are often so eager to "cover the content" and get through the extending and application tasks they have prepared, they pass over the refinements. It is important to take the time to ensure that students are performing the skills correctly and successfully—through the use of refinements—before moving on to the next extension or application.

A teacher who does a good job of using cues and refinements is Janet N., who teaches at a suburban elementary school in the southern United States. Janet always uses specific cues to make sure students perform tasks correctly, and she doesn't move on until they do. In one lesson on jumping and landing, Janet continued to do one specific task, refining it until her students were swinging and springing correctly on the jump, and landing softly by bending the knees. It took about eight different refinements, but all students were successful in the end.

The use of refinements helps students experience success and enjoyment in class. More information about developing and using a content development, and more examples of content developments, are found in *Teaching Physical Education for Learning* by Judy Rink (2002).

One reason Jamal displays very little interest in and value for his physical education class might be the lack of challenge he experiences in class. The tasks his teacher asks him to perform are the same ones he did in earlier grades (e.g., stationary passing in basketball). Jamal's teachers could greatly enhance his situational interest and subjective task value by using a comprehensive content development of tasks for each activity unit. Then tasks could be individualized for Jamal and his classmates using techniques like teaching by invitation and intratask variation (see below), challenging Jamal by making tasks harder for him in activities like basketball.

focus point

A good content development in action consists of all three types of tasks: extending, refining, and application tasks.

Use Teaching by Invitation and Intratask Variations

Having a comprehensive written content development allows physical educators to use two important instructional skills: teaching by invitation and intratask variation (Graham et al., 2004). In **teaching by invitation,** two or three options are presented to the whole class: "You may try your cartwheel on the mat, or on a floor line, or on the low balance beam"; "You may choose to practice the forearm pass with the trainer volleyball, or with the regulation volleyball." Such invitations allow students to choose tasks that more closely match their skill level, so they can be challenged as well as successful.

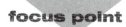

Barbara P., a physical educator at an urban elementary school in the southern United States, frequently used teaching by invitation. For example, during a rhythms unit, she invited 5th grade students who were ready to use the rhythm sticks; those who didn't feel ready would continue to use their hands.

In **intratask variation,** the physical educator decides to privately make the task easier or harder for individual students or groups (Graham et al., 2004). Perhaps 7th graders are working on hitting a forearm pass to a partner from the partner's toss; the partner is to catch the ball before tossing it back to the hitter. If one group is doing this task well, the teacher can provide an intratask variation for that group by telling them to try continuous forearm passes, without a partner catching the ball.

Another way to use intratask variation is to adjust the challenge given to students in application tasks. For example, students who are skilled at catching fly balls in softball can be challenged to catch 9 of 10 fly balls that are tossed to them, while students with a lower level of skill can be challenged to catch 6 of 10. In addition, students can do an application task and then be challenged to beat their own previous score on the application task.

Ben M., a student teacher at a suburban middle school in the southern United States, frequently used this strategy during his 6th grade soccer unit. For example, while practicing heading the ball, Ben had the students see how many tosses out of 10 they could hit directly back to their partner. After the task, instead of asking the class who got the most, he then asked them to do it again and try to beat the score they got the previous time.

Intratask variations can increase students' chances for success and adequate challenge, thus enhancing interest in and subjective task value for physical education.

Diminish Gender-Role Stereotyping

One important source of students' subjective task values is the gender-role stereotypes held by significant others and found in society. Research clearly indicates that such stereotypes often inhibit females from being physically active or participating in activities that might be personal interests. Such stereotypes could also prevent males from participating in activities they might find personally interesting but are stereotypically thought of as for females. Obviously, physical educators cannot address all gender-role stereotyping students might encounter in their lives. But teachers can examine their own beliefs and behaviors to determine if they are promoting physical activity for one gender over the other, or promoting specific activities as more appropriate for certain genders. For example, when two physical educators combine their 8th grade classes during a class period, and one teacher instructs the girls in volleyball while the other instructs the boys in flag football (and the students do not have a choice of activity), gender stereotyping is occurring. A simple change would be to offer students a choice of learning volleyball or flag football, regardless of gender. As another example, motivating the boys by yelling, "Come on, you guys! Don't let those girls beat you!" insinuates that girls should not be as good as boys at physical activities. Carefully monitoring words and actions ensures that physical activities of all kinds are promoted and acceptable to all students.

connected CONCEPTS

Other means of enhancing students' subjective task value for physical education and activities are described in other chapters: (1) gain parental support in encouraging students—especially females—to be physically active (Chapter 10), (2) establish a task-involving climate (Chapter 5), (3) enhance students' success (positive affect) and self-perceptions (Chapter 6), and (4) reduce the costs associated with being physically active (e.g., reduce body image concerns—Chapter 9; teach students self-management skills—Chapter 10).

Summary

Student interest and subjective task value are very important to student effort and persistence in physical education. Research shows that two main types of interest, personal and situational interest, are important to student achievement and motivated learning behaviors. One's subjective task value in a domain has four components: attainment value, intrinsic value, utility value, and cost. Student interest in and value for physical activity varies with certain student characteristics, such as skill level, stage of learning, age, gender, race, self-perceptions, and task involvement. Such characteristics should be considered when determining how to enhance student interest in and value for physical education. Some of the ways to enhance student interest in and value for physical education include the following: meeting students' personal interests, using technology, communicating to students the various meanings associated with activities, using the inquiry and tactical games instructional models, creating and using a content development, utilizing teaching by invitation and intratask variation, and diminishing gender-role stereotyping.

KEY concepts

Interest	Subjective task value
Value	Attainment value
Personal interest	Intrinsic value
Situational interest	Utility value
Catching interest	Cost
Holding interest	Motivated learning behaviors
Personal meaning	Exploration intention
Expectancy-value theory	Movement analysis curriculum

Movement elements   Extensions

Perceptual elements   Refinements

Conceptual elements   Applications

Inquiry model   Teaching by invitation

Tactical games model   Intratask variation

Content development

application exercises

1. Scott is a high school sophomore who plays on the varsity soccer team. He is a very talented soccer player. But during the soccer unit in physical education class, Scott just plays around and doesn't give much effort. Based on what you learned in this chapter, why might Scott behave this way? Using strategies discussed in this chapter, name two things you could do to increase Scott's interest in and subjective task value for the soccer unit.

2. Mary is an overweight 7th grader who despises physical education. She often has a note from her parents asking that she be excused from physical education for the day. When Mary does dress and participate, she does as little as possible. According to the information on interest in this chapter, describe what might be happening in physical education class that contributes to Mary's behavior. What strategies could you use to change her behavior?

3. Using the same scenario as in question 2, describe Mary's subjective task value components and what is happening in physical education class in relation to those components that might contribute to Mary's behavior. How might you change the environment to enhance each of those value components?

4. Ms. Hernandez is getting ready to teach a folk dance unit to her 6th graders, but she remembers how much these students disliked folk dance as 5th graders last year. Using what you learned in this chapter, what advice would you give Ms. Hernandez to help increase the students' interest in and value for folk dance this time around?

9

Motivation

Mr. Weaver is a physical education teacher at a suburban high school. His biggest problem is motivating his students; he feels it's like pulling teeth to get the students to do anything, especially those in his required lifestyle fitness class. Most students are late coming out of the locker room. They are supposed to run two laps around the gym before beginning the day's scheduled activities, but most students walk. Anything Mr. Weaver asks them to do is met with sighs, rolled eyes, and little effort. He often hears complaints of boredom; "We've done that already," they say. Some students, like Andy, work hard only if threatened with some kind of punishment, such as extra push-ups or laps. Other students, like Gisell, are motivated by rewards; letting students listen to the music of their choice as they worked out increased her effort. Mr. Weaver's greatest challenge is Mara, who rarely dresses for class, or participates at all even when she does dress; "I don't care," is her response when Mr. Weaver tells her she's failing the course. Interestingly, many students in Mr. Weaver's elective weight training class work very hard during class, the same individuals who were clearly unmotivated when they were in his lifestyle fitness class two years earlier. Chris, for example, told Mr. Weaver he enjoys class because strength training helps him achieve his goal of being fit and healthy. Murray pushes himself in class because his football coach wants him to increase his strength, and Murray doesn't want to let the coach down. Trisha just seems to enjoy the process of improving herself; she mentioned once that she really likes how it feels to push herself to lift more.

introduction ▶

Student motivation is a major concern of many physical educators. Although low student motivation seems to be more common at the middle and high school levels, it can also be a problem with some elementary children. Nearly every chapter in this book includes some information about increasing student motivation; however, in this chapter the concept of motivation and a frequently used motivation theory will be examined. Research in physical education and youth sport on motivation will be presented. Finally, means of enhancing student motivation, based on the theory and research, will be described.

Motivation Defined

Motivation has been defined as the direction and intensity of behavior (Gill, 2000; Sage, 1977). Both aspects are critical to motivation in physical education. Direction refers to the activities in which students choose to participate. For example, do high school students choose to participate in elective physical education or not? If they do choose to take elective physical education, do they choose a dance, team sports, or fitness class? Within a fitness class, do they choose to ride a stationary bicycle for an aerobic activity or walk? When students are required to attend physical education, as in elementary and middle school and high school classes required for graduation, direction of effort may mean whether a student chooses to perform the task as directed by the teacher or whether the student decides to perform an off-task behavior.

Intensity of effort refers to how hard students work on the activities in which they choose to or are required to engage. For example, during the progressive aerobic test, do students work really hard, or do they quit before they have done their best? While practicing the volleyball overhead pass, do students quickly retrieve a ball when it is hit away from them so they can make more attempts, or do they walk slowly to retrieve balls? Obviously, both direction and intensity of effort are important to motivation in physical education.

Self-Determination Theory

A number of theories about the process of motivation have emerged over the years. The motivational theory presented here is **self-determination theory,** which is increasingly used in youth sport and physical education settings to study motivation. Self-determination theory proposes three basic psychological needs to produce human motivation: competence, autonomy, and relatedness (Deci & Ryan, 1991, 1994, 2000; Ryan & Deci, 2000). In other words, in any given situation (e.g., physical education class), the extent to which individuals feel they are competent and effective, that their behavior is self-determined and based on their own initiative, and that they are socially connected to others will determine their motivation. This statement implies that, in physical education, students will show the highest levels of motivation when they believe that these three needs have been met: they experience success, are given choices, and are helped to feel like part of a group. For example, one reason Mr. Weaver's students showed higher levels of motiva-

connected CONCEPTS

Other theories or concepts already described in this book that contribute to our knowledge about motivation in physical education include achievement goal (see Chapter 5); competence motivation, self-efficacy (see Chapter 6); attribution (see Chapter 7); and personal and situational interest (see Chapter 8). Achievement goal and competence motivation theories, especially, have similar aspects to self-determination theory. In both self-determination and competence motivation theories, a person's desire to show competence and to be autonomous (have internal control) are proposed to influence one's motivation. Demonstrating competence is also a major part of achievement goal theory; in task involvement, competence is demonstrated by improving one's performance, while in ego involvement, a person shows competence by performing better than others. The motivational climate in achievement goal theory is an important part of the social context described in self-determination theory that can influence perceptions of competence, autonomy, and relatedness.

tion in the weight training class than in the lifestyle fitness class may be that the former was an elective class the students chose to take, whereas the latter was required.

Another tenet of self-determination theory is that there are several kinds of motivational orientations, based on the reasons people engage in an activity (Deci & Ryan, 1991, 1994, 2000; Ryan & Deci, 2000). These reasons fall on a continuum, based on their degree of autonomy or self-determination, from totally self-determined to totally externally determined (see Exhibit 9.1).

Intrinsic Motivation

At one end of the continuum, with the greatest self-determination, is **intrinsic motivation.** In intrinsic motivation, activities are engaged in for the inherent satisfaction the behavior affords the individual. In the absence of external contingencies, the activity would still be performed because the

EXHIBIT 9.1 Motivational orientations and their degree of self-determination.

MOTIVATIONAL ORIENTATION	REASONS FOR ENGAGING IN ACTIVITY	DEGREE OF SELF-DETERMINATION	CONSEQUENCES
Intrinsic motivation	Inherent pleasure, satisfaction, enjoyment, challenge, curiosity, interest, fun, for its own sake	Highest self-determination	Most positive/ adaptive
Extrinsic motivation			
■ Integrated regulation	"Want" to engage; activity is valued and important; greater incorporation with self than identified regulation		
■ Identified regulation	"Want" to engage; activity is valued as means to an end		
■ Introjected regulation	"Should" engage; to avoid guilt or experience pride; for self- or others' approval		
■ External regulation	Completely external; to receive a reward; avoid punishment or threats; "must" engage	Lowest self-determination	Least positive/ adaptive
Amotivation	None		No engagement in activities

individual wants to satisfy her curiosity, enjoys the challenge, finds the activity fun, is interested in it, or simply experiences pleasure. The activity is done for its own sake, not for any external reward or because it contributes to a goal. Trisha, in the opening scenario, seemed intrinsically motivated, because she mentioned pleasure and enjoyment at the process and challenge of weight training. The behavior of an intrinsically motivated student is totally self-determined and fully internalized and integrated with the student's sense of self.

Vallerand (1997) suggests there are three forms of intrinsic motivation: to know, to experience stimulation, and toward accomplishments. Intrinsic motivation to know involves participating in an activity for the ". . . pleasure and satisfaction that one experiences while learning, exploring, or trying to understand something new" (p. 280). When a person participates in an activity because she enjoys the physical and/or aesthetic sensations she experiences during the activity, she is displaying intrinsic motivation for stimulation. A person who is motivated to participate and work hard because she enjoys the satisfaction she experiences in improving herself, reaching her potential, or creating something has intrinsic motivation toward accomplishments. Trisha seems intrinsically motivated to experience stimulation (i.e., she likes how it feels to push herself) as well as to accomplish (i.e., she likes improving herself).

Extrinsic Motivation

The remaining motivational orientations are forms of extrinsic motivation. In **extrinsic motivation,** a person's behavior is directed by some separable consequence, not just performing the behavior for its own sake (Deci & Ryan, 1991, 1994, 2000; Ryan & Deci, 2000). The activity is performed as a means to an end, not an end in itself. Each form of extrinsic motivation varies in its degree of self-determination, but all have less self-determination than intrinsic motivation.

External regulation

At the far end of the continuum from intrinsic motivation is **external regulation,** or what many people typically think of as extrinsic motivation. With external regulation, an individual's actions are completely controlled by external forces, such as a reward, threat, or punishment. For example, a physical education student who works hard only because the teacher gives students a free day if they show high effort is showing external regulation. Likewise, a student is externally regulated when she completes the two-lap warm-up at the start of class without walking only to avoid having to run another lap. Even students who work at skills because they want praise from the teacher are being externally regulated. Andy and

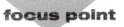

focus point

Intrinsic motivation is the motivational orientation with the greatest self-determination.

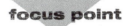

focus point

Intrinsic motivation can take three forms: to know, to experience stimulation, and toward accomplishments.

Gisell, two of Mr. Weaver's students, are externally regulated through punishments and rewards. The problem with external regulation is that when the reward, threat, or punishment is gone, the individual is likely to withdraw from the activity.

Introjected regulation

Next to external regulation, with the second highest level of external control, is **introjected regulation.** When a person is motivated by introjected regulation, external control is internalized. Whereas with external regulation, a person feels she "must" participate in an activity, with introjected regulation, the person feels like she "should" or "ought to" participate. So individuals engage in activities to gain approval from oneself or others. They participate to avoid feeling guilty or to experience pride. A student is motivated by introjected regulation when he works hard during the fitness tests so other students will see his high ability. The same is true for a student who dresses and gets out of the locker room quickly at the start of class, because she knows the whole class will have to run extra laps in the warm-up if anyone is late, which would make her feel guilty. Murray, in Mr. Weaver's weight training class, is motivated by introjected regulation, because he works hard to avoid guilt about letting his football teammates down.

Identified regulation

In **identified regulation,** a behavior is still performed as a means to an end, but now the person sees the activity as valuable and important to her. The activity is engaged in freely, but it is not in and of itself enjoyable to the person. Whereas external and introjected regulation reflect external motives that I "must" and "ought" to do this activity, respectively, identified regulation is the first motivational orientation to reflect an intrinsic choice—I "want" to do this activity. So, although identified regulation is internally regulated, it is still not completely self-determined as is intrinsic motivation. When a student works hard during the fitness part of class because it will help him reach the goal of losing weight, identified regulation is at work. This behavior is unlike intrinsic motivation toward accomplishments, in which the fitness activity is done because the person enjoys the process of maximizing his potential—it isn't just a means to the end of losing weight.

Integrated regulation

The extrinsic motivational orientation that lies closest to intrinsic motivation is **integrated regulation.** Indeed, the lines between identified and integrated regulation, and between integrated regulation and intrinsic motivation, are quite blurry. With all three of those motivational orientations, individuals "want" to perform the activity—it is an intrinsic choice—so there is autonomy and self-determination. Though individuals with identified or integrated regulation would both freely engage in activities because the activities are viewed as valuable and important to them, the two orientations differ in that the goals have been even more incorporated with one's definition of self with integrated regulation. But integrated regulation differs from intrinsic motivation in that, with integrated regulation, the activity is still seen as a means to an end—to achieve a personal, valued goal—and not simply engaged in for its inherent pleasure, as in intrinsic motivation. A student who willingly gives high effort because he believes physical activity is vital to health is motivated by integrated regulation. Chris, the student who works hard in weight training class because he knows strength training is part of being fit and healthy, is probably motivated by integrated regulation, because strength training is part of his self-identity. If he were motivated by identified regulation, he would willingly work hard in class only because it helps him achieve the goal of being fit and healthy, and strength training is not part of his identity. Moreover, he is still not motivated by intrinsic motivation, because the goal of being fit and healthy is why he works hard, not because he just enjoys weight training in itself.

focus point

The extrinsic motivational orientations vary on a continuum of self-determination, with integrated regulation having the highest self-determination and external regulation the least.

Amotivation

Outside of the motivational continuum is **amotivation**, which is when individuals are not motivated, either intrinsically or extrinsically, to engage in specified activities. A student with amotivation in physical education would not participate because he has no good reason to do so, may not believe he can be successful, or doesn't think he has control over his participation and its outcome. In fact, amotivated high school students often will not even sign up for elective physical education classes. Amotivation is a serious problem in physical education, especially with older students. Mara, in Mr. Weaver's lifestyle fitness class, is displaying amotivation.

focus point

An amotivated student cannot come up with a good reason to participate, may not believe he can be successful, or thinks he has no control over his participation and its outcome.

Consequences of the Motivational Orientations

These various motivational orientations are important because they differentially affect three types of consequences: affective, cognitive, and behavioral (Vallerand, 1997; Vallerand & Losier, 1999). Affective consequences can include enjoyment, interest, satisfaction, mood, emotions, and

connected   CONCEPTS

A severe form of amotivation is learned helplessness, the belief that there is no relationship between one's actions and an outcome (see Chapter 7).

The affective, cognitive, and behavioral consequences of the various motivational orientations are believed to be more positive as the level of self-determination increases, with intrinsic motivation having the most positive outcomes.

anxiety, while cognitive consequences include a person's attention, concentration, and memory. Behaviors that may be affected include choice of activities, effort, persistence, adherence, and eventually performance. In self-determination theory, intrinsic motivation is predicted to produce the most positive consequences, and consequences become less positive as self-determination decreases (see Exhibit 9.1). Thus, high intrinsic motivation should yield positive emotions; high levels of interest, enjoyment, satisfaction, effort, persistence, and performance; better concentration; and low levels of anxiety and negative emotions. Amotivation and external regulation are predicted to yield the least adaptive consequences. Even though integrated and identified regulation are forms of extrinsic motivation, they are still believed to lead to more positive consequences, although to a slightly lesser degree than intrinsic motivation.

Role of the Social Context

Deci and Ryan (1991) assert that three aspects of the social context can influence a person's self-determination and, in turn, his motivational orientation: autonomy support, structure, and involvement. Self-determination is enhanced in an autonomy-supportive environment, in which individuals are given choices, initiation is encouraged, and pressure to perform in specific ways is minimized. A context with a clear structure—clear consequences and expectations, and helpful feedback—also promotes self-determination. High involvement by significant others such as parents and teachers—by spending time with and showing sincere interest in a child—is another part of the social context that can produce high self-determination.

Similarly, Vallerand and Losier (1999) propose three major contextual influences on self-determination and perceptions of competence, autonomy, and relatedness: significant others' behaviors, success versus failure, and cooperation versus competition. Similar to Deci and Ryan's (1991) assertion, a context in which significant others (e.g., parents and teachers) utilize an autonomy-supportive style is proposed to yield greater self-determination than a controlling style. Success at tasks is expected to produce higher perceptions of competence, autonomy, and relatedness—and thus self-determination—than failure. Perceived autonomy and relatedness, and self-determination, are believed to be higher with cooperative activities than competitive ones.

According to these theorists, therefore, more self-determined forms of motivation (intrinsic motivation, integrated and identified regulation) can be developed by doing the following:

- Giving students choices
- Providing opportunities for students to initiate activities and be self-directed

- Allowing freedom of expression and flexibility in criteria for success
- Establishing clear expectations and consequences (positive and negative)
- Giving positive feedback for good performances and corrective feedback for less successful performances
- Providing social support by showing interest in students, before and after school
- Offering opportunities to demonstrate competence as well as become successful
- Using cooperative activities and stressing the cooperation inherent in competitive sports

focus point

Various aspects of the social context are predicted to influence perceptions of competence, autonomy, and relatedness, and in turn motivational orientation, in a situation.

The Motivational Process in Self-Determination Theory

The process of motivation described in self-determination theory is shown in Exhibit 9.2. The context established in physical education (e.g., degree of social support, clear structure, success, cooperation) influences a student's perceptions of competence, autonomy, and relatedness. Those perceptions influence the student's motivational orientation, which in turn yields affective, cognitive, and behavioral consequences (e.g., effort, persistence, and enjoyment). This process clearly shows that physical education teachers can influence their students' motivational orientations and behaviors through the context they set up.

Process of motivation in self-determination theory. **EXHIBIT 9.2**

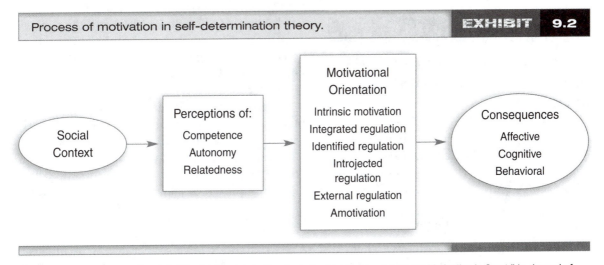

Adapted from R. J. Vallerand and G. F. Losier, "An Integrative Analysis of Intrinsic and Extrinsic Motivation in Sport," in *Journal of Applied Sport Psychology, 11,* 142–169. Copyright 1999, Taylor & Francis, Philadelphia. Reprinted with permission.

Motivation Research

Numerous studies have examined children's motivation in physical activity settings. This section will review some of that research, paying special attention to studies based on self-determination theory. First, various student characteristics and their relationships to motivation and the motivational orientations will be described. Next will be an examination of the consequences of the motivational orientations, and how satisfaction of the needs for competence, autonomy, and relatedness may influence the motivational orientations and related factors. This section concludes with a description of research on the social context as it is associated with perceived need satisfaction, motivational orientations, and consequences.

Student Characteristics

Age

A common observation of physical education teachers is that motivation to participate in physical activities in class decreases with age. But is this true? Although few studies have specifically addressed this issue in physical education, research in other areas indicates that student motivation and attitudes toward school in general and specific academic subjects decline as children get older (Anderman & Maehr, 1994; Jacobs, Lanza, Osgood, Eccles, & Wigfield, 2002). The decline in children's physical activity levels as they become older is well documented (e.g., Sallis, 2000; Trost et al., 2002), which in part may indicate a decline in motivation. Other researchers discovered that elementary students' intrinsic motivation toward motor skill learning (Weiss, Bredemeier, & Shewchuk, 1985) and their intentions to participate in future physical education activities (Xiang et al., 2006; Xiang, McBride, & Guan, 2004; Xiang, McBride, Guan, & Solmon, 2003) decline with time.

connected CONCEPTS

Research reviewed in Chapter 8 shows that older students have less interest and value for physical education than younger students.

More research is needed that specifically investigates in physical education how the motivational orientations described in self-determination theory change as children age. But, physical education teachers cannot assume that students will be motivated to participate in activities in class and so should be prepared with strategies to motivate children of all ages.

Gender

Most researchers discovered that boys have higher levels of intrinsic motivation for physical activity than girls (Ntoumanis, 2005; Rose, Larkin, & Berger, 1998; Wang & Biddle, 2001; Wang et al., 2002). For example, in a study specifically examining intrinsic motivation in physical education, 11- to 14-year-old boys scored slightly higher than girls on identified regulation and intrinsic motivation, whereas the girls scored higher on amotivation (Wang et al., 2002). Physical educators should be aware that while efforts to enhance the intrinsic motivation of all students in physical education are important, special attention to females may be necessary.

Dispositional goal orientation

Another student characteristic that might influence motivation is the type of goals they prefer to set in physical activity settings such as physical education—their dispositional goal orientation (see Chapter 5). Most researchers found that task orientation is positively correlated with various intrinsic motivation measures (Cury et al., 1996; Ferrer-Caja & Weiss, 2000; Goudas, Biddle, & Fox, 1994b; Standage, Duda, & Ntoumanis, 2003b; Standage & Treasure, 2002; Wang et al., 2002; Williams & Gill, 1995), identified regulation (Standage et al., 2003b; Standage & Treasure, 2002; Wang et al., 2002), and introjected regulation (Standage et al., 2003b) in physical education. Physical education students who score high in task orientation also tend to exhibit low external regulation and amotivation (Standage & Treasure, 2002; Wang et al., 2002).

But the relationships between ego orientation and the motivational orientations are less clear. Some studies show that students high in ego orientation tend to have low levels of intrinsic motivation (Ferrer-Caja & Weiss, 2000) and identified regulation (Standage et al., 2003b), as well as high amotivation (Standage & Treasure, 2002) and external regulation (Standage & Treasure, 2002; Wang et al., 2002). However, other research indicates that a high ego orientation is related to high levels of intrinsic motivation, identified regulation, and introjected regulation (Wang et al., 2002). Middle school students in one study who were highly motivated in physical education scored high in both task and ego orientations (Wang et al., 2002).

A student's level of task orientation appears to be a stronger influence on his motivation level than his degree of ego orientation (Goudas, Biddle, & Fox, 1994a; Standage & Treasure, 2002). For example, Standage and Treasure (2002) found that students who demonstrated high scores in task orientation, whether they scored high or low in ego orientation, had the highest levels of intrinsic motivation and identified regulation in physical education. But students who exhibited low task orientation along with high ego orientation had the lowest levels of intrinsic motivation and identified regulation in physical education, as well as the highest levels of external regulation and amotivation.

focus point

Researchers have evidence that children's motivation in physical education declines as they get older and that girls have lower intrinsic motivation for physical activity than boys.

It appears that a high task goal orientation enhances intrinsic motivation and other more self-determined motivational orientations, regardless of the person's ego orientation level. Physical educators should help students become more task oriented by emphasizing their own improvement, especially students who focus on comparing themselves to and beating others.

Dispositional ability conceptions

As described in Chapter 6, people adopt either an entity or incremental view about ability (Dweck, 1999, 2002). In the entity view, ability is fixed and unchangeable, while in the incremental view, ability is seen as changeable and improvable with effort and practice. So far researchers discovered that an incremental conception of ability tends to promote more self-determined forms of motivation (e.g., intrinsic motivation, identified regulation) than an entity conception (Li, Lee, & Solmon, 2005; Wang et al., 2002), while entity beliefs are associated with amotivation (Biddle, Wang, Chatzisarantis, & Spray, 2003). For example, high entity beliefs in 11- to 14-year-old children were related to high levels of external and introjected regulation and amotivation, but low levels of intrinsic motivation in physical education (Wang et al., 2002). Conversely, incremental beliefs were positively related to intrinsic motivation and identified and introjected regulation, but negatively related to amotivation. In addition, students in the low motivation group had lower incremental beliefs about ability than students in the high motivation group. Consistent reminders to students that everyone can improve their performance by working hard can help them adopt an incremental view of ability.

connected   CONCEPTS

Research on the relationships between the types of attributions students give for outcomes in physical education and their motivational orientations is limited. But research reviewed in Chapter 7 indicates that learned helpless students, who are extremely amotivated, tend to attribute their performances to uncontrollable factors. This finding suggests teachers may enhance student motivation by helping students attribute successful and less successful performances to factors they can control and are able to change, like how hard they try and practice strategies.

Motivational Orientations and Consequences

Different affective, cognitive, and behavioral consequences are proposed to result from the various motivational orientations. According to self-determination theory, consequences should be more positive and adaptive with more self-determined forms of motivational orientations, such as intrinsic motivation and identified regulation, and less adaptive with less self-determined forms, like external regulation and amotivation. Most research findings in physical education and youth sport settings, with 10- to 19-year-olds, support these contentions.

Self-determined and intrinsic motivation

In some studies, an overall self-determined motivation score was computed by subtracting extrinsic motivational orientation scores (identified regulation, introjected regulation, and/or external regulation) from an intrinsic motivation score. In other studies, intrinsic motivation and the other motivational orientations were measured separately. Researchers generally found high levels of self-determined or intrinsic motivation are associated with:

- Stronger intentions to participate in physical activity or optional physical education in the future (Ntoumanis, 2001, 2005; Standage, Duda, & Ntoumanis, 2003a)
- Greater actual participation in optional physical education or physical activity outside of physical education (Hagger, Chatzisarantis, Culverhouse, & Biddle, 2003; Ntoumanis, 2005; Wang et al., 2002)
- Better concentration (Ntoumanis, 2005; Standage, Duda, & Ntoumanis, 2005)
- Greater effort and persistence (Ferrer-Caja & Weiss, 2000; Ntoumanis, 2001, 2002, 2005; Standage, Duda, & Ntoumanis, 2006)
- Lower intentions to drop out of an activity (Sarrazin, Vallerand, Guillet, Pelletier, & Cury, 2002)
- Stronger preference for challenging tasks (Ferrer-Caja & Weiss, 2000; Standage et al., 2005)
- Higher levels of positive affect (Ntoumanis, 2002; Standage et al., 2005; Ullrich-French & Smith, 2006)
- Lower levels of negative affect (Ntoumanis, 2001, 2002, 2005; Standage et al., 2005; Ullrich-French & Smith, 2006)

Extrinsic motivational orientations

Like intrinsic motivation, even some forms of extrinsic motivation correlate with adaptive consequences. Adaptive consequences (e.g., high effort and enjoyment and low boredom) are more likely to result in student learning than maladaptive consequences (e.g., boredom, unhappiness, and low effort and enjoyment). Of the extrinsic motivational orientations, researchers found the most adaptive consequences (higher effort and enjoyment, low boredom, higher levels of participation in physical activity outside of physical education) with identified and introjected regulation (Ntoumanis, 2002; Wang et al., 2002). Identified regulation was more strongly correlated with those outcomes than introjected regulation, as indicated in self-determined motivation theory.

The least adaptive consequences (high boredom and unhappiness; low effort, enjoyment, and concentration; low intentions for and actual participation in physical activities outside of physical education) were found with external regulation and amotivation (Ntoumanis, 2001, 2002; Sarrazin, Vallerand, et al., 2002; Standage et al., 2003a, 2005; Wang et al., 2002). Students with high levels of amotivation in physical education avoided physical education (through low attendance and excuses to miss class), displayed low involvement (i.e., disruptive behavior, passive attitude and behavior), and showed little desire to participate in future physical activity (Ntoumanis, Pensgaard, Martin, & Pipe, 2004).

Implications

The research indicates that more adaptive consequences occur with intrinsic motivation, but that the more self-determined extrinsic motivational orientations, especially identified regulation, can also result in positive outcomes. As expected, the least adaptive outcomes result from external regulation and amotivation. Thus physical educators should minimize the use of threats and punishments, which can contribute to students' sense of external regulation. External rewards, which also contribute to an external regulation orientation, should be used only when students seem to be amotivated or are initially unmotivated by less tangible benefits. Teachers should strive to develop students' intrinsic motivation, integrated regulation, or identified regulation in physical education. Thus if external rewards are used, concurrent emphases should include the pleasure, challenge, fun, and intricacies of an activity (to enhance intrinsic motivation); and how an activity can be valuable to students, help them achieve goals, and become a meaningful part of their lives and sense of self (to enhance identified and integrated regulation). Other ways to move the students' focus from the external rewards to less tangible, internal factors are to make sure students receive rewards only if they are earned (e.g., they are contingent upon students' behavior), and to fade rewards by making them harder to earn.

focus point

More adaptive affective, behavioral, and cognitive consequences result from intrinsic motivation and more self-determined forms of extrinsic motivation than from external regulation and amotivation.

Need Satisfaction and Motivation

According to self-determination theory, students will show higher intrinsic motivation in physical education if they believe their needs to show competence, autonomy, and relatedness are met. In some studies involving these constructs, the various perceptions and motivational orientations were analyzed separately, but in other studies, these constructs were combined to form a combined need satisfaction and/or overall self-determination motivation score.

Combined need satisfaction

When students perceived that their needs for competence, autonomy, and relatedness were being met in physical education, they exhibited higher self-determined motivation, intrinsic motivation, and introjected regulation but lower external regulation and amotivation than when students believed those needs were not being met (Ntoumanis, 2005; Standage et al., 2005).

Perceptions of competence

In studies in physical education with students 11 through 19 years of age, high perceptions of competence tend to be associated with higher levels of intrinsic motivation (Cury et al., 1996; Ferrer-Caja & Weiss, 2000; Goudas & Biddle, 1994; Ntoumanis, 2001; Standage et al., 2003b; Wang et al., 2002), identified regulation (Ntoumanis, 2001; Standage et al., 2003b; Wang et al., 2002), introjected regulation (Ntoumanis, 2001; Standage et al., 2003a, 2003b; Wang et al., 2002), and self-determined motivation (Standage et al., 2003a, 2006). Conversely, high perceptions of competence were associated with low levels of amotivation (Ntoumanis, 2001; Standage et al., 2003a, 2003b, 2006; Wang et al., 2002) and external regulation (Ntoumanis, 2001) in physical education. Similarly, in a qualitative study, 14- to 15-year-old students identified as amotivated in physical education claimed that one cause of their low motivation was their low perceptions of competence (Ntoumanis et al., 2004).

Perceptions of autonomy

Researchers in physical education confirm that high perceptions of autonomy in 11- to 19-year-old students are associated with high levels of self-determined motivation (Standage et al., 2003a, 2006), intrinsic motivation (Ferrer-Caja & Weiss, 2000; Hagger et al., 2003; Hassandra, Goudas, & Chroni, 2003), identified regulation (Hagger et al., 2003), and introjected regulation (Standage et al., 2003a). Researchers also found that low perceptions of autonomy in physical education are associated with high levels of amotivation (Ntoumanis et al., 2004; Standage et al., 2006) and external regulation (Ntoumanis, 2001).

Perceptions of relatedness

According to self-determination theory, the degree to which students feel socially connected will influence their motivation. Researchers examined the impact of children's overall perceptions of relatedness in a situation, as well as more specific perceptions of peer relationships, on children's motivation. The teacher may also influence students' perceptions of relatedness in physical education, through their interactions with students, feedback, and the type of climate they establish. That research will be reviewed in the section on social context.

Perceptions of relatedness in physical education. In studies with students 11 through 19 years of age, high perceptions of relatedness in physical education were related to higher levels of self-determined motivation (Standage et al., 2003a, 2006), introjected regulation (Ntoumanis, 2001; Standage et al., 2003a), identified regulation, and intrinsic motivation in females (Ntoumanis, 2001). Conversely, low perceptions of relatedness were associated with high levels of amotivation (Ntoumanis, 2005; Ntoumanis et al., 2004; Standage et al., 2003a, 2006).

Peers. In physical education, a student's relationships with his classmates make a vital contribution to his perception of relatedness. Several studies in general activity settings, sport, and physical education show that positive relationships with peers can positively impact intrinsic motivation and related variables (Duncan, 1993; Hassandra et al., 2003; Kunesh, Hasbrook, & Lewthwaite, 1992; Patrick et al., 1999; Smith, 1999; Ullrich-French & Smith, 2006; Vazou, Ntoumanis, & Duda, 2006; Weiss & Smith, 2002a). For example, Duncan (1993) found that 7th and 8th graders' perceptions of companionship and reassurance of worth from peers in physical education were positively related to their choice to participate in physical activity outside of class. But this influence may be age related, as other researchers discovered that 11- to 13-year-olds' intrinsic motivation in physical education was more strongly predicted by the influence of parents than by peers or teachers, while the opposite was true for 14- to 17-year-olds (Carr, Weigand, & Hussey, 1999). Unfortunately, 11- to 12-year-old girls report more negative treatment from peers while in physical activity at school than at home, especially from boys during physical education (Kunesh et al., 1992). The girls claimed this negative treatment at school contributed to their decision not to participate in physical activity at school.

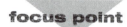

focus point

Studies in several types of physical activity settings show that positive relationships with peers can positively affect children's intrinsic motivation and related variables.

Implications

These studies show that when students' needs for competence, autonomy, and relatedness are met, intrinsic motivation and some forms of extrinsic motivational orientations (e.g., identified and introjected regulation) are higher than when these needs are not met. Conversely, when students perceive low competence, autonomy, and relatedness in situations, amotivation and external regulation are higher. Students can develop intrinsic motivation and more self-determined forms of extrinsic motivation if they feel successful and competent at physical education activities; have more responsibilities, choices, and decisions to make in class; and experience opportunities in class to develop positive relationships with peers as well as the teacher.

Social Context

The social context is an important element in the motivational process in self-determination theory (refer back to Exhibit 9.2). Specifically, the con-

focus point

Students who believe their needs for competence, autonomy, and relatedness are met in physical education have higher intrinsic motivation and more self-determined forms of extrinsic motivation, and lower external regulation and amotivation, than if they perceive those needs are not being met.

text directly influences the satisfaction of individuals' needs to show competence, autonomy, and relatedness. Social context can also affect the other elements in self-determination theory—motivational orientations and consequences—although a more indirect impact through perceived need satisfaction is predicted.

Relationships to perceptions of competence, autonomy, and relatedness

Researchers investigated various aspects of the social context in physical education and physical activity settings that may influence children's perceptions. In studies examining the overall context, students' general perceptions that their physical education teacher created a context that supported their needs for competence, relatedness, and/or autonomy positively predicted the students' perceptions that those needs were being satisfied (Ntoumanis, 2005; Standage et al., 2003a, 2005, 2006).

Specific contextual factors. Other studies, looking at more specific aspects of the social context, revealed factors that may enhance students' perceptions of competence, autonomy, and relatedness:

- High student perceptions of choice in physical education were associated with high perceptions of autonomy (Ntoumanis, 2005).

- Sharing decision making with students is associated with higher self-concepts (Martinek, Zaichkowsky, & Cheffers, 1977; Schempp, Cheffers, & Zaichkowsky, 1983) and greater future participation in physical education (Ferrer-Caja & Weiss, 2000).

- Perceptions of cooperation or actual participation in cooperative activities are linked with high perceived relatedness (Ntoumanis, 2001), self-perceptions (Ebbeck & Gibbons, 1998), and perceptions of success (Ennis, 1999; Ennis et al., 1999); conversely, competition is associated with low perceptions of competence in children who believe they lost (Vallerand, Gauvin, & Halliwell, 1986a).

- An emphasis on self-improvement is related to higher perceptions of competence and expectations for performance (Ntoumanis, 2001; Rudisill, 1990).

- High perceptions of challenge are associated with high perceived competence (Koka & Hein, 2003).

- A lower basketball hoop and a smaller ball were related to higher self-efficacy (Chase et al., 1994).

focus point

Specific contextual factors shown to enhance children's perceived need satisfaction include choices, shared decision making, cooperative activities, challenging and successful experiences, developmentally appropriate equipment, and emphasis on self-improvement.

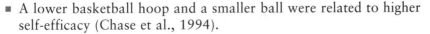

connected CONCEPTS

Research described in Chapter 5 indicates a task-involving climate is associated with high self-perceptions, while the relationships between an ego-involving climate and self-perceptions is unclear.

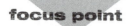

Motivational climate. A task-involving motivational climate actually has many of the characteristics of the social context that are predicted in self-determination theory to positively influence students' perceptions of competence, autonomy, and relatedness:

- Students are given choices, freedom of expression, and opportunities to make decisions, be self-directed, demonstrate competence, and work at their own level.
- Flexible/self-referenced criteria are used to define success.
- Tasks emphasize cooperation instead of competition among students.
- Students receive information/feedback on how to improve.

Researchers found that female handballers' perceptions of a task-involving climate positively predicted their perceived competence, autonomy, and relatedness (Sarrazin, Vallerand, et al., 2002).

connected CONCEPTS

Teacher feedback is an important part of the physical education context that can influence students' self-perceptions. Research reviewed in Chapter 2 shows that perceptions of competence can be enhanced by giving the following types of feedback: praise for success, corrective information for lack of success, and contingent (matches their performance level).

Implications. The research conducted to date confirms the impact the social context can have on students' perceptions of competence, autonomy, and relatedness. To yield a positive influence, studies suggest physical education teachers do the following:

- Establish a task-involving motivational climate.
- Give students choices and decision-making responsibilities.
- Emphasize cooperation and caring among students, and include cooperative activities.
- Emphasize self-improvement.
- Help students experience and perceive success.
- Provide tasks that challenge students—tasks slightly more difficult than they've performed in the past—rather than having students perform tasks they can already do.
- Use developmentally appropriate equipment.
- Give appropriate feedback.

Relationships to motivational orientations and consequences

Besides investigating the impact of the social context on need satisfaction, researchers also examined how the social context influences motivational orientations and various consequences such as effort, persistence, and on-task behaviors.

Motivational climate. Researchers confirmed that student perceptions of a task-involving climate in physical education, as well as actual participation in task-involving lessons, result in higher intrinsic motivation, more positive affect, less negative affect, and higher persistence and effort than an ego-involving climate (e.g., Goudas & Biddle, 1994; Mitchell, 1996; Papaioannou, 1994; Standage et al., 2003b; Vallerand, Gauvin, & Halliwell, 1986a, 1986b; Wallhead & Ntoumanis, 2004). In a qualitative study, students high in amotivation confirmed that one contextual factor causing their amotivation was a high ego-involving and low task-involving climate (Ntoumanis et al., 2004).

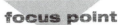

Compared to an ego-involving climate, a task-involving climate has been associated with high intrinsic motivation, low amotivation, and more positive behavioral and affective consequences.

Reinforcement. Teacher feedback and extrinsic rewards are aspects of the social context that influenced intrinsic motivation and related behaviors. Positive feedback from the teacher or coach about performance has been shown to positively impact children's intrinsic motivation (Koka & Hein, 2003; Vallerand, 1983; Whitehead & Corbin, 1991). As expected, extrinsic rewards, an integral part of external regulation, have been found to negatively influence children's intrinsic interest in an activity (Orlick & Mosher, 1978). The key seems to be whether or not the reward was actually earned, because contingent rewards increased intrinsic interest (Thomas & Tennant, 1978) and productive behaviors, and decreased nonproductive behaviors (Hume & Crossman, 1992) more so than noncontingent rewards (see Chapter 2).

Positive feedback has been shown to enhance children's intrinsic motivation, whereas contingent rewards have enhanced children's intrinsic interest and productive behaviors.

Other contextual elements. Researchers discovered other contextual factors that can influence students' intrinsic motivation and related outcomes:

- High perceived challenge in tasks is associated with high intrinsic motivation (Koka & Hein, 2003).
- Perceptions of a cooperative environment are associated with high intrinsic motivation and identified regulation, but low amotivation and external regulation (Ntoumanis, 2002).
- Perceptions of unequal recognition in physical education are associated with low intrinsic motivation and identified regulation, and high amotivation and external regulation (Ntoumanis, 2002).
- Choice of activities results in higher intrinsic motivation and identified regulation, but lower external regulation and amotivation (Prusak, Treasure, Darst, & Pangrazi, 2004).
- Poor teacher-student relationships can negatively affect students' motivation (Hassandra et al., 2003; Ntoumanis et al., 2004).

■ Being able to interact with friends (Hassandra et al., 2003), planning activities to coincide with the outdoor climate (e.g., when cold, do indoor activities not outdoor ones), increasing the lesson duration (to have enough time to increase fitness levels), and reducing body image concerns (e.g., let students wear what they want, give them more time to dress) (Ntoumanis et al., 2004) can positively affect motivation.

Implications. Many of the same contextual features that enhance students' perceptions of competence, autonomy, and relatedness also seem to benefit their intrinsic motivation, identified regulation, affect, and persistence: establishing a task-involving motivational climate, giving students choices, emphasizing cooperation and self-improvement instead of competition, providing challenging tasks, and making feedback and rewards contingent upon performance. Other aspects of the physical education context that can be adjusted to positively influence students' motivation and behaviors include the following:

■ Recognize all students, not just the highly skilled, for their achievements in class.

■ Purposely get to know all students, in order to develop more positive teacher–student relationships.

■ Give students opportunities to interact with peers during class.

■ Plan so that outdoor activities are performed in warmer, good weather, and indoor activities occur when weather is worse.

■ If possible, establish longer class periods, especially for older students, so they can be given more time to change clothes and actually improve their fitness and skills.

■ Decrease students' body concerns by allowing them to wear clothing that covers their body (e.g., allow students to wear sweatpants instead of requiring them to wear shorts).

Strategies to Influence Student Motivation Positively in Physical Education

According to self-determination theory and related research, intrinsic motivation can be developed by enhancing students' perceptions of competence, autonomy, and relatedness; these needs are affected by the social context. Research reveals strategies teachers can use to satisfy students' needs and in turn, their intrinsic motivation and related outcomes in physical education.

Moving Students from Amotivation to Intrinsic Motivation

Students who are amotivated—do not participate in any form or just go through the motions—are a challenge for physical education teachers. Although intrinsic motivation is the ideal motivational orientation, many students in physical education who actually do participate do so for reasons other than the sheer joy of the activity and movement. So how do teachers move students from amotivation to some form of motivation, and then move them from less self-determined forms of motivation to the most self-determined form, intrinsic motivation?

One reason students might be amotivated in physical education is because they do not believe they have any control in the situation, thus they avoid participation. So methods to increase their sense of autonomy (e.g., alternative assessments, choices, sport education, peer teaching, and PSI model) could help; when these methods are used, you should clearly point out to students that they are being given some control.

Another cause of students' amotivation in class may be that they do not have any good reasons to participate. Instead of simply saying to students, "Do this," remind them why it would be to their benefit to engage in certain activities or tasks. When teachers do this, they are actually trying to move students from amotivation all the way to identified regulation, which may only be effective with a few students.

Another way to give students a reason to participate is through some form of external factor such as rewards, which would be an attempt to move a student from amotivation to external regulation. Minimize the use of threats and punishments because they create an unpleasant, aversive learning environment that is not conducive to developing a joy of movement. The use of rewards for participating may move students from amotivation to external regulation, but these rewards must be desired by students. Rewards are also likely to be more motivating to students if criteria for earning the rewards are clear; rewards are based on self-improvement instead of the performance of others; and students receive the rewards only if they have truly earned them (i.e., contingent). These kinds of reward structures can actually give students positive information about their performances in physical education, which may in turn enhance their perceptions of competence—a precursor of intrinsic motivation in self-determination theory. Try to use extrinsic rewards only when students seem to be amotivated; giving extrinsic rewards to students who are already intrinsically motivated may change their reasons for participating from internal ones to external ones, and then their engagement suffers when the rewards are no longer there.

connected CONCEPTS

Several methods of positively influencing student motivation in physical education were described in previous chapters: establishing a task-involving climate (Chapter 5), enhancing students' self-perceptions (Chapter 6), helping students make adaptive attributions (Chapter 7), and using various instructional models (personalized system of instruction—Chapter 2; peer teaching—Chapter 3; taking personal and social responsibility, cooperative learning, sport education, and adventure-based learning—Chapter 4; inquiry and tactical games—Chapter 8).

focus point

Students who are amotivated in physical education may be moved to external regulation through the use of extrinsic rewards.

Once students have gone from amotivation to at least being externally regulated to participate in class, the physical educator can move them toward more self-determined forms of motivation. One way to do that is to fade the use of rewards; in other words, try to make the students less dependent on rewards by making it harder to earn rewards. For example, require students to complete more minutes of cardiovascular exercise, or more repetitions of a task before giving them the reward. At the same time, try to gradually change the reinforcer currently controlling the students' participation (e.g., the extrinsic reward) to a different, less tangible one. For example, praise the students for their hard work and accomplishments as they participate in class for the rewards. Although the students may still be externally regulated by teacher praise, that reward is less tangible than other rewards and is more readily transferred into other more self-directed forms of motivation.

Students may be helped to develop identified or integrated regulation ("I want to participate") when teachers stress how their actions will help them reach goals the students value (e.g., being fit, healthy). Of course, students might not initially understand the value of physical education activities for them, so you should regularly point out these benefits to students. Strive to help students develop intrinsic motivation by pointing out the fun in trying and learning new activities (intrinsic motivation to know), the satisfaction of challenging and improving oneself with physical activities (intrinsic motivation to accomplish), and the pleasurable sensations one can experience when participating in physical activities (intrinsic motivation for stimulation).

connected CONCEPTS

Guidelines for the appropriate use of punishments and external rewards are described in Chapter 2.

The use of extrinsic rewards might effectively move Mara from being amotivated to external regulation. Mr. Weaver should try to find out what kinds of extrinsic rewards might motivate Mara, and set up a reward system for her based on the guidelines found in Chapter 2. In addition, Mr. Weaver should find some kind of reward that works to engage Andy in class, rather than the threats that currently move him to participate (an undesirable form of external regulation). Once these students, like Gisell, are at least participating due to external regulation, then Mr. Weaver can help them develop more self-directed forms of motivation. For example, he might require them to dress out or complete more full workouts per week before receiving the reward. Mr. Weaver should also praise the students for their accomplishments and stress the satisfaction they may experience when pushing their bodies harder than they have before. He could try to help them see the value in their participation. For example, Mr. Weaver could point out to Gisell, who wants to be a doctor someday, what physical activity does at the cellular level and how it works to prevent disease—which is a major part of being a doctor. And Andy, who loves to surf, might be helped to understand how specific parts of his workout will help his balance and endurance on the surfboard, and thus make him a better surfer.

Reduce Students' Body Image Concerns

Many middle and high school students are self-conscious about their bodies; indeed, such concerns about body image can start as early as elementary school. Oftentimes, clothing styles can make physical education a negative experience for some students even before any activities are attempted. Intrinsic motivation for physical activity cannot develop under such circumstances. Although students must be given some guidelines for appropriate clothing in class (e.g., athletic shoes instead of street shoes, ability to move comfortably), allowing students to wear clothing that appropriately covers their bodies (e.g., sweatpants) helps reduce their body image concerns.

Developing flexible showering policies can eliminate stress for some students. For example, if a class period consists of low physical activity (so the students haven't sweat), showers should not be required of students. When students need to shower, they should be given adequate time to do so and as much privacy as possible. When class periods are short and showering time cannot be extended, consider allowing some students (with high body concerns) to leave class early so they can shower privately. Physical educators often cringe at the suggestion to decrease class time for longer shower times, as we are ingrained with the idea of maximizing activity time and making the most of our physical education time. However, we must keep in mind that in the long run, it might be worth giving up a few minutes of activity time if students feel more comfortable about physical education, as this could enhance their motivation for future physical activity.

Finally, locker rooms should always be monitored. This is necessary for physical safety as well as psychological safety. Students should not be allowed to make fun of others in the locker room, and the teacher's presence can often curtail such teasing. But if harassment still occurs, action is needed to eliminate such behaviors. For example, tell students to stop if you hear or see such harassment taking place; if it continues, then apply negative consequences for the offending student.

Mr. Weaver and his colleagues require all students to wear the same physical education uniform every day in class, regardless of the activity. It consists of a pair of school shorts, the school T-shirt, white socks, and athletic shoes. It is one of the main reasons Mara doesn't like to participate in class; she is very self-conscious about her weight and doesn't want to be seen in shorts. Developing a more flexible dress policy—such as allowing students to wear sweat pants instead of shorts, or not having to change clothes for activities like golf or bocce ball—would go a long way in helping Mara feel comfortable in class.

focus point

Flexible dress and showering policies, along with effective locker room supervision, may reduce some students' body image concerns and enhance their motivation in physical education.

Establish Strong Teacher–Student Relationships

Although relatedness with fellow classmates is a major factor influencing students' perceptions of relatedness, the quality of students' relationships with the teacher can also affect the satisfaction of this need and eventual motivation for physical education. This is especially true for middle and high school students. As a physical education teacher, you can take several steps to enhance interpersonal relationships with students (Buskist & Saville, 2001):

- *Learn and use student names.* There are numerous methods of learning names, but perhaps the easiest is for students to wear name tags at the beginning of the semester.

- *Chat with students.* Learn about students' interests, hobbies, and goals.

- *Make eye contact with students.* Eye contact is a direct way of connecting with students.

- *Smile!* Smiling helps teachers seem more approachable to students. It makes students think you like your job and them.

- *Be respectful of students.* The golden rule is important: treat students as you would want to be treated. Most people don't enjoy being yelled at, so avoid yelling at students. Manners ("please," "thank you") go a long way in showing respect.

- *Use humor.* Telling jokes (even bad ones) and gentle teasing (once you know students) can help students feel more comfortable in class. But avoid biting sarcasm or ridicule.

- *Attend student extracurricular activities.* This lets students know that you are interested in and care about them. Be sure to comment about the activity when you see them again.

- *Be an active listener.* An active listener is someone who maintains eye contact with the speaker, uses nonverbal actions (e.g., head nodding, facial expressions), and paraphrases what was said (e.g., "so it sounds like you are having a difficult time in English class"; "so you really enjoyed your weekend with your brother") (Darst & Pangrazi, 2006).

- *Maintain confidentiality.* Students may confide personal information to you (e.g., problems with a boyfriend or family member; health concerns). This information should stay between the teacher and student and not be shared with other faculty or students. Exceptions include information about student abuse or illegal activity; in such cases, let the student know that this information will be shared with the proper authorities, and then do so.

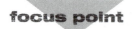

focus point

Students' perceptions of relatedness in physical education, especially for middle school and high school students, may be enhanced through good student–teacher relationships.

real world

Michal S. is a high school physical education teacher at an urban high school in the southern United States who establishes very strong relationships with her students. Within one week of the semester, she knows all of her students' names. Michal's ready smile is catching; that smile and her gentle teasing often gets return smiles from students. She can frequently be seen in the hallways, as well as before and after class, talking with students. Probably Michal's most effective means of establishing good relationships with her students is to attend their extracurricular activities. She spends many evenings attending sporting events, plays, and musical performances, supporting her students in those activities and praising them on their efforts when she sees them again.

Mr. Weaver's relationships with some students, particularly the more highly skilled ones, are pretty good, but he needs to work on relating better to lower skilled students. If he truly wants students like Mara, Andy, and Gisell to show more motivation in class, it will take a concentrated effort on his part to interact more with them, get to know them better, and show them that he truly cares about their welfare.

Emphasize the Cooperation Within Competition

One characteristic of the physical education context found to enhance students' perceptions of relatedness and competence, as well as intrinsic motivation and identified regulation, is an emphasis on cooperation. While this can happen by using the cooperative learning instructional model (see Chapter 4), you can also do this by clearly pointing out to students the cooperation needed in competitive activities. It would be very difficult, but also unnecessary, to completely eliminate competition from physical education; after all, competition is inherent in all kinds of sports. But students need to also understand that considerable cooperation is necessary for competition to occur. In team sports, teammates must work together if their team is to be successful. Competition in any kind of sport—team, individual, dual—cannot occur unless the participants cooperate regarding rules, traditions, and opportunities to play. For example, a golf competition would not be possible if some players decide they aren't going to cooperate regarding the order of play, or that they aren't going to follow all of the rules. Strive to specifically praise students for cooperating with each other in order to make competition possible. Although the classes Mr. Weaver teaches do not include much competition, he does play games like aerobic kickball or ultimate Frisbee some days; so he could stress the importance of cooperating both within and between teams on such days.

focus point

Cooperation, and perceptions of relatedness, can be emphasized in physical education by pointing out to students how cooperation is a necessary part of competitive events.

Promote an Incremental View of Ability

Research shows that students who believe their motor skill ability level is changeable (i.e., an incremental view of ability) are likely to have higher levels of intrinsic motivation and identified regulation and lower levels of amotivation than students who believe their ability level cannot be changed (i.e., an entity view of ability). Therefore, regularly emphasize that everyone, regardless of how good or poor they are at an activity, can get better as long as they practice hard at relevant tasks.

For example, while student teaching middle school students at a school in the midwestern United States, Matt W. gave regular skills tests to his students throughout a soccer unit. These skills tests allowed students to see their continual improvement throughout the unit. Some of his students played on the soccer team; others had never touched a soccer ball before. Matt promoted an incremental view of ability through his frequent reminders that all of his students, regardless of their ability levels, could improve their soccer skills.

Mr. Weaver could also utilize this strategy, especially for students who don't even try because they say they just aren't any good at sports (i.e., have an entity view of ability).

Physical educators can promote an incremental view of ability, which can enhance intrinsic motivation, by emphasizing that all students, regardless of ability, can improve their skills.

Establish a Structured Learning Environment

According to Deci and Ryan (1991), a context with a clearly defined structure can promote a sense of self-determination. Although it appears to be counterproductive to perceptions of autonomy, structure allows students to know what to expect, which can actually enhance their sense of control. One way to create structure in physical education is to utilize routines and procedures. For example, you might establish a routine for starting class and taking role (e.g., come out of the locker room within five minutes of the class bell and sit in your assigned squad), or for what students are to do when they hear the stop signal (e.g., put any equipment down, sit or kneel, and listen to the teacher). Such routines need to be taught to students and practiced at the beginning of the school year. A structured learning environment will result by establishing rules and clearly communicating and carrying out consequences for following and breaking the rules. Rules should be stated positively, be few in number, and be posted for all students to see (Rink, 2002). When you go over rules at the beginning of the school year, also review the consequences for not following as well as following the rules. In addition, when you give students choices (as is suggested by self-determination theory to create a sense of autonomy), those choices should be made within specified guidelines; giving students choices doesn't mean a "free-for-all" or "anything goes" for students. For example, when volleyball teams in the sport education model are allowed to start designing and carrying out their own practices, designate which particular skills to work on each day and/or require all students to be involved.

Many excellent physical education teachers know how to help students develop a sense of autonomy while still establishing a structured learning environment.

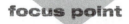

Creating a structured learning environment in physical education can help develop students' perceptions of autonomy because they know what to expect in class, which enhances their sense of control.

For example, Carolyn T., a middle school teacher in the mid-Atlantic states, regularly spends the first couple weeks of each semester going over rules, consequences (positive and negative), and routines with her students. In fact, she purposely engages them in many different activities in those first two weeks, just so they can practice things like getting and putting away different kinds of equipment, quickly forming different-size groups, and so on. Students are then familiar with all rules and routines, and she can start her actual instructional units. Within each unit, students are given many choices, but students must choose within the rules and guidelines. For example, she lets students choose if they want to participate in a competitive tournament at the end of the volleyball unit, or just play games for fun. But if they choose to participate in the competitive games, the students cannot give up during games or just mess around; they must try their best.

Mr. Weaver already has a structured learning environment; he posts and explains rules and consequences each semester, and routines for getting equipment like jump ropes and exercise bands are clearly explained to students, practiced, and enforced. Mr. Weaver now needs to give his students choices within that structured environment, like the type of aerobic exercise to do in a day, in order to enhance their perceptions of autonomy and intrinsic motivation.

Summary

Motivation is a significant concern of many physical education teachers. Motivation can be defined as the direction and intensity of effort and is the subject of many theories. According to self-determination theory, people's motivation in a situation is the result of their perceptions of competence, autonomy, and relatedness in that situation. People have different reasons for participating in activities, called motivational orientations, which vary in their level of self-determination. Intrinsic motivation is the most self-determined form of motivation and yields the most adaptive behaviors like high effort, persistence, and enjoyment. The social context affects whether individuals believe their needs for competence, autonomy, and relatedness have been met, and in turn a person's motivational orientation. Research shows that students' motivational orientations may vary depending on their age, gender, goal orientation, and dispositional ability conception. Studies confirm that intrinsic motivation and more self-determined forms of extrinsic motivation yield more adaptive consequences than amotivation or external regulation.

There are no magical solutions to motivating students in physical education. Students are, after all, human beings, and humans are quite complex—influenced by many factors. But self-determination theory and related research suggest several means of enhancing students' perceptions of competence, autonomy, and relatedness, and moving them toward intrinsic motivation, such as using rewards appropriately, reducing students' body image concerns, establishing positive teacher-student relationships, emphasizing cooperation within competition, promoting an incremental view of ability, and establishing a structured learning environment. These strategies should not be considered surefire solutions, but part of an arsenal of possible weapons to use in the fight to develop students' intrinsic motivation.

KEY concepts

Motivation

Self-determination theory

Intrinsic motivation

Extrinsic motivation

External regulation

Introjected regulation

Identified regulation

Integrated regulation

Amotivation

application exercises

1. Describe activities or events in which your reason for participating matches each of the motivational orientations described in self-determination theory (intrinsic motivation, external regulation, introjected regulation, identified regulation, integrated regulation). In addition, describe an activity or event for which you display amotivation. Explain why you believe your reason for participating (or not, in the case of amotivation) fits that motivational orientation. (Your answer should include a total of six activities or events.)

2. Two physical education teachers in a high school have very different approaches to motivating their students. Mr. Sanchez is primarily concerned with getting students to complete the tasks/activities required in each class period; he isn't concerned about the students' motivation to be active outside of physical education or later in life. Ms. Bandero, however, is more concerned about the students' long-term motivation than whether they complete tasks during class. Describe three activities/strategies each teacher would utilize in order to achieve their desired goals. What type or types of motivational orientations is each activity or strategy likely to develop?

3. As a middle school physical education teacher, you understand that enhancing students' perceptions of competence, autonomy, and relatedness can increase their intrinsic motivation. Although you have always used direct instruction in your classes, you decide to implement a new instructional model in order to increase their intrinsic motivation. Which instructional model best meets all three of those student needs? How does it do that?

Physical Activity and Lifestyle Enhancement

Mr. Olson is a physical education teacher at an urban elementary school. He is very concerned about children's physical activity levels and knows that physical education is one important means of getting children physically active. He has worked hard to increase the time his students spend in moderate to vigorous physical activity in class. Unfortunately, his children have physical education only two days each week for 45 minutes each class period. Even though the students get lots of physical activity during class, Mr. Olson knows that isn't enough time. Julia and Sneha are two 5th grade girls in one of his classes. He isn't worried about Sneha's physical activity levels; he knows Sneha participates in a local soccer league, sees her playing kickball and tag at recess, and has overheard her discussing her ballet class and regular trips to a local park with her family. Julia, however, is a different story. Mr. Olson has noticed that she tends to stand against the wall outside at recess, and she rarely mentions doing anything active outside of physical education. Mr. Olson wonders what else he could do to help students like Julia be physically active outside of physical education time. He also wants his students to be physically active throughout their lifetime and questions how to help that happen.

introduction

focus point

Developing physically active youth who desire lifetime activity is a major goal of physical education programs, but it is difficult to achieve this during physical education alone.

Lifetime physical activity is a primary goal of physical education programs (NASPE, 2004b). In fact, NASPE defines a physically educated person as one who "participates regularly in physical activity" and "values physical activity for health, enjoyment, challenge, self-expression, and/or social interaction" (2004b, p. 11). Two goals named in the *Healthy People 2010* statement are to increase the proportion of adolescents participating in moderate physical activity for at least 30 minutes each day 5 of 7 days each week, and to increase the proportion of adolescents participating in vigorous physical activity for at least 20 minutes each day on 3 of 7 days in a week (United States Department of Health and Human Services [USDHHS], 2000). Unfortunately, in many schools physical education is not offered enough days per week, or minutes per day, to reach these objectives. Even when it is, managerial factors (e.g., taking role, showering) take time away from activity; thus, the ability of physical education alone to meet those objectives is restricted. So, if physical education teachers want to help their students become physically educated individuals for a lifetime, they need to help them value and enjoy physical activity and help them be active outside of as well as inside physical education.

The purpose of this chapter is to help physical educators develop physically active students who desire a lifetime of physical activity. A framework for conceptualizing youth participation in physical activity will be presented. This will be followed by a review of research conducted on factors that may influence youth activity levels, and the effectiveness of various interventions to increase young people's physical activity levels outside of physical education. The chapter will conclude with strategies physical education teachers can use to enhance students' physical activity levels and help them become physically active adults.

The Youth Physical Activity Promotion Model

Numerous theoretical frameworks have been used to explain lifetime physical activity involvement. Theories that may be useful in explaining youth participation in physical activity outside of physical education and in the future are shown in Appendix B. Most of these frameworks, however, were developed for adults, not children, and only a few have been used to conceptualize research on children's physical activity. An exception, however, is the **Youth Physical Activity Promotion Model** (Welk, 1999). Greg Welk developed this model using existing theoretical frameworks and research to explain factors that could influence school-age children's physical activity, as well as to design interventions to enhance youth activity. The model includes factors from other theories that researchers found affect youth physical activity. According to Welk (1999), youth physical activity levels are the result of interactions among four categories of factors: predisposing, reinforcing, enabling, and personal demographics (see Exhibit 10.1).

connected CONCEPTS

Several theories and concepts from previous chapters also explained how people learn to be physically active: social learning theory (through the socialization process of modeling and reinforcement of physical activity by significant others—Chapters 3 and 4), self-determination theory (by demonstrating competence, perceiving autonomy, and experiencing relatedness in physical activities—Chapter 9), achievement goal theory (by a dispositional task goal orientation and by experiencing task-involving physical activity settings—Chapter 5), competence motivation theory (by high perceived competence and internal sense of control in physically active situations), self-efficacy theory (by developing high self-efficacy in physical activities through successful performances, similar role models, verbal persuasion, and positive physiological arousal, emotional states, and imagery—Chapter 6), attribution theory (by attributing successful outcomes of physical activity attempts to controllable, internal, and stable causes, and attributing negative outcomes to external, controllable, and unstable causes—Chapter 7), high personal and situational interest in physical activities, and expectancy-value theory (by expecting to be successful when being physically active and valuing that success—Chapter 8).

Predisposing Factors

Predisposing factors are those that "collectively increase the likelihood that a person will be physically active on a regular basis" (Welk, 1999, p. 11). These factors answer two questions: Am I able? Is it worth it? (Fox, 1991; Welk, 1999).

EXHIBIT   10.1   The Youth Physical Activity Promotion Model.

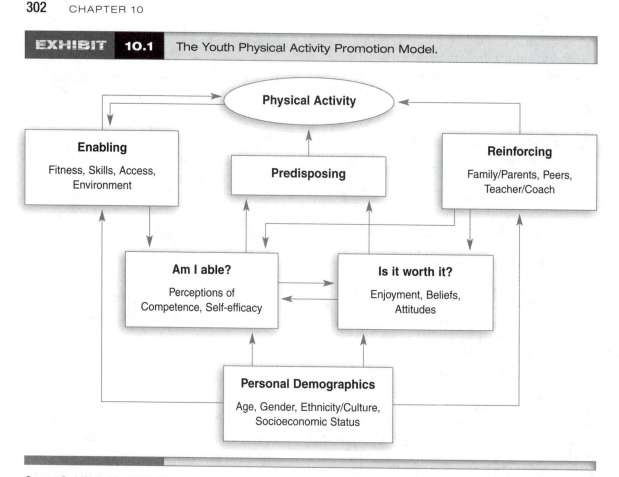

Source: G. J. Welk, "The Youth Physical Activity Promotion Model: A Conceptual Bridge between Theory and Practice," in *Quest, 51,* 5–23. Copyright 1999, Human Kinetics, Champaign, IL. Reprinted with permission.

Am I able?

focus point

The Youth Physical Activity Promotion Model was developed using existing theoretical frameworks and research to explain factors that could influence school-age children's physical activity and to design interventions to enhance their physical activity.

A person's beliefs about their physical or motor skill abilities—perceived competence or physical self-efficacy—are predicted to have a strong impact on their choices to be physically active. Young people who believe they are capable of performing or learning an activity are more likely to participate in that activity than those who do not. Perhaps one reason Sneha is more physically active than Julia during recess is because Sneha believes she can be successful while playing tag and kickball, while Julia doesn't believe she would be successful.

Is it worth it?

The answer to this question addresses the value a student places on the expected outcomes of being physically active. An individual goes through a decision-making process, wherein the benefits of participating in an activity are weighed against the costs of or barriers to participating. When the balance favors the benefits, the student is likely to participate in physical activity. One factor that influences the assessment of benefits is the enjoyment experienced in physical education or specific physical activities. Other benefits can include being with friends, learning skills, improving fitness, and improving one's body shape. Costs of or barriers to participating can include a lack of time or interest, getting sweaty/tired/dirty, or a fear of being teased. Sneha may be active because she values being with her friends (who are involved in the activities) and has fun when she participates, whereas Julia's dislike for tag games and kickball and her desire to talk to her friends during recess leads to less value on physical activity.

The answers to the two questions—Am I able? Is it worth it?—likely influence each other. If a student believes she is capable of doing something successfully, she may believe the effort of being physically active is worth it. Conversely, if a student believes there is value in an activity, participating in it may enhance the student's perceived competence and motor abilities.

connected   CONCEPTS

The two questions answered by the predisposing factors likely stem from the expectancy-value theory (see Chapter 8); one's expectations for success in a domain determine if one is able, and the value one places on success in that domain reveals whether it is worth it.

focus point

Children are more likely to be physically active if they believe they can be successful and that the benefits to participating outweigh the costs or barriers.

Reinforcing Factors

Factors that support or encourage a person's physical activity (Welk, 1999) fall into the **reinforcing** category of influences. Such reinforcement comes from three main sources: parents/family, peers, and teachers. Parents and families may affect young people's physical activity engagement in several ways, which include modeling physical activity (i.e., being active themselves), encouraging their children to be active ("Why don't you go outside and play?"), praising their children for being active, signing them up for activity programs, or transporting them to such programs or play areas. Peers can positively influence physical activity levels by encouraging their friends to participate with them or praising friends for their efforts. Physical education teachers may influence students' activity participation by presenting lessons that maximize activity time, giving students activity homework, or relating the benefits of physical activity. Sneha's high activity level is strongly affected by her parents; they are very active, and they signed her up for and take her to ballet class as well as to the park. Sneha's friends also like to play games at recess, which helps her be active. On the other hand, Julia's friends prefer more sedentary activities; in addition, neither her parents nor her siblings are involved in activity. Of course, Mr. Olson reinforces the girls' physical activity levels

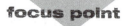
by providing active physical education lessons, as well as encouraging his students to be active outside of class.

Sometimes these factors directly influence youth activity levels; for example, Sneha participates in ballet because her parents signed her up and take her there. But the factors may indirectly influence physical activity by affecting the person's answers to the questions Am I able? Is it worth it? For example, Sneha's parents praise her after dance recitals, so her perceived competence increases, but Julia may not value activity because her friends are not involved.

Enabling Factors

"Factors that allow youth to be physically active" (Welk, 1999, p. 14) are **enabling factors**. This category encompasses environmental factors as well as biological ones. Environmental influences include their access to parks, gyms, physical activity programs (like youth sports, intramurals), sidewalks, and a safe neighborhood; the weather can also affect youth physical activity. Biological influences can include the student's motor skills, fitness level, and body composition. These factors are necessary but not sufficient to result in a student's being physically active. In other words, it would be very difficult for a young person to be active if they do not have a place where they can be active; but just because that space is available doesn't mean an individual will be active. Both Sneha and Julia have good motor skill abilities in many activities, but that is not sufficient to get Julia physically active. An environmental factor working in Sneha's favor is the safe neighborhood where she lives; her parents are comfortable letting her play outside without constant supervision. This is unlike Julia's neighborhood; her parents do not want her playing outside without their supervision, and they have to work late into the evening.

Like the reinforcing factors, these enabling factors may have a direct or indirect influence on physical activity levels. A student whose school provides numerous intramural activities from which to choose and transportation home is more likely to be active than a student in a school without such opportunities (a direct influence). Students with high motor skill abilities are more likely to feel like they are able to participate successfully in an activity, which then leads them to participate; this illustrates an indirect influence on perceptions of competence (Am I able?).

Personal Demographics

Various personal factors may affect youth physical activity participation, such as age, gender, racial/ethnic group, and socioeconomic status. Welk (1999) further asserts that this influence is indirect through the other factors. For example, a girl might receive less support from parents to be physically active than a boy, and a particular ethnic group may put less importance on being active than others, thus affecting the child's beliefs about the value of physical activity. The main reason Julia's parents do not encourage her to be physically active is because they believe that detracts from her femininity, and so Julia similarly believes sweating is something to avoid. Conversely, Sneha's parents believe girls should be just as active as boys, so she values physical activity. In addition, the socioeconomic status of the families affects the girls' physical activity levels; Sneha's parents have the money to buy her sports equipment and pay for ballet lessons, while Julia's parents lack the discretionary funds to provide such opportunities for her.

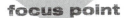

focus point

Personal demographics—gender, race/ethnicity, and socioeconomic status—may indirectly affect a child's physical activity by influencing predisposing, reinforcing, and enabling factors.

Designing Interventions

According to the Youth Physical Activity Promotion Model (Welk, 1999), once the predisposing, reinforcing, and enabling factors have been identified in a situation, along with relevant personal demographics, interventions can be planned based on the available resources and likely barriers. According to the Centers for Disease Control and Prevention (CDC, 1997), a **coordinated school health program** is a good model to use to promote youth physical activity. The model consists of eight components that should interact to enhance youth activity levels: (a) health education, (b) physical education, (c) health services, (d) nutrition services, (e) counseling and psychological services, (f) healthy school environment, (g) health promotion for staff, and (h) family and community involvement. Welk (1999) believes that the two main means within the coordinated school health program model of influencing youth physical activity levels are the physical education program and family and community involvement.

Physical education

According to Welk (1999), physical education is best positioned to enhance students' physical activity levels by influencing the predisposing and enabling factors. Physical educators may be able to improve students' fitness and motor skill levels (enabling factors) such that their perceptions of competence and enjoyment of physical activity (predisposing factors) increase.

Family and community involvement

Parents and siblings play key reinforcing roles in impacting youth physical activity. Parents need to understand ways to directly influence their child's activity levels (e.g., take them to parks, buy them equipment), as well as the indirect impact of their praise and encouragement.

Community programs primarily influence youth physical activity levels by affecting the enabling and predisposing factors. Welk (1999) describes the need for more facilities such as bike paths, skate parks, and playgrounds (enabling factors), as well as recreational activity programs that focus on self-improvement of skills rather than comparison to others through competition. The increased availability of activity programs for youth is another way of increasing enabling factors, while changing the focus to self-improvement can enhance perceptions of competence and enjoyment, which are predisposing factors.

The Youth Physical Activity Promotion Model provides an excellent means of organizing the myriad of research that has recently emerged on factors influencing young people's physical activity. In the next section, this research will be summarized, along with descriptions of research on the long-term effects of physical activity in youth, physical education and physical activity, and intervention programs designed to enhance youth activity levels.

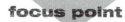

focus point

Within a coordinated school health program, major means of influencing students' physical activity levels include the physical education program, families, and community programs.

Youth Physical Activity Research

Research on variables that might influence youth physical activity levels has proliferated in the past two decades. Because of this fact, reviews of research and other studies not included in such reviews, primarily those conducted since 2000 and those that provide further information about a variable or topic, form the basis of this section. Throughout this section, the following terms will be used: "children" will refer to individuals 12 years old and younger, "adolescents" are individuals 13 to 18 years of age, and "youth," "young people," or "students" will refer to all school-age persons, from kindergarten through high school.

Does Early Participation Lead to Participation Later in Life?

One reason physical educators will want students to be active is because physically active youth will become physically active in the future, particularly as adults. But is that true? Several reviewers found that previous participation in physical activity positively influenced children's and adolescents' later participation as children and adolescents (Biddle et al., 2005; Daley, 2002; Malina, 2001; Sallis et al., 2000). Researchers also found that participation in physical activity as a child or adolescent is positively related to adult participation, but the impact is much weaker (Beunen et al., 2004; Kraut, Melamed, Gofer, & Froom, 2003; Malina, 2001; Telama, Yang, Hirvensalo, & Raitakari, 2006; Trudeau, Laurencelle, & Shephard, 2004). Interestingly, adolescent participation in sports was a better predictor of adult sport participation in females than males (Biddle et al., 2005; Malina, 2001).

The research points to a weakening association with time between previous physical activity and current physical activity. Even though the relationship between youth and adult physical activity is small, the fact that there is any kind of association at all still makes early participation important. Physical educators should strive to help students become physically active in a consistent manner not only because it is vital to their current health, but also because such activity may influence their future lifestyle. It seems especially important to help girls find organized physical activities in which they can participate and enjoy.

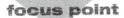

focus point

Research indicates that participation in physical activity during childhood and adolescence is significantly but weakly related to adult physical activity levels.

Demographics

Several demographics were examined for their relationship to youth physical activity levels, as well as how such demographics might impact the predisposing, reinforcing, and enabling factors. Although teachers cannot change demographics, subgroups may require special attention by physical educators. The demographic factors most consistently found to influence physical activity are age, gender, ethnicity/race, and some disabilities.

Most reviewers and researchers found that physical activity levels tend to decline as children get older (e.g., Anderssen, Wold, & Tonsheim, 2005; Biddle et al., 2005; Corbin, Pangrazi, & LeMasurier, 2004; Iannotti et al., 2005; Norman et al., 2006), especially in adolescence (Sallis, 2000; Sallis et al., 2000). This is also true of youth with various disabilities (e.g., Ayvazoglu, Oh, & Kozub, 2006; Kozub, 2003; Pan & Frey, 2005). In one study the least active adolescents were also those least likely to change activity levels in their teenage years (Anderssen et al., 2005), showing the importance of getting them active early in life.

Most reviews and studies of factors related to physical activity levels show that boys are more active than girls during childhood as well as adolescence (e.g., Biddle et al., 2005; Corbin et al., 2004; Iannotti et al., 2005; Sallis et al., 2000; Welk, Wood, & Morss, 2003). Researchers confirmed this with youth from various countries or ethnic groups (e.g., Crocker, Eklund, & Kowalski, 2000; Hagger et al., 1998; Loucaides et al., 2004; Morgan et al., 2003; Raudsepp et al., 2002; Santos, Matos, & Mota, 2005; Wu & Jwo, 2005) and with youth who have various disabilities (Sit, Lindner, & Sherrill, 2002). But interviews with 15-year-old girls revealed that they will be very active outside of physical education when they are doing activities they enjoy (Flintoff & Scraton, 2001).

Most studies and reviews show that Caucasian youth tend to be more active than non-Caucasians, especially girls (Hagger et al., 1998; Norman et al., 2006) and during adolescence (Biddle et al., 2005; Kann & Warren, 1996; Morgan et al., 2003; Sallis et al., 2000). Children with developmental coordination disorder, spastic diplegia, physical disabilities, visual impairments, and intellectual disabilities have displayed lower levels of

focus point

Evidence suggests that physical activity levels are lower in adolescents, girls, non-Caucasian youth, and students with developmental coordination disorder, spastic diplegia, physical disabilities, and visual impairments.

activity than children without those disabilities or children with hearing impairments (e.g., Cairney et al., 2005; Faison-Hodge & Porretta, 2004; Sit et al., 2002; Steele et al., 1996; Stuart, Lieberman, & Hand, 2006; Suzuki et al., 1991; Van den Berg-Emons et al., 1995), and children with physical disabilities were less active than children with intellectual disabilities (Suzuki et al., 1991). But children with self-reported disabilities (Hogan, McLellan, & Bauman, 2000) and with autistic spectrum disorder (Sandt & Frey, 2005) were as physically active as children without disabilities.

A religion may enhance physical activity and other healthy habits via its prohibitions (e.g., drinking of alcohol, sex before marriage) or prescriptions (e.g., live within walking distance of a synagogue). But a religion could also inhibit physical activity (e.g., forbid physical work on certain days). Kahan (2004) discovered that Jewish adolescents' physical activity on Saturday decreased as their observance of religious laws strengthened. In addition, Kahan found that non-Orthodox Jewish adolescents engaged in significantly greater levels of physical activity on Saturday than Orthodox adolescents. The researcher reasoned that the Orthodox adolescents, in observing the Sabbath and refraining from work, participated in less strenuous activities than the non-observant adolescents, who could engage in secular pursuits like organized sport.

Although the socioeconomic status of families is proposed to influence youth physical activity levels, the evidence on this factor is mixed; some reviews and studies indicate higher activity levels with higher socioeconomic status (Biddle et al., 2005; M. J. Duncan, Al-Nakeeb, Nevill, & Jones, 2004; S. C. Duncan, Duncan, Strycker, & Chaumeton, 2004; Macdonald et al., 2004; Santos, Esculcas, & Mota, 2004), while others show no influence of socioeconomic status on activity participation (Kalakanis, Goldfield, Paluch, & Epstein, 2001; Sallis et al., 2000).

Implications

The results of research suggest it is especially important that physical educators help adolescents, females, non-Caucasian youth (especially females), and students with physical disabilities, spastic diplegia, developmental coordination disorder, and visual impairments become and stay physically active both in and out of school. It appears crucial to enhance young children's activity levels, because research shows that once students become inactive, it is difficult to change their participation levels. Because girls will be active if they find activities they enjoy, physical educators should help girls develop the motor skills to be successful in activities and either provide activities they enjoy or help them find chances to participate in those activities outside of class. Although more information is needed on the influence of other religions on physical activity, physical educators can help students of various faiths become more active by learning about the religion's principles regarding physical activity, which could help them make informed suggestions to those students about how to increase their activity levels. In the case of socioeconomic status, although it may be that low parental income can negatively affect youth participation, it doesn't have to. Physical education teachers should present a wide variety of opportunities for physical activity to students, including those that don't require participation fees (for example, a local bowling alley that offers free bowling to youth accompanied by an adult during the summer). It is imperative to find out about such events and make students aware of them.

Predisposing Factors

Among the many predisposing factors researchers examined on youth physical activity levels are attitudes toward physical activity and physical education, perceived barriers and benefits, intentions to be active, beliefs about the value significant others place on physical activity (subjective norm), and perceptions of control, time, and body image.

Attitudes

An individual's attitudes toward physical activity in general and physical education specifically are believed to affect the answer to the question, Is it worth it? Although researchers often distinguish among various attitude constructs, for our purposes the term "attitudes" will include the following: enjoyment, fun, interest, likes, preferences, attraction, and value.

connected   CONCEPTS

Self-perceptions of various kinds are proposed to formulate young people's answers to the question, Am I able? Research reviewed in Chapter 6 indicates that positive self-perceptions are related to higher activity levels in youth. Another factor that might predispose an individual to be physically active is one's motivation. Research reviewed in Chapter 9 shows that high intrinsic motivation and more self-determined forms of extrinsic motivation are associated with high levels of physical activity in youth.

Attitudes toward physical activity. Youth physical activity levels were found to be positively related to several attitudes: enjoyment (Biddle et al., 2005; Dishman, Motl, Saunders, et al., 2005; Schilling, 2001; Spink et al., 2006; Watkinson et al., 2005; Welk, 1999), preference for physical activity (Sallis et al., 2000), attraction to physical activity (Welk & Schaben, 2004), and value for physical activity (Whitehead, Biddle, O'Donovan, & Nevill, 2006). In their review, Biddle et al. (2005) found that adolescent girls' low interest in physical activity was associated with lower activity levels. The activities in which children participate were influenced by their levels of interest in those activities (Macdonald et al., 2004; Watkinson et al., 2005). Other researchers found that attraction to physical activity positively influenced 9- to 14-year-olds' perceived physical competence, which in turn yielded greater participation (Paxton et al., 2004). Several researchers discovered that positive attitudes regarding physical activity result in stronger intentions to be active (Downs, Graham, Yang, Bargainnier, & Vasil, 2006; Hagger et al., 2007; Martin, Oliver, & McCaughtry, 2007; Mummery, Spence, & Hudec, 2000; Thompson, Romanow, & Horne, 1998).

Attitudes toward physical education. It is hoped that students' participation in physical education is positive, and that positive attitudes toward physical education would result in greater physical activity overall—but do they? Some researchers found that positive attitudes toward and enjoyment of physical education positively affected children's and adolescents' physical activity (Chung & Phillips, 2002; Dishman, Motl, Saunders et al., 2005; Sallis, Prochaska, Taylor, Hill, & Geraci, 1999; Wallhead & Buckworth, 2004), either directly or by influencing their self-perceptions. In one study (Chung & Phillips, 2002), females had less positive attitudes than males, which might help explain their lower activity levels. Similarly, teenage girls who were interviewed said they valued physical activity but they did not like physical education (Flintoff & Scraton, 2001). The girls said the activities were out of date and not challenging, the boys dominated play, and teachers had negative attitudes toward and low expectations of girls.

Most recent research suggests students' attitudes toward physical activity in general and physical education specifically can influence their overall physical activity levels. Physical educators must make their classes positive and enjoyable for all students, especially females. The research indicates that students will engage in physical activities they enjoy and in which they are interested. This suggests that a variety of activities—beyond traditional team sports—should be offered in physical education, especially at the middle school and high school levels, and that students have choices of activities in which they will participate. This ensures they are engaging in activities they enjoy and gives them the sense of control that affects their intentions to be active. As a physical educator, you can support all students' attempts to be active by asking them about their after-school and weekend physical activity, encouraging and praising them for being active, and helping students find ways to be active.

Perceived barriers/benefits

According to the Youth Physical Activity Promotion Model (Welk, 1999), students go through a decision-making process, weighing the barriers to participating in activity with the benefits, when determining whether to be physically active. This helps them answer the question, Is it worth it? When youth perceive that the benefits are greater than the costs, they will be active, but will choose to be inactive if they perceive greater costs than benefits. Most research indicates that youth activity levels are higher when

focus point

According to recent research, students' positive attitudes toward physical activity in general and physical education specifically can positively influence their physical activity levels.

the overall perceived benefits are high and the perceived barriers are low (Biddle et al., 2005; Kimm et al., 2006; Sallis et al., 2000; Spink et al., 2006; Watkinson et al., 2005). In other studies, adolescents who perceived more benefits of exercise were more consistent exercisers, while those who perceived more costs were more likely to be non-exercisers, still thinking about starting an exercise program, or inconsistent exercisers (Maddison & Prapavessis, 2006; Nigg & Courneya, 1998; Prapavessis et al., 2004). Females have reported more barriers and fewer benefits than boys (Wu & Jwo, 2005), and Mexican American youth reported more barriers to activity than Caucasian Americans (Morgan et al., 2003). Specific barriers (e.g., lack of time, facilities, money, transportation, and low motor skills) and benefits and their relationships to activity levels are discussed later in this chapter.

Physical educators should help students of all ages identify benefits of physical activity in general and of specific activities, and help them find ways to overcome barriers to or costs of participating. Such assistance may be especially necessary for females and non-Caucasians.

Intentions to be active, subjective norm, and perceived control

Intentions to be active imply a belief that physical activity is worth it and should lead to actual activity (Ajzen, 1985). Some researchers found that intentions predict exercise behavior and activity levels, particularly in adolescents (Downs et al., 2006; Downs & Hausenblas, 2005; Hagger et al., 2007; Hagger et al., 2003; Martin et al., 2007; Sallis et al., 2000). Downs et al. (2006) found that boys' intentions to be active were higher than girls', which could help explain girls' lower activity levels.

The **subjective norm** refers to an individual's beliefs about significant others' views and typical expectations for physical activity and the individual's motivation to comply with those expectations (Ajzen, 1985). Such beliefs should affect one's intentions to be active and could impact the answer to the question, Is it worth it? Most research indicates that the subjective norm, while not directly affecting activity levels, can positively influence young people's intentions to be active (Downs et al., 2006; Martin et al., 2005; Martin et al., 2007; Mummery et al., 2000; Thompson et al., 1998). But Mummery et al. (2000) found the subjective norm to be a stronger predictor of intentions for physical activity in 3rd graders than in older students.

Another predisposing factor believed to influence physical activity levels is one's beliefs about the degree of control a person has over her physical activity (Ajzen, 1985). Some researchers found that high perceptions of control positively affected adolescents' activity levels (Downs et al., 2006) and children's and adolescents' intentions to be active (Downs et al., 2006;

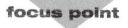

Hagger et al., 2007; Martin et al., 2005; Martin et al., 2007; Mummery et al., 2000), especially in girls and adolescents (Mummery et al., 2000).

While the subjective norm and perceptions of control may not directly impact physical activity levels, these beliefs do appear to influence youth intentions to be active. Physical educators can enhance students' sense of control by giving students choices of activities or tasks in which to participate in class. Help students perceive that their significant others want them to be physically active by encouraging them to be active and praising their efforts, as well as asking parents to encourage and help their children be physically active.

Perception of available time

Youth physical activity levels, especially for adolescent girls, are lower if they perceive they do not have the available time for activity (Biddle et al., 2005; Kimm et al., 2006). Physical education teachers should help all students, but especially adolescent girls, realize that physical activity does not have to be time consuming. Small but consistent efforts to be active—like parking far away from and walking to the mall entrance—can increase students' physical activity levels.

Body image

An individual's perception of his or her body might influence the answer to the question, Is it worth it? A person who does not feel good about his body may believe that the cost of showing one's body in public in physical activity is not worth the benefits that can be obtained through the activity, and not make the attempt. Reviewers of research on factors affecting youth activity levels concluded that adolescent girls' perceptions of body attractiveness were positively related with their activity levels (Biddle et al., 2005), but that body image did not impact children's participation (Sallis et al., 2000). Indeed, fewer high school girls than boys indicated being comfortable with their bodies (Azzarito & Solmon, 2006a). So, body image may have a greater influence on the activity levels of adolescent girls than other students. Physical educators can help girls develop positive perceptions of their bodies, regardless of their current physical condition, by pointing out the unhealthy and unrealistic body weights of most models seen in ads, and call attention to famous and successful individuals with more realistic body shapes.

Reinforcing Factors

The main sources of support and encouragement for young people's engagement in physical activity are their parents/families, peers, and teachers/coaches.

Parents/family

Parents and families are believed to exert a significant influence on youth physical activity levels (Welk, 1999). But is that true? And if so, how? Researchers examined the various ways by which families and parents affect young people's participation, including parental role modeling and involvement, support and encouragement, and sibling impact.

Role modeling and involvement. Parents role-model physical activity when they are physically active themselves. Similarly, parents who participate in physical activity with their child are exhibiting involvement. Some researchers found that youth physical activity levels could be positively influenced by their parents' participation in and/or role modeling of physical activity (Biddle et al., 2005; Davison, Cutting, & Birch, 2003; Kalakanis et al., 2001; Loucaides & Chedzoy, 2005); other researchers did not find such an impact (Ayvazoglu et al., 2006; Biddle et al., 2005; Davison, 2004; Iannotti et al., 2005; Kozub, 2003; Pan & Frey, 2005; Sallis et al., 2000). These conflicting findings are illustrated in a study conducted by Whitehead and his colleagues (Whitehead et al., 2006), who discovered that physically active 11- to 13-year-old girls, but not 14- to 16-year-old girls, had more physically active mothers than low active girls.

Support and encouragement. Parents and families may provide emotional support by prompting their children to be active ("You may watch 30 minutes of television after school, and then you need to go outside and play"), encouraging them to be active ("Why don't you go shoot some hoops?"), and praising them for activity ("You're doing a great job in your ballet lessons"). Another way support can be given is by facilitating involvement, such as transporting children to activities, paying for equipment or lessons, or enrolling them in sports leagues. Such parental support and encouragement positively affects youth engagement in physical activity (Biddle et al., 2005; Davison, 2004; Davison et al., 2003; Davison, Downs, & Birch, 2006; Sallis et al., 2000; Spink et al., 2006; Welk et al., 2003; Wu & Jwo, 2005). For example, 9-year-old girls who received greater parental support for physical activity were found to be more active when they were 11 years old than girls with less parental support (Davison et al., 2006). In case studies of young people with visual impairments, the parents reported that they provided facilitative support for their child's physical activity more so than actually participating with them (Ayvazoglu et al., 2006). Other visually impaired children had higher expectations for success in and value for physical activity when their parents also had high expectations for the children's success (Stuart et al., 2006).

The research suggests that parental support and encouragement of children's physical activity has a positive impact on children's engagement. Physical educators should help parents understand how to prompt and encourage their children to be active, as well as praise them for being active. Teachers should also help parents facilitate their children's participation by identifying ways for children to be active; perhaps a newsletter to parents can include lists of sports leagues, dance and gymnastic lessons, and low- or no-cost activity opportunities. Although the effect of parental role modeling and involvement in physical activity with their children is unclear, parents could still be encouraged to be active, preferably with their children, because it will still benefit the parents even if it doesn't positively affect the students' activity levels.

Siblings. Some researchers discovered that higher activity levels in siblings corresponded with higher levels of physical activity in pre-teens (S.C. Duncan et al., 2004), adolescents (Sallis et al., 2000), and youth with visual impairments (Ayvazoglu et al., 2006). Higher levels of support from siblings and families also showed positive relationships to youth physical activity levels (Davison, 2004; S.C. Duncan et al., 2004). Simply having siblings even seems to positively impact children's physical activity, especially for girls in two-parent families and for boys with a brother who is more than three years older (Bagley, Salmon, & Crawford, 2006).

Though the presence of siblings is not a factor anyone can change, as a physical education teacher, you will want to be aware of how students' families can affect their activity levels; students without siblings, for example, might need special encouragement and assistance to be engaged.

Peers

In addition to parents and families, recent studies suggest that peers are important to young people's physical activity levels. Support from friends to be physically active (Davison, 2004; Duncan, 1993; Spink et al., 2006), the availability of friends with whom one can play (Ayvazoglu et al., 2006; Kozub, 2003; Loucaides & Chedzoy, 2005; Voorhees et al., 2005), the physical activity levels of friends (Loucaides et al., 2004; Spink et al., 2006), and the number of physically active friends (Voorhees et al., 2005) were all found to positively influence youth activity levels. Furthermore, the activities in which children choose to participate are influenced by whether their friends are participating (Macdonald et al., 2004).

Unfortunately, peers can also have a negative impact on children's physical activity. Middle school girls, in particular, report less social support for physical activity from peers than boys (Wu & Jwo, 2005), claim more negative treatment from peers during physical education than when playing at home, and avoid physical activity in settings where boys ridicule them and criticize their motor skills (Kunesh et al., 1992).

The results of research suggest physical educators should help students find activities in which they can participate with their friends. Even if friends aren't participating in the same activities, physical educators should show them how to encourage their friends in their activities. Sadly, being treated negatively by peers, such as being teased for one's level of skill, can lead students to avoid participation. The fact that this negative treatment seemed to happen more during physical education than in other settings is telling. Every effort should be made to stop such treatment immediately. Establishing a task-involving climate, where students strive for self-improvement rather than comparing themselves to others, should create a positive environment in which such negative treatment is abhorred.

Teachers and coaches

Compared to research on the impact of parents, families, and peers, there is surprisingly little research that has specifically examined how teachers and coaches affect youth activity levels. Some researchers found that coach support positively affected adolescents' activity levels in structured activities (Spink et al., 2006), and that kindergarten children with greater interest in being physically active were taught by physical education teachers with more years' teaching experience than children with less interest (Chen & Zhu, 2005). Unfortunately, parents of visually impaired and/or blind children believe that their children's physical activity levels are hindered by physical educators or recreation leaders who lack knowledge about those disabilities and cannot help their children be physically active in class (Lieberman & MacVicar, 2003; Stuart et al., 2006). Adolescent children with physical disabilities also claim they are excluded from participating in physical education by their teacher (Taub & Greer, 2000). Ways to influence students' activity levels will be presented later in this chapter.

Enabling Factors

As described earlier in the chapter, enabling factors allow youth to be active. Welk (1999) describes biological (i.e., body composition, fitness/health levels, motor skill abilities) and environmental (i.e., access to facilities and equipment, safety when engaged, availability of recess, transportation to school, season of the year, type of community and schooling) enabling factors. But behavioral elements (i.e., time spent in sedentary and outdoor activities, skills to overcome obstacles to physical activity) might also be considered enabling factors.

Biological factors

It seems logical that youth with lower levels of body fat would be more active than those with higher levels. Similarly, young people who are fit or healthy should be more active than those who are not, and youth with bet-

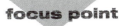

focus point

Recent research suggests support from and engagement with peers can positively affect youth engagement, but ridicule and other negative treatment from peers can inhibit participation.

ter motor skill abilities might be more active, since they have the skills to be successful in their activity attempts. But so far there is conflicting evidence about the impact that these biological factors have on youth physical activity levels, with some researchers and reviewers finding a small influence on activity levels (e.g., Biddle et al., 2005; Malina, 2001; Patterson, Anderson, & Klavora, 1997; Spink et al., 2005) and others finding no relationships (e.g., McKenzie et al., 2002; Mota, Ribeiro, Santos, & Gomes, 2006; Sallis et al., 2000). So, biological factors are not clear predictors of youth physical activity; perhaps environmental or behavior skills play a bigger role in enabling youth activity.

Environmental factors

Access. Most schools do not offer enough extracurricular physical activity opportunities for students; one study found that middle schools only offered an average of 30 minutes of such activities per week per student, and that only 5 percent of students who attended school each day attended an extracurricular physical activity on that day (Powers, Conway, McKenzie, Sallis, & Marshall, 2002). Yet, several studies and reviews of research show that having access to equipment and facilities and opportunities to be active enhance youth physical activity levels (Duncan, Duncan, Strycker, & Chaumeton, 2002; Jago, Baranowski, & Harris, 2006; Loucaides et al., 2004; Sallis et al., 2000; Spink et al., 2006; Stuart et al., 2006; Whitehead et al., 2006). For example, having a park nearby was positively related to adolescent boys' physical activity (Jago et al., 2006), while the parents of visually impaired children and the children themselves believed that a lack of activity opportunities was a barrier to the children's involvement (Stuart et al., 2006). Access may help explain gender and racial differences in activity levels, because female adolescents and Mexican American adolescents reported less access to sport teams and facilities than males and Caucasian Americans (Morgan et al., 2003).

Physical educators should make students aware of all available physical activity sites in the students' neighborhoods. Elementary physical education teachers should ensure plenty of equipment is available for students to use during recess. In addition, physical educators at all levels can work with other school personnel to open school facilities for students during non-class times and find ways to offer more activity opportunities outside of physical education class and interscholastic sports.

Safety. The belief that neighborhoods or physical activities are unsafe could inhibit youth engagement in physical activity, and several researchers found evidence to support this idea (Ayvazoglu et al., 2006; Chen & Zhu, 2005; Loucaides & Chedzoy, 2005; Macdonald et al., 2004; Stuart et al., 2006). For example, parents report that neighborhood safety and fear of injury affects their children's physical activity (Macdonald

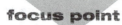

focus point

Biological factors such as body composition, fitness/health levels, and motor skill ability levels are not clear predictors of youth activity levels.

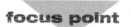

focus point

Most research shows that access to facilities and equipment enhances youth activity levels.

et al., 2004). Parents of visually impaired youth also cite environmental safety and fear of injury as barriers to their child's participation (Ayvazoglu et al., 2006; Stuart et al., 2006). Neighborhood safety is cited as a barrier to activity more often by Mexican American adolescents (Morgan et al., 2003) and African American adolescent girls (Kimm et al., 2006) than their Caucasian American counterparts, another factor that might explain ethnic activity differences. One place usually considered safe is the schools, and schools need to provide opportunities beyond physical education class and interscholastic sports for students to be active. Before school, after school, and lunch hour activity space and activities should be provided and supervised to enhance safety. Such occasions could be especially important to the activity levels of non-Caucasian adolescents.

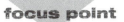

focus point

Concerns about safety, either within the neighborhood or the activity itself, can negatively affect young people's participation in physical activity.

Recess. Recess is a part of younger students' school days that impacts their activity levels. Urban students (Johns & Ha, 1999) and students with and without autistic spectrum disorder (Sandt & Frey, 2005) were found to be more active during recess than when they were at home after school. Other children showed higher activity levels during recess than during physical education class (Faison-Hodge & Porretta, 2004), which may be due to the instructional nature of physical education. For various reasons, some schools are decreasing recess time or eliminating it altogether. But 3rd and 4th grade children whose activity opportunities were restricted at school did not compensate with greater after-school physical activity (Dale, Corbin, & Dale, 2000). In fact, those students were actually more active after school on days they had physical education and outdoor recess at school than days when they did not have those opportunities. These studies indicate that both recess and physical education are vital to students' activity levels; physical educators should help parents and school administrators understand that fact and vigorously oppose any efforts to reduce or eliminate recesses for young students.

focus point

Recess makes an important contribution to children's activity levels; when recess is taken away, the students do not compensate with greater activity after school.

Transport to school. The use of **active transport,** transportation involving physical activity (e.g., walking, riding bicycle), to school has been found to influence students' physical activity levels. For example, 5th graders who walked to school obtained more moderate to vigorous physical activity (MVPA) per day than children who used other modes of transportation (Sirard, Riner, McIver, & Pate, 2005). Other researchers found that the use of active transport to get to school is greater in neighborhoods with sidewalks, in boys, and in students younger than 10th grade (Fulton, Shisler, Yore, & Caspersen, 2005). The use of active transport is probably related, at least in part, to safety; active transport is used more in neighborhoods with sidewalks because it is safer to walk or ride on sidewalks than on streets. It may also be unsafe to use active transport in some neighborhoods because of concerns about crime. When it is a safe alternative, however, physical education teachers should encourage stu-

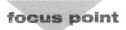

focus point

Students who use active transport to get to school tend to have higher levels of physical activity than students who do not.

dents—especially girls and high school students—to ride their bicycles or walk to school, because this can increase their activity levels. In addition, physical educators should encourage parents to require their children to use active transport, if it can be safely done, instead of driving them or allowing them to drive to school.

Behavioral factors

One behavioral factor determined to negatively influence youth physical activity levels is the time they spend doing sedentary activities (Jago, Baranowski, Thompson, Baranowski, & Greaves, 2005; Loucaides & Chedzoy, 2005; Pan & Frey, 2005; Sallis et al., 2000; Spink et al., 2005). One specific sedentary pursuit is watching television, which is often associated with decreased MVPA time (Clocksin, Watson, & Ransdell, 2002). Other researchers found that the time children spend playing outdoors (Loucaides et al., 2004; Sallis et al., 2000) and the number of activities in which children are involved (Spink et al., 2005) positively affect their activity levels. The use of self-management skills, like counterconditioning and self-liberation, also positively affects youth activity levels. In **counterconditioning,** an individual actively substitutes alternatives for the problem behavior. So, an adolescent whose problem behavior is a sedentary behavior like watching television might substitute mall-walking with friends. **Self-liberation** is the choice and commitment to change the problem behavior. For example, an adolescent might make a contract with his physical education teacher to play basketball with his friends for one hour three nights a week instead of playing video games. Studies show that the more these two skills are used by adolescents, the more consistently they exercise (Maddison & Prapavessis, 2006; Nigg & Courneya, 1998; Prapavessis et al., 2004). Similarly, middle school girls' use of self-management strategies like positive self-talk about exercise and finding ways to make exercise enjoyable positively affected their activity levels (Dishman, Motl, Sallis et al., 2005).

Encourage parents to limit their children's video game playing, Internet surfing, and television watching and prompt the children to perform outside activities instead. Self-management skills (e.g., positive self-talk, counterconditioning, self-liberation) should also be taught to middle and high school students to help them become more physically active.

The Impact of Physical Education on Physical Activity Levels

Physical education has the potential to be a vital enabling factor for students' physical activity, but is it? In this section, research on the levels of physical activity in traditional physical education, the impact of interven-

focus point

Student participation in sedentary activities contributes to lower activity levels, and self-management skills help older students become more consistent participants in physical activity.

tions to enhance activity levels in physical education, and the impact of physical education participation on activity later in life will be reviewed.

Physical activity levels in physical education class

Reviewers of research on the physical activity levels of students in physical education classes concluded that elementary students in non-intervention classes (e.g., traditional classes where no special attempt to increase physical activity has been made) engaged in MVPA about 34 percent of class time, while middle and high school students in non-intervention classes engaged in MVPA between 27 percent and 47 percent of class time (Fairclough & Stratton, 2005, 2006). These percentages fall short of the *Healthy People 2010* objective of 50 percent MVPA time in physical education class (USDHHS, 2000). The reviewers attributed the low activity time to the educational nature of physical education; the goal is for students to learn motor skills, which requires time for instruction, demonstration, and organization. Unlike the overall physical activity levels of boys and girls, these reviewers found that boys and girls tended to be equally active during physical education, except in activities preferred by boys. Elementary students tended to become more active in class as they became older (Fairclough & Stratton, 2006). The type of activity influenced the activity levels of the middle and high school students; specifically, fitness-oriented activities (e.g., aerobics, strength training) and team invasion games (e.g., soccer, basketball) were associated with higher MVPA than movement activities (e.g., dance, gymnastics) and net games (e.g., tennis, volleyball) (Fairclough & Stratton, 2005).

Because most students do not get sufficient levels of physical activity during traditional physical education class, physical educators must help students find other opportunities for physical activity, as well as find ways to enhance activity during class, especially for older students. Even though some research suggests fitness and team sports yield higher student engagement levels than other activities during class, it is not desirable to only include such activities in a physical education program; students tend to find fitness activities less enjoyable than other activities, and most team sports are generally not considered lifetime activities.

Interventions to increase physical activity levels in physical education

Because of the insufficient levels of activity experienced by students in traditional physical education, interventions—such as curricular modifications and teacher training—have been employed to increase student activity during class, and many have been successful (Cale & Harris, 2006; Fairclough & Stratton, 2005, 2006; Kahn et al., 2002; Pate et al.,

focus point

Reviews of research on activity time in traditional physical education show that students do not get sufficient levels of activity, boys and girls are equally active, and the type of activity influences engagement.

2006; Ringuet & Trost, 2001; Stone, McKenzie, Welk, & Booth, 1998; Wallhead & Buckworth, 2004). At the high school level, interventions that were most successful at enhancing student activity and fitness levels used high-intensity and training activities (Fairclough & Stratton, 2005). But such activities "did not appear to consider the wider educational focus of PE" (Fairclough & Stratton, 2005, p. 229). In fact, when given a choice in walking activities in physical education, adolescent females chose social activities over exercise and fitness activities (Prusak & Darst, 2002).

Other effective interventions that did maintain an educational focus included the following:

- Using an integration of fitness, skill development tasks, and game play
- Promoting MVPA as an additional lesson objective
- Training teachers in active supervision techniques
- Implementing a health-related curriculum and teacher encouragement
- Providing curricular materials and teacher training to revise existing instructional strategies

focus point

Although all kinds of interventions can enhance students' physical activity levels during physical education, the educational focus of physical education can be maintained by integrating enhanced physical activity with other learning objectives (e.g., motor skill development).

Reviewers of elementary program interventions also concluded that programs simply incorporating more vigorous activities were successful at helping children be more active during class, but the educational nature—and enjoyment—of such lessons is questionable (Fairclough & Stratton, 2006). Equally effective at the elementary level were programs integrating motor skill learning with increased health-related activities, learning of self-management skills, enjoyable activities, and training of teachers to provide those lessons, such as the Sports, Play, and Active Recreation for Kids (SPARK) program (Sallis et al., 1997). SPARK, used for two years with 4th and 5th graders, effectively enhanced the students' MVPA during physical education. Importantly, Sallis et al. found that the MVPA of students taught by specialist physical education teachers and classroom teachers trained to implement active lessons were much higher than students taught by regular, untrained classroom teachers.

Impact of physical education on later physical activity

Researchers found that students who take high school physical education (Everhart et al., 2005), or who participate in high-quality high school physical education classes (Hildebrand & Johnson, 2001) tend to be more active in college than students who did not participate in such programs. Similarly, 9th grade students who took a special, yearlong conceptual physical education class were more active later in high school than students who had taken traditional physical education (Dale, Corbin, & Cuddihy, 1998). In addition, fewer students who took the special class reported being sedentary one or two years following graduation than students in a national survey (Dale & Corbin, 2000). The curriculum, called "Project Active Teens," consisted of:

- One classroom day per week teaching concepts and skills related to activity and fitness
- One gym day per week teaching students to assess their own fitness levels, design a fitness program, and perform lifelong physical activities
- Three days per week performing sport-based activities (as in traditional physical education) (Dale et al., 1998)

Other researchers discovered the positive relationship between childhood activity and activity 25 years later was stronger for individuals taught by a physical education specialist five hours per week than those taught by a classroom teacher 40 minutes per week (Trudeau et al., 2004), especially in females (Trudeau, Laurencelle, Tremblay, Rajic, & Shephard, 1999).

The preceding findings underscore the importance of daily physical education taught by specialists, including at the elementary level, and for programs (especially at the secondary level) that incorporate more individual and lifetime activities than traditional team sports.

Other Interventions to Enhance Students' Overall Physical Activity Levels

Interventions to increase student knowledge of, value for, and actual activity levels outside of physical education have been attempted. Some programs were comprehensive and used multiple school and/or community components, while others were small scale and compared isolated strategies for increasing engagement.

Comprehensive interventions

Recently, reviewers of research on physical activity interventions for youth (e.g., Cale & Harris, 2006; Pate et al., 2006; Ringuet & Trost, 2001; Stone et al., 1998; Wallhead & Buckworth, 2004) came to similar conclusions:

- Interventions focused on enhancing physical activity levels during physical education class were more effective than those focused on increasing overall physical activity levels.
- Interventions to enhance student knowledge and attitudes related to physical activity were mostly effective.
- Interventions employing multiple components were more effective at enhancing overall physical activity than single component ones.
- Classroom-based health education interventions enhanced physical activity levels in some interventions but not all.

focus point

Participation in physical education can positively affect individuals' activity levels later in life, especially if participation is frequent, classes are taught by specialists, and content (at the secondary level) focuses on physical activity concepts and lifetime activities.

Two programs, one short term and one longer term, serve as examples of effective comprehensive activity interventions. A New Zealand elementary school implemented an integrated curriculum approach with 5th and 6th graders (Oliver, Schofield, & McEvoy, 2006). A common theme, a virtual walk around New Zealand, was integrated during a four-week unit into English, social studies, mathematics, statistics, and physical education. Using pedometers, the teachers recorded the students' number of steps each morning. The activity levels of students with initially low activity levels, especially females, were effectively increased.

Another intervention increased the activity levels of 9th grade girls by changing the instructional program and school environment (Dishman, Motl, Saunders, et al., 2005). The Lifestyle Education for Activity Program utilized six of the eight components of the Coordinated School Health Program model: physical education, school environment, health education, school health services, faculty/staff health promotion, and family/community involvement. Physical education instruction changed in the following ways: more choices, gender sensitive, sometimes gender segregated, emphasis on small group interactions, and a de-emphasis on competition and the use of elimination games. Self-management skills were taught during health and physical education classes. The school environment changed by providing girls more opportunities to be active outside of physical education, encouraging faculty and staff physical activity (and thus modeling), placing posters around the school promoting physical activity, and involving the school nurse. The program increased the girls' MVPA, enjoyment of physical education and physical activity, and self-efficacy (Dishman, Motl, Saunders, et al., 2005; Felton et al., 2005).

Small-scale interventions to enhance students' physical activity

Less comprehensive interventions usually were effective in enhancing children's or adolescents' physical activity levels, or their attitudes toward activity and intentions to be active:

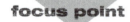

focus point

Interventions to enhance youth overall activity levels are most effective when they incorporate multiple components, such as found in the coordinated school health program model, but several small-scale strategies can also be effective.

- Setting daily activity goals based on either the number of pedometer steps or number of minutes (Schofield, Mummery, & Schofield, 2005)
- Using television watching time as a reward for meeting activity goals (Roemmich, Gurgol, & Epstein, 2004)
- Providing parents with information on the benefits of physical activity for children, and ideas about how to get children active (Saakslahti et al., 2004)
- Regularly reminding adolescent students of age-appropriate reasons to be physically active (i.e., have fun, stay fit, improve skills) (Chatzisarantis & Hagger, 2005)

According to the reviews, interventions to enhance students' overall activity levels will be most effective when they employ multiple components, such as physical education, health education, school health services, faculty and staff, school-based activity opportunities outside of physical education, and parental and community involvement. The coordinated school health program is an excellent model to follow in implementing a comprehensive intervention. But recent smaller-scale interventions were effective at enhancing youth activity levels. The following strategies can enhance students' overall activity levels: set daily goals based on number of pedometer steps or activity time; enlist parents to reward their children for physical activity with television watching time; increase parental knowledge about the benefits of and how to help children be active; and emphasize reasons important to students for being active.

Enhancing Student Physical Activity Levels

As a physical educator, you can play a significant role in enhancing students' current physical activity levels, as well as helping them develop the lifetime habit of physical activity.

Increase Physical Activity Levels During Physical Education Class

Physical education was named by Welk (1999) as a key means of influencing youth physical activity levels. One obvious way physical education teachers will want to enhance students' engagement is to increase their activity during physical education class.

Assess current physical activity levels

First determine how much time your students currently spend in MVPA. The System for Observing Fitness Instruction Time (SOFIT; McKenzie, Sallis, & Nader, 1991) is one means of doing that. Although SOFIT was designed to assess three different aspects of physical education lessons, only the dimension that measures student activity levels will be described here. Student activity levels are coded according to 5 levels:

1: the student is lying down
2: the student is sitting down

connected   CONCEPTS

Several means of enhancing students' activity levels were described in previous chapters: reinforce/ reward and give appropriate feedback to students for being physically active (Chapter 2); create a task-involving climate in physical education (including offer students choices) (Chapter 5); enhance students' self-perceptions regarding physical activity (Chapter 6); catch and hold student situational interest, take advantage of their personal activity interests, and increase value for physical activity (Chapter 8); help students develop intrinsic motivation for physical activity (Chapter 9); and avoid using physical activity as punishment (Chapter 2).

3: the student is standing

4: the student is walking

5: the student is more active than walking

Four students in the class are randomly chosen as the target students to observe. Target Student A is observed for 4 minutes, then Target Student B is observed for 4 minutes, followed by Target Student C, and then Target Student D. This rotation continues until the end of the lesson. The observer records the activity level the target student is doing at the end of every 20 seconds.

Exhibit 10.2 shows a completed worksheet for a 30-minute 5th grade class observed by a fellow teacher and Appendix A.11 provides a blank form. At the end of the first 20 seconds, Target Student A was walking into class, so a "4" was recorded under the PA Level column. Every 20 seconds Target Student A's activity level was recorded; when 12 observations (4 minutes) were done, Target Student B was watched. This process continued until the end of the lesson. The summary shows that only 37 percent of class time was spent in MVPA (the number of 4s plus the number of 5s), below the desired 50 percent.

Decrease management and instruction time

If activity levels are below the *Healthy People 2010* (USDHHS, 2000) goal of 50 percent class time in MVPA, find ways to increase student engagement in physical activity. One way is to decrease management time during class. How long do students spend in the locker room? Getting and putting equipment away? Forming groups? Also look at your instruction time: how long does it take to explain and demonstrate tasks and activities? Although a certain amount of instruction time is warranted to maintain the educational focus of physical education, instruction time need not be excessive. Ask colleagues for suggestions on more efficient means of performing management tasks and task presentations. Consider using pictures, task cards, or videos for task presentations. Spending less time on management and instruction results in more activity time.

Change task structure and/or activities

Teachers should also examine the task structure and activities used in lessons. Tasks in which students wait for a chance to participate do not maximize activity levels; therefore, change the structure of such tasks so as to use the minimum number of students, and keep other students active. For example, a common volleyball task is to put seven or eight students in a circle with one ball and practice the pass or set; but that does not maximize activity time. For a better task structure, have students pair up and

| Recording sheet for SOFIT student physical activity levels. | EXHIBIT | 10.2 |

Date: 9-12-xx

Grade Level: 5th

Class: Gonzalez

PA Levels: 1 = Lying down   2 = Sitting   3 = Standing   4 = Walking   5 = Very active

TARGET STUDENT	OBSERVATION #	PA LEVEL	OBSERVATION #	PA LEVEL	OBSERVATION #	PA LEVEL
A	1	4	49	3	97	
	2	3	50	3	98	
	3	4	51	3	99	
	4	4	52	4	100	
	5	5	53	3	101	
	6	5	54	3	102	
	7	3	55	4	103	
	8	3	56	5	104	
	9	4	57	5	105	
	10	5	58	4	106	
	11	5	59	4	107	
	12	4	60	5	108	
B	13	3	61	3	109	
	14	4	62	3	110	
	15	2	63	3	111	
	16	2	64	4	112	
	17	2	65	4	113	
	18	2	66	5	114	
	19	2	67	4	115	
	20	2	68	3	116	
	21	2	69	5	117	
	22	2	70	5	118	
	23	2	71	3	119	
	24	2	72	3	120	
C	25	2	73	3	121	
	26	2	74	3	122	

(continued)

| EXHIBIT | 10.2 | Recording sheet for SOFIT student physical activity levels, *continued*. |

TARGET STUDENT	OBSERVATION #	PA LEVEL	OBSERVATION #	PA LEVEL	OBSERVATION #	PA LEVEL
	27	2	75	3	123	
	28	4	76	3	124	
	29	3	77	3	125	
	30	5	78	3	126	
	31	5	79	3	127	
	32	3	80	4	128	
	33	3	81	2	129	
	34	3	82	1	130	
	35	5	83	2	131	
	36	3	84	2	132	
D	37	4	85	2	133	
	38	4	86	2	134	
	39	3	87	2	135	
	40	3	88	2	136	
	41	3	89	2	137	
	42	3	90	2	138	
	43	3	91		139	
	44	3	92		140	
	45	4	93		141	
	46	4	94		142	
	47	4	95		143	
	48	3	96		144	

Total # of observations: 90

# of 1s =   1

# of 2s =   22

# of 3s =   34

# of 4s =   20

# of 5s =   13

4s + 5s =   33

Divide the total of 4s + 5s, 33 in this case, by the total # of observations (90) = 37 % class time in MVPA.

practice the same skills; use foam balls if there aren't enough volleyballs. Similarly, when 30 4th grade students are all participating in the same kickball game, there is lots of standing around. Organize several games at once, using a smaller space for each game; smaller numbers of students on each team means more activity for the students.

Combine motor skill instruction with physical activity

Another way physical educators enhance student activity levels combines instruction in motor skills with physical activity. As described earlier, certain curricula, like the SPARK curriculum, are designed to provide high levels of physical activity as well as promote motor skill development (McKenzie & Rosengard, 2000; Rosengard & McKenzie, 2000; Rosengard, McKenzie, & Short, 2000). But teachers could also develop their own means of combining activity with motor tasks.

For example, several years ago the physical education teachers at Woodland Heights Elementary in South Carolina developed lessons that began with a 15- to 18-minute teacher-led fitness activity, followed by a 15- to 18-minute motor skill lesson (Steller & Young, 1994). The two class segments shared the same motor skills and maximized movement. For example, the first segment of a 5th grade lesson consisted of an aerobic routine during which students dribbled a ball with their hands. During the second segment, the students practiced a dribbling task in which they dribbled the length of the gym while being guarded by a partner; students were encouraged to keep moving in those tasks.

As mentioned in the opening scenario, Mr. Olson does a good job of maximizing activity time for his students. He uses pictures, task cards, and demonstrations for task presentations (to minimize his instruction time), as well as the most efficient ways of performing management tasks like getting and putting equipment away. In addition, Mr. Olson uses only individual, partner, or small-group activities—no large-group games—in order to maximize activity time.

Emphasize Physical Activity over Physical Fitness

Physical fitness testing has been an important part of many physical education programs. In fact, physical educators often use fitness test results to justify the value of their program. But teachers should emphasize physical activity in their programs over physical fitness (Corbin, 2002; Freedson & Row- land, 1992) for several reasons:

1. Fitness testing in children and adolescents is unreliable. It is hard to motivate students to perform their best and get a true measure of their fitness.

real world

focus point

Students' activity levels during physical education can be enhanced by decreasing management and instruction time, using the minimum number of students for tasks, and combining motor skill instruction with physical activity.

2. Students' fitness levels are influenced by many factors, including heredity, age, and maturation (Corbin, 2002). Claiming that a physical education program helped students improve their fitness over a school year is difficult because of those factors; conversely, a program should not be blamed if students' fitness levels don't improve or decline.

3. Many students do not partake in physical education often enough or long enough to influence greatly their physical fitness.

4. Youth fitness levels are not a good indicator of their activity levels (Corbin, 2002); just because a student is fit doesn't mean she is active and has the habit of physical activity.

5. Students often find traditional fitness activities (e.g., jogging, stretching, push-ups) boring (Rikard & Banville, 2006), which doesn't develop a desire to remain active for a lifetime.

The above reasons do not suggest avoiding fitness testing altogether. When fitness testing is conducted, health-related tests—those that assess elements such as cardiovascular fitness, muscular strength and endurance, and flexibility—should be used instead of tests of motor skill fitness (e.g., speed, agility) (CDC, 1997). Moreover, with proper instruction, students can assess their own fitness levels and develop an activity program based on their current fitness levels (Nahas, Goldfine, & Collins, 2003).

real world

A high school physical education teacher in the midwest United States, Carole D., had her students assess themselves on health-related fitness items and develop goals and activity programs to reach those goals; she emphasized appropriate activity to enhance health-related fitness, not the results of the tests. Self-assessment and program planning are self-management skills that enable students to be active in the future. These self- or peer-assessments can occur periodically throughout the school year, so students can see results, adjust their activity programs, and use the results for goal setting. Thus, fitness testing becomes an educational tool related to physical activity that is integrated into the curriculum (CDC, 1997). Avoid fitness testing that is conducted only once or twice a year with the sole purpose of giving awards.

Even though Mr. Olson does emphasize being physically active to his elementary students, his use of fitness tests needs improvement. He formally tests his 5th grade students at the beginning and end of the school year and gives awards to those who meet the health-related fitness criteria. There is nothing wrong with this practice, but his students undoubtedly would benefit if he were to

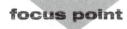
focus point

Physical education teachers should emphasize physical activity over physical fitness.

- Use something like the Activitygram® (The Cooper Institute, 2006) so that students like Julia are rewarded for being active, regardless of fitness levels

- Teach his 5th graders, and maybe even the 3rd and 4th graders, how to assess each other on health-related fitness elements, like the push-up or curl-up tests

- Set up stations that include health-related fitness tests so that students could test each other on those elements to see if they are improving

- Emphasize to the students that the test results are meant to help them identify elements on which they might be weak

- Help the students find activities to help them improve those areas where they need attention

Teach Students Self-Management Skills

Physical education teachers can also help students become more physically active by teaching them self-management skills (e.g., Cale & Harris, 2006; CDC, 1997; McKenzie, 2001; Nahas et al., 2003). Such skills help students address many of the costs or barriers to being active, such as a lack of time or a desire to be with friends.

Because lack of time is often cited as a barrier to being physically active by adolescent girls, one self-management skill to teach middle school and high school students is time management. Students can first be made aware of how they use their time

connected CONCEPTS

Self-management skills described in previous chapters that physical education teachers could teach to students include imagery, arousal regulation (Chapter 6), and goal setting (Chapter 5).

by completing a 24-hour time use assignment (see Exhibit 10.3 for a completed example and Appendix A.12 for a blank form). Once students have completed the form, help them schedule time for physical activity. For example, students can combine time spent socializing with friends with activity, so friends are active with each other. Or they can combine time spent listening to music with activity. Sometimes, students need to replace time spent in one activity with physical activity; for example, a student who spends three hours each night watching television can replace one of those hours with skateboarding with his friends.

As mentioned earlier, two self-management skills shown to be related to more consistent exercise behavior in adolescents are counterconditioning and self-liberation. When teaching counterconditioning, help students identify problem behaviors, such as watching television, surfing the Internet, or driving to school. Then help the students identify alternatives to those problem behaviors, such as walking or riding bicycle to school, walking around the mall, or joining a bowling league with friends. In self-liberation, after they identify a problem behavior, encourage each student to make a behavioral contract with someone who will hold him or her accountable (such as an active friend, parent, or physical education teacher). For example, the written contract might state: "I pledge to walk

EXHIBIT 10.3 Awareness of time use sheet.

Name: Sherry Armstrong   Grade: 10

Date Completed: Monday, Feb. 10

Time	Activity
7:00 am	Get up, shower & dress, breakfast, catch bus to school
8:00 am	Homeroom; Band
9:00 am	Algebra
10:00 am	American Literature
11:00 am	Government
Noon	Lunch
1:00 pm	Study Hall
2:00 pm	Physiology
3:00 pm	Work on set for the play
4:00 pm	To Jenny's house
5:00 pm	To home; Watch TV & help with dinner
6:00 pm	Dinner & dishes
7:00 pm	Homework
8:00 pm	Watch TV, talk on the phone
9:00 pm	" "
10:00 pm	" "
11:00 pm	To bed/sleep
Midnight	"
1:00 am	"
2:00 am	"
3:00 am	"
4:00 am	"
5:00 am	"
6:00 am	"

around my neighborhood for 30 minutes after school for at least three days each week. This will replace 30 minutes of Internet activity after school. If I do this for 8 weeks in a row, I will reward myself by purchasing a CD of my choice." The student and the accountable person both sign the contract, and the accountable person checks in with the student to make sure she is following the contract.

Other self-management skills that you as a physical education teacher can teach your students include

- *Self-monitoring.* Students should learn how to self-monitor or keep track of their physical activity participation, especially if they are doing more traditional exercise like walking, jogging, or weight lifting. Simply recording on a calendar or in a notebook how long a student walked is self-monitoring. You may also give students sheets for recording weight training exercises; the sheet could include a place for recording the date, exercise name, weight used, and number of sets and repetitions done (see Exhibit 10.4).

- *Self-reinforcement.* Self-monitoring is a simple means of reinforcing one's physical activity; seeing the time or exercise sessions accumulate can be quite rewarding. Students can also be taught to reinforce themselves using simple rewards (e.g., computer time or movies) for achieving goals they set.

- *Using a decision-balance sheet.* A decision-balance sheet requires students to recognize and record all of the benefits of physical activity as well as all of the costs or barriers to activity. See Exhibit 10.5 for a partially completed form and Appendix A.13 for a blank form. If the costs or barriers outweigh the benefits, you or even other students can help students identify more benefits, as well as identify means of overcoming the costs or barriers.

- *Varying activity routines.* Students who perform regular exercise routines need to understand the importance of varying their routines; you may give students options for various activities. For example, students who walk or jog around their neighborhood should be encouraged to try different routes; a student who regularly walks or jogs should occasionally play basketball or do an aerobics videotape.

Self-assessing fitness levels and activity program planning are two additional self-management skills described in the previous section.

Self-management skills were an integral part of the Lifestyle Education for Activity Program designed to increase activity levels of adolescent girls (Felton et al., 2005). Positive self-talk, goal setting, planning for physical activity, developing options for physical activities, and making physical activity enjoyable were part of instruction in both health and physical education (Dishman, Motl, Sallis, et al., 2005). The use of such skills helped increase

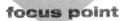
focus point

Self-management skills like time management, counterconditioning, self-liberation, self-monitoring and self-assessing, and program planning may help students stay active for a lifetime.

EXHIBIT 10.4 Weight training recording sheet.

Name: _____

| Exercise | | | | | | | | | | | | | | |
Date	Sets	Reps	Weight	Sets	Reps	Weight	Sets	Reps	Weight	Sets	Reps	Weight	Sets	Reps	Weight

EXHIBIT	10.5

Example partially completed decision-balance sheet.

Name: Alonzo   Date: 9-12-XX

Grade: Junior

Directions: In the first column, write down all of the reasons to be physically active that are important to you. In the second column, write down anything that prevents you from being physically active, or reasons why you don't like or want to be physically active. When you are done with the first two columns, get together with a one or two other students and brainstorm some ways to overcome some of the costs or barriers to physical activity that you put in the second column, and to identify other benefits to physical activity.

BENEFITS OF PHYSICAL ACTIVITY	COSTS OF/BARRIERS TO PHYSICAL ACTIVITY	WAYS TO OVERCOME COSTS/BARRIERS
Gets me in shape for baseball	Don't have time	Play BB with friends instead of hanging out at mall
Look good for the girls	Don't have money for a club membership	Ask coach if I can workout in weight room during lunch
Hang out with friends	Don't know best weights to lift to get me ready for baseball	Find out from coach some weight lifting exercises
Some of it's fun		

the girls' activity levels. Self-management skills are also integral to the SPARK curriculum described previously. Even though Mr. Olson's students are young, his upper elementary students—like Julia and Sneha—could still learn simple self-management skills. He could set up a "buddy system," in which the students pair themselves with another student and each partner is responsible for helping the other find ways to be active, encouraging their partner to be active, praising their partner for being active, and being active together. As mentioned earlier, Mr. Olson could also teach his upper elementary students to self-assess their health-related fitness levels.

Inform Students About Physical Activity Opportunities Available Outside of School

Some students may not participate in adequate levels of physical activity because they are unaware of available opportunities outside of school. In fact, lack of information about how and where to participate inhibited the physical activity levels of children with hearing impairments (Tsai & Fung, 2005). Find out about these prospective sites and programs and convey that information to students (CDC, 1997; McKenzie, 2001). Include information about sites and facilities students may use on an informal basis, the days and times of availability, and specific, formal activity programs such as after-school programs, sports leagues, and dance classes. Find activities that do not require money (e.g., outdoor basketball courts in parks, free summer bowling for youth) and those that require only a nominal fee. Include rules associated with opportunities, such as the rule that a person must live in a neighborhood in order to use the neighborhood swimming pool. By being informed, students are better able to participate in activity outside of school.

Physical educators can convey this information to students in several ways. Describe opportunities to students at the beginning or end of class. Create a flyer or brochure of community physical activity opportunities (if the community is small enough, all information regarding available activities could be put on one flyer; otherwise the teacher may need several different flyers). Exhibit 10.6 is an example of a flyer that contains parks and recreation department summer activities; other flyers could convey information for other times of the year, for school interscholastic and intramural activities, or for private activity lessons/leagues. Similar information could make up bulletin boards, or the school or physical education website, or be mailed/e-mailed to parents. The Centers for Disease Control (1997) even suggests that the school or physical education program sponsor an information fair in which community sports and recreation programs present their various opportunities to students. Such a fair could occur one day during physical education classes; tables with representatives from various programs could be set up in the gym all day long and all students in the physical education classes visit the tables. Or tables might be set up in the school hallways, so all students could find out about community activity programs.

Mr. Olson could easily develop brochures describing physical activity opportunities in his community, because he has lived there many years and is familiar with the area. The brochures could be given to students periodically, as well as made available in the school office and at parent–teacher conferences. Because Julia's family doesn't have the money to spend on lessons or activity fees, information about free physical activities might help her become more active.

Promote Peer Involvement

The support and encouragement of peers seem to be vital reinforcing factors for students' physical activity. Stress to students that activity should be fun, and being with friends can help make it fun. Present activities to students they can do together: team sports, dual sports, walking around a park or

---

focus point

Physical education teachers can verbally inform their students about physical activity opportunities outside of class, or use brochures, flyers, posters, or an information fair to do so.

focus point

Increasing peer involvement in physical education would enhance the peer reinforcing factor for physical activity.

A sample flyer of community summer physical activity opportunities.   **EXHIBIT**   **10.6**

Summer Physical Activity Opportunities for Kids
Through Lafayette Parks & Rec

Available Parks & Facilities *(open sunrise to sunset)*

Armstrong Park *(9th St. & Beck Lane)*
- 2/3 mile paved trail
- Multi-age playground
- 5 lighted tennis courts
- 3 baseball fields
- Open green space

CAT Park *(east of Sagamore Parkway, west of Creasy Lane)*
- 8 soccer fields

McCaw Park *(Union & Creasy Lane)*
- Tot & multi-age playground
- 3 baseball fields
- Open green space

Munger Park *(Between Greenbush & Union Streets)*
- 1 mile paved trail
- Multi-age playground
- Open space

Murdock Park *(18th & Ferry Streets)*
- .9 mile interpretive trail
- Tot & multi-age playground
- Disc golf course
- Softball field

Shamrock Park *(Wabash Avenue)*
- Tot & multi-age playground
- Outdoor roller-hockey rink
- Basketball court
- Horseshoes
- Open green space

Swimming Facilities

Tropicanoe Cove *(Columbia Park)*
- Open Memorial Day through Labor Day
- Hours: Daily 11–7 PM; Wednesdays (Family night) 11–8 PM
- Rates: Season Pass $100; each additional family member $25
  - Under 48"—Weekday $4 ($2.50 after 4:30 PM); Weekend/holidays $5.50 ($4 after 4:30 PM); Family night $1.50
  - Over 48"—Weekday $5 ($3.50 after 4:30 PM); Weekend/holidays $6.50 ($5 after 4:30 PM); Family night $2.50

Castaway Bay *(Armstrong Park)*
- Hours: Noon–7 PM; Family night—Tuesday, noon–8 PM
- Rates: Season Pass $75; each additional family member $20
  - Youth (3–17 years)—$3.50
  - Adults (18+)—$4
  - Family night—$2 (Tuesday 4–8 PM)
  - Save $1 on all admissions after 4 PM

Vinton Pool *(3111 Prairie Lane)*
- Hours: Noon–7 PM; Family night—Thursday, noon–8 PM
- Rates: Season Pass $55; each additional family member $20
  - Youth/Adult—$3
  - Family night—$1.25 (Thursday 4–8 PM)

(continued)

EXHIBIT   10.6   A sample flyer, *continued.*

Workreation

This Lafayette Parks & Rec volunteer program is for children 8–17 years of age. Children can earn "Rec Bucks" for performing light cleaning and maintenance work in the parks. The "Rec Bucks" can then be used to purchase admission to pools, the zoo, or for registration fees for other Parks & Rec programs. Children earn $5 "Rec Bucks" for each hour of work. Call 807-1500 for more information and to register.

Hours of Workreation: Columbia Park—MWF 9:30–10:30 AM

Vinton Pool—T 10:30–11:30 AM

Castaway Bay—Th 10:30–11:30 AM

McAllister Recreation Center *(2351 N. 20th Street; 807-1360)*

Outdoor Facilities

- Outside basketball court
- Children's playground area
- Ball field
- Soccer field
- Open green space

Indoor Facilities

- Weights and fitness equipment
- Gymnasium
- Game room

Center Pass

- $5 per year
- Allows access to game room and gymnasium; needed to register for other programs at the center

Youth Programs *(call 807-1360 for more information)*

Super Summer Community Bowl

- Free bowling for youth Fridays noon–3 PM in summer
- At Market Square Lanes, Star Lanes, Mike Aulby's Arrowhead Bowl
- Free shoes and games

Cross Country & Track & Field

- 3–14 years of age
- June—1 hour per day—5 days per week
- $30 for first child in family, $15 for each additional child

Summer Tennis Classes

- Start in June
- Fee involved

Sports for Shorties

- 4–6 years of age
- Registration fee
- Instructional lessons for young children; in summer, the activities are golf and tee-ball

Summer Camp

- 6–12 years of age
- 12 weeks in summer
- Registration fee
- Campers visit park aquatic facilities, and go to movies, bowling, and on nature field trips, to name a few things

mall, skateboarding, and jogging a 5K together. Teach students the importance of encouraging, not demeaning, their friends' activity efforts. In addition, students could help friends set physical activity goals, and then hold their friends accountable for reaching those goals, giving an extrinsic reward when a goal is met (Nahas et al., 2003). The "buddy system" already described is one way Mr. Olson could increase peer involvement and reinforcement of physical activity.

connected CONCEPTS

Several instructional models described in previous chapters can also promote peer involvement: peer teaching (Chapter 3), cooperative learning, sport education, and adventure-based learning (Chapter 4).

Ensure All Students Are Included

As physical education teachers, we must ensure all students are physically active during class, and that includes students with disabilities. If you are not sure how to get them involved, many resources are available to you. For example, the PE Central website (www.pecentral.org/adapted /adaptedmenu.html) includes links to:

- means of adapting activities for students with disabilities,
- assessment instruments,
- information on working with paraprofessionals, and
- adapted physical education books.

You'll find a separate link for adapted physical education (www.pelinks4u .org/sections/adapted/adapted.htm) on the PELinks4U website. You may also contact local colleges and universities to see if they have an adapted physical education specialist willing to give advice on including all students. Convey to students the various opportunities outside of physical education for students with disabilities to be physically active. For example, the brochures, flyers, posters, or website created to convey community physical activity opportunities for students might include a section on activities for students with disabilities. In addition, discuss with students the many role models of physically active persons who have disabilities. For example, Brenda Levy was born with spina bifida, which left her paralyzed from the waist down. However, she is a world-class athlete who medaled in swimming in the 1996 Paralympic Games (among others) and won the wheelchair division of the Marine Corps Marathon in 1991.

An elementary physical education teacher in the Midwest who does an excellent job of including students with disabilities is Dave W. In a 1st grade class, a wheelchair-bound girl took her place around a parachute. She moved clockwise and counterclockwise with the students as they worked on locomotor skills while holding on to the parachute. Dave later lifted her out of her chair and put her in a seated position around the

real world

parachute along with the other children as they performed arm strengthening exercises with the parachute. Similarly, Mr. Olson always finds a way to make sure his students with disabilities are included in class activities.

Identify Religious and Cultural Principles Related to Physical Activity

Communities and schools in the United States and other countries are often quite diverse; students of all cultures and ethnic groups are educated in schools. If you are not aware of religious and cultural principles concerning physical activity, you may inadvertently require your students to perform activities or follow class rules that are contrary to their cultural customs or religious beliefs. This could make physical education—and physical activity participation—a negative experience for those students. To create a "more inviting physical activity culture" (Kahan, 2003, p. 52), physical educators should learn about principles related to physical activity for cultural and religious groups represented by students. This information can be obtained on the internet, or by asking students and/or their parents about any cultural or religious restrictions or guidelines. You may then make appropriate accommodations for students. For example, David Kahan (2003) described several ways physical educators could help Muslim students feel more comfortable in physical education: allow female students to wear the *hijab*, refrain from fitness testing during the month of Ramadan when Muslim students fast, and allow female adolescents to wear long-sleeved shirts and loose sweats under the physical education uniform. Moreover, it may be necessary for you to educate all students about the cultural and religious principles being accommodated, and discourage students from making fun of others.

focus point

Physical education teachers should find ways to include all students—such as those with disabilities and of various religious and cultural backgrounds—in physical activities.

real world

As a high school physical education teacher in the midwestern United States, Carole D. worked hard to include all students in physical activity, including girls who were members of a particular religious faith. According to the principles of their faith, the girls were required to wear long skirts and could not wear tennis shoes. Carole accommodated these requirements by letting the girls wear shorts under their skirts and soft-soled, flat leather shoes. Similarly, another teacher in the Midwest, Katie M., accommodated Amish girls in physical education by allowing them to wear their skirts during class and to face away from other students when doing curl-ups (because they were not allowed to wear shorts under their skirts).

Mr. Olson could easily find out about students' cultural and religious restrictions related to physical activity by asking students and their parents at the beginning of the school year, then making appropriate accommodations.

Model a Physically Active Lifestyle

As one important reinforcing factor for students' physical activity, you as a physical education teacher should strive to be an effective role model of a physically active lifestyle. Students need to hear about your current activities: walking in the local 5K, riding a bike in the park, or playing disc golf with friends. Such talks may take place before or after school, during lunch breaks or breaks between classes, or at the start or end of class. You might even participate in a warm-up with students at the start of class; just be sure that you are still able to supervise and ensure a safe environment. Physical educators who are not physically active should become so. The message of lifelong activity will likely be ineffective if heard from someone not modeling such behavior.

Many physical education teachers are effective role models of physical activity, such as Kevin J., a secondary physical education and health teacher at a private school in the midwestern United States. Kevin plays in a local basketball league and enjoys lifting weights among many other means of being physically active.

Likewise, Mr. Olson enjoys playing in a year-round tennis league; his students know about his participation and often ask him about his matches.

Include Lifetime Physical Activities

Team sports are a much bigger part of secondary physical education curricula than lifetime activities (Fairclough, Stratton, & Baldwin, 2002; Pate et al., 1995). Competitive sports, primarily team sports, also dominate school extramural activities (Cale, 2000). But recently scholars called for the renewal of physical education curricula by placing a stronger emphasis on lifetime activities (Clocksin et al., 2002; Green, 2002, 2004; Pate et al., 1995) or health-related fitness activities and concepts (Daley, 2002). Adults are more likely to participate in recreational lifestyle activities such as swimming, aerobics, weight training, walking, outdoor pursuits, golf, and cycling than competitive team sports; therefore, secondary physical education and extracurricular programs that desire to facilitate lifelong participation should offer such activities. This will help students develop a desire to remain physically active for a lifetime.

Team sports and traditional sports-based physical education curricula do little to promote lifelong participation (Daley, 2002; Green, 2004). High school students themselves want a wider variety of sport and fitness activities than those offered in most physical education programs (Rikard & Banville, 2006). Females of all ages tend to prefer lifetime activities over team sports (Telford, Salmon, Timperio, & Crawford, 2005). Moreover,

real world

focus point

When physical educators role-model a physically active lifestyle, students see their teachers "walk the talk," which could influence their desire for lifetime physical activity.

parents of adolescents with mental retardation (Kozub, 2003) and children with visual impairments (Ayvazoglu et al., 2006) claim the most important skills schools could teach students in physical education are lifetime activities. A program that goes beyond team sports is in Naperville, Illinois. Several years ago, the program was changed from a sports-based curriculum to a curriculum focused on lifetime activities, health, and wellness. While team sports are still offered as options, high school students can take other activities, such as fitness, dance, aquatics, high ropes, and kayaking. Because Mr. Olson teaches elementary students, his focus of helping students become skilled in a wide variety of basic motor skills is appropriate and should help his students develop a physically active lifestyle. Mr. Olson includes many individual and partner activities in class, but he could explain to older students how the skills being learned contribute to lifetime activity.

Collaborate with Other School Staff

One consistent suggestion made by scholars as a means of enhancing physical activity in youth is for physical educators to collaborate with other school faculty, administrators, and staff (e.g., Cale & Harris, 2005, 2006; CDC, 1997; McKenzie, 2001; Pate et al., 1995). Although physical education teachers can do a lot to promote students' physical activity, the impact will be greater if the message of regular, lifetime activity is heard from many different sources. Moreover, opportunities to be active must be provided to students outside of physical education, because in most schools those classes do not meet often enough for students to obtain the suggested levels of activity. All teachers, especially health teachers, should regularly promote the need for daily physical activity. Physical education and health teachers can coordinate lessons regarding health-related activity and fitness. For example, a health teacher will want to teach about cardiovascular fitness, which is then repeated and expanded on during physical education by doing activities that promote cardiovascular fitness. Elementary physical education teachers can help classroom teachers develop lessons that include physical activity. For example, students given a math problem could indicate their answer by doing the correct number of push-ups (or jumping jacks or scissor-steps). The school nurse or other health specialists can distribute information regarding physical activity to parents. In order to offer more extracurricular activities, school staff other than the physical educator can be encouraged to supervise such activities.

One way you can enlist the assistance of other school faculty and staff and parents is to offer them physical activity and fitness advice. Simple fitness tests for faculty and parents (e.g., flexibility tests, abdominal or upper body endurance assessments) can be given after school, along with advice for enhancing weak areas. Cale and Harris (2005) also suggest that physical educators offer activity opportunities for school staff and parents (e.g., a walking club). These activities help educate the staff and parents about the need for physical activity, and may establish their regular participation, which results in other active role models for students.

Besides enhancing students' activity levels during physical education, the physical education teachers at Woodland Heights Elementary School in South Carolina also worked with other school staff, parents, and students to enhance students' engagement (Steller & Young, 1994). One method used was the activity Physical Exercise Revives Kids (PERK). At the start of each day, all students in the school engaged in five minutes of classroom PERK. During PERK, music was played simultaneously over the public address system in all classrooms, and pairs of 5th grade students led each class in choreographed exercises to the music. A parent-volunteer developed the routines and trained the 5th graders to lead the routines, and the 5th grade teachers and physical educators supervised the student leaders. Parents and classroom teachers supervised two other activities for 3rd, 4th, and 5th graders: before-school activities (e.g., tetherball, small-group basketball, and jump rope) and an after-school PE Club (in which students interested in running, jumping rope, or sports met one hour per week).

real world

Mr. Olson can strengthen the message of regular physical activity by obtaining the help of his fellow teachers, staff, and administrators. Other teachers know that he infuses concepts from their courses (e.g., math, language, and social studies) into physical education, so that should help gain their help. At a faculty meeting, he can explain the need for regular activity for children and adults and suggest ways teachers can support and encourage student activity. Mr. Olson can also recommend ways teachers can incorporate activity into their lessons, show them websites where they can get ideas for such lessons (e.g., www.pecentral.org), and offer his help in creating ideas. In addition, Mr. Olson can send a survey to the faculty and staff to determine who has expertise in various activities, and recruit those individuals to teach lessons or run clubs for extracurricular activities. In order to have an extracurricular physical activity program after school for students, some buses would need to run later than immediately after school, so Mr. Olson would need to gain cooperation from school administrators as well as bus drivers.

Increase Physical Activity Opportunities at School

Access to safe spaces and facilities in which to be physically active is a vital enabling factor affecting youth activity. Schools are a logical place to provide more activity opportunities for students for several reasons: (1)

students are already there, (2) most schools are relatively safe places, and (3) facilities are often underutilized. Some suggestions for establishing such activities include the following:

- *Offer activities for free or at minimal cost to students.* All students, regardless of income, should be able to participate.

- *Provide a wide variety of activities.* Organized activities might include clubs, lessons, and intramural sports. Both competitive and noncompetitive activities, and perhaps different divisions for different skill levels, should be offered. As described above, more than just team sports should be offered. Students can be surveyed to find out the activities in which they want to participate, so that activities offered meet their needs and interests. School physical activity space should be opened up whenever it isn't being used (e.g., before and after school, lunch hour) so kids can play pick-up games, etc.

- *Provide qualified, adult supervision.* Obviously, physical educators alone will not be able to supervise all the activities provided. Other faculty and staff and parents will need to supervise activities. Physical educators can provide simple training for activity leaders on such topics as establishing a safe movement environment, maximizing participation, and creating a positive atmosphere.

- *Provide school-sponsored, out-of-school activity events/trips* (Cale & Harris, 2005). Rollerblading or hiking in a state park could be activities sponsored by the school but held on a Saturday off-campus.

- *Conduct physically active fund-raising events* (Cale & Harris, 2005). Jump Rope for Heart, Hoops for Heart, walkathons, bikathons, and car washes are ways of raising funds—either for charitable organizations or for school projects—that can encourage student activity.

- *Ensure safe, well-marked, clean activity facilities and areas.* Middle school students tend to be more active in play areas that have permanent improvements (e.g., basketball hoops, tennis courts, softball diamonds, soccer goals) (Sallis et al., 2001). Equipment should be checked regularly to make sure it is safe. Playgrounds should be marked with lines for recreational activities and sports (e.g., four-square, hopscotch, basketball). Changing/showering facilities should also be adequate and safe.

- *Make sure equipment is available.* Physical education teachers can work with other teachers and school staff to make sure each elementary classroom has enough play equipment for students to use during recess. Sport and play equipment should also be available to middle school and high school students for use during open gym time.

- *Encourage teachers not to take away recess or physical education as punishment.* Research shows that recess is an important avenue of physical activity for students, so classroom teachers should be encouraged to find other means of punishing students.

Kim Q., an elementary physical education teacher in the midwestern United States, increases her students' physical activity levels by running an Early Morning Fitness Walkers club. Kim arrives at school 20 minutes early, and the 4th and 5th grade students who arrive early go to the gym and walk with Kim. This gives these students a little extra activity time, and Kim enjoys it because she would walk in the morning anyway.

real world

There is currently no extracurricular physical activity program at Mr. Olson's elementary school. One activity he could start during lunch recess is a jump rope club, as two teachers indicated expertise in that activity and were willing to be the instructors. Because Julia seems to enjoy rope jumping, she might participate in that activity. If buses were available, other activities could be offered after school, because that is when most students have inactive free time. A couple of parents offered to supervise four-square games one afternoon each week, while another parent volunteered to offer an hour's workshop on hacky sack. Mr. Olson could also commit to conducting a Jump Rope for Heart event each year.

Involve Parents/Caretakers and Other Family Members

Research indicates that parents and siblings can be vital reinforcing factors for students' physical activity. Parents can also impact two predisposing factors—subjective norm and intentions to be active—by helping their children perceive that activity is important to parents. Physical educators can enlist parental help in supporting their child's physical activity in various ways. First, parents should be given information about physical activity and children, including the following:

- The importance of physical activity for children and adults
- School and community physical activity opportunities for children and families
- Means of limiting children's inactive recreational activities (e.g., limit video game play, computer use, and television watching)
- Ways parents can prompt, encourage, and praise children for physical activity (e.g., buy play equipment, transport children to lessons,

set physical activity goals with children and reward their achievement, provide ideas for family physical activity outings)

- The importance of parental role modeling of activity and being active with their children

- The importance of active transport to school, when safely possible

Newsletters, brochures, e-mails, websites, parent–teacher conferences, or parent nights are all possible avenues through which parents can be given such information.

Second, as described previously, parents should be encouraged to serve as volunteer supervisors of nonorganized activity time at school or leaders of extracurricular activities, such as a four-square club or rope jumping lessons. As described earlier, physical educators should train parents to be effective leaders in activities.

Third, provide space for parents to be active with their children. When gyms are not being used in the evenings, the space can be open for parents and their children to shoot hoops together or play badminton. Such activities should be monitored to make sure the adults do not take over play and that the children are actually physically active.

Fourth, as described previously, physical activity and fitness advice, as well as simple fitness testing, can be offered to parents/guardians.

Fifth, you may assign physical activity homework to students that must be done with the students' parents/guardians. For instance, Mr. Olson could give his 5th graders, who have been learning about upper body strength and endurance, an assignment to tell a parent/guardian three principles related to that fitness component, and to show their parent three exercises that can be done with canned goods to enhance arm strength/endurance. Such an assignment would help Julia be more active outside of school and involve her parents as well.

focus point

When physical education teachers collaborate with other school staff and involve parents, more activity opportunities outside of physical education can be offered to students at school.

real world

As the elementary physical education teacher at a school in the mid-western United States, Kim Q. has done several activities to inform her students' parents about the importance of physical activity and involve them in enhancing the students' activity levels. For example, during class, her 5th grade students learned exercises that correspond to the components of fitness. Then on Family Fitness Night, 5th graders and their parents came to the gym and the students acted as the parents' personal fitness trainers, showing the parents how to use equipment correctly and exercising together.

Right now Mr. Olson sends a newsletter home to parents each month; it contains information about activities being performed in the program. He could easily include information related to physical activity and children like that described above, as well as put out a request for parent volunteers to supervise and instruct extracurricular activities.

Encourage Active Transport to School

One way to increase the amount of physical activity students engage in is to have them use active transport, such as walking or riding bicycle, to school. School leaders and physical education teachers can work together to promote this in several ways:

- *Work with community leaders to make sure students have safe routes to school* (Pate et al., 2006). This might include the following: sidewalks in neighborhoods, crosswalks with crossing guards, traffic lights, bicycle lanes, and bike racks.
- *Inform students about the importance of active transport.* This can be done verbally during classes, or in written form on posters around the school or flyers.
- *Inform parents about the importance of active transport.* This can be done in a physical education or school newsletter, at parent–teacher conferences, or on the physical education or school website.

Although most of the students in Mr. Olson's school ride the school bus to school, many students' parents drive them to and from school. Yet most neighborhoods around the school have sidewalks and are relatively safe. Mr. Olson plans an "Active Transport" campaign to encourage students and parents to walk or ride a bike to school. He plans to bombard students and parents with information about how active transport to school can greatly increase activity levels, by discussing it during class, sending brochures and newsletters home, putting up posters around school, and posting the information on the school website. Mr. Olson has noticed that few streets around the school have bicycle lanes, so he and the school administrators plan to talk to the mayor and street commissioner to see if anything can be improved. There are also few bicycle racks at school, so the school board has approved installing more. Mr. Olson has also observed that many 5th grade students, like Julia, carry several items to and from school, like a bookbag, band instrument, and their lunch; this makes it prohibitive to walk or ride bicycle to school. Mr. Olson will talk to the principal about this to see whether a school van could be used to transport the band instruments to specific drop-off points at specific times (after the students would have reached their homes) so that the students might be more able to use active transport to and from school.

focus point

Students and parents should be told about the value of active transport, and physical educators and school officials should work with community leaders to ensure safe routes to school.

Summary

Important goals of most physical educators are to get students active and help them develop a habit of lifetime physical activity. According to the Youth Physical Activity Promotion Model, youth activity levels are the result of interactions among four categories of factors: predisposing, reinforcing, enabling, and personal demographics. Predisposing factors incline a person to be physically active and answer two questions: Am I able? Is it worth it? Positive attitudes toward physical activity and physical education, high perceived benefits, and low perceived barriers are among the predisposing factors that positively influence students' activity levels. Factors that encourage or support a person to be physically active are reinforcing factors, including parental support and encouragement, sibling activity levels, peer support and involvement, and teacher support and behaviors. Enabling factors allow youth to be physically active, such as biological, environmental, and behavioral factors. Although biological factors such as motor skills and body composition are not clear predictors of youth activity, environmental (e.g., access to facilities and equipment, safety, recess availability, and using active transport to school) and behavioral (e.g., time spent in sedentary and outdoor activities, self-management skills) factors seem to influence activity levels. Demographic research shows that older, female, non-Caucasian students tend to be less active than younger, male, Caucasian students.

You as a physical education teacher can use many strategies on your own to increase students' activity levels and the habit of physical activity. These strategies include increasing activity levels during class, emphasizing physical activity over physical fitness, teaching students self-management skills, informing students about activity opportunities outside of school, promoting peer involvement, including students with disabilities, accommodating activities and class procedures for students of various cultural and religious backgrounds, role-modeling an active lifestyle, and including more lifetime activities in the curriculum. But you can impact students' current and future activity levels by working with other school staff, parents, and community leaders to increase activity opportunities at school (via before- and after-school programs) and encourage active transport to school. Many strategies require much work, organization, and creativity, but the development of physically active students who desire a lifetime of physical activity is well worth the effort.

KEY concepts

Youth Physical Activity Promotion Model

Predisposing factors

Reinforcing factors

Enabling factors

Coordinated school health program

Subjective norm

Active transport

Counterconditioning

Self-liberation

application exercises

1. Use the Youth Physical Activity Promotion Model to explain your current physical activity level. Be sure to describe elements in each of the four categories of factors: predisposing, reinforcing, enabling, and personal demographics.

2. Ricardo is a visually impaired 5th grader in your school. Even though he has good motor skill abilities, he doesn't participate in much physical activity outside of physical education class. His parents and siblings don't allow him to do too much because they are afraid he will get hurt. Describe five strategies you would use in working with Ricardo's parents to enhance their support and encouragement of his physical activity.

3. You are teaching in a middle school in an affluent area. There is little chance of working with other teachers, school administrators, or parents to enhance students' activity levels because they highly emphasize academics, to the exclusion of other activities. First, describe three specific strategies you would use on your own to strengthen students' predisposing factors toward physical activity. Second, describe three actions you could take to gain the help of other adults in promoting students' activity levels.

4. You are a new physical education teacher in a high school where students have low activity levels. Describe two reinforcing and two enabling factors you will target in your attempts to increase the students' engagement. For each factor chosen, describe one specific means of positively affecting the factor to enhance the students' activity levels.

APPENDIX A

Instructional Tools

APPENDIX   A.1

Survey to Determine Elementary Students' Perceptions of Rewards

REWARDS SURVEY

Name: _____   Date: _____

Class: _____

Please put a check beside two items in each category that you would enjoy receiving/doing the most.

Activities

☐ Extra game play at the end of class

☐ 10 minutes of activity choice at the end of class

☐ Being a peer assistant in PE class with younger children

☐ Doing a treasure hunt around the playground

☐ Being able to pick/bring the music listened to in class

☐ Being the designated "teaching assistant" in PE class for the day (demonstrating tasks, getting equipment out, etc.)

Material

☐ Trophy

☐ Stickers

☐ Certificate

☐ Stuffed animals

☐ School T-shirt

Social

☐ Verbal praise from the teacher

☐ Getting high-fives or fist bumps from the teacher

☐ Having your name read over the school loudspeaker

☐ Having your name put on a public poster

☐ Having your picture taken and put on a public poster

☐ Having your name put in the school newsletter

Form for Assessing Prosocial Behaviors in Physical Education

Class

Date   Lesson Content

✓+ = *Consistently demonstrates*   ✓ = *Sometimes demonstrates*   ✓− = *Rarely demonstrates*

STUDENT NAME	SUPPORTS TEAMMATES	ACCEPTS OFFICIATING	PRAISES OPPONENTS	LISTENS TO INSTRUCTIONS	TAKES TURNS	SHARES EQUIPMENT

| APPENDIX   A.3 | **Scoring Sheet for a Daily Point System for Sport Education Units** |

Sport Education Unit: _____   Date: _____

	POINTS EARNED/DEDUCTED				
BEHAVIOR DISPLAYED	**TEAM 1**	**TEAM 2**	**TEAM 3**	**TEAM 4**	**TEAM 5**
Team wears team colors Yes = +5 pts. No = 0					
Team warms up correctly +1 to 5 pts.					
Team performs daily roles +1 to 5 pts.					
Team is enthusiastic (e.g., performs team cheer) +1 to 5 pts.					
Obeys the instructor +1 to 5 pts.					
Sportspersonship behaviors noticed by instructor +2 pts. each occurrence	*2 = _____	*2 = _____	*2 = _____	*2 = _____	*2 = _____

Application contests
    +5 pts. for overall winner for day
    +4 pts. for second place
    +3 pts. for third place
    +2 pts. for fourth place
    +1 pt. for fifth place					

Unsportsmanlike behaviors –5 pts. each occurrence	*-5 = _____	*-5 = _____	*-5 = _____	*-5 = _____	*-5 = _____

*Note: A team cannot earn more than 25 points per day.

Scoring sheet based on one by Tony Pritchard, Georgia Southern University, with permission.

Goal-Setting Sheet

Name: _____   Class: _____

Contract set date: _____   Target date: _____

GOAL DEFINED:

_____

_____

_____

STRATEGIES TO ACHIEVE GOALS:

_____

_____

_____

_____

DAILY PROGRESS NOTES:

_____

_____

_____

_____

_____

_____

_____

_____

_____

_____

APPENDIX   A.5

Closed-Response Exit Slip

Class: _____

Name: _____   Date: _____

On a scale of 1 to 5, with 5 being very successful and 1 being not successful at all, how would you rate your performance in class today? *(Circle the number.)*

1	2	3	4	5
Not successful at all				*Very successful*

What are some possible reasons for your level of success today? *(Put a check beside all that apply)*

_____ I have lots of athletic ability.   _____ I have little athletic ability.

_____ I tried hard today.   _____ I didn't try hard today.

_____ Today's activity was an easy skill.   _____ Today's activity was hard.

_____ I had good luck.   _____ I had bad luck.

_____ I used a good practice strategy.   _____ I used a poor practice strategy.

_____ Others (please name)   _____ I liked today's activity a lot.

_____

_____

"Getting to Know You" Survey

Your Name: _____

Class Period: _____

Date: _____

The purpose of this survey is to help your teacher get to know more about you outside of physical education class. You may choose not to complete this survey if you want, or choose not to answer specific questions if you want. Your teacher will not share your responses with any other students or school faculty/staff.

1. What is your favorite meal at school? Why is that your favorite meal?

   _____

   _____

2. If you could take a vacation anywhere in the world (and had the money to do that), where would you go? Why do you want to go there?

   _____

   _____

3. What do you think is your best subject at school? Why do you think it is your best subject?

   _____

   _____

4. What do you think is your worst subject at school? Why do you think it is your worst subject?

   _____

   _____

5. Think back to last week. In what school subject did you do your best/worst? Why do you think that was your best/worst school subject last week?

   _____

   _____

APPENDIX A.7   "Reasons for Outcomes" Form

REASONS FOR OUTCOMES

Class: _____

Time/Period: _____   Date: _____

STUDENT NAME	SUCCESSFUL OUTCOMES	UNSUCCESSFUL OUTCOMES
1.		
2.		
3.		
4.		
5.		
6.		
7.		
8.		
9.		
10.		
11.		
12.		
13.		
14.		
15.		
16.		
17.		
18.		
19.		
20.		
21.		
22.		
23.		
24.		
25.		

Unlimited-Choice Survey to Identify
Students' Personal Activity Interests

Class Period: _____   Date: _____

Directions: Please respond to the following questions.

1. Age as of last birthday in years *(please circle)*

   9   10   11   12   13   14   15

2. Gender

   Male   Female

3. List the five physical activities in which you would most like to participate.

1. _____

2. _____

3. _____

4. _____

5. _____

Source: From D. S. Fleming, M. Mitchell, J. J. Gorecki, & M. M. Coleman, "Students change and so do good programs: Addressing the interests of multicultural secondary students," in *Journal of Physical Education, Recreation, and Dance, 70* (2), 79–83. Copyright 1999, American Alliance for Health, Physical Education, Recreation, and Dance, Reston, VA. Reprinted with permission.

APPENDIX A.9

Limited-Choice Survey to Identify Students' Personal Activity Interests

Class Period: _____   Date: _____

Directions: Please respond to the following questions.

1. Age as of last birthday in years *(please circle)*

   9   10   11   12   13   14   15

2. Gender

   Male   Female

3. Check all of the activities in which you would enjoy participating.

   ____ Aerobics   ____ Rackets (tennis/badminton)

   ____ Basketball   ____ Rugby

   ____ Bowling   ____ Soccer

   ____ Cycling   ____ Softball

   ____ Dance   ____ Swimming

   ____ Football   ____ Team handball

   ____ Golf   ____ Ultimate Frisbee

   ____ Gymnastics   ____ Volleyball

   ____ Hockey (field or floor)   ____ Weight/strength training

   ____ Outdoor pursuits (archery, orienteering, canoeing, hiking)

   ____ Other _____ (fill in)

Ranked-Choice Survey to Identify Students' Personal Activity Interests

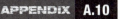
APPENDIX A.10

Class Period: _____   Date: _____

Directions: Please respond to the following questions.

1. Age as of last birthday in years *(please circle)*

   9   10   11   12   13   14   15

2. Gender

   Male   Female

3. Below is a list of different activities. Read the entire list, then use the following scale to rank the top four in which you would like to participate.

   0 = I know what this activity is, but it is not one of my top 4 choices

   1 = My first choice (please choose only one activity)

   2 = My second choice (please choose only one activity)

   3 = My third choice (please choose only one activity)

   4 = My fourth choice (please choose only one activity)

   5 = I don't know what this activity is

TEAM SPORTS

_____ Basketball   _____ Hockey (Field or Floor)

_____ Football   _____ Team handball

_____ Softball   _____ Ultimate Frisbee

_____ Rugby   _____ Volleyball

_____ Soccer   _____ Other team sport _____ *(fill in)*

Below is another list of different activities. Again, read the entire list, then use the previous scale to rank the top four activities in which you would like to participate.

OTHER ACTIVITIES

_____ Aerobics   _____ Outdoor pursuits (archery, orienteering, canoeing, hiking)

_____ Bowling   _____ Rackets (tennis/badminton)

_____ Cycling   _____ Swimming

_____ Dance   _____ Weight/strength training

_____ Golf   _____ Wrestling

_____ Gymnastics   _____ Other activity _____ *(fill in)*

Source: D. S. Fleming, M. Mitchell, J. J. Gorecki, & M. M. Coleman, "Students change and so do good programs: Addressing the interests of multicultural secondary students," in *Journal of Physical Education, Recreation, and Dance, 70* (2), 79–83. Copyright 1999, American Alliance for Health, Physical Education, Recreation, and Dance, Reston, VA. Reprinted with permission.

APPENDIX A.11	**Recording Sheet for SOFIT Student Physical Activity Levels**

Date: _____

Grade Level: _____

Class: _____

PA Levels: *1 = Lying down*   *2 = Sitting*   *3 = Standing*   *4 = Walking*   *5 = Very active*

TARGET STUDENT	OBSERVATION #	PA LEVEL	OBSERVATION #	PA LEVEL	OBSERVATION #	PA LEVEL
A	1		49		97	
	2		50		98	
	3		51		99	
	4		52		100	
	5		53		101	
	6		54		102	
	7		55		103	
	8		56		104	
	9		57		105	
	10		58		106	
	11		59		107	
	12		60		108	
B	13		61		109	
	14		62		110	
	15		63		111	
	16		64		112	
	17		65		113	
	18		66		114	
	19		67		115	
	20		68		116	
	21		69		117	
	22		70		118	
	23		71		119	
	24		72		120	
C	25		73		121	
	26		74		122	

	27		75	123
	28		76	124
	29		77	125
	30		78	126
	31		79	127
	32		80	128
	33		81	129
	34		82	130
	35		83	131
	36		84	132
D	37		85	133
	38		86	134
	39		87	135
	40		88	136
	41		89	137
	42		90	138
	43		91	139
	44		92	140
	45		93	141
	46		94	142
	47		95	143
	48		96	144

Total # of observations: _____

# of 1s = _____

# of 2s = _____

# of 3s = _____

# of 4s = _____

# of 5s = _____

4s + 5s = _____

Divide the total of 4s + 5s by the total # of observations = _____ % class time in MVPA.

APPENDIX A.12

Awareness of Time Use Sheet

Name: _____   Grade: _____

Date Completed: _____

Time	Activity
7:00 am	
8:00 am	
9:00 am	
10:00 am	
11:00 am	
Noon	
1:00 pm	
2:00 pm	
3:00 pm	
4:00 pm	
5:00 pm	
6:00 pm	
7:00 pm	
8:00 pm	
9:00 pm	
10:00 pm	
11:00 pm	
Midnight	
1:00 am	
2:00 am	
3:00 am	
4:00 am	
5:00 am	
6:00 am	

Decision-Balance Sheet

Name: _____   Date: _____

Grade: _____

Directions: In the first column, write down all of the reasons to be physically active that are important to you. In the second column, write down anything that prevents you from being physically active, or reasons why you don't like to or want to be physically active. When you are done with the first two columns, get together with one or two other students and brainstorm ways to overcome some of the costs or barriers to physical activity that you put in the second column, and to identify other benefits to physical activity.

BENEFITS OF PHYSICAL ACTIVITY	COSTS OF/BARRIERS TO PHYSICAL ACTIVITY	WAYS TO OVERCOME COSTS/BARRIERS

Theory	Principles/Process by Which a Physically Active Lifestyle Is Developed
Theories of Reasoned Action/Planned Behavior (Ajzen, 1985; Ajzen & Fishbein, 1980)	Intentions to be physically active directly impact physical activity levels, as long as people perceive they have the ability and opportunities to do so (perceived behavioral control). Our intentions are influenced by three factors: our attitudes toward physical activity, the subjective norm (beliefs about significant others' opinions toward exercise), and perceived behavioral control over participation.
Transtheoretical Model (Prochaska, DiClemente, & Norcross, 1992)	Individuals pass through five stages when adopting a physically active lifestyle: (1) precontemplation (no intentions to exercise); (2) contemplation (thinking about starting to exercise within the next 6 months); (3) preparation (exercise, but not regularly); (4) action (regular exercise for less than 6 months); and (5) maintenance (regularly active for more than 6 months). Cognitive (e.g., consciousness raising, self-reevaluation) and behavioral (e.g., stimulus control, reinforcement) processes are proposed as strategies of change.
Health-Belief Model (Rosenstock, 1974)	The adoption of a health-related behavior (e.g., physical activity) is based on one's perceptions of (a) how susceptible one is to a particular disease or health threat, (b) the severity of that disease or condition, (c) the benefits of taking steps to reduce the threat, and (d) the barriers to or costs of taking those steps.

APPENDIX B

Exercise and Physical Activity Theories

GLOSSARY

Academic learning time The amount of time a student spends in class engaged in learning activities at an appropriate level of difficulty.

Accommodation phase The second phase in the interactional theory of moral development; an individual gives preference to the needs and interests of others.

Achievement goal theory Asserts that individuals define ability and success differently and set different kinds of goals in achievement situations, based on their individual dispositions and situational factors. The different goal perspectives influence individual motivation and behaviors.

Active transport Transportation involving physical activity, such as walking, riding a bicycle, and skateboarding.

Adventure-based learning The deliberate use of sequenced games, trust activities, and problem-solving initiatives for the personal, social, and moral development of students; activities involve challenge and risk.

Amotivation Lack of motivation, either intrinsic or extrinsic, to participate in an activity.

Application A type of task in which students use or apply a skill or skills they have practiced; can be games, self- or group challenges, or performances.

Approach goal Goal characterized by a desire to achieve a positive outcome; a type of task- and ego-involvement.

Assimilation phase The first phase in the interactional theory of moral development; an individual's own needs and interests take priority.

Attainment value A component of subjective task value; the personal importance placed on a task because achievement confirms aspects of the person's identity.

Attribution A perceived cause of a performance outcome, or how individuals explain their successes and failures.

Attribution retraining The deliberate process of training students to change their maladaptive attributions to adaptive attributions.

Attribution theory Asserts that one's motivation is influenced by the types of attributions made in a situation.

Auditory modeling The use of sound (e.g., clapping hands, hitting rhythm sticks or a drum) to model the timing in motor skills.

Augmented feedback Information that a performer receives about a movement from an outside source.

Avoidance goal Goal characterized by a desire to avoid a negative outcome; a type of task and ego involvement.

Behavior modification The deliberate and systematic use of reinforcement to develop desirable behaviors and eliminate undesirable behaviors. Also known as behavior management, contingency management, or behavioral coaching.

Behavioral theory Proposes that behaviors and skills are learned via interactions between individuals and the environment; essentially, the consequences that follow the display of a behavior will determine whether that behavior is repeated and learned or not.

Catching interest The elements in the environment or activity that initially attract a person to an activity; because it is short-lived, it must be acted upon to increase the initial interest.

Cognitive evaluation theory Proposes that external rewards will harm intrinsic motivation if the receiver believes the reward is given to control him or her, but external rewards will enhance intrinsic motivation if the reward is perceived as providing positive information about the receiver's competence.

Cognitive mediation theory Asserts that modeling influences learning through four processes: (1) attention, (2) retention, (3) behavior reproduction, and (4) motivation.

Competence motivation One's desire to show mastery and make task attempts.

Competence motivation theory Asserts that one's perceptions of competence and control influence that person's emotions, competence motivation, and achievement in a situation. Perceptions of competence and control are influenced by performance outcomes, reinforcement from significant others, and motivational and goal orientations.

Competent bystander A student who avoids participation in physical education activities without drawing attention to him- or herself.

Conceptual elements A category of skill elements that may be similar among skills; these elements refer to similar strategies, rules, or concepts that exist between activities.

Concurrent feedback Feedback that is given to a student while a movement is being made (also *see* verbal guidance).

Congruent feedback Feedback that matches the focus of the task.

Content development A series of tasks designed to move students from one skill level to another; consists of extensions, refinements, and applications.

Contingent feedback Feedback that matches the student's performance level.

Continuous reinforcement A schedule of reinforcement in which a person is reinforced every time the desired behavior is produced.

Controllability A method of classifying attributions; causes of performance outcomes can be seen as changeable or unchangeable by a person.

Cooperative learning An instructional model in which students are placed onto learning teams and must work together to complete a learning task.

Coordinated school health program A model consisting of eight components that should interact to enhance youth activity levels: health education, physical education, health services, nutrition services, counseling and psychological services, healthy school environment, health promotion for staff, and family and community involvement.

Coping model A model who first has trouble performing a skill but gradually shows improvement until correct performance is demonstrated; in addition, they initially verbalize high task difficulty, a negative attitude, and low confidence, which gradually become more positive and confident.

Coping processes More mature moral reasoning capabilities such as being empathetic, being able to suppress one's primitive impulses to display socially acceptable behavior, and conducting a logical and accurate analysis of a situation.

Cost A component of subjective task value; the negative aspects of participating in an activity.

Counterconditioning Self-management skill in which an individual actively substitutes alternatives for the problem behavior.

Defending processes Less mature moral reasoning processes that yield an inaccurate evaluation of a situation, such as rationalizing or denying one's actions, or projecting one's motives onto others.

Delayed feedback Feedback given to a learner about a task attempt (or several) after a period of time has elapsed (several seconds or minutes).

Demonstration Another term for modeling; frequently used in physical education to describe the visual presentation of how to perform a motor skill or task.

Differentiated view of ability Ability to distinguish ability from effort; a person understands that ability is highest when one performs better than others with less effort.

Dispositional goal orientation Part of a person's character; a person's tendency to choose one type of goal (self-referenced or other-referenced) over another in an achievement situation.

Ego involvement The goal perspective in which a person's definition of ability is other- or norm-referenced, meaning that one's performance compared to others is the main determinant of competence and success; the goal is to perform better than others.

Ego-involving climate The social climate established when a teacher constantly compares students to each other, encourages them to perform better than each other, and stresses a normative definition of success.

Ego orientation The dispositional goal orientation in which the individual prefers to define success as performing better than others; uses the norm-referenced definition of success.

Emotional state A person's situational mood, such as happiness, exhilaration, tranquility, sadness, anxiety, or depression. A source of efficacy information in self-efficacy theory.

Enabling factors Factors that allow individuals to be physically active; include environmental and biological factors.

Entity conception of ability View of ability as fixed and unchangeable regardless of one's effort and practice.

Equilibration phase The third phase in the interactional theory of moral development; the individual seeks a balance among the rights and needs of everyone within the situation.

Expectancy–value theory Proposes a person's behavior in an achievement situation is determined by the degree to which a person expects to be successful, and the subjective value placed on success in that situation.

Exploration intention A desire to learn more about an activity and discover all of the different aspects of the activity.

Extension A type of task that increases or decreases in difficulty or complexity.

External regulation The extrinsic motivational orientation with the lowest self-determination; an individual's actions are completely controlled by external forces, such as a reward, threat, or punishment.

Extrinsic motivation Type of motivation that exists when someone performs a task or behavior in order to receive some outcome separate from the activity.

Extrinsic motivational orientation An orientation toward performing activities to receive external rewards such as trophies or praise from others.

Fading The process of gradually changing a reinforcer that controls a behavior so the behavior eventually occurs in response to a new reinforcer.

Fixed ratio schedule A schedule of reinforcement in which a behavior must be exhibited a set number of times before being reinforced.

Flow A positive affective state in which a person has total concentration, a sense of control, loss of self-consciousness, and a merging of action and awareness.

Goal perspective The type of goal that one adopts in an achievement situation. It is determined by the person's definition of ability in that situation and is influenced by the individual's dispositional goal orientation and the motivational climate.

Holding interest An individual's continued attraction to an activity that remains after catching interest declines; it can be enhanced by increasing personal meaning and involvement.

Identified regulation The extrinsic motivational orientation in which an individual freely engages in an activity, but the activity is valued solely as a means to an end.

Imagery Using all of the senses to create or re-create an experience in the mind. A source of efficacy information in self-efficacy theory.

Immediate feedback Information given to a learner about a skill immediately after making a task attempt.

Incremental conception of ability View of ability as changeable, capable of being improved through effort and practice.

Inquiry model An instructional model in which question asking is the exclusive method of task presentation, and students are invited to think and produce a wide range of correct movement responses.

Integrated regulation The extrinsic motivational orientation with the highest level of self-determination; the individual freely chooses to engage in an activity, and the activity is more integrated with the individual's self-identity than with identified regulation.

Interactional theory A structural developmental theory of moral development that describes moral development as a series of phases and levels of moral reasoning through which individuals progress; individuals move from self-interests to mutual interests as the basis of moral reasoning.

Interest An individual's feelings or attitudes of concern, involvement, or curiosity, as aroused by something or someone.

Intermittent reinforcement Schedule of reinforcement where some instances of a behavior are reinforced but others are not.

Intratask variation Instructional skill in which the teacher makes the decision to privately make the task easier or harder for individual students or groups.

Intrinsic feedback Information that a performer receives about a movement through the various senses just by making the movement.

Intrinsic motivation An internal desire to show competence and be self-determining; performing an activity for its own sake, for the pleasure and excitement derived from participation, and for the desire to master a task.

Intrinsic motivational orientation An orientation toward performing activities to seek challenges or for one's own curiosity or interest.

Intrinsic value A component of subjective task value; the enjoyment or pleasure derived from participating in an activity for its own sake.

Introjected regulation The extrinsic motivational orientation with the second highest external control; an individual feels obligated to engage in activity in order to gain approval and pride or to avoid guilt.

Learned helplessness The belief that there is no relationship between one's actions and a performance outcome; the belief that one has no control over that person's performance outcomes.

Locus of causality A method of classifying attributions; causes of performance outcomes can be seen internal or external to an individual.

Maladaptive attributions Attributions for performance outcomes that inhibit students' motivation and effort and produce negative emotions.

Mastery model A model who demonstrates a skill correctly, along with making statements during the demonstration that convey confidence, ease, and a positive attitude.

Modeling Communicating a visual or auditory representation of a motor skill, prosocial behavior, or psychological skill to someone in order to convey information about performing that skill or behavior.

Moral balance The state of basic agreement about rights and/or responsibilities among all individuals involved.

Moral development levels The moral levels are within three phases of development and describe the reasoning used by someone at that level to decide whether an action is right or wrong.

Moral dialogue The process through which moral balance is achieved, which may involve verbal negotiation of rights or nonverbal interactions.

Moral reasoning The aspect of sportspersonship concerning the rationale used to judge the rightness or wrongness of behaviors.

Motivated learning behaviors Behaviors that suggest a person is engaged in the content, is making a high effort to learn the content, and is persistent in doing so.

Motivation The direction and intensity of effort.

Motivational climate The social climate in a situation that leads a person to perceive one goal perspective is more important than the other. It is established in part by actions taken by the teacher that emphasize one goal perspective over the other.

Movement analysis curriculum Type of curriculum that encourages students to find new and different ways of moving and applying principles of movement (i.e., movement education).

Movement elements A category of skill elements that may be similar among skills; these elements refer to the form or movement patterns used to perform skills.

Negative reinforcement A stimulus perceived as negative or aversive that is removed, which then serves to increase the occurrence of or strengthens the behavior it follows.

Observational learning The process of learning to perform a motor skill, prosocial behavior, or psychological skill by observing someone perform the skill or behavior.

Optimally challenging tasks Tasks that are neither too hard nor too easy for an individual.

Peer teaching An instructional model in which students pair up and take turns teaching other.

Perceptions of competence/perceived ability A person's description of and evaluation of her abilities in a specific domain. Perceptions of competence are less global and less stable than one's self-esteem.

Perceptions of control A person's beliefs about who or what controls one's performance or learning; these perceptions can be internal or external to oneself.

Perceptual elements A category of skill elements that may be similar among skills; these elements refer to the environmental stimuli produced during a skill that a person must detect and correctly interpret in order to be successful.

Performance accomplishments The most influential source of efficacy information in self-efficacy theory. Past successes are proposed to increase self-efficacy, whereas repeated failures decrease self-efficacy.

Personal interest An individual's unique disposition to participate in and seek out certain activities, events, and objects; stable preferences for activities that develop over time when an individual has repeated, positive interactions with those activities.

Personal meaning A perception that what is being learned is important in an individual's life today.

Personalized system of instruction (PSI) An instructional model in which task presentations for a unit occur via written workbooks or video-recordings, allowing students to progress at their own rate.

Physiological state A person's somatic response to task attempts or stressful situations (e.g., increased heart rate, being out of breath, sweaty palms, muscle fatigue, and soreness). A source of efficacy information in self-efficacy theory.

Positive reinforcement A stimulus that acts to increase or strengthen a behavior after it is received because it is perceived as desirable or positive by the person receiving it.

Predisposing factors Factors that collectively increase the likelihood that a person will be physically active on a regular basis; these factors answer two questions: Am I able? Is it worth it?

Prosocial behaviors One aspect of sportsmanship consisting of behaviors generally deemed desirable by society and that help one function in and contribute to society, such as cooperation, generosity, sympathy, honesty, and helping.

Psychology The study of the mind and behavior.

Psychology of teaching physical education The study of human behavior in physical education, and the practical application of that knowledge in physical education settings; information that can help physical educators enhance student learning and enjoyment.

Punishment A stimulus designed to decrease the occurrence of a behavior it follows. This can happen either by presenting a negative or aversive stimulus to a person following the behavior or by removing a stimulus the person perceives as positive.

Refinements Tasks or cues that help a student achieve a quality performance; address the critical elements of skill performance.

Reinforcement Any stimulus that increases the occurrence of or strengthens a behavior it immediately follows.

Reinforcing factors Factors that support or encourage a person's physical activity; come from three main sources: parents/family, peers, and teachers/coaches.

Sandwich approach Method of giving verbal feedback that consists of three sequential elements: a positive statement, future-oriented technical instructions, and a compliment.

Schedules of reinforcement The timing and frequency with which a person is reinforced.

Self-concept A person's relatively stable, global description of herself without any evaluation of worth. It is multidimensional, meaning it consists of many different elements or domains.

Self-confidence The strength of a person's belief that he will actually be successful in a particular domain or context.

Self-determination theory Asserts motivation will be highest when the psychological needs for competence, autonomy, and relatedness are met; also asserts that there are different types of motivational orientations, based on the reasons for engaging in activity and the level of self-determination.

Self-efficacy Situation-specific self-confidence; one's degree of confidence in her capability to achieve a specific performance level or outcome in a particular situation.

Self-efficacy theory Asserts that one's self-efficacy will influence that person's behaviors, thought patterns, emotional reactions, and eventual performance.

Self-esteem One's personal assessment or judgment of her value or worth as a person, based on domain-specific self-conceptions and the importance one places on the domains.

Self-liberation A self-management skill in which a person makes a choice and commitment to change the problem behavior (e.g., making a contract).

Self-perceptions All of the thoughts and feelings individuals have about themselves, both specific to particular domains and overall as persons in general.

Shaping Process of rewarding successful approximations of or progressive small improvements in a skill or behavior.

Situational interest An individual's perception of the appealing characteristics of an activity; it is generated primarily by conditions or objects in the environment. This interest is temporary but if maintained over time, it could develop into personal interest.

Social learning theory Asserts that people learn thoughts and behaviors through the socialization process of modeling, and reinforcement by and social comparison to significant others.

Sport and exercise psychology The scientific study of human behavior in sport and exercise, and the practical application of that knowledge in sport and exercise settings.

Sport education A curriculum and instructional model in which activity units simulate actual sport seasons; the model is characterized by long units, team membership, students learning roles other than player, formal competition, a culminating event, record keeping, and festivity.

Sportspersonship The prosocial behaviors deemed acceptable by society in sport and movement settings.

Stability A method of classifying attributions; causes of performance outcomes can be seen as stable and permanent (the same outcome can be expected in the future) or unstable and temporary (a different outcome is possible in the future).

Structural developmental An approach to moral development that focuses on the reasoning behind behaviors, which then affects a person's judgments of behaviors and the actual behaviors exhibited by the person.

Subjective norm An individual's beliefs about significant others' views and typical expectations for physical activity and the individual's motivation to comply with those expectations.

Subjective task value The importance of being successful in a domain; consists of four components: attainment value, intrinsic value, utility value, and cost.

Tactical games model An instructional model that focuses on teaching students tactics and skills through modified game forms.

Taking personal and social responsibility Curriculum and instructional model that focuses on helping children take personal responsibility for their own actions and contribute to the welfare of others; primary components include five goals of student responsibility, a daily lesson format, and strategies to promote self-responsibility at each level.

TARGET Acronym that stands for the structures in an achievement situation that can be altered to foster task involvement: task, authority, reward, grouping, evaluation, and time.

Task involvement A goal perspective in which a person's definition of ability is self-referenced and improving one's own performance is the basis for perceptions of ability; the goal is to master a task.

Task-involving climate The social climate established when a teacher focuses on each student's improvement and stresses a self-referenced definition of success.

Task orientation The dispositional goal orientation in which the individual prefers to define success as improving that person's own performance and mastering tasks; uses the self-referenced definition of success.

Teacher expectations A teacher's beliefs about what a student can achieve; these expectations can affect the teacher's behaviors toward students and the students' eventual performances.

Teaching by invitation Instructional skill in which a teacher presents two or three task options from which the students choose.

Theory A system of ideas developed to explain an event, a behavior, or a phenomenon.

Undifferentiated view of ability The inability to distinguish between ability and effort; ability is self-referenced, and higher effort means higher ability.

Utility value A component of subjective task value; the value placed on a task because it helps a person achieve current and/or future goals.

Value The desirability or worth of an object, event, or performance.

Variable ratio schedule A schedule of reinforcement in which the number of times a person must produce the desired behavior in order to earn a reward varies, so the person doesn't know when the reward will be received.

Verbal guidance Verbal information given to a learner about a movement as the movement is being made (also *see* concurrent feedback).

Verbal persuasion Process whereby significant others try to convince an individual that the person can be successful at a task. The persuasion may consist of motivational statements or information about correct performance on the task. A source of efficacy information in self-efficacy theory.

Verbal rehearsal The act of repeating, either out loud or to oneself, the important cues for a skill or task.

Vicarious experiences Observations of someone else demonstrating or modeling a skill or behavior. A source of efficacy information in self-efficacy theory.

Youth physical activity promotion model Asserts that school-age children's physical activity is the result of interactions among four categories of factors: predisposing, reinforcing, enabling, and personal demographics.

REFERENCES

Abramson, L. Y., Seligman, M. E. P., & Teasdale, J. D. (1978). Learned helplessness in humans: Critique and reformulation. *Journal of Abnormal Psychology, 87,* 49–74.

Adams, J. A. (1986). Use of the model's knowledge of results to increase the observer's performance. *Journal of Human Movement Studies, 12,* 89–98.

Ajzen, I. (1985). From intentions to actions: A theory of planned behavior. In J. Kuhl & J. Beckmann (Eds.), *Action control: From cognition to behavior* (pp. 11–40). Berlin, Germany: Springer-Verlag.

Ajzen, I., & Fishbein, M. (1980). *Understanding attitudes and predicting social behavior.* Englewood Cliffs, NJ: Prentice Hall.

Alexander, K., Taggart, A., & Thorpe, S. (1996). A spring in their steps? Possibilities for professional renewal through sport education in Australian schools. *Sport, Education and Society, 1,* 23–46.

Alexander, P. A., Jetton, T. L., & Kulikowich, J. M. (1995). Interrelationship of knowledge, interest, and recall: Assessing a model of domain learning. *Journal of Educational Psychology, 87,* 559–575.

Allen, J. B., & Howe, B. L. (1998). Player ability, coach feedback, and female adolescent athletes' perceived competence and satisfaction. *Journal of Sport and Exercise Psychology, 20,* 280–299.

Allison, M. G., & Ayllon, T. (1980). Behavioral coaching in the development of skills in football, gymnastics, and tennis. *Journal of Applied Behavior Analysis, 13,* 297–314.

American Psychological Association. (n. d.). *About the American Psychological Association.* Retrieved July 7, 2007, www.apa.org/about/.

Ames, C. (1992a). Achievement goals, motivational climate, and motivational processes. In G. Roberts (Ed.), *Motivation in sport and exercise* (pp. 161–176). Champaign, IL: Human Kinetics.

Ames, C. (1992b). Classrooms: Goals, structures, and student motivation. *Journal of Educational Psychology, 84,* 261–272.

Amorose, A. J., & Smith, P. J. K. (2003). Feedback as a source of physical competence information: Effects of age, experience and type of feedback. *Journal of Sport and Exercise Psychology, 25,* 341–359.

Amorose, A. J., & Weiss, M. R. (1998). Coaching feedback as a source of information about perceptions of ability: A developmental examination. *Journal of Sport and Exercise Psychology, 20,* 395–420.

Anderman, E. M., & Maehr, M. L. (1994). Motivation and schooling in the middle grades. *Review of Educational Research, 64,* 287–309.

Anderssen, N., Wold, B., & Torsheim, T. (2005). Tracking of physical activity in adolescence. *Research Quarterly for Exercise and Sport, 76,* 119–129.

Arntzen, E., Halstadtro, A. M., & Halstadtro, M. (2003). Training play behavior in a 5-year-old boy with developmental disabilities. *Journal of Applied Behavior Analysis, 36,* 367–370.

Atkinson, J. W. (1964). *An introduction to motivation.* New York: Van Nostrand Reinhold.

Ayvazoglu, N. R., Oh, H. K., & Kozub, F. M. (2006). Explaining physical activity in children with visual impairments: A family systems approach. *Exceptional Children, 72,* 235–248.

Azzarito, L., & Solmon, M. A. (2006a). A feminist poststructuralist view on student bodies in physical education: Sites of compliance, resistance, and transformation. *Journal of Teaching in Physical Education, 26,* 200–225.

Azzarito, L., & Solmon, M. A. (2006b). A poststructural analysis of high school students' gendered and racialized bodily meanings. *Journal of Teaching in Physical Education, 25,* 75–98.

Babkes, M. L., & Weiss, M. R. (1999). Parental influence on children's cognitive and affective responses to competitive soccer participation. *Pediatric Exercise Science, 11,* 44–62.

Bagley, S., Salmon, J., & Crawford, D. (2006). Family structure and children's television viewing and physical activity. *Medicine & Science in Sports & Exercise, 38,* 910–918.

Bandura, A. (1977). *Social learning theory.* Englewood Cliffs, NJ: Prentice-Hall.

Bandura, A. (1986). *Social foundations of thought and actions: A social cognitive theory.* Englewood Cliffs, NJ: Prentice-Hall.

Bandura, A. (1997). *Self-efficacy: The exercise of control.* New York: W. H. Freeman & Co.

Bar-Eli, M., Pie, J. S., & Chait, T. (1995). Perceived competence among adolescents participating in enriched versus regular physical education classes. *European Physical Education Review, 1,* 74–82.

Barrett, T. (2005). Effects of cooperative learning on the performance of sixth-grade physical education students. *Journal of Teaching in Physical Education, 24,* 88–102.

Behets, D. (1990). Concerns of preservice physical education teachers. *Journal of Teaching in Physical Education, 10,* 66–75.

Beunen, G. P., Lefevre, J., Philippaerts, R. M., Delvaux, K., Thomis, M., Claessens, A. L., et al. (2004). Adolescent correlates of adult physical activity: A 26-year follow-up. *Medicine & Science in Sports & Exercise, 36,* 1930–1936.

Biddle, S. J. H. (2001). Enhancing motivation in physical education. In G. C. Roberts (Ed.), *Advances in motivation in sport and exercise* (pp. 101–127). Champaign, IL: Human Kinetics.

Biddle, S., Cury, F., Goudas, M., Sarrazin, P., Famose, J. P., & Durand, M. (1995). Development of scales to measure perceived physical education class climate: A cross-national project. *British Journal of Educational Psychology, 65,* 3341–3358.

Biddle, S., Page, A., Ashford, B., Jennings, D., Brooke, R., & Fox, K. (1993). Assessment of children's physical self-perceptions. *International Journal of Adolescence and Youth, 4,* 93–109.

Biddle, S. J. H., Wang, C. K. J., Chatzisarantis, N. L. D., & Spray, C. M. (2003). Motivation for physical activity in young people: Entity and incremental beliefs about athletic ability. *Journal of Sports Sciences, 21,* 973–989.

Biddle, S. J. H., Whitehead, S. H., O'Donovan, T. M., & Nevill, M. E. (2005). Correlates of participation in physical activity for adolescent girls: A systematic review of recent literature. *Journal of Physical Activity and Health, 2,* 423–434.

Bird, A. M., & Williams, J. M. (1980). A developmental-attributional analysis of sex-role stereotypes for sport performance. *Developmental Psychology, 16,* 319–322.

Black, S. J., & Weiss, M. R. (1992). The relationship among perceived coaching behaviors, perceptions of ability, and motivation in competitive age-group swimmers. *Journal of Sport and Exercise Psychology, 14,* 309–325.

Blandin, Y., Lhuisset, L., & Proteau, L. (1999). Cognitive processes underlying observational learning of motor skills. *The Quarterly Journal of Experimental Psychology, 52A,* 957–979.

Blandin, Y., & Proteau, L. (2000). On the cognitive basis of observational learning: Development of mechanisms for the detection and correction of errors. *The Quarterly Journal of Experimental Psychology, 53A,* 846–867.

Blankenship, B. T. (2007). The stress process in physical education. *Journal of Physical Education, Recreation, and Dance, 78*(6), 39–44.

Boggess, T. E., McBride, R. E., & Griffey, D. C. (1985). The concerns of physical education student teachers: A developmental view. *Journal of Teaching in Physical Education, 4,* 202–211.

Bouffard, M., & Dunn, J. G. H. (1993). Children's self-regulated learning of movement sequences. *Research Quarterly for Exercise and Sport, 64,* 393–403.

Bredemeier, B. J. (1995). Divergence in children's moral reasoning about issues in daily life and sport specific contexts. *International Journal of Sport Psychology, 26,* 453–463.

Bredemeier, B. J., & Shields, D. L. (1984). Divergence in moral reasoning about sport and everyday life. *Sociology of Sport Journal, 1,* 348–357.

Bredemeier, B. J., & Shields, D. L. (1986a). Game reasoning and interactional morality. *Journal of Genetic Psychology, 147,* 257–275.

Bredemeier, B. J., & Shields, D. L. (1986b). Moral growth among athletes and nonathletes: A comparative analysis. *The Journal of Genetic Psychology, 147,* 7–18.

Bredemeier, B. J., Weiss, M. R., Shields, D. L., & Shewchuk, R. M. (1986). Promoting moral growth in a summer sport camp: The implementation of theoretically grounded instructional strategies. *Journal of Moral Education, 15,* 212–220.

Brobst, B., & Ward, P. (2002). Effects of public posting, goal setting, and oral feedback on the skills of female soccer players. *Journal of Applied Behavior Analysis, 35,* 247–257.

Brown, M. (2006). Adventure education and physical education. In D. Kirk, D. Macdonald, & M. O'Sullivan (Eds.), *Handbook of physical education* (pp. 685–702). London: Sage.

Browne, J. (1992). Reasons for the selection or nonselection of physical education studies by year 12 girls. *Journal of Teaching in Physical Education, 11,* 402–410.

Brustad, R. J. (1993). Who will go out and play? Parental and psychological influences on children's attraction to physical activity. *Pediatric Exercise Science, 5,* 210–223.

Brustad, R. J. (1996). Attraction to physical activity in urban schoolchildren: Parental socialization and gender influences. *Research Quarterly for Exercise and Sport, 67,* 316–323.

Buskist, W., & Saville, B. K. (2001) Rapport building: Creating positive emotional contexts for enhancing teaching and learning. *APS Observer, 14*(3), 12–13, 19.

Buzas, H. P., & Ayllon, T. (1981). Differential reinforcement in coaching tennis skills. *Behavior Modification, 5,* 372–385.

Cadopi, M., Chatillon, J. F., & Baldy, R. (1995). Representation and performance: Reproduction of form and quality of movement in dance by eight- and 11-year-old novices. *British Journal of Psychology, 86,* 217–225.

Cairney, J., Hay, J., Faught, B., Mandigo, J., & Flouris, A. (2005). Developmental coordination disorder, self-efficacy toward physical activity and play: Does gender matter? *Adapted Physical Activity Quarterly, 22,* 67–82.

Cale, L. (2000). Physical activity promotion in secondary schools. *European Physical Education Review, 6,* 71–90.

Cale, L., & Harris, J. (2005). Promoting physical activity within schools. In L. Cale & J. Harris (Eds.), *Exercise and young people: Issues, implications, and initiatives* (pp. 162–190). New York: Palgrave Macmillan.

Cale, L., & Harris, J. (2006). School-based physical activity interventions: Effectiveness, trends, issues, implications and recommendations for practice. *Sport, Education, and Society, 11,* 401–420.

Carlson, T. B., & Hastie, P. A. (1997). The student social system within sport education. *Journal of Teaching in Physical Education, 16,* 176–195.

Carpenter, P. J., & Morgan, K. (1999). Motivational climate, personal goal perspectives, and cognitive and affective responses in physical education classes. *European Journal of Physical Education, 4,* 31–44.

Carr, S., Weigand, D. A., & Hussey, W. (1999). The relative influence of parents, teachers, and peers on children and adolescents' achievement and intrinsic motivation and perceived competence in physical education. *Journal of Sport Pedagogy, 5,* 28–51.

Centers for Disease Control and Prevention. (1997). Guidelines for school and community programs to promote lifelong physical activity among young people. *Journal of School Health, 67*(6), 202–219.

Chase, M. A. (1998). Sources of self-efficacy in physical education and sport. *Journal of Teaching in Physical Education, 18,* 76–89.

Chase, M. A. (2001a). Children's accuracy of self-appraisal of ability and motivational beliefs in physical education. *The Physical Educator, 58,* 103–112.

Chase, M. A. (2001b). Children's self-efficacy, motivational intentions, and attributions in physical education and sport. *Research Quarterly for Exercise and Sport, 72,* 47–54.

Chase, M. A., Ewing, M. E., Lirgg, C. D., & George, T. R. (1994). The effects of equipment modification on children's self-efficacy and basketball shooting performance. *Research Quarterly for Exercise and Sport, 65,* 159–168.

Chatzisarantis, N. L. D., & Hagger, M. S. (2005). Effects of a brief intervention based on the theory of planned behavior on leisure-time physical activity participation. *Journal of Sport and Exercise Psychology, 27,* 470–487.

Chen, A. (1996). Student interest in activities in a secondary physical education curriculum: An analysis of student subjectivity. *Research Quarterly for Exercise and Sport, 67,* 424–432.

Chen, A. (1998). Meaningfulness in physical education: A description of high school students' conceptions. *Journal of Teaching in Physical Education, 17,* 285–306.

Chen, A. (2001). A theoretical conceptualization for motivation research in physical education: An integrated perspective. *Quest, 53,* 35–58.

Chen, A., & Darst, P. W. (2001). Situational interest in physical education: A function of learning task design. *Research Quarterly for Exercise and Sport, 72,* 150–164.

Chen, A., & Darst, P. W. (2002). Individual and situational interest: The role of gender and skill. *Contemporary Educational Psychology, 27,* 250–269.

Chen, A., Darst, P. W., & Pangrazi, R. P. (1999). What constitutes situational interest? Validating a construct in physical education. *Measurement in Physical Education and Exercise Science, 3*(3), 157–180.

Chen, A., Darst, P. W., & Pangrazi, R. P. (2001). An examination of situational interest and its sources. *British Journal of Educational Psychology, 71,* 383–400.

Chen, A., & Shen, B. (2004). A web of achieving in physical education: Goals, interest, outside-school activity and learning. *Learning and Individual Differences, 14,* 169–182.

Chen, A., & Zhu, W. (2005). Young children's intuitive interest in physical activity: Personal, school, and home factors. *Journal of Physical Activity and Health, 2,* 1–15.

Chung, M., & Phillips, D. A. (2002). The relationship between attitude toward physical education and leisure-time exercise in high school students. *The Physical Educator, 59,* 126–138.

Clark, S. E., & Ste-Marie, D. M. (2002). Peer mastery versus peer coping models: Model type has differential effects on psychological and physical performance measures. *Journal of Human Movement Studies, 43,* 179–196.

Clocksin, B. D., Watson, D. L., & Ransdell, L. (2002). Understanding youth obesity and media use: Implications for future intervention programs. *Quest, 54,* 259–275.

The Cooper Institute. (2006). *Fitnessgram/ Activitygram 8.0 test kit.* Champaign, IL: Human Kinetics.

Corbin, C. B. (2002). Physical activity for everyone: What every physical educator should know about promoting lifelong physical activity. *Journal of Teaching in Physical Education, 21,* 128–144.

Corbin, C. B., Pangrazi, R. P., & LeMasurier, G. C. (2004). Physical activity for children: Current patterns and guidelines. *President's Council on Physical Fitness and Sports Research Digest, 5*(2), 1–8.

Cosgriff, M. (2000). Walking our talk: Adventure based learning and physical education. *Journal of Physical Education New Zealand, 33*(2), 89–98.

Cousineau, W. J., & Luke, M. D. (1990). Relationships between teacher expectations and academic learning time in sixth grade physical education basketball classes. *Journal of Teaching in Physical Education, 9,* 262–271.

Crocker, P. R. E., Eklund, R. C., & Kowalski, K. C. (2000). Children's physical activity and physical self-perceptions. *Journal of Sports Sciences, 18,* 383–394.

Csikszentmihalyi, M. (1975). *Beyond boredom and anxiety.* San Francisco: Jossey-Bass.

Cury, F., Biddle, S. J. H., Famose, J., Goudas, M., Sarrazin, P., & Durand, M. (1996). Personal and situational factors influencing intrinsic interest of adolescent girls in school physical education: A structural equation modeling analysis. *Educational Psychology, 16,* 305–315.

Cury, F., Biddle, S., Sarrazin, P., & Famose, J. P. (1997). Achievement goals and perceived ability predict investment in learning a sport task. *British Journal of Educational Psychology, 67,* 293–309.

Dale, D., & Corbin, C. B. (2000). Physical activity participation of high school graduates following exposure to conceptual or traditional physical education. *Research Quarterly for Exercise and Sport, 71,* 61–68.

Dale, D. I., Corbin, C. B., & Cuddihy, T. F. (1998). Can conceptual physical education promote physically active lifestyles? *Pediatric Exercise Science, 10,* 97–109.

Dale, D., Corbin, C. B., & Dale, K. S. (2000). Restricting opportunities to be active during school time: Do children compensate by increasing physical activity levels after school? *Research Quarterly for Exercise and Sport, 71,* 240–248.

Daley, A. J. (2002). School based physical activity in the United Kingdom: Can it create physically active adults? *Quest, 54,* 21–33.

Daley, A. J., & Buchanan, J. (1999). Aerobic dance and physical self-perceptions in female adolescents: Some implications for physical education. *Research Quarterly for Exercise and Sport, 70,* 196–200.

Darst, P. W., & Pangrazi, R. P. (2006). *Dynamic physical education for secondary school students* (5th ed.). San Francisco: Pearson Benjamin Cummings.

Davison, K. K. (2004). Activity-related support from parents, peers, and siblings and adolescents' physical activity: Are there gender differences? *Journal of Physical Activity and Health, 1,* 363–376.

Davison, K. K., Cutting, T. M., & Birch, L. L. (2003). Parents' activity-related parenting practices predict girls' physical activity. *Medicine & Science in Sports & Exercise, 35,* 1589–1595.

Davison, K. K., Downs, D. S., & Birch, L. L. (2006). Pathways linking perceived athletic competence and parental support at age 9 years to girls' physical activity at age 11 years. *Research Quarterly for Exercise and Sport, 77,* 23–31.

Deakin, J. M., & Proteau, L. (2000). The role of scheduling in learning through observation. *Journal of Motor Behavior, 32,* 268–276.

DeBusk, M., & Hellison, D. (1989). Implementing a physical education self-responsibility model for delinquency-prone youth. *Journal of Teaching in Physical Education, 8,* 104–112.

Deci, E. L., & Ryan, R. M. (1985). *Intrinsic motivation and self-determination in human behavior.* New York: Plenum Press.

Deci, E. L., & Ryan, R. M. (1991). A motivational approach to self: Integration in personality. *Nebraska Symposium on Motivation, 38,* 237–288.

Deci, E. L., & Ryan, R. M. (1994). Promoting self-determined education. *Scandinavian Journal of Educational Research, 38,* 3–41.

Deci, E. L., & Ryan, R. M. (2000). The "what" and "why" of goal pursuits: Human needs and the self-determination of behavior. *Psychological Inquiry, 11,* 227–268.

DeLuca, R. V., & Holborn, S. W. (1992). Effects of a variable-ratio reinforcement schedule with changing criteria on exercise in obese and nonobese boys. *Journal of Applied Behavior Analysis, 25,* 671–679.

Diener, C. I., & Dweck, C. S. (1978). An analysis of learned helplessness: Continuous changes in performance, strategy, and achievement cognitions following failure. *Journal of Personality and Social Psychology, 36,* 451–462.

Diener, C. I., & Dweck, C. S. (1980). An analysis of learned helplessness II: The processing of success. *Journal of Personality and Social Psychology, 39,* 940–952.

Dishman, R. K., Motl, R. W., Sallis, J. F., Dunn, A. L., Birnbaum, A. S., Welk, G. J., et al. (2005). Self-management strategies mediate self-efficacy and physical activity. *American Journal of Preventive Medicine, 29,* 10–18.

Dishman, R. K., Motl, R. W., Saunders, R., Felton, G., Ward, D. S., Dowda, M., et al. (2005). Enjoyment mediates effects of a school-based physical activity intervention. *Medicine & Science in Sports & Exercise, 37,* 478–487.

Doody, S. G., Bird, A. M., & Ross, D. (1985). The effect of auditory and visual models on acquisition of a timing task. *Human Movement Science, 4,* 271–281.

Downs, D. S., Graham, G. M., Yang, S., Bargainnier, S., & Vasil, J. (2006). Youth exercise intention and past exercise behavior: Examining the moderating influences of sex and meeting exercise recommendations. *Research Quarterly for Exercise and Sport, 77,* 91–99.

Downs, D. S., & Hausenblas, H. A. (2005). The theories of reasoned action and planned behavior applied to exercise: A meta-analytic update. *Journal of Physical Activity and Health, 2,* 76–97.

Duncan, M. J., Al-Nakeeb, Y., Nevill, A., & Jones, M. V. (2004). Body image and physical activity in British secondary school children. *European Physical Education Review, 10,* 243–260.

Duncan, S. C. (1993). The role of cognitive appraisal and friendship provisions in adolescents' affect and motivation toward activity in physical education. *Research Quarterly for Exercise and Sport, 64,* 314–323.

Duncan, S. C., Duncan, T. E., Strycker, L. A., & Chaumeton, N. R. (2002). Neighborhood physical activity opportunity: A multilevel contextual model. *Research Quarterly for Exercise and Sport, 73,* 457–463.

Duncan, S. C., Duncan, T. E., Strycker, L. A., & Chaumeton, N. R. (2004). A multilevel analysis of sibling physical activity. *Journal of Sport and Exercise Psychology, 26,* 57–68.

Duncan, T. E., & Duncan, S. C. (1991). A latent growth curve approach to investigating developmental dynamics and correlates of change in children's perceptions of physical competence. *Research Quarterly for Exercise and Sport, 64,* 314–323.

Dunn, J. C. (2000). Goal orientations, perceptions of the motivational climate, and perceived competence of children with movement difficulties. *Adapted Physical Activity Quarterly, 17,* 1–19.

Dunn, J. L. C., & Watkinson, E. J. (1994). A study of the relationship between physical awkwardness and children's perceptions of physical competence. *Adapted Physical Activity Quarterly, 11,* 275–283.

Dunton, G. F., Jamner, M. S., & Cooper, D. M. (2003). Physical self-concept in adolescent girls: Behavioral and physiological correlates. *Research Quarterly for Exercise and Sport, 74,* 360–365.

Dweck, C. S. (1980). Learned helplessness in sport. In C. H. Nadeau, W. R. Halliwell, K. M. Newell, & G. C. Roberts (Eds.), *Psychology of motor behavior and sport—1979* (pp. 1–11). Champaign, IL: Human Kinetics.

Dweck, C. S. (1986). Motivational processes affecting learning. *American Psychologist, 41,* 1040–1048.

Dweck, C. S. (1999). *Self-theories: Their role in motivation, personality, and development.* Philadelphia: Taylor & Francis/Psychology Press.

Dweck, C. S. (2002). The development of ability conceptions. In A. Wigfield & J. S. Eccles (Eds.), *Development of achievement motivation* (pp. 57–88). New York: Academic.

Dyson, B. P. (1995). Students' voices in two alternative elementary physical education programs. *Journal of Teaching in Physical Education, 14,* 394–407.

Dyson, B. P. (1996). Two physical education teachers' experience of Project Adventure. *Journal of Experiential Education, 19,* 90–97.

Dyson, B. (2001). Cooperative learning in an elementary physical education program. *Journal of Teaching in Physical Education, 20,* 264–281.

Dyson, B. (2002). The implementation of cooperative learning in an elementary physical education program. *Journal of Teaching in Physical Education, 22,* 69–85.

Dyson, B. P., & Harper, M. L. (1997). Cooperative learning in an elementary physical education program. *Research Quarterly for Exercise and Sport, 68* (Suppl.), A-68.

Dyson, B., & Strachan, K. (2000). Cooperative learning in a high school physical education program. *Waikato Journal of Education, 6,* 19–37.

Ebbeck, V., & Gibbons, S. L. (1998). The effect of a team building program on the self-conceptions of grade 6 and 7 physical education students. *Journal of Sport and Exercise Psychology, 20,* 300–310.

Ebbeck, V., & Stuart, M. E. (1993). Who determines what's important? Perceptions of competence and importance as predictors of self-esteem in youth football players. *Pediatric Exercise Science, 5,* 253–262.

Ebbeck, V., & Weiss, M. R. (1998). Determinants of children's self-esteem: An examination of perceived competence and affect in sport. *Pediatric Exercise Science, 10,* 285–298.

Eccles, J. S. (2005). Subjective task value and the Eccles et al. model of achievement-related choices. In A. J. Elliot & C. S. Dweck (Eds.), *Handbook of competence and motivation* (pp. 105–121). New York: Guilford Publications.

Eccles, J. S., Adler, T. F., Futterman, R., Goff, S. B., Kaczala, C. M., Meece, J. L., et al. (1983). Expectancies, values, and academic behaviors. In J. T. Spence (Ed.), *Achievement and achievement motivation* (pp. 75–146). San Francisco: W. H. Freeman.

Eccles, J. S., & Harold, R. D. (1991). Gender differences in sport involvement: Applying the Eccles' expectancy-value model. *Journal of Applied Sport Psychology, 3,* 7–35.

Eccles, J. S., & Wigfield, A. (2002). Motivational beliefs, values, and goals. *American Review of Psychology, 5,* 109–132.

Eccles, J., Wigfield, A., Harold, R. D., & Blumenfeld, P. (1993). Age and gender differences in children's self- and task perceptions during elementary school. *Child Development, 64,* 830–847.

Elliot, A. J., & McGregor, H. A. (2001). A 2 X 2 achievement goal framework. *Journal of Personality and Social Psychology, 80,* 501–519.

Emmanouel, C., Zervas, Y., & Vagenas, G. (1992). Effects of four physical education teaching methods on development of motor skill, self-concept, and social attitudes of fifth-grade children. *Perceptual and Motor Skills, 74,* 1151–1167.

Ennis, C. D. (1999). Creating a culturally relevant curriculum for disengaged girls. *Sport, Education and Society, 4,* 31–49.

Ennis, C. D., Solmon, M. A., Satina, B., Loftus, S. J., Mensch, J., & McCauley, M. T. (1999). Creating a sense of family in urban schools using the "Sport for Peace" curriculum. *Research Quarterly for Exercise and Sport, 70,* 273–285.

Entzion, B. J. (1991). A child's view of fairplay. *Strategies, 5*(2), 16–19.

Epstein, J. (1988). Effective schools or effective students? Dealing with diversity. In R. Haskins & B. MacRae (Eds.), *Policies for America's public schools* (pp. 89–126). Norwood, NJ: Ablex.

Epstein, J. (1989). Family structures and student motivation: A developmental perspective. In C. Ames & R. Ames (Eds.), *Research on motivation in education* (Vol. 3, pp. 259–295). New York: Academic Press.

Everhart, B., Kernodle, M., Ballard, K., McKey, C., Eason, B., & Weeks, M. (2005). Physical activity patterns of college students with and without high school physical education. *Perceptual and Motor Skills, 100,* 1114–1120.

Ewert, A., & Garvey, D. (2006). Philosophy and theory of adventure education. In D. Prouty, J. Panicucci, & R. Collinson (Eds.), *Adventure education: Theory and applications* (pp. 19–32). Champaign, IL: Human Kinetics.

Fairclough, S., & Stratton, G. (2005). Physical activity levels in middle and high school physical education: A review. *Pediatric Exercise Science, 17,* 217–236.

Fairclough, S., & Stratton, G. (2006). A review of physical activity levels during elementary school physical education. *Journal of Teaching in Physical Education, 25,* 239–257.

Fairclough, S., Stratton, G., & Baldwin, G. (2002). The contribution of secondary school physical education to lifetime physical activity. *European Physical Education Review, 8,* 69–84.

Faison-Hodge, J., & Porretta, D. L. (2004). Physical activity levels of students with mental retardation and students without disabilities. *Adapted Physical Activity Quarterly, 21,* 139–152.

Felton, G., Saunders, R. P., Ward, D. S., Dishman, R. K., Dowda, M., & Pate, R. R. (2005). Promoting physical activity in girls: A case study of one school's success. *Journal of School Health, 75,* 57–62.

Feltz, D. L. (1982). The effects of age and number of demonstrations on modeling of form and performance. *Research Quarterly for Exercise and Sport, 53,* 291–296.

Feltz, D. L. (1984). Self-efficacy as a cognitive mediator of athletic performance. In W. F. Straub & J. M. Williams (Eds.), *Cognitive sport psychology* (pp. 191–198). Lansing, MI: Sport Science Associates.

Feltz, D. L., & Brown, E. W. (1984). Perceived competence in soccer skills among youth soccer players. *Journal of Sport Psychology, 6,* 385–394.

Feltz, D. L., & Chase, M. A. (1998). The measurement of self-efficacy and confidence in sport. In J. L. Duda (Ed.), *Advances in sport and exercise psychology measurement* (pp. 65–80). Morgantown, WV: Fitness Information Technology.

Feltz, D. L., & Landers, D. M. (1977). Informational-motivational components of a model's demonstration. *Research Quarterly, 48,* 525–533.

Ferrer-Caja, E., & Weiss, M. R. (2000). Predictors of intrinsic motivation among adolescent students in physical education. *Research Quarterly for Exercise and Sport, 71*, 267–279.

Fielstein, E., Klein, M. S., Fischer, M., Hanan, C., Koburger, P., Schneider, M. J., et al. (1985). Self-esteem and causal attributions for success and failure in children. *Cognitive Therapy and Research, 9*, 381–398.

Fitterling, J. M., & Ayllon, T. (1983). Behavioral coaching in classical ballet. *Behavior Modification, 3*, 345–368.

Fleming, D. S., Mitchell, M. F., Coleman, M. M., & Gorecki, J. J. (1997). Gender and race differences in rural student preferences for physical education. *Research Quarterly for Exercise and Sport, 68*(Suppl.), A78–79.

Fleming, D. S., Mitchell, M., Gorecki, J. J., & Coleman, M. M. (1999). Students change and so do good programs: Addressing the interests of multicultural secondary students. *Journal of Physical Education, Recreation, and Dance, 70*(2), 79–83.

Flintoff, A., & Scraton, S. (2001). Stepping into active leisure? Young women's perceptions of active lifestyles and their experiences of school physical education. *Sport, Education, and Society, 6*, 5–21.

Fox, K. R. (1988). The self-esteem complex and youth fitness. *Quest, 40*, 230–246.

Fox, K. (1991). Motivating children for physical activity: Towards a healthier future. *Journal of Physical Education, Recreation, and Dance, 62*(7), 34–38.

Fredenburg, K. B., Lee, A. M., & Solmon, M. (2001). The effects of augmented feedback on students' perceptions and performance. *Research Quarterly for Exercise and Sport, 72*, 232–242.

Fredricks, J. A., & Eccles, J. S. (2002). Children's competence and value beliefs from childhood through adolescence: Growth trajectories in two male-sex-typed domains. *Developmental Psychology, 38*, 519–533.

Fredricks, J. A., & Eccles, J. S. (2005). Family socialization, gender, and sport motivation and involvement. *Journal of Sport and Exercise Psychology, 27*, 3–31.

Freedson, P. S., & Rowland, T. W. (1992). Youth activity versus youth fitness: Let's redirect our efforts. *Research Quarterly for Exercise and Sport, 63*, 133–136.

Fry, M. D. (2000a). A developmental analysis of children's and adolescents' understanding of luck and ability in the physical domain. *Journal of Sport and Exercise Psychology, 22*, 145–166.

Fry, M. D. (2000b). A developmental examination of children's understanding of task difficulty in the physical domain. *Journal of Applied Sport Psychology, 12*, 180–202.

Fry, M. D., & Duda, J. L. (1997). A developmental examination of children's understanding of effort and ability in the physical and academic domains. *Research Quarterly for Exercise and Sport, 68*, 331–344.

Fuller, F. F. (1969). Concerns of teachers: A developmental conceptualization. *American Educational Research Journal, 6*, 207–226.

Fulton, J. E., Shisler, J. L., Yore, M. M., & Caspersen, C. J. (2005). Active transportation to school: Findings from a national survey. *Research Quarterly for Exercise and Sport, 76*, 352–357.

Fung, L. (1993). Concerns among physical educators with varying years of teaching experience. *The Physical Educator, 50*(1), 1–12.

Gallagher, J. D., French, K. E., Thomas, K. T., & Thomas, J. R. (2002). Expertise in youth sport: Relations between knowledge and skill. In F. L. Smoll & R. E. Smith (Eds.), *Children and youth in sport: A biopsychosocial perspective* (pp. 475–500). Dubuque, IA: Kendall/Hunt.

George, T. R., Feltz, D. L., & Chase, M. A. (1992). Effects of model similarity on self-efficacy and muscular endurance: A second look. *Journal of Sport and Exercise Psychology, 14*, 237–248.

Gernigon, C., Fleurance, P., & Reine, B. (2000). Effects of uncontrollability and failure on the development of learned helplessness in perceptual-motor tasks. *Research Quarterly for Exercise and Sport, 71*, 44–54.

Gibbons, S. L., & Ebbeck, V. (1997). The effect of different teaching strategies on the moral development of physical education students. *Journal of Teaching in Physical Education, 17*, 85–98.

Gibbons, S. L., Ebbeck, V., & Weiss, M. R. (1995). Fair Play for Kids: Effects on the moral development of children in physical education. *Research Quarterly for Exercise and Sport, 66,* 247–255.

Giebink, M. P., & McKenzie, T. L. (1985). Teaching sportsmanship in physical education and recreation: An analysis of interventions and generalization effects. *Journal of Teaching in Physical Education, 4,* 167–177.

Gill, D. L. (2000). *Psychological dynamics of sport and exercise* (2nd ed.). Champaign, IL: Human Kinetics.

Gilligan, C. (1977). In a different voice: Women's conceptions of self and morality. *Harvard Educational Review, 17,* 481–517.

Goodway, J. D., & Rudisill, M. E. (1996). Influence of a motor skill intervention program on perceived competence of at-risk African American preschoolers. *Adapted Physical Activity Quarterly, 13,* 288–301.

Goodway, J. D., & Rudisill, M. E. (1997). Perceived physical competence and actual motor skill competence of African American preschool children. *Adapted Physical Activity Quarterly, 14,* 314–326.

Goudas, M., & Biddle, S. (1994). Perceived motivational climate and intrinsic motivation in school physical education classes. *European Journal of Psychology of Education, 9,* 241–250.

Goudas, M., Biddle, S. J. H., & Fox, K. R. (1994a). Achievement goal orientations and intrinsic motivation in physical fitness testing. *Pediatric Exercise Science, 6,* 159–167.

Goudas, M., Biddle, S., & Fox, K. (1994b). Perceived locus of causality, goal orientations, and perceived competence in school physical education classes. *British Journal of Educational Psychology, 64,* 453–463.

Gould, D., & Damarjian, N. (1996). Imagery training for peak performance. In J. L. Van Raalte & B. W. Brewer (Eds.), *Exploring sport and exercise psychology* (pp. 25–50). Washington, DC: American Psychological Association.

Gould, D. R., & Weiss, M. R. (1981). The effects of model similarity and model talk on self-efficacy and muscular endurance. *Journal of Sport Psychology, 3,* 17–29.

Graham, G., Holt/Hale, S. A., & Parker, M. (2004). *Children moving: A reflective approach to teaching physical education* (6th ed.). New York: McGraw-Hill.

Green, K. (2002). Physical education and 'the couch potato society'—part one. *European Journal of Physical Education, 7,* 95–107.

Green, K. (2004). Physical education, lifelong participation and the 'couch potato society.' *Physical Education and Sport Pedagogy, 9,* 73–86.

Griffin, L. L., Mitchell, S. A., & Oslin, J. L. (1997). *Teaching sport concepts and skills: A tactical games approach.* Champaign, IL: Human Kinetics.

Grineski, S. (1989). Children, games, and prosocial behavior—insight and connections. *Journal of Physical Education, Recreation, and Dance, 60*(8), 20–25.

Grineski, S. (1996). *Cooperative learning in physical education.* Champaign, IL: Human Kinetics.

Grineski, S. (1997). The effect of cooperative games on the promotion of prosocial behaviors of preschool students. *Research Quarterly for Exercise and Sport, 68*(Suppl.), A67–68.

Guan, J., Xiang, P., McBride, R., & Bruene, A. (2006). Achievement goals, social goals, and students' reported persistence and effort in high school physical education. *Journal of Teaching in Physical Education, 25,* 58–74.

Guillet, E., Sarrazin, P., Fontayne, P., & Brustad, R. J. (2006). Understanding female sport attrition in stereotypical male sport within the framework of Eccles' expectancy-value model. *Psychology of Women Quarterly, 30,* 358–368.

Guinn, B., Vincent, V., Semper, T., & Jorgensen, L. (2000). Activity involvement, goal perspective, and self-esteem among Mexican American adolescents. *Research Quarterly for Exercise and Sport, 71,* 308–311.

Guralnik, D. B. (Ed.). (1979). *Webster's new world dictionary* (Modern desk ed.). New York: Prentice-Hall.

Haan, N. (1977). *Coping and defending: Processes of self-environment organization.* New York: Academic Press.

Haan, N., Aerts, E., & Cooper, B. A. B. (1985). *On moral grounds: The search for practical morality.* New York: New York University Press.

Hagger, M., Ashford, B., & Stambulova, N. (1998). Russian and British children's physical self-perceptions and physical activity participation. *Pediatric Exercise Science, 10,* 137–152.

Hagger, M. S., Chatzisarantis, N. L. D., Barkoukis, V., Wang, J. C. K., Hein, V., Pihu, M., et al. (2007). Cross-cultural generalizability of the theory of planned behavior among young people in a physical activity context. *Journal of Sport and Exercise Psychology, 29,* 1–20.

Hagger, M. S., Chatzisarantis, N. L. D., Culverhouse, T., & Biddle, S. J. H. (2003). The processes by which perceived autonomy support in physical education promotes leisure-time physical activity intentions and behavior: A trans-contextual model. *Journal of Educational Psychology, 95,* 784–795.

Halliburton, A. L., & Weiss, M. R. (2002). Sources of competence information and perceived motivational climate among adolescent female gymnasts varying in skill level. *Journal of Sport and Exercise Psychology, 24,* 396–419.

Harter, S. (1978). Effectance motivation reconsidered. *Human Development, 21,* 34–64.

Harter, S. (1981). A model of intrinsic mastery motivation in children: Individual differences and developmental change. In W. A. Collins (Ed.), *Minnesota Symposium on Child Psychology* (Vol. 14, pp. 215–255). Hillsdale, NH: Erlbaum.

Harter, S. (1987). The determinants and mediational role of global self-worth in children. In N. Eisenberg (Ed.), *Contemporary topics in developmental psychology* (pp. 219–242). New York: Wiley.

Harter, S. (1999). *The construction of the self: A developmental perspective.* New York: Guilford Press.

Hassandra, M., Goudas, M., & Chroni, S. (2003). Examining factors associated with intrinsic motivation in physical education: A qualitative approach. *Psychology of Sport and Exercise, 4,* 211–223.

Hastie, P. A., & Buchanan, A. M. (2000). Teaching responsibility through sport education: Prospects of a coalition. *Research Quarterly for Exercise and Sport, 71,* 25–35.

Hastie, P. A., & Sharpe, T. (1999). Effects of a sport education curriculum on the positive social behavior of at-risk rural adolescent boys. *Journal of Education for Students Placed at Risk, 4,* 417–430.

Hebert, E. P., & Landin, D. (1994). Effects of a learning model and augmented feedback on tennis skill acquisition. *Research Quarterly for Exercise and Sport, 65,* 250–257.

Hellison, D. (2003). *Teaching responsibility through physical activity* (2nd ed.). Champaign, IL: Human Kinetics.

Hellison, D., Cutforth, N., Kallusky, J., Martinek, T., Parker, M., & Stiehl, J. (2000). *Youth development and physical activity: Linking universities and communities.* Champaign, IL: Human Kinetics.

Hellison, D. R., Martinek, T. J., & Cutforth, N. J. (1996). Beyond violence prevention in inner-city physical activity programs. *Peace and Conflict: Journal of Peace Psychology, 2,* 321–337.

Hidi, S. (2000). An interest researcher's perspective: The effects of extrinsic and intrinsic factors on motivation. In C. Sansone & J. M. Harackiewicz (Eds.), *Intrinsic and extrinsic motivation: The search for optimal motivation and performance* (pp. 309–339). San Diego, CA: Academic Press.

Hidi, S., & Anderson, V. (1992). Situational interest and its impact on reading and expository writing. In K. A. Renninger, S. Hidi, & A. Krapp (Eds.), *The role of interest in learning and development* (pp. 215–238). Hillsdale, NJ: Erlbaum.

Hildebrand, K. M., & Johnson, D. J. (2001). Determinants of college physical activity class enrollment: Implications for high school physical education. *Physical Educator, 58*(1), 51–56.

Hogan, A., McLellan, L., & Bauman, A. (2000). Health promotion needs of young people with disabilities—a population study. *Disability and Rehabilitation, 22,* 352–357.

Horn, T. S. (1984). Expectancy effects in the interscholastic athletic setting: Methodological considerations. *Journal of Sport Psychology, 6,* 60–76.

Horn, T. S. (1985). Coaches' feedback and changes in children's perceptions of their physical competence. *Journal of Educational Psychology, 77,* 174–186.

Horn, T. S. (2004). Developmental perspectives on self-perceptions in children and adolescents. In M. R. Weiss (Ed.), *Developmental sport and exercise psychology: A lifespan perspective* (pp. 101–143). Morgantown, WV: Fitness Information Technology.

Horn, T. S., Glenn, S. D., & Wentzell, A. B. (1993). Sources of information underlying personal ability judgments in high school athletes. *Pediatric Exercise Science, 5,* 263–274.

Horn, T. S., & Hasbrook, C. A. (1986). Informational components influencing children's perceptions of their physical competence. In M. R. Weiss & D. Gould (Eds.), *Sport for children and youths* (pp. 81–88). Champaign, IL: Human Kinetics.

Horn, T. S., & Hasbrook, C. A. (1987). Psychological characteristics and the criteria children use for self-evaluation. *Journal of Sport Psychology, 9,* 208–221.

Horn, T. S., Lox, C. L., & Labrador, F. (2001). The self-fulfilling prophecy theory: When coaches' expectations become reality. In J. M. Williams (Ed.), *Applied sport psychology: Personal growth to peak performance* (4th ed., pp. 63–81). Mountain View, CA: Mayfield.

Horn, T. S., & Weiss, M. R. (1991). A developmental analysis of children's self-ability judgments. *Pediatric Exercise Science, 3,* 312–328.

Hume, K. M., & Crossman, J. (1992). Musical reinforcement of practice behaviors among competitive swimmers. *Journal of Applied Behavior Analysis, 25,* 665–670.

Hume, K. M., Martin, G. L., Gonzalez, P., Cracklen, C., & Genthon, S. (1985). A self-monitoring feedback package for improving freestyle figure skating practice behaviors. *Journal of Sport Psychology, 7,* 333–345.

Iannotti, R. J., Sallis, J. F., Chen, R., Broyles, S. L., Elder, J. P., & Nader, P. R. (2005). Prospective analyses of relationships between mothers' and children's physical activity. *Journal of Physical Activity and Health, 2,* 16–34.

Ille, A., & Cadopi, M. (1999). Memory for movement sequences in gymnastics: Effects of age and skill level. *Journal of Motor Behavior, 31,* 290–300.

Jacobs, J. E., Lanza, S., Osgood, D. W., Eccles, J. S., & Wigfield, A. (2002). Changes in children's self-competence and values: Gender and domain differences across grades one through twelve. *Child Development, 73,* 509–527.

Jago, R., Baranowski, T., & Harris, M. (2006). Relationships between GIS environmental features and adolescent male physical activity: GIS coding differences. *Journal of Physical Activity and Health, 3,* 230–242.

Jago, R., Baranowski, T., Thompson, D., Baranowski, J., & Greaves, K. A. (2005). Sedentary behavior, not TV viewing, predicts physical activity among 3- to 7-year-old children. *Pediatric Exercise Science, 17,* 364–376.

James, W. (1892). *Psychology: Briefer course.* New York: Holt.

Janelle, C. M., Champenoy, J. D., Coombes, S. A., & Mousseau, M. B. (2003). Mechanisms of attentional cueing during observational learning to facilitate skill acquisition. *Journal of Sports Sciences, 21,* 825–838.

Jantz, R. K. (1975). Moral thinking in male elementary pupils as reflected by perception of basketball rules. *Research Quarterly, 46,* 414–421.

Jewett, A. E., Bain, L. L., & Ennis, C. D. (1995). *The curriculum process in physical education* (2nd ed.). Boston: WCB McGraw-Hill.

Johns, D. P., & Ha, A. S. (1999). Home and recess physical activity of Hong Kong children. *Research Quarterly for Exercise and Sport, 70,* 319–323.

Johnson, M., & Ward, P. (2001). Effects of class-wide peer tutoring on correct performance of striking skills in 3rd grade physical education. *Journal of Teaching in Physical Education, 20,* 247–263.

Kahan, D. (2003). Islam and physical activity: Implications for American sport and physical educators. *Journal of Physical Education, Recreation, and Dance, 74*(3), 48–54.

Kahan, D. (2004). Relationships among religiosity, physical activity, and sedentary behavior in Jewish adolescents. *Pediatric Exercise Science, 16,* 54–63.

Kahn, E. B., Ramsey, L. R., Brownson, R. C., Heath, G. W., Howze, E. H., Powell, K. E., et al. (2002). The effectiveness of interventions to increase physical activity. *American Journal of Preventive Medicine, 22*(4S), 73–107.

Kalakanis, L. E., Goldfield, G. S., Paluch, R. A., & Epstein, L. H. (2001). Parental activity as a determinant of activity level and patterns of activity in obese children. *Research Quarterly for Exercise and Sport, 72,* 202–209.

Kann, L., & Warren, C. W. (1996). Youth risk behavior surveillance—United States, 1995. *Journal of School Health, 10,* 365–377.

Karper, W. B., & Martinek, T. J. (1983). The differential influence of instructional factors on motor performance among handicapped and non-handicapped children in mainstreamed physical education classes. *Educational Research Quarterly, 8*(3), 40–46.

Karper, W. B., & Martinek, T. J. (1985). Teachers' expectations in a mainstreamed physical activity program. *Palaestra, 1*(3), 19–21, 41.

Katz, R. C., & Singh, N. N. (1986). Increasing recreational behavior in mentally retarded children. *Behavior Modification, 10,* 508–519.

Kauss, D. R. (1980). *Peak performance.* Englewood Cliffs, NJ: Prentice-Hall.

Kavussanu, M., & Roberts, G. C. (1996). Motivation in physical activity contexts: The relationship of perceived motivational climate to intrinsic motivation and self-efficacy. *Journal of Sport and Exercise Psychology, 18,* 264–280.

Kavussanu, M., & Roberts, G. C. (2001). Moral functioning in sport: An achievement goal perspective. *Journal of Sport and Exercise Psychology, 23,* 37–54.

Keller, F. S. (1968). Good-bye, teacher. *Journal of Applied Behavior Analysis, 1,* 79–89.

Keller, F. S., & Sherman, J. G. (1982). *The PSI handbook: Essays on personalized instruction.* Lawrence, KS: T. R. I. Publications.

Kimiecik, J. C., Horn, T. S., & Shurin, C. S. (1996). Relationships among children's beliefs, perceptions of their parents' beliefs, and their moderate-to-vigorous physical activity. *Research Quarterly for Exercise and Sport, 67,* 324–336.

Kimm, S. Y. S., Glynn, N. W., McMahon, R. P., Voorhees, C. C., Striegel-Moore, R. H., & Daniels, S. R. (2006). Self-perceived barriers to activity participation among sedentary adolescent girls. *Medicine & Science in Sports & Exercise, 38,* 534–540.

Kitsantas, A., Zimmerman, B. J., & Cleary, T. (2000). The role of observation and emulation in the development of athletic self-regulation. *Journal of Educational Psychology, 92,* 811–817.

Klomsten, A. T., Marsh, H. W., & Skaalvik, E. M. (2005). Adolescents' perceptions of masculine and feminine values in sport and physical education: A study of gender differences. *Sex Roles: A Journal of Research, 52,* 625–636.

Kohlberg, L. (1976). Moral stages and moralization: The cognitive-developmental approach. In T. Lickona (Ed.), *Moral development and behavior: Theory, research, and social issues* (pp. 31–53). New York: Holt, Rinehart & Winston.

Koka, A., & Hein, V. (2003). Perceptions of teacher's feedback and learning environment as predictors of intrinsic motivation in physical education. *Psychology of Sport and Exercise, 4,* 333–346.

Kolb, D. A. (1984). *Experiential learning.* Englewood Cliffs, NJ: Prentice-Hall.

Komaki, J., & Barnett, F. (1977). A behavioral approach to coaching football: Improving the play execution of the offensive backfield on a youth football team. *Journal of Applied Behavioral Analysis, 10,* 657–664.

Koop, S., & Martin, G. L. (1983). Evaluation of a coaching strategy to reduce swimming stroke errors with beginning age-group swimmers. *Journal of Applied Behavior Analysis, 16,* 447–460.

Kowalski, E. M., & Sherrill, C. (1992). Motor sequencing of boys with learning disabilities: Modeling and verbal rehearsal strategies. *Adapted Physical Activity Quarterly, 9,* 261–272.

Kozub, F. M. (2002). Expectations, task persistence, and attributions in children with mental retardation during integrated physical education. *Adapted Physical Activity Quarterly, 19,* 334–349.

Kozub, F. M. (2003). Explaining physical activity in individuals with mental retardation: An exploratory study. *Education and Training in Developmental Disabilities, 38,* 302–313.

Krapp, A., Hidi, S., & Renninger, K. A. (1992). Interest, learning, and development. In K. A. Renninger, S. Hidi, & A. Krapp (Eds.), *The role of interest in learning and development* (pp. 3–25). Hillsdale, NJ: Lawrence Erlbaum.

Kraut, A., Melamed, S., Gofer, D., & Froom, P. (2003). Effect of school age sports on leisure time physical activity in adults: The CORDIS Study. *Medicine & Science in Sports & Exercise, 35,* 2038–2042.

addux, J. E., & Meier, L. J. (1995). Self-efficacy and depression. In J. E. Maddux (Ed.), *Self-efficacy, adaptation, and adjustment: Theory, research, and application* (pp. 143–172). New York: Plenum Press.

agill, R. A. (1993). Modeling and verbal feedback influences on skill learning. *International Journal of Sport Psychology, 24*, 358–369.

agill, R. A. (2004). *Motor learning and control: Concepts and applications* (7th ed.). New York: McGraw-Hill.

agill, R. A., & Schoenfelder-Zohdi, B. (1996). A visual model and knowledge of performance as sources of information for learning a rhythmic gymnastics skill. *International Journal of Sport Psychology, 27*, 7–22.

alina, R. M. (2001). Adherence to physical activity from childhood to adulthood: A perspective from tracking studies. *Quest, 53*, 346–355.

arsh, H. W. (1989). Age and sex effects in multiple dimensions of self-concept: Preadolescence to early adulthood. *Journal of Educational Psychology, 81*, 417–430.

arsh, H. W. (1998). Age and gender effects in physical self-concepts for adolescent elite athletes and nonathletes: A multicohort-multioccasion design. *Journal of Sport and Exercise Psychology, 20*, 237–259.

arsh, H. W., Papaioannou, A., & Theodorakis, Y. (2006). Causal ordering of physical self-concept and exercise behavior: Reciprocal effects model and the influence of physical education teachers. *Health Psychology, 25*, 316–328.

artens, R. (1987). *Coaches guide to sports psychology*. Champaign, IL: Human Kinetics.

artens, R., Burwitz, L., & Zuckerman, J. (1976). Modeling effects on motor performance. *Research Quarterly, 47*, 277–291.

artens, R., Christina, R. W., Harvey, J. S., & Sharkey, B. J. (1981). *Coaching young athletes*. Champaign, IL: Human Kinetics.

artin, G., & Pear, J. (2003). *Behavior modification: What it is and how to do it*. Upper Saddle River, NJ: Prentice-Hall.

artin, J. J., Kulinna, P. H., McCaughtry, N., Cothran, D., Dake, J., & Fahoome, G. (2005). The theory of planned behavior: Predicting phys-ical activity and cardiorespiratory fitness in African American children. *Journal of Sport and Exercise Psychology, 27*, 456–469.

Martin, J. J., Oliver, K., & McCaughtry, N. (2007). The theory of planned behavior: Predicting physical activity in Mexican American children. *Journal of Sport and Exercise Psychology, 29*, 225–238.

Martinek, T. J. (1981). Physical attractiveness: Effects of teacher expectations and dyadic interactions in elementary age children. *Journal of Sport Psychology, 3*, 196–205.

Martinek, T. J. (1988). Confirmation of a teacher expectancy model: Student perceptions and causal attributions of teaching behaviors. *Research Quarterly for Exercise and Sport, 59*, 118–126.

Martinek, T. J. (1989). Children's perceptions of teaching behaviors: An attributional model for explaining teacher expectancy effects. *Journal of Teaching in Physical Education, 8*, 318–328.

Martinek, T. J. (1996). Fostering hope in youth: A model for explaining learned helplessness in physical activity. *Quest, 48*, 409–421.

Martinek, T. J., & Griffith, J. B. (1994). Learned helplessness in physical education: A developmental study of causal attributions and task persistence. *Journal of Teaching in Physical Education, 13*, 108–122.

Martinek, T. J., & Johnson, S. (1979). Teacher expectations: Effects on dyadic interactions and self-concept in elementary age children. *Research Quarterly, 50*, 60–70.

Martinek, T. J., & Karper, W. B. (1981). Teachers' expectations for handicapped and nonhandicapped children in mainstreamed physical education classes. *Perceptual and Motor Skills, 53*, 327–330.

Martinek, T. J., & Karper, W. B. (1982). Canonical relationships among motor ability, expression of effort, teacher expectations and dyadic interactions in elementary age children. *Journal of Teaching in Physical Education, 2*, 26–39.

Martinek, T. J., & Karper, W. B. (1983). The influence of teacher expectations on ALT in physical education instruction. *Journal of Teaching in Physical Education, Monograph 1*, 48–52.

Kunesh, M. A., Hasbrook, C. A., & Lewthwaite, R. (1992). Physical activity socialization: Peer interactions and affective responses among a sample of sixth grade girls. *Sociology of Sport Journal, 9,* 385–396.

Lai, Q., Shea, C. H., Bruechert, L., & Little, M. (2002). Auditory model enhances relative-timing learning. *Journal of Motor Behavior, 34,* 299–307.

Lai, Q., Shea, C. H., & Little, M. (2000). Effects of modeled auditory information on a sequential timing task. *Research Quarterly for Exercise and Sport, 71,* 349–356.

Landers, D. M., & Landers, D. M. (1973). Teacher versus peer models: Effects of model's presence and performance level on motor behavior. *Journal of Motor Behavior, 5,* 129–139.

Lee, A. M., Keh, N. C., & Magill, R. A. (1993). Instructional effects of teacher feedback in physical education. *Journal of Teaching in Physical Education, 12,* 228–243.

Lee, T. D., & White, M. A. (1990). Influence of an unskilled model's practice schedule on observational motor learning. *Human Movement Science, 9,* 349–367.

Lepper, M. R., & Greene, D. (1975). Turning play into work: Effects of adult surveillance and extrinsic rewards on children's intrinsic motivation. *Journal of Personality and Social Psychology, 28,* 129–137.

Lewis, S. (1974). A comparison of behavior therapy techniques in the reduction of fearful avoidance behavior. *Behavior Therapy, 5,* 648–655.

Li, W., Lee, A. M., & Solmon, M. A. (2005). Relationships among dispositional ability conceptions, intrinsic motivation, perceived competence, experience, persistence, and performance. *Journal of Teaching in Physical Education, 24,* 51–65.

Lieberman, L. J., & MacVicar, J. M. (2003). Play and recreational habits of youths who are deaf-blind. *Journal of Visual Impairment & Blindness, 97,* 755–768.

Lirgg, C. D. (1993). Effects of same-sex versus coeducational physical education on the self-perceptions of middle and high school students. *Research Quarterly for Exercise and Sport, 64,* 324–334.

Lirgg, C. D., & Feltz, D. L. (1991). Teac[ ] peer models revisited: Effects on mo[ ] mance and self-efficacy. *Research Q[ ] Exercise and Sport, 62,* 217–224.

Li-Wei, Z., Qi-Wei, M., Orlick, T., & Zit[ ] L. (1992). The effect of mental-imag[ ] on performance enhancement with 7[ ] children. *The Sport Psychologist, 6, [ ]*

Lloyd, J., & Fox, K. R. (1992). Achievem[ ] and motivation to exercise in adolesc[ ] preliminary intervention study. *Britis[ ] Physical Education Research Supplen[ ]* 12–16.

Logsdon, B. J., Barrett, K. R., Ammons, [ ] M. R., Halverson, L. E., McGee, R.[ ] (1984). *Physical education for childre[ ] on the teaching process.* Philadelphia[ ] Febiger.

Loucaides, C. A., & Chedzoy, S. M. (200[ ] influencing Cypriot children's physica[ ] levels. *Sport, Education, and Society,[ ]* 101–118.

Loucaides, C. A., Chedzoy, S. M., Bennett[ ] Walshe, K. (2004). Correlates of phys[ ] in a Cypriot sample of sixth-grade chi[ ] *atric Exercise Science, 16,* 25–36.

Luke, M. D., & Sinclair, G. D. (1991). Ge[ ] ences in adolescents' attitudes towar[ ] physical education. *Journal of Teachin[ ] cal Education, 11,* 31–46.

Lund, J. L., & Kirk, M. F. (2002). *Perform[ ] assessment for middle and high school[ ] education.* Human Kinetics: Champaig[ ]

Macdonald, D., Rodger, S., Ziviani, J., Jenk[ ] Batch, J., & Jones, J. (2004). Physical[ ] as a dimension of family life for lowe[ ] school children. *Sport, Education, and [ ]* 307–325.

Maddison, R., & Prapavessis, H. (2006). E[ ] behavior among New Zealand adolesc[ ] of the transtheoretical model. *Pediatric [ ] Science, 18,* 351–363.

Maddux, J. E. (1995). Self-efficacy theory: A[ ] duction. In J. E. Maddux (Ed.), *Self-ef[ ] adaptation, and adjustment: Theory, res[ ] and application* (pp. 3–33). New York: [ ] Press.

Martinek, T. J., & Karper, W. B. (1984a). The effects of noncompetitive and competitive social climates on teacher expectancy effects in elementary physical education classes. *Journal of Sport Psychology, 8,* 408–421.

Martinek, T. J., & Karper, W. B. (1984b). Multivariate relationships of specific impression cues with teacher expectations and dyadic interactions in elementary physical education classes. *Research Quarterly for Exercise and Sport, 55,* 32–40.

Martinek, T. J., & Karper, W. B. (1986). Motor ability and instructional contexts: Effects on teacher expectations and dyadic interactions in elementary physical education classes. *Journal of Classroom Interaction, 21*(2), 16–25.

Martinek, T., & Williams, L. (1997). Goal orientation and task persistence in learned helplessness and mastery oriented students in middle school physical education classes. *International Sports Journal, 1,* 63–76.

Martinek, T. J., Zaichkowsky, L. D., & Cheffers, J. T. F. (1977). Decision-making in elementary age children: Effects on motor skills and self-concept. *The Research Quarterly, 48,* 349–357.

Masser, L. S. (1990). Teaching for affective learning in physical education. *Journal of Physical Education, Recreation, and Dance, 62*(7), 18–19.

Masser, L. S. (1993). Critical cues help first-grade students' achievement in handstands and forward rolls. *Journal of Teaching in Physical Education, 12,* 301–312.

Matanin, M., & Tannehill, D. (1994). Assessment and grading in physical education. *Journal of Teaching in Physical Education, 13,* 395–405.

McAuley, E. (1985). Modeling and self-efficacy: A test of Bandura's model. *Journal of Sport Psychology, 7,* 283–295.

McBride, R. E. (1984). An intensive study of a systematic teacher training model in physical education. *Journal of Teaching in Physical Education, 4,* 3–16.

McBride, R. E. (1993). The TCQ-PE: An adaptation of the Teacher Concerns Questionnaire instrument to a physical education setting. *Journal of Teaching in Physical Education, 12,* 188–196.

McBride, R. E., Boggess, T. E., & Griffey, D. C. (1986). Concerns of inservice physical education teachers as compared with Fuller's concern model. *Journal of Teaching in Physical Education, 5,* 149–156.

McCullagh, P. (1987). Model similarity effects on motor performance. *Journal of Sport Psychology, 9,* 249–260.

McCullagh, P., & Caird, J. K. (1990). Correct and learning models and the use of model knowledge of results in the acquisition and retention of a motor skill. *Journal of Human Movement Studies, 18,* 107–116.

McCullagh, P., & Little, W. S. (1989). A comparison of modalities in modeling. *Human Performance, 2,* 107–116.

McCullagh, P., & Meyer, K. N. (1997). Learning versus correct models: Influence of model type on the learning of a free-weight squat. *Research Quarterly for Exercise and Sport, 68,* 56–61.

McCullagh, P., Stiehl, J., & Weiss, M. R. (1990). Developmental modeling effects on the quantitative and qualitative aspects of motor performance. *Research Quarterly for Exercise and Sport, 61,* 344–350.

McCullagh, P., & Weiss, M. R. (2002). Observational learning: The forgotten psychological method in sport psychology. In J. L. Van Raalte & B. W. Brewer (Eds.), *Exploring sport and exercise psychology* (2nd ed., pp. 131–149). Washington, DC: American Psychological Association.

McKenzie, T. L. (2001). Promoting physical activity in youth: Focus on middle school environments. *Quest, 53,* 326–334.

McKenzie, T. L., & Rosengard, P. F. (2000). *Sports, play, and active recreation for kids! Physical education program grades 3–6.* San Diego, CA: San Diego State University Foundation.

McKenzie, T. L., & Rushall, B. S. (1974). Effects of self-recording on attendance and performance in a competitive swimming training environment. *Journal of Applied Behavior Analysis, 7,* 199–206.

McKenzie, T. L., Sallis, J. F., Broyles, S. L., Zives, M. M., Nader, P. R., Berry, C. C., et al. (2002). Childhood movement skills: Predictors of physical activity in Anglo American and Mexican American adolescents? *Research Quarterly for Exercise and Sport, 73,* 238–244.

McKenzie, T. L., Sallis, J. F., & Nader, P. R. (1991). SOFIT: System for observing fitness instruction time. *Journal of Teaching in Physical Education, 11,* 195–205.

McKiddie, B., & Maynard, I. W. (1997). Perceived competence of school children in physical education. *Journal of Teaching in Physical Education, 16,* 324–339.

Meaney, K. S. (1994). Developmental modeling effects on the acquisition, retention, and transfer of a novel motor skill. *Research Quarterly for Exercise and Sport, 65,* 31–39.

Meaney, K. S., & Edwards, R. (1996). Ensenanzas en un gimnasio: An investigation of modeling and verbal rehearsal on the motor performance of Hispanic limited English proficient children. *Research Quarterly for Exercise and Sport, 67,* 44–51.

Meaney, K. S., Griffin, L. K., & Hart, M. A. (2005). The effect of model similarity on girls' motor performance. *Journal of Teaching in Physical Education, 24,* 165–178.

Meek, G. A. (1996). The Teacher Concerns Questionnaire with preservice physical educators in Great Britain: Being concerned with concerns. *Journal of Teaching in Physical Education, 16,* 20–29.

Meers, A., & Blankenship, B. T. (2005). Developing sportsmanship in elementary physical education through social learning. *Indiana AAHPERD Journal, 34*(3), 6–9.

Mender, J., Kerr, R., & Orlick, T. (1982). A cooperative games program for learning disabled children. *International Journal of Sport Psychology, 13,* 222–233.

Metzler, M. W. (2005). *Instructional models for physical education* (2nd ed.). Scottsdale, AZ: Holcomb Hathaway.

Metzler, M. W., & Sebolt, D. (1998). *Instructor's manual for the Personalized Sport Instruction Series.* Dubuque, IA: Kendall Hunt.

Miserandino, M. (1998). Attributional retraining as a method of improving athletic performance. *Journal of Sport Behavior, 21,* 286–297.

Mitchell, M. (1993). Situational interest: Its multifaceted structure in the secondary school mathematics classroom. *Journal of Educational Psychology, 85,* 424–436.

Mitchell, M. F., Fleming, D. S., Coleman, M. M., & Gorecki, J. J. (1997). Gender and race differences in urban student preferences for physical education. *Research Quarterly for Exercise and Sport, 68*(Suppl.), A84–85.

Mitchell, S. A. (1996). Relationships between perceived learning environment and intrinsic motivation in middle school physical education. *Journal of Teaching in Physical Education, 15,* 369–383.

Mitchell, S. A., Oslin, J. L., & Griffin, L. L. (2003). *Sport foundations for elementary physical education: A tactical games approach.* Champaign, IL: Human Kinetics.

Morgan, C. F., McKenzie, T. L., Sallis, J. F., Broyles, S. L., Zive, M. M., & Nader, P. R. (2003). Personal, social, and environmental correlates of physical activity in a bi-ethnic sample of adolescents. *Pediatric Exercise Science, 15,* 288–301.

Morgan, L. K., Griffin, J., & Heyward, V. H. (1996). Ethnicity, gender, and experience effects on attributional dimensions. *The Sport Psychologist, 10,* 4–16.

Mosston, M., & Ashworth, S. (2002). *Teaching physical education* (5th ed.). San Francisco: Benjamin Cummings.

Mota, J., Ribeiro., J., Santos, M. P., & Gomes, H. (2006). Obesity, physical activity, computer use, and TV viewing in Portuguese adolescents. *Pediatric Exercise Science, 17,* 113–121.

Mullan, E., Albinson, J., & Markland, D. (1997). Children's perceived physical competence at different categories of physical activity. *Pediatric Exercise Science, 9,* 237–242.

Mummery, W. K., Spence, J. C., & Hudec, J. C. (2000). Understanding physical activity intention in Canadian school children and youth: An application of the theory of planned behavior. *Research Quarterly for Exercise and Sport, 71,* 116–124.

Nahas, M. V., Goldfine, B., & Collins, M. A. (2003). Determinants of physical activity in adolescents and young adults: The basis for high school and college physical education to promote active lifestyles. *The Physical Educator, 60*(1), 42–56.

National Association for Sport and Physical Education. (2000). *Appropriate practices for elementary school physical education.* Reston, VA: Author.

National Association for Sport and Physical Education. (2001). *Appropriate practices for middle school physical education.* Reston, VA: Author.

National Association for Sport and Physical Education. (2004a). *Appropriate practices for high school physical education.* Reston, VA: Author.

National Association for Sport and Physical Education. (2004b). *Moving into the future: National standards for physical education* (2nd ed). Reston, VA: Author.

National Association for Sport and Physical Education (2004c). *Position on dodgeball in physical education.* Retrieved October 28, 2005, from www.aahperd.org/naspe/template.cfm?template=position-papers.html.

Nicholls, J. G. (1978). The development of the concepts of effort and ability, perception of academic attainment, and the understanding that difficult tasks require more ability. *Child Development, 49*(3), 800–814.

Nicholls, J. G. (1984). Achievement motivation: Conceptions of ability, subjective experience, task choice, and performance. *Psychological Review, 91,* 328–346.

Nicholls, J. G. (1989). *The competitive ethos and democratic education.* Cambridge, MA: Harvard University Press.

Nicholls, J. G., & Miller, A. T. (1984). Reasoning about the ability of self and others: A developmental study. *Child Development, 55,* 1990–1999.

Nigg, C. R., & Courneya, K. S. (1998). Transtheoretical model: Examining adolescent exercise behavior. *Journal of Adolescent Health, 22,* 214–224.

Norman, G. J., Nutter, S. K., Ryan, S., Sallis, J. F., Calfas, K. J., & Patrick, K. (2006). Community design and access to recreational facilities as correlates of adolescent physical activity and body-mass index. *Journal of Physical Activity and Health, 3*(Suppl 1), S118–S128.

Ntoumanis, N. (2001). A self-determination approach to the understanding of motivation in physical education. *British Journal of Educational Psychology, 71,* 225–242.

Ntoumanis, N. (2002). Motivational clusters in a sample of British physical education classes. *Psychology of Sport and Exercise, 3,* 177–194.

Ntoumanis, N. (2005). A prospective study of participation in optional school physical education using a self-determination theory framework. *Journal of Educational Psychology, 97,* 444–453.

Ntoumanis, N., Pensgaard, A. M., Martin, C., & Pipe, K. (2004). An idiographic analysis of amotivation in compulsory school physical education. *Journal of Sport and Exercise Psychology, 26,* 197–214.

Oliver, M., Schofield, G., & McEvoy, E. (2006). An integrated curriculum approach to increasing habitual physical activity in children: A feasibility study. *Journal of School Health, 76,* 74–79.

Orbach, I., Singer, R. N., & Murphey, M. (1997). Changing attributions with an attribution training technique related to basketball dribbling. *The Sport Psychologist, 11,* 294–304.

Orbach, I., Singer, R. N., & Price, S. (1999). An attribution training program and achievement in sport. *The Sport Psychologist, 13,* 69–82.

Orlick, T. (1981a). Cooperative play socialization among preschool children. *Journal of Individual Psychology, 37,* 54–63.

Orlick, T. D. (1981b). Positive socialization via cooperative games. *Developmental Psychology, 17,* 426–429.

Orlick, T. D., & Mosher, R. (1978). Extrinsic awards and participant motivation in a sport related task. *International Journal of Sport Psychology, 9,* 27–39.

Pan, C., & Frey, G. C. (2005). Identifying physical activity determinants in youth with autistic spectrum disorders. *Journal of Physical Activity and Health, 2,* 412–422.

Pangrazi, R. P., Beighle, A., & Sidman, C. L. (2003). *Pedometer power: 67 lessons for k–12.* Champaign, IL: Human Kinetics.

Papaioannou, A. (1994). Development of a questionnaire to measure achievement orientations in physical education. *Research Quarterly for Exercise and Sport, 65,* 11–20.

Papaioannou, A. (1995). Differential perceptual and motivational patterns when different goals are adopted. *Journal of Sport and Exercise Psychology, 17,* 18–34.

Papaioannou, A. (1998a). Goal perspectives, reasons for being disciplined, and self-reported discipline in physical education lessons. *Journal of Teaching in Physical Education, 17,* 421–441.

Papaioannou, A. (1998b). Students' perceptions of the physical education class environment for boys and girls and the perceived motivational climate. *Research Quarterly for Exercise and Sport, 69,* 267–275.

Papaioannou, A., & Kouli, O. (1999). The effect of task structure, perceived motivational climate, and goal orientations on students' task involvement and anxiety. *Journal of Applied Sport Psychology, 11,* 51–71.

Papaioannou, A., & Macdonald, A. I. (1993). Goal perspectives and purposes of physical education as perceived by Greek adolescents. *Physical Education Review, 16,* 41–48.

Papaioannou, A., & Theodorakis, Y. (1996). A test of three models for the prediction of intention for participation in physical education lessons. *International Journal of Sport Psychology, 27,* 383–399.

Parish, L. E., & Treasure, D. C. (2003). Physical activity and situational motivation in physical education: Influence of the motivational climate and perceived ability. *Research Quarterly for Exercise and Sport, 74,* 173–182.

Pate, R. R., Davis, M. G., Robinson, T. N., Stone, E. J., McKenzie, T. L., & Young, J. C. (2006, August 14). Promoting physical activity in children and youth: A leadership role for schools. *Circulation, 114,* 1–11. Retrieved August 15, 2006, from http://circ.ahajournals.org/subscriptions/.

Pate, R. R., Small, M. W., Ross, J. G., Young, J. C., Flint, K. H., & Warren, C. S. (1995). School physical education. *Journal of School Health, 63,* 312–318.

Patrick, C. A., Ward, P., & Crouch, D. W. (1998). Effects of holding students accountable for social behaviors during volleyball games in elementary physical education. *Journal of Teaching in Physical Education, 17,* 143–156.

Patrick, H., Ryna, A. M., Alfeld-Liro, C., Fredricks, J. A., Hruda, L. Z., & Eccles, J. S. (1999). Adolescents' commitment to developing talent: The role of peers in continuing motivation for sports and arts. *Journal of Youth and Adolescence, 28,* 741–763.

Patterson, S. B., Anderson, A., & Klavora, P. (1997). Investigating the relationships between physical skill development and active living: A review of literature. *CAHPERD Journal,* Winter, 4–9.

Paxton, R. J., Estabrooks, P. A., & Dzewaltowski, D. (2004). Attraction to physical activity mediates the relationship between perceived competence and physical activity in youth. *Research Quarterly for Exercise and Sport, 75,* 107–111.

Pellet, T. L., & Harrison, J. M. (1995). The influence of a teacher's specific, congruent, and corrective feedback on female junior high school students' immediate volleyball practice success. *Journal of Teaching in Physical Education, 15,* 53–63.

Pollock, B. J., & Lee, T. D. (1992). Effects of the model's skill level on observational motor learning. *Research Quarterly for Exercise and Sport, 63,* 25–29.

Pope, C. C., & Grant, B. C. (1996). Student experiences in sport education. *Waikato Journal of Education, 2,* 103–118.

Porretta, D. L., & Surburg, P. R. (1995). Imagery and physical practice in the acquisition of gross motor timing of coincidence by adolescents with mild mental retardation. *Perceptual and Motor Skills, 80,* 1171–1183.

Portman, P. A. (1995). Who is having fun in physical education classes? Experiences of sixth-grade students in elementary and middle schools. *Journal of Teaching in Physical Education, 14,* 445–453.

Powers, H. S., Conway, T. L., McKenzie, T. L., Sallis, J. F., & Marshall, S. J. (2002). Participation in extracurricular physical activity programs at middle schools. *Research Quarterly for Exercise and Sport, 73,* 187–192.

Prapavessis, H., Maddison, R., & Brading, F. (2004). Understanding exercise behavior among New Zealand adolescents: A test of the transtheoretical model. *Journal of Adolescent Health, 35,* 346, e17–e27.

Prochaska, J. O., DiClemente, C. C., & Norcross, J. (1992). In search of how people change. *American Psychologist, 47,* 1102–1114.

Prouty, D., Panicucci, J., & Collinson, R. (Eds.) (2006). *Adventure education: Theory and applications.* Champaign, IL: Human Kinetics.

Prusak, K. A., & Darst, P. W. (2002). Effects of types of walking activities on actual choices by adolescent female physical education students. *Journal of Teaching in Physical Education, 21,* 230–241.

Prusak, K. A., Treasure, D. C., Darst, P. W., & Pangrazi, R. P. (2004). The effects of choice on the motivation of adolescent girls in physical education. *Journal of Teaching in Physical Education, 23,* 19–29.

Rainey, D. W., Santilli, N. R., & Fallon, K. (1992). Development of athletes' conceptions of sport officials' authority. *Journal of Sport and Exercise Psychology, 14,* 392–404.

Raudsepp, L., Liblik, R., & Hannus, A. (2002). Children's and adolescents' physical self-perceptions as related to moderate to vigorous physical activity and physical fitness. *Pediatric Exercise Science, 14,* 97–106.

Reitman, D., Hupp, S. D. A., O'Callaghan, P. M., Gulley, V., & Northup, J. (2001). The influence of a token economy and methylphenidate on attentive and disruptive behavior during sports with ADHD-diagnosed children. *Behavior Modification, 25,* 305–323.

Renninger, K. A., Hidi, S., & Krapp, A. (Eds.). (1992). *The role of interest in learning and development.* Hillsdale, NJ: Erlbaum.

Rikard, G. L. (1991). The short-term relationship of teacher feedback on student practice. *Journal of Teaching in Physical Education, 10,* 275–285.

Rikard, G. L., & Banville, D. (2006). High school student attitudes about physical education. *Sport, Education, and Society, 11,* 385–400.

Rikard, G. L., & Knight, S. M. (1997). Obstacles to professional development: Interns' desire to fit in, get along, and be real teachers. *Journal of Teaching in Physical Education, 16,* 440–453.

Ringuet, C. J., & Trost, S. G. (2001). Effects of physical activity intervention in youth: A review. *International Sports Medicine Journal, 2*(5), 1–10.

Rink, J. E. (2002). *Teaching physical education for learning* (4th ed.). New York: McGraw-Hill.

Roberton, M. A., Halverson, L. E., & Harper, C. J. (1997). Visual/verbal modeling as a function of children's developmental levels in hopping. In J. E. Clark & J. H. Humphrey (Eds.), *Motor development: Research and reviews* (Vol. 1, pp. 122–147). Reston, VA: NASPE.

Roberts, G. C. (2001). Understanding the dynamics of motivation in physical activity: The influence of achievement goals on motivational processes. In G. C. Roberts (Ed.), *Advances in motivation in sport and exercise* (pp. 1–50). Champaign, IL: Human Kinetics.

Robinson, D. W. (1990). An attributional analysis of student demoralization in physical education settings. *Quest, 42,* 27–39.

Robinson, D. W., & Howe, B. L. (1989). Appraisal variable/affect relationships in youth sport: A test of Weiner's attributional model. *Journal of Sport and Exercise Psychology, 11,* 431–443.

Roemmich, J. N., Gurgol, C. M., & Epstein, L. H. (2004). Open-loop feedback increases physical activity of youth. *Medicine & Science in Sports & Exercise, 36,* 668–673.

Romance, T. J., Weiss, M. R., & Bockoven, J. (1986). A program to promote moral development through elementary school physical education. *Journal of Teaching in Physical Education, 5,* 126–136.

Rose, B., Larkin, D., & Berger, B. G. (1997). Coordination and gender influences on the perceived competence of children. *Adapted Physical Activity Quarterly, 14,* 210–221.

Rose, B., Larkin, D., & Berger, B. G. (1998). The importance of motor coordination for children's motivational orientation in sport. *Adapted Physical Activity Quarterly, 15,* 316–327.

Rosengard, P. F., & McKenzie, T. L. (2000). *Sports, play, and active recreation for kids! Physical education program grades 6–8.* San Diego, CA: San Diego State University Foundation.

Rosengard, P. F., McKenzie, T. L., & Short, K. (2000). *Sports, play, and active recreation for kids! Physical education program grades k–2.* San Diego, CA: San Diego State University Foundation.

Rosenholtz, S. J., & Simpson, C. (1984). Classroom organization and student stratification. *The Elementary School Journal, 85,* 21–37.

Rosenstock, I. (1974). Historical origins of the health belief model. *Health Education Monographs, 2,* 328–335.

Rosenthal, R., & Jacobson, L. (1968). *Pygmalion in the classroom: Teacher expectations and pupils' intellectual development*. New York: Holt, Rinehart & Winston.

Rudisill, M. E. (1990). The influence of various achievement goal orientations on children's perceived competence, expectations, persistence, and performance for three motor tasks. *Journal of Human Movement Studies, 19,* 131–149.

Rudisill, M. E., Mahar, M. T., & Meaney, K. S. (1993). The relationship between children's perceived and actual motor competence. *Perceptual and Motor Skills, 76,* 895–906.

Rudisill, M. E., & Singer, R. N. (1988). Influence of causal dimension orientation on persistence, performance and expectations of performance during perceived failure. *Journal of Human Movement Studies, 15,* 215–228.

Rush, D. B., & Ayllon, T. (1984). Peer behavioral coaching: Soccer. *Journal of Sport Psychology, 6,* 325–334.

Ryan, R. M., & Deci, E. L. (2000). Self-determination theory and the facilitation of intrinsic motivation, social development, and well-being. *American Psychologist, 55,* 68–78.

Ryan, S., Ormond, T., Imwold, C., & Rotunda, R. J. (2002). The effects of a public address system on the off-task behavior of elementary physical education students. *Journal of Applied Behavior Analysis, 35,* 305–308.

Ryan, S., & Yerg, B. (2001). The effects of cross-group feedback on off-task behavior in a physical education setting. *Journal of Teaching in Physical Education, 20,* 172–188.

Saakslahti, A., Numminen, P., Salo, P., Tuominen, J., Helenius, H., & Valimaki, I. (2004). Effects of a three-year intervention on children's physical activity from age 4 to 7. *Pediatric Exercise Science, 16,* 167–180.

Sage, G. (1977). *Introduction to motor behavior: A neuropsychological approach* (2nd ed.). Reading, MA: Addison-Wesley.

Sallis, J. F. (2000). Age-related decline in physical activity: A synthesis of human and animal studies. *Medicine & Science in Sports & Exercise, 32,* 1598–1600.

Sallis, J. F., Conway, T. L., Prochaska, J. J., McKenzie, T. L., Marshall, S. J., & Brown, M. (2001). The association of school environments with youth physical activity. *American Journal of Public Health, 91,* 618–620.

Sallis, J. F., McKenzie, T. L., Alcaraz, J. E., Kolody, B., Faucette, N., & Hovell, M. F. (1997). The effects of a 2-year physical education programme (SPARK) on physical activity and fitness in elementary school students. *American Journal of Public Health, 87,* 1328–1334.

Sallis, J. F., Prochaska, J. J., & Taylor, W. C. (2000). A review of correlates of physical activity of children and adolescents. *Medicine & Science in Sports & Exercise, 32,* 963–975.

Sallis, J. F., Prochaska, J. J., Taylor, W. C., Hill, J. O., & Geraci, J. C. (1999). Correlates of physical activity in a national sample of girls and boys in grades 4 through 12. *Health Psychology, 18,* 410–415.

Salmoni, A. W., Schmidt, R. A., & Walter, C. B. (1984). Knowledge of results and motor learning: A review and reappraisal. *Psychological Bulletin, 95,* 355–386.

Sandt, D. D. R., & Frey, G. C. (2005). Comparison of physical activity levels between children with and without autistic spectrum disorders. *Adapted Physical Activity Quarterly, 22,* 146–159.

Santos, M. P., Esculcas, C., & Mota, J. (2004). The relationship between socioeconomic status and adolescents' organized and nonorganized physical activities. *Pediatric Exercise Science, 16,* 210–218.

Santos, M. P., Matos, M., & Mota, J. (2005). Seasonal variations in Portuguese adolescents' organized and nonorganized physical activities. *Pediatric Exercise Science, 17,* 390–398.

Sariscsany, M. J., Darst, P. W., & van der Mars, H. (1995). The effects of three teacher supervision patterns on student on-task and skill performance in secondary physical education. *Journal of Teaching in Physical Education, 14,* 179–197.

Sarrazin, P., Roberts, G., Cury, F., Biddle, S., & Famose, J. (2002). Exerted effort and performance in climbing among boys: The influence of achievement goals, perceived ability, and task difficulty. *Research Quarterly for Exercise and Sport, 73,* 425–436.

Sarrazin, P., Vallerand, R., Guillet, E., Pelletier, L., & Cury, F. (2002). Motivation and dropout in female handballers: A 21-month prospective study. *European Journal of Social Psychology, 32,* 395–418.

Schempp, P. G., Cheffers, J. T. F., & Zaichkowsky, L. D. (1983). Influence of decision-making on attitudes, creativity, motor skills, and self-concept in elementary children. *Research Quarterly for Exercise and Sport, 54,* 183–189.

Schiefele, U., Krapp, A., & Winteler, A. (1992). Interest as a predictor of academic achievement: A meta-analysis of research. In K. A. Renninger, S. Hidi, & A. Krapp (Eds.), *The role of interest in learning and development* (pp. 183–212). Hillsdale, NJ: Erlbaum.

Schilling, T. A. (2001). An investigation of commitment among participants in an extended day physical activity program. *Research Quarterly for Exercise and Sport, 72,* 355–365.

Schmidt, R. A., & Lee, T. D. (2005). *Motor control and learning: A behavioral emphasis* (4th ed.). Champaign, IL: Human Kinetics.

Schmidt, R. A., & Wrisberg, C. A. (2000). *Motor learning and performance* (2nd ed.). Champaign, IL: Human Kinetics.

Schofield, L., Mummery, W. K., & Schofield, G. (2005). Effects of a controlled pedometer intervention trial for low-active adolescent girls. *Medicine & Science in Sports & Exercise, 37,* 1414–1420.

Schunk, D. H. (1995). Self-efficacy and education and instruction. In J. E. Maddux (Ed.), *Self-efficacy, adaptation, and adjustment: Theory, research, and application* (pp. 281–303). New York: Plenum Press.

Screws, D. P., & Surburg, P. R. (1997). Motor performance of children with mild mental disabilities after using mental imagery. *Adapted Physical Activity Quarterly, 14,* 119–130.

Scully, D. M., & Newell, K. M. (1985). Observational learning and the acquisition of motor skills: Toward a visual perception perspective. *Journal of Human Movement Studies, 11,* 169–186.

Shapiro, D. R., & Ulrich, D. A. (2001). Social comparisons of children with and without learning disabilities when evaluating physical competence. *Adapted Physical Activity Quarterly, 18,* 273–288.

Shapiro, D. R., & Ulrich, D. A. (2002). Expectancies, values, and perceptions of physical competence of children with and without learning disabilities. *Adapted Physical Activity Quarterly, 19,* 318–333.

Shapiro, E. S., & Shapiro, S. (1985). Behavioral coaching in the development of skills in track. *Behavior Modification, 9,* 211–224.

Sharpe, T., Brown, M., & Crider, K. (1995). The effects of a sportsmanship curriculum intervention on generalized positive social behavior of urban elementary school students. *Journal of Applied Behavior Analysis, 28,* 401–416.

Sharpe, T., Crider, K., Vyhlidal, T., & Brown, M. (1996). Description and effects of prosocial instruction in an elementary physical education setting. *Education and Treatment of Children, 19,* 435–357.

Shea, C. H., Wright, D. L., Wulf, G., & Whitacre, C. (2000). Physical and observational practice afford unique learning opportunities. *Journal of Motor Behavior, 32,* 27–36.

Shea, C. H., Wulf, G., Park, J. H., & Gaunt, B. (2001). Effects of an auditory model on the learning of relative and absolute timing. *Journal of Motor Behavior, 33,* 127–138.

Shea, C. H., Wulf, G., & Whitacre, C. (1999). Enhancing training efficiency and effectiveness through the use of dyad training. *Journal of Motor Behavior, 31,* 119–125.

Shen, B., & Chen, A. (2006). Examining the interrelations among knowledge, interests, and learning strategies. *Journal of Teaching in Physical Education, 25,* 182–199.

Shen, B., & Chen, A. (2007a). An examination of learning profiles in physical education. *Journal of Teaching in Physical Education, 26,* 145–160.

Shen, B., & Chen, A. (2007b). Using achievement goals and interest to predict learning in physical education. *Journal of Experimental Education, 75,* 89–108.

Shen, B., Chen, A., Scrabis, K. A., & Tolley, H. (2003). Gender and interest-based motivation in learning dance. *Journal of Teaching in Physical Education, 22,* 396–409.

Shields, D. L. L., & Bredemeier, B. J. L. (1989). Moral reasoning, judgment, and action in sport.

In J. Goldstein (Ed.), *Sports, games and play: Social and psychological viewpoints* (pp. 59–81). Hillsdale, NJ: Erlbaum.

Shields, D. L., & Bredemeier, B. L. (2001). Moral development and behavior in sport. In R. N. Singer, H. A. Hausenblaus, & C. M. Janelle (Eds.), *Handbook of sport psychology* (2nd ed., pp. 585–603). New York: John Wiley & Sons.

Sidaway, B., & Hand, M. J. (1993). Frequency of modeling effects on the acquisition and retention of a motor skill. *Research Quarterly for Exercise and Sport, 64,* 122–126.

Siedentop, D. (Ed.). (1994). *Sport education: Quality PE through positive sport experiences.* Champaign, IL: Human Kinetics.

Siedentop, D., Hastie, P., & van der Mars, H. (2004). *Complete guide to sport education.* Champaign, IL: Human Kinetics.

Silverman, S. J., & Ennis, C. D. (2003). Enhancing learning: An introduction. In S. J. Silverman & C. D. Ennis (Eds.), *Student learning in physical education: Applying research to enhance instruction* (2nd ed., pp. 3–7). Champaign, IL: Human Kinetics.

Silverman, S., Tyson, L., & Krampitz, J. (1992). Teacher feedback and achievement in physical education: Interaction with student practice. *Teaching and Teacher Education, 8,* 333–344.

Silverman, S., Woods, A. M., & Subramaniam, P. R. (1999). Feedback and practice in physical education: Interrelationships with task structures and student skill level. *Journal of Human Movement Studies, 35,* 203–224.

Simons, J., Dewitte, S., & Lens, W. (2003). "Don't do it for me, do it for yourself!" Stressing the personal relevance enhances motivation in physical education. *Journal of Sport and Exercise Psychology, 25,* 145–160.

Singer, R. N., Grove, J. R., Cauraugh, J., & Rudisill, M. (1985). Consequences of attributing failure on a gross motor task to lack of effort or ineffective strategy. *Perceptual and Motor Skills, 61,* 299–306.

Sinnott, K., & Biddle, S. (1998). Changes in attributions, perceptions of success and intrinsic motivation after attribution retraining in children's sport. *International Journal of Adolescence and Youth, 7,* 137–144.

Sirard, J. R., Riner, W. F., Jr., McIver, K. L., & Pate, R. R. (2005). Physical activity and active commuting to elementary school. *Medicine & Science in Sports & Exercise, 37,* 2062–2069.

Sit, C. H. P., Lindner, K. J., & Sherrill, C. (2002). Sport participation of Hong Kong Chinese children with disabilities in special schools. *Adapted Physical Activity Quarterly, 19,* 453–471.

Skinner, B. F. (1953). *Science and human behavior.* New York: The Free Press.

Skinner, B. F. (1974). *About behaviorism.* New York: Alfred A. Knopf.

Smith, A. L. (1999). Perceptions of peer relationships and physical activity participation in early adolescence. *Journal of Sport and Exercise Psychology, 21,* 329–350.

Smith, B., Markley, R., & Goc Karp, G. (1997). The effect of a cooperative learning intervention on the social skill enhancement of a third grade physical education class. *Research Quarterly for Exercise and Sport, 68*(Suppl), A-68.

Smith, D. S., & Nagle, R. J. (1995). Self-perceptions and social comparison among children with LD. *Journal of Learning Disabilities, 28,* 364–371.

Smith, R. E., & Smoll, F. L. (1996). *Way to go, coach: A scientifically-proven approach to coaching effectiveness.* Portola Valley, CA: Warde.

Solmon, M. A. (1996). Impact of motivational climate on students' behaviors and perceptions of a physical education setting. *Journal of Educational Psychology, 88,* 731–738.

Solmon, M. A., Lee, A. M., Belcher, D., Harrison, L., Jr., & Wells, L. (2003). Beliefs about gender appropriateness, ability, and competence in physical activity. *Journal of Teaching in Physical Education, 22,* 261–279.

Southall, J. E., Okely, A. D., & Steele, J. R. (2004). Actual and perceived physical competence in overweight and nonoverweight children. *Pediatric Exercise Science, 16,* 15–24.

Spink, K. S., Chad, K., Muhajarine, N., Humbert, L., Odnokon, P., Gryba, C., et al. (2005). Intrapersonal correlates of sufficiently active youth and adolescents. *Pediatric Exercise Science, 17,* 124–135.

Spink, K. S., Shields, C. A., Chad, K., Odnokon, P., Muhajarine, N., & Humbert, L. (2006). Correlates of structured and unstructured activity among sufficiently active youth and adolescents: A new approach to understanding physical activity. *Pediatric Exercise Science, 18,* 203–215.

Spray, C. M. (2000). Predicting participation in non-compulsory physical education: Do goal perspectives matter? *Perceptual and Motor Skills, 90,* 1207–1215.

Spray, C. M., & Biddle, S. J. H. (1997). Achievement goal orientations and participation in physical education among male and female sixth form students. *European Physical Education Review, 3,* 83–90.

Spray, C. M., Biddle, S. J. H., & Fox, K. R. (1999). Achievement goals, beliefs about the cause of success and reported emotion in post-16 physical education. *Journal of Sports Sciences, 17,* 213–219.

Standage, M., & Duda, J. L. (2004). Motivational processes among older adults in sport and exercise settings. In M. R. Weiss (Ed.), *Developmental sport and exercise psychology: A lifespan perspective* (pp. 357–381). Morgantown, WV: Fitness Information Technology.

Standage, M., Duda, J. L., & Ntoumanis, N. (2003a). A model of contextual motivation in physical education: Using constructs from self-determination and achievement goal theories to predict physical activity intentions. *Journal of Educational Psychology, 95,* 97–110.

Standage, M., Duda, J. L., & Ntoumanis, N. (2003b). Predicting motivational regulations in physical education: The interplay between dispositional goal orientations, motivational climate and perceived competence. *Journal of Sports Sciences, 21,* 631–647.

Standage, M., Duda, J. L., & Ntoumanis, N. (2005). A test of self-determination theory in school physical education. *British Journal of Educational Psychology, 75,* 411–433.

Standage, M., Duda, J. L., & Ntoumanis, N. (2006). Students' motivational processes and their relationship to teacher ratings in school physical education: A self-determination theory approach. *Research Quarterly for Exercise and Sport, 77,* 100–110.

Standage, M., & Treasure, D. C. (2002). Relationship among achievement goal orientations and multi-dimensional situational motivation in physical education. *British Journal of Educational Psychology, 72,* 87–103.

Steele, C. A., Kalnins, I. V., Jutai, J. W., Stevens, S. E., Bortolussi, J. A., & Biggar, W. D. (1996). Lifestyle health behaviors of 11- to 16-year-old youth with physical disabilities. *Health Education Research, 11,* 173–186.

Steller, J. J., & Young, D. B. (1994). Moving to success: A comprehensive approach to physical education. In R. R. Pate & R. C. Hohn (Eds.), *Health and fitness through physical education* (pp. 177–184). Champaign, IL: Human Kinetics.

Stephens, D. E. (1998). The relationship of goal orientation and perceived ability to enjoyment and value in youth sport. *Pediatric Exercise Science, 10,* 236–247.

Stipek, D., & MacIver, D. (1989). Developmental change in children's assessment of intellectual competence. *Child Development, 60,* 521–538.

Stone, E. J., McKenzie, T. L., Welk, G. J., & Booth, M. L. (1998). Effects of physical activity interventions in youth: Review and synthesis. *American Journal of Preventive Medicine, 15,* 298–315.

Strachan, K., & MacCauley, M. (1997). Cooperative learning in a high school physical education program. *Research Quarterly for Exercise and Sport, 68*(Suppl), A-69.

Stroot, S. A., & Oslin, J. L. (1993). Use of instructional statements by preservice teachers for overhand throwing performance of children. *Journal of Teaching in Physical Education, 13,* 24–45.

Stuart, M. E. (1997). *An examination of adolescents' sources of subjective task value in sport.* Unpublished doctoral dissertation, Oregon State University, Corvallis.

Stuart, M. E., Lieberman, L., & Hand, K. E. (2006). Beliefs about physical activity among children who are visually impaired and their parents. *Journal of Visual Impairment and Blindness, 100,* 223–234.

Suzuki, M., Saitoh, S., Tasaki, Y., Shimomura, Y., Makishima, R., & Hosoya, N. (1991). Nutritional status and daily physical activity of handicapped students in Tokyo metropolitan schools for deaf, blind, mentally retarded, and physically handicapped individuals. *American Journal of Clinical Nutrition, 54,* 1101–1111.

Taggart, A. C., Taggart, J., & Siedentop, D. (1986). Effects of a home-based activity program: A study with low fitness elementary school children. *Behavior Modification, 10,* 487–507.

Tannehill, D., & Zakrajsek, D. (1993). Student attitudes towards physical education: A multicultural study. *Journal of Teaching in Physical Education, 13,* 78–84.

Taub, D. E., & Greer, K. R. (2000). Physical activity as a normalizing experience for school-age children with physical disabilities. *Journal of Sport and Social Issues, 24,* 395–414.

Telama, R., Yang, X., Hirvensalo, M., & Raitakari, O. (2006). Participation in organized youth sport as a predictor of adult physical activity: A 21-year longitudinal study. *Pediatric Exercise Science, 17,* 76–88.

Telford, A., Salmon, J., Timperio, A., & Crawford, D. (2005). Examining physical activity among 5- to 6- and 10- to 12-year-old children: The children's leisure activities study. *Pediatric Exercise Science, 17,* 266–280.

Theeboom, M., DeKnop, P., & Weiss, M. R. (1995). Motivational climate, psychological responses, and motor skill development in children's sport: A field-based intervention study. *Journal of Sport and Exercise Psychology, 17,* 294–311.

Thomas, J. R., & Tennant, L. K. (1978). Effects of rewards on children's motivation for an athletic task. In F. L. Smoll & R. E. Smith (Eds.), *Psychological perspectives in youth sports* (pp. 123–144). Washington, DC: Hemisphere.

Thompson, L. P., Romanow, S. K. E., & Horne, T. E. (1998). Factors influencing intentions and motor engagement behaviour of children in an instructional physical activity program. *Avante, 4,* 23–42.

Tjeerdsma, B. L. (1991). Imagery in elementary physical education. *Strategies, 4*(4), 25–28.

Todorovich, J. R., & Curtner-Smith, M. D. (2002). Influence of the motivational climate in physical education on sixth grade pupils' goal orientations. *European Physical Education Review, 8,* 119–138.

Todorovich, J. R., & Curtner-Smith, M. D. (2003). Influence of the motivational climate in physical education on third grade students' task and ego orientations. *Journal of Classroom Interaction, 38*(1), 36–46.

Tousignant, M., & Siedentop, D. (1983). A qualitative analysis of task structures in required secondary physical education classes. *Journal of Teaching in Physical Education, 3*(1), 47–57.

Treanor, L., Graber, K., Housner, L., & Wiegand, R. (1998). Middle school students' perceptions of coeducational and same-sex physical education classes. *Journal of Teaching in Physical Education, 18,* 43–56.

Treasure, D. (1997). Perceptions of the motivational climate and elementary school children's cognitive and affective response. *Journal of Sport and Exercise Psychology, 19,* 278–290.

Treasure, D. C., & Roberts, G. C. (1995). Applications of achievement goal theory to physical education: Implications for enhancing motivation. *Quest, 47,* 475–489.

Tremblay, M. S., Inman, J. W., & Williams, J. D. (2000). The relationship between physical activity, self-esteem, and academic achievement in 12-year-old children. *Pediatric Exercise Science, 12,* 312–323.

Trost, S. G., Pate, R. R., Sallis, J. F., Freedson, P. S., Taylor, W. C., Dowda, M., et al. (2002). Age and gender differences in objectively measured physical activity in youth. *Medicine & Science in Sports & Exercise, 34,* 350–355.

Trudeau, F., Laurencelle, L., & Shephard, R. J. (2004). Tracking of physical activity from childhood to adulthood. *Medicine & Science in Sports & Exercise, 36,* 1937–1943.

Trudeau, F., Laurencelle, L., Tremblay, J., Rajic, M., & Shephard, R. J. (1999). Daily primary school physical education: Effects on physical activity during adult life. *Medicine and Science in Sports and Exercise, 31,* 111–117.

Tsai, E., & Fung, L. (2005). Perceived constraints to leisure time physical activity participation of students with hearing impairment. *Therapeutic Recreation Journal, 39*(3), 192–206.

Ullrich-French, S., & Smith, A. L. (2006). Perceptions of relationships with parents and peers in youth sport: Independent and combined prediction of motivational outcomes. *Psychology of Sport and Exercise, 7,* 193–214.

Ulrich, B. D. (1987). Perceptions of physical competence, motor competence, and participation in organized sport: Their interrelationships in young children. *Research Quarterly for Exercise and Sport, 58,* 57–67.

United States Department of Health and Human Services. (2000). *Tracking Healthy People 2010.* Washington, DC: United States Government Printing Office.

Urdang, L. (Ed.). (1995). *The Oxford desk dictionary: American edition.* New York: Oxford University Press.

Valentini, N., Rudisill, M., & Goodway, J. (1999). Incorporating a mastery climate into physical education: It's developmentally appropriate. *Journal of Physical Education, Recreation, and Dance, 70,* 28–32.

Vallerand, R. J. (1983). The effect of differential amounts of positive verbal feedback on the intrinsic motivation of male hockey players. *Journal of Sport Psychology, 5,* 100–107.

Vallerand, R. J. (1997). Toward a hierarchical model of intrinsic and extrinsic motivation. *Advances in Experimental Social Psychology, 29,* 271–360.

Vallerand, R. J., Gauvin, L. I., & Halliwell, W. R. (1986a). Effects of zero-sum competition on children's intrinsic motivation and perceived competence. *Journal of Social Psychology, 126,* 465–472.

Vallerand, R. J., Gauvin, L. I., & Halliwell, W. R. (1986b). Negative effects of competition on children's intrinsic motivation. *Journal of Social Psychology, 126,* 649–657.

Vallerand, R. J., & Losier, G. F. (1999). An integrative analysis of intrinsic and extrinsic motivation in sport. *Journal of Applied Sport Psychology, 11,* 142–169.

Van den Berg-Emons, H. J. G., Saris, W. H. M., de Barbanson, D. C., Westerterp, K. R., Huson, A., & van Baak, M. A. (1995). Daily physical activity of schoolchildren with spastic diplegia and of health control subjects. *Journal of Pediatrics, 127*(4), 578–584.

van der Mars, H. (1989). Effects of specific verbal praise on off-task behavior of second-grade students in physical education. *Journal of Teaching in Physical Education, 8,* 162–169.

Van Dongen-Melman, J. E. W. M., Koot, H. M., & Verhulst, F. C. (1993). Cross-validation of Har-

ter's self-perception profile for children in a Dutch sample. *Educational and Psychological Measurement, 53,* 739–753.

Van Wersch, A., Trew, K., & Turner, I. (1992). Post-primary school pupils' interest in physical education: Age and gender differences. *British Journal of Educational Psychology, 62,* 56–72.

Vazou, S., Ntoumanis, N., & Duda, J. L. (2006). Predicting young athletes' motivational indices as a function of their perceptions of the coach- and peer-created climate. *Psychology of Sport and Exercise, 7,* 215–233.

Vintere, P., Hemmes, N. S., Brown, B. L., & Poulson, C. L. (2004). Gross-motor skill acquisition by preschool dance students under self-instruction procedures. *Journal of Applied Behavior Analysis, 37,* 305–322.

Vlachopoulos, S., & Biddle, S. J. H. (1997). Modeling the relation of goal orientation to achievement-related affect in physical education: Does perceived ability matter? *Journal of Sport and Exercise Psychology, 19,* 169–187.

Vlachopoulos, S., Biddle, S., & Fox, K. (1996). A social-cognitive investigation into the mechanisms of affect generation in children's physical activity. *Journal of Sport and Exercise Psychology, 18,* 174–193.

Vlachopoulos, S., Biddle, S., & Fox, K. (1997). Determinants of emotion in children's physical activity: A test of goal perspectives and attribution theories. *Pediatric Exercise Science, 9,* 65–79.

Voorhees, C. C., Murray, D., Welk, G., Birnbaum, A., Ribisl, K. M., Johnson, C. C., et al. (2005). The role of peer social network factors and physical activity in adolescent girls. *American Journal of Health Behavior, 29,* 183–190.

Wallhead, T. L., & Buckworth, J. (2004). The role of physical education in the promotion of youth physical activity. *Quest, 56,* 285–301.

Wallhead, T. L., & Ntoumanis, N. (2004). Effects of a sport education intervention on students' motivational responses in physical education. *Journal of Teaching in Physical Education, 23,* 4–18.

Walling, M. D., & Duda, J. L. (1995). Goals and their associations with beliefs about success in and perceptions of the purposes of physical education. *Journal of Teaching in Physical Education, 14,* 150–156.

Walling, M. D., & Martinek, T. J. (1995). Learned helplessness: A case study of a middle school student. *Journal of Teaching in Physical Education, 14,* 454–466.

Wang, C. K. J., & Biddle, S. J. H. (2001). Young people's motivational profiles in physical activity: A cluster analysis. *Journal of Sport and Exercise Psychology, 23,* 1–22.

Wang, C. K. J., Chatzisarantis, N. L. D., Spray, C. M., & Biddle, S. J. H. (2002). Achievement goal profiles in school physical education: Differences in self-determination, sport ability beliefs, and physical activity. *British Journal of Educational Psychology, 72,* 433–445.

Wang, L., & Hart, M. A. (2005). Influence of auditory modeling on learning a swimming skill. *Perceptual and Motor Skills, 100,* 640.

Ward, P., & Lee, M. (2005). Peer-assisted learning in physical education: A review of theory and research. *Journal of Teaching in Physical Education, 24,* 205–225.

Watkinson, E. J., Dwyer, S. A., & Nielsen, A. B. (2005). Children theorize about reasons for recess engagement: Does expectancy-value theory apply? *Adapted Physical Activity Quarterly, 22,* 179–197.

Weeks, D. L., & Anderson, L. P. (2000). The interaction of observational learning with overt practice: Effects on motor skill learning. *Acta Psychologica, 104,* 259–271.

Weigand, D. A., & Broadhurst, C. J. (1998). The relationship among perceived competence, intrinsic motivation, and control perceptions in youth soccer. *International Journal of Sport Psychology, 29,* 324–338.

Weinberg, R. S., & Gould, D. (2003). *Foundations of sport and exercise psychology* (3rd ed.). Champaign, IL: Human Kinetics.

Weiner, B. (1985). An attributional theory of achievement motivation and emotion. *Psychological Review, 92,* 548–573.

Weiner, B. (1986). *An attributional theory of motivation and emotion.* New York: Springer-Verlag.

Weiner, B., Frieze, I., Kukla, A., Reed, L., Rest, S., & Rosenbaum, R. M. S. (1972). Perceiving the causes of success and failure. In E. E. Jones, D. E. Kanouse, H. H. Kelley, R. E. Nisbett, S. Valins, & B. Weiner (Eds.), *Attribution: Perceiving the causes of behavior* (pp. 95–120). Morristown, NJ: General Learning Corporation.

Weir, P. L., & Leavitt, J. L. (1990). Effects of model's skill level and model's knowledge of results on the performance of a dart throwing task. *Human Movement Science, 9,* 369–383.

Weiss, M. R. (1983). Modeling and motor performance: A developmental perspective. *Research Quarterly for Exercise and Sport, 54,* 190–197.

Weiss, M. R. (1987). Teaching sportsmanship and values. In V. Seefeldt (Ed.), *Handbook for youth sports coaches* (pp. 137–151). Reston, VA: American Alliance for Health, Physical Education, Recreation, and Dance.

Weiss, M. R. (1991). Psychological skill development in children and adolescents. *The Sport Psychologist, 5,* 335–354.

Weiss, M. R., & Amorose, A. J. (2005). Children's self-perceptions in the physical domain: Between- and within-age variability in level, accuracy, and sources of perceived competence. *Journal of Sport and Exercise Psychology, 27,* 226–244.

Weiss, M. R., Bredemeier, B. J., & Shewchuk, R. M. (1985). An intrinsic/extrinsic motivation scale for the youth sport setting: A confirmatory factor analysis. *Journal of Sport Psychology, 7,* 75–91.

Weiss, M. R., & Ebbeck, V. (1996). Self-esteem and perceptions of competence in youth sport: Theory, research, and enhancement strategies. In O. Bar-Or (Ed.), *The encyclopedia of sports medicine: Vol. VI. The child and adolescent athlete* (pp. 364–382). Oxford, UK: Blackwell Science.

Weiss, M. R., Ebbeck, V., & Horn, T. S. (1997). Children's self-perceptions and sources of physical competence information: A cluster analysis. *Journal of Sport and Exercise Psychology, 19,* 52–70.

Weiss, M. R., Ebbeck, V., & Rose, D. J. (1992). "Show and tell" in the gymnasium revisited: Developmental differences in modeling and verbal rehearsal effects on motor skill learning and performance. *Research Quarterly for Exercise and Sport, 63,* 292–301.

Weiss, M. R., & Ferrer-Caja, E. (2002). Motivational orientations and sport behavior. In T. S. Horn

(Ed.), *Advances in sport psychology* (2nd ed., pp. 101–183). Champaign, IL: Human Kinetics.

Weiss, M. R., & Horn, T. S. (1990). The relation between children's accuracy estimates of their physical competence and achievement-related characteristics. *Research Quarterly for Exercise and Sport, 61,* 250–258.

Weiss, M. R., & Klint, K. A. (1987). "Show and tell" in the gymnasium: An investigation of developmental differences in modeling and verbal rehearsal of motor skills. *Research Quarterly for Exercise and Sport, 58,* 234–241.

Weiss, M. R., McAuley, E., Ebbeck, V., & Wiese, D. M. (1990). Self-esteem and causal attributions for children's physical and social competence in sport. *Journal of Sport and Exercise Psychology, 12,* 21–36.

Weiss, M. R., McCullagh, P., Smith, A. L., & Berlant, A. R. (1998). Observational learning and the fearful child: Influence of peer models on swimming skill performance and psychological responses. *Research Quarterly for Exercise and Sport, 69,* 380–394.

Weiss, M. R., & Smith, A. L. (2002a). Friendship quality in youth sport: Relationship to age, gender, and motivation variables. *Journal of Sport and Exercise Psychology, 24,* 420–437.

Weiss, M. R., & Smith, A. L. (2002b). Moral development in sport and physical activity: Theory, research, and intervention. In T. Horn (Ed.), *Advances in sport psychology* (2nd ed., pp. 243–280). Champaign, IL: Human Kinetics.

Weiss, M. R., & Williams, L. (2004). The why of youth sport involvement: A developmental perspective on motivational process. In M. R. Weiss (Ed.), *Developmental sport and exercise psychology: A lifespan perspective* (pp. 223–268). Morgantown, WV: Fitness Information Technology.

Welk, G. J. (1999). The youth physical activity promotion model: A conceptual bridge between theory and practice. *Quest, 51,* 5–23.

Welk, G. J., & Schaben, J. A. (2004). Psychosocial correlates of physical activity in children: A study of relationships when children have similar opportunities to be active. *Measurement in Physical Education and Exercise Science, 8,* 63–81.

Welk, G. J., Wood, K., & Morss, G. (2003). Parental influences on physical activity in children: An exploration of potential mechanisms. *Pediatric Exercise Science, 15,* 19–33.

Wendt, J. C., & Bain, L. L. (1989). Concerns of preservice and inservice physical educators. *Journal of Teaching in Physical Education, 8,* 177–180.

White, S. A. (1993). The effect of gender and age on causal attributions in softball players. *International Journal of Sport Psychology, 24,* 49–58.

Whitehead, J. R., & Corbin, C. B. (1991). Youth fitness testing: The effect of percentile-based evaluation feedback on intrinsic motivation. *Research Quarterly for Exercise and Sport, 62,* 225–231.

Whitehead, S. H., Biddle, S. J. H., O'Donovan, T. M., & Nevill, M. E. (2006). Social-psychological and physical environmental factors in groups differing by levels of physical activity: A study of Scottish adolescent girls. *Pediatric Exercise Science, 18,* 226–239.

Wiese-Bjornstal, D. M., & Weiss, M. R. (1992). Modeling effects on children's form, kinematics, performance outcome, and cognitive recognition of a sport skill: An integrated perspective. *Research Quarterly for Exercise and Sport, 63,* 67–75.

Wigfield, A., & Eccles, J. S. (2000). Expectancy-value theory of achievement motivation. *Contemporary Educational Psychology, 25,* 58–81.

Wigfield, A., Eccles, J. S., MacIver, D., Reuman, D. A., & Midgley, C. (1991). Transitions during early adolescence: Changes in children's domain-specific self-perceptions and general self-esteem across the transition to junior high school. *Developmental Psychology, 27,* 552–565.

Wigfield, A., Eccles, J. S., Yoon, K. S., Harold, R. D., Arbreton, A. J., Freedman-Doan, C., et al. (1997). Change in children's competence beliefs and subjective task values across the elementary school years: A 3-year study. *Journal of Educational Psychology, 89,* 451–469.

Williams, L., & Gill, D. L. (1995). The role of perceived competence in the motivation of physical activity. *Journal of Sport and Exercise Psychology, 17,* 363–378.

Wolko, K. I., Hrycaiko, D. W., & Martin, G. L. (1993). A comparison of two self-management packages to standard coaching for improving performance of gymnasts. *Behavior Modification, 17,* 209–223.

Wright, P. M., White, K., & Gaebler-Spira, D. (2004). Exploring the relevance of the personal and social responsibility model in adapted physical activity: A collective case study. *Journal of Teaching in Physical Education, 23,* 71–87.

Wrisberg, C. A., & Anshel, M. H. (1989). The effect of cognitive strategies on the free throw shooting performance of young athletes. *The Sport Psychologist, 3,* 95–104.

Wu, T., & Jwo, J. (2005). A prospective study on changes of cognitions, interpersonal influences, and physical activity in Taiwanese youth. *Research Quarterly for Exercise and Sport, 76,* 1–10.

Wuyts, I. J., & Buekers, M. J. (1995). The effects of visual and auditory models on the learning of a rhythmical synchronization dance skill. *Research Quarterly for Exercise and Sport, 66,* 105–115.

Xiang, P., Chen, A., & Bruene, A. (2005). Interactive impact of intrinsic motivators and extrinsic rewards on behavior and motivation outcomes. *Journal of Teaching in Physical Education, 24,* 179–197.

Xiang, P., & Lee, A. (1998). The development of self-perceptions of ability and achievement goals and their relations in physical education. *Research Quarterly for Exercise and Sport, 69,* 231–241.

Xiang, P., Lee, A., & Williamson, L. (2001). Conceptions of ability in physical education: Children and adolescents. *Journal of Teaching in Physical Education, 20,* 282–294.

Xiang, P., McBride, R., & Bruene, A. (2003). Relations of parents' beliefs to children's motivation in an elementary physical education running program. *Journal of Teaching in Physical Education, 22,* 410–425.

Xiang, P., McBride, R. E., & Bruene, A. (2004). Fourth graders' motivation in an elementary physical education running program. *The Elementary School Journal, 104,* 253–266.

Xiang, P., McBride, R. E., & Bruene, A. (2006). Fourth-grade students' motivational changes in an elementary physical education running program. *Research Quarterly for Exercise and Sport, 77,* 195–207.

Xiang, P., McBride, R., & Guan, J. (2004). Children's motivation in elementary physical education: A longitudinal study. *Research Quarterly for Exercise and Sport, 75,* 71–80.

Xiang, P., McBride, R., Guan, J., & Solmon, M. (2003). Children's motivation in elementary physical education: An expectancy-value model of achievement choice. *Research Quarterly for Exercise and Sport, 74,* 25–35.

Yun, J., & Ulrich, D. A. (1997). Perceived and actual physical competence in children with mild mental retardation. *Adapted Physical Activity Quarterly, 14,* 285–297.

Zelaznik, H. N., Shapiro, D. C., & Newell, K. M. (1978). On the structure of motor recognition memory. *Journal of Motor Behavior, 10,* 313–323.

Ziglar, Z. (1985). *Raising positive kids in a negative world.* Nashville, TN: Oliver Nelson.

SUBJECT INDEX